The Literary Politics of
Scottish Devolution

For Brigid

And in memory of Tom Leonard

The Literary Politics of Scottish Devolution

Voice, Class, Nation

Scott Hames

EDINBURGH
University Press

Edinburgh University Press is one of the leading university presses in the UK. We publish academic books and journals in our selected subject areas across the humanities and social sciences, combining cutting-edge scholarship with high editorial and production values to produce academic works of lasting importance. For more information visit our website: edinburghuniversitypress.com

Edinburgh University Press Ltd
The Tun – Holyrood Road
12(2f) Jackson's Entry
Edinburgh EH8 8PJ

Typeset in 11/13 Bembo by
IDSUK (DataConnection) Ltd, and
printed and bound in Great Britain

A CIP record for this book is available from the British Library

ISBN 978 1 4744 1813 3 (hardback)
ISBN 978 1 4744 1815 7 (webready PDF)
ISBN 978 1 4744 1814 0 (paperback)
ISBN 978 1 4744 1816 4 (epub)

Contents

Preface

A poet is the creator of a nation around himself: he gives them a world to see and has their souls in his hand, to lead them there.
  – Herder, 'The Influence of Poetry on the Customs of Modernity' (1777)[1]

Thanks for your letter. I'll be happy to do reviews [. . .] The one area I couldn't touch would be contemporary Scottish writers, or the recent past. The place is too small, and I like to relax when I go a walk.
  – Tom Leonard, Letter to enquiring editor (1989)[2]

The Canongate Wall forms the northern edge of the Scottish Parliament building, at the very foot of Edinburgh's Royal Mile. Designed by Sora Smithson, the wall symbolically grounds the witty angles of Holyrood within local geology. Rough extrusions of dolerite burst through the façade at street level, as though enacting the architect's vision of a parliament that 'arrives into the city almost surging out of the rock'.[3] Embedded in the wall are twenty-six decorative panels of Scottish stone including Iona marble, Lewisian gneiss and Easdale slate.[4] If this motif hints at inexorable forces underpinning – and likely to outlast – the elegance and self-conscious modernity of the building, the inscriptions on each panel also gesture to a 'bedrock' of national culture and identity. These citations gather a kind of pebbledash pantheon of modern Scottish literature, an upmarket weather-proof coverage including Robert Burns (twice), Walter Scott, Robert Louis Stevenson, Hugh MacDiarmid (thrice), Hamish Henderson, Norman MacCaig, Edwin Morgan and Alasdair Gray. The first version of Gray's stone – bearing the unofficial credo of devolutionary nationalism, 'work as if you were living in the early days of a better nation' – misspelled his first name, and had to be re-made. But the 'vernacular', hand-crafted particularities of the wall make errors of this kind seem forgivably natural. No element of the design places democracy on a solemn neoclassical pedestal, or encourages hushed reverence for governing power; indeed, the human faults and frailties of parliamentarians are a running theme. In pride of place, the left-most stone quotes Mrs Howden from Scott's *Heart of Midlothian*: 'When we had a king, and a chancellor, and parliament-men o' our ain, we could aye peeble them wi' stanes when they werena gude bairns – But naebody's nails can reach the length o' Lunnon.' A firm reminder, in demotic Scots, that the parliament is accountable to the local voices and dissenting energies of its immediate lifeworld. Far from monumentalising their power, the wall reminds MSPs of the socially limited character of their role. These Psalms, verses and songs anchor the young institution in deep folkways and geological time, but these same stones might quickly be con-verted to missiles for enforcing, or withdrawing, a conditional popular mandate.

Andrew Fletcher of Saltoun's inscription reads: 'If a man were permitted to make all the ballads, he need not care who should make the laws of a nation.' On these terms Scottish literature is directly incorporated into the fabric of the parliament, claiming an authority which precedes, and authenticates, that of the elected members inside the chamber. This patchwork of stone and script – including several Gaelic inscriptions, works by English authors, and religious texts – might be held to embody the 'diversity of voices' the building exists to represent, and yet it would be impos-sible to read the wall as democratically reflecting the nation. Of the twenty-six panels, twenty feature quotations by men. There are four authorless proverbs and songs, a Psalm, and just one stone featuring the name of a woman, the songwriter and communist mill-worker Mary Brooksbank.[5] All the named authors are white. If we pursue this thought, and think critically about the imagery of national representation, the Canongate façade begins to take on a rather different countenance. Its oblique planes and irregular surfaces might even begin to suggest handholds and footholds: potential means of scaling the outer skin of Holyrood, perhaps to seek another point of entry, from an angle discouraged by the confident architecture. That thought is close to the impulse behind this book.

Literature and/as politics

A few weeks prior to the 2014 referendum on Scottish independence, Colin Kidd argued that 'Scottish literature is for the SNP not a frill, but a matter of central concern.'

> For [First Minister Alex] Salmond, literature is a kind of QED: Anglo-Scottish differences in diction, lilt, sensitivity and worldview prove the grand truths of nationalism. He has argued, plausibly enough, that it is impossible to mistake the differences between a Scottish novel and an English novel. Novels, he believes, reveal fundamental differences in the values and ethos of Scots and English.[6]

In the summer of 2014 one did hear such arguments, among many others. And yet few prominent Scottish writers who supported the campaign for independence would accept this firm equation between literary Scottishness and the demand for statehood, as though one predicated the other.[7] The modern SNP is noted for its 'a-cultural' nationalism, placing far greater emphasis – particularly under Salmond's leadership – on economic powers, and confining to Burns Night its appetite for literary inspiration. Indeed, Cairns Craig notes with regret 'that there is probably no nationalist party in the world that has been less focused on mobilising culture as part of its political strategy than the SNP', despite Scotland's bounteous possession of 'cultural wealth' ripe for the purpose.[8] But the minimal presence of programmatic literary patriotism is only one part of the story, with the potential to conceal another. There really has been a complex and pervasive intermingling of Scottish literature and politics over the past few decades, with far-reaching consequences in both domains: for how we read (and over-read) the politics of Scottish writing, and for how we conceive the place of cultural and literary 'identity' within the project of Scottish nationalism. That is, broadly, what this book is about. In sketching its purview, we must begin by amending Kidd's history: it is precisely in the *absence* of an official literary nationalism that Scottish writers and artists have claimed – and been burdened with – special 'representative' clout.

This is particularly the case in the post-1979 period on which this study is mainly focused, but is also evident in earlier debates. Jack Brand's 1978 study of the *National Movement in Scotland* found, in Christopher Harvie's paraphrase,

> that although literature may have mobilized members of the party elite – and was interesting for this reason – the intellectual trend in Scotland had really been away from nationalism towards socialism. Paradoxically, Brand argued, this aided SNP organization. Political mobilization did not conflict with an existing scale of literary values – or with literary nationalists throwing their weight around.[9]

This too was only half-true: there were plenty of bellicose literary nationalists in the 1970s, many spoiling for a fight with Scotland's 'deracinated' political class, but they kept a wary distance from the SNP. For some, this was indeed an expression of socialist distrust of 'bourgeois nationalism'; for others, the SNP weren't nationalist enough (or indeed nationalist at all). But such debates occurred at the fringe of Scottish politics. They only gained purchase in the political mainstream following the failed referendum on a Scottish Assembly held in March 1979. While the SNP vote crashed following the 40 per cent rule debacle, Harvie continues, 'the 1980s saw a nationalist stance become general among the Scottish intelligentsia. [. . .] The orthodoxy now is that the revival in painting, film and the novel, in poetry and drama – staged and televised – kept a "national movement" in being.'[10]

As we shall see, this 'orthodoxy' has an extensive history of its own – Harvie was writing in 1991, at the height of its influence and plausibility – and is less a neutral historical description of how things transpired than a mobilising narrative constructed *within* the diffuse, campaign-like process and milieu it describes. As Jonathan Hearn observes in his partly ethnographic study of this world (based on doctoral research conducted in the mid-1990s), 'members of the intelligentsia have an interest in treating Scotland as an object of concern, study and discussion'.[11] The political utterances of literary figures such as William McIlvanney, James Kelman, Irvine Welsh and Alasdair Gray are thus located by Hearn within a broader 'network of intellectuals, academics, artists, writers, journalists and media figures through whom the ideas of the [self-government] movement are constantly being articulated and re-articulated'[12] in this period: the 'committed' (and preferably outspoken) Scottish writer was a key and prominent contributor to the pro-devolution social consensus which so strongly conditioned the critical reception of his or her art. Their eminent roles in the 'discursive reinforcement' and cultural authentication of devolution profoundly shaped the scholarly and journalistic perspectives through which these writers' literary output was read, as part of – or as often as not, *in place of* – that larger social articulation.[13]

Intellectuals and constitutional politics

This presents a certain dilemma, for literary critic and political historian alike. The established narrative of *literary and critical vanguardism* – in which writers, thinkers and artists established and secured the space for renewing Scottish democracy – is usually 'reported' by interested protagonists and fellow-travellers, just as much of the best writing on Scotland's nationalist intelligentsia involves a degree of self-portraiture. Few of the key scholars and commentators cited in this study have remained aloof from the events and investments at issue, but (once acknowledged) this does not diminish the interest of their reflections and analysis. On the contrary: post-war Scotland is an enormously rich and well-documented case of what Michael D. Kennedy and Ronald

Grigor Suny call the 'mutual articulation of national discourses and intellectuals'. As we shall see, a whole constellation of writers, journalists, artists and thinkers embraced their role 'as constitutive of the nation itself' during the period this book examines, with several overtly committing themselves to (re-)establishing 'the very language and universe of meaning in which nations become possible'.[14] The majority of these figures remain active in Scottish cultural debate, so it is with a degree of unease that I take up a critical stance on their work of several decades – work which I respect, whose political motivation I largely share, and the fruits of which have undoubtedly benefitted me personally. Nonetheless, there must be a space for critique 'within-and-against' nationalist intellectualism, if any of its liberating and clarifying energies are to be realised within the scholarly fields it helped to consolidate. Kennedy and Suny observe that

> intellectuals face a double risk when enveloped by the nation. On one hand, as patriots they lose their credentials as critical or independent. On the other hand, as critical intellectuals questioning the very 'authenticity' of the nation, they are either ignored, marginalized, or cast out altogether.[15]

Analysis of their role in the discursive reproduction of nationhood 'is likely to draw hostility from "true" nationalists', as many historic examples attest, but I am optimistic this study will be received in a spirit which lives up to the finer moments in the history it traces. To be clear from the outset, this study is not an exercise in debunking Harvie's 'orthodoxy' or exposing the self-interest of its proponents. It is a critical exploration of what this story – the story of 'cultural devolution' prior to the 1998 Scotland Act – means to us in devolved Scotland two decades later: as an historical account of how and why the Scottish Parliament came to be; as a paradigm guiding critical practice in Scottish literary studies (and cultural studies more generally); and as a political narrative presenting the *meaning* of devolution in culturally expressive terms.

But what is 'cultural devolution'? The concluding section of my introduction traces the hegemonic status of this notion over the past twenty years, but as a handy starting-point, we might take the writer and activist Kevin Williamson's forthright claim that

> Scotland's musicians, singers, poets, writers and artists had paved the way for the re-opening of the Scottish Parliament. They had reasserted their sense of Scottish identity, and their democratic aspirations, and from 1999 Scots had a political structure which could begin to convey the democratic wishes of the Scottish people.[16]

I will often refer to this story as 'The Dream': a story of cultural vanguardism in which writers and artists play the starring role in the recuperation of national identity, cultural confidence and democratic agency. It contrasts sharply with the less inspiring story I will call 'The Grind': the longer, thinner political history of devolution as a shrewd and sometimes grubby saga of electoral expediency, characterised less by stirring visions of democratic rebirth than ploys of cynical circumspection (such as a Royal Commission on the Constitution appointed to do, or rather to recommend, as little as politically possible). Tellingly, it is the establishment of Harold Wilson's Royal Commission in 1969 – not any electoral breakthrough for Scottish or Welsh nationalists, or any of the constitutional novelties of the 1990s – which is commemorated in the new stained-glass tribute to UK devolution in the Palace of Westminster.[17] This book explores the difference and interaction of these parallel stories – one determinedly Scottish, the other inescapably British – with an interest in tracing moments where one seems to illuminate, puncture, or redeem the other. My aim is to critically examine the conflation of these narratives and processes, and the consequences which follow for Scottish literary history and criticism; not to throw stones at what the Canongate Wall seems to signify, but to examine the logic of its construction.

Notes

1. Cited and translated by Karl Menges, 'Particular universals: Herder on national literature, popular literature, and world literature', p. 195.
2. Tom Leonard, Letter to 'John', 12 June 1989.

3. Enric Miralles, quoted in Archello entry for the Scottish Parliament.
4. McAdam, 'Canongate Wall', pamphlet.
5. The original twenty-four quotations were chosen by a panel of three (male) MSPs, and included zero women. Brooksbank's stone was added in 2010, with Norman MacCaig's, after a public competition held in 2009, marking a decade of parliamentary devolution. Scottish Parliament, 'Canongate Wall'.
6. Kidd, 'Scottish independence: literature and nationalism', *The Guardian*, 19 July 2014.
7. For several examples, see my edited collection *Unstated: Writers on Scottish Independence*.
8. Craig, *The Wealth of the Nation*, p. 20.
9. Harvie, 'Nationalism, journalism and cultural politics', p. 30.
10. Ibid. p. 30.
11. Hearn, *Claiming Scotland*, p. 39.
12. Ibid. p. 78.
13. Ibid. p. 78.
14. Kennedy and Suny, *Intellectuals and the Articulation of the Nation*, p. 3.
15. Ibid. p. 5.
16. Williamson, 'Language and culture in a rediscovered Scotland', p. 57.
17. My thanks to David Torrance of the House of Commons Library for this detail.

Acknowledgements

This project draws on archival research and two interdisciplinary workshops supported by a British Academy/Leverhulme Small Research Grant in 2014–16 (ref. SG132334). My thanks to the writers, critics, thinkers and politicians who took part in 'Narrating Scottish Devolution: Literature, Politics and the Culturalist Paradigm'. (For a podcast based on workshop recordings, see <https://narratingdevolution.wordpress.com>.)

The analysis presented here was developed in several earlier publications, including my article 'On Vernacular Scottishness and its Limits: Devolution and the Spectacle of "Voice"' for *Studies in Scottish Literature* (2013), and in a summary of workshop findings published as 'Narrating Devolution: Politics and/as Scottish Fiction' in *C21: Journal of Twenty-First Century Writings* (2017). My thanks to their editors and publishers, especially Patrick Scott of *SISL*. Elements of Chapter 7 appeared as 'The New Scottish Renaissance?' in Peter Boxall and Bryan Cheyette (eds), *The Oxford History of the Novel in English, Volume Seven: British and Irish Fiction Since 1940* (2016), pp. 494–511, reproduced with permission of Oxford University Press.

For assistance with various sources and archives, thanks are owed to the staff of the National Archives, the National Library of Scotland, the University of Edinburgh's Special Collections, and the Scottish Political Archive at the University of Stirling. The expertise of Sarah Bromage at SPA was vital, and I am particularly indebted to James Mitchell for his assistance navigating the Kew archival material on 1970s devolution. Thank you to David M. Black and Michael Keating for permission to quote from their unpublished correspondence.

For various prompts and helpful conversations along the way, my thanks to Eleanor Bell, Bethan Benwell, David Borthwick, John Corbett, James Costa, Cairns Craig, Stephen Dornan, Cailean Gallagher, Michael Gardiner, Ewan Gibbs, Suzanne Gilbert, Harry Josephine Giles, Gerry Hassan, Dominic Hinde, Adrian Hunter, Arianna Introna, Kathleen Jamie, Carole Jones, Karen Lowing, Peter Lynch, Graeme Macdonald, Meghan McAvoy, David McCrone, Liam McIlvanney, Tom Nairn, Laura Paterson, Douglas Robertson, Stewart Sanderson, Carla Sassi, Michael Shaw, Jim Smyth, Andrew Sneddon, Alex Thomson, David Torrance, Rory Watson, Amy Westwell, Matt Wickman, and students of Stirling's MLitt in Scottish Literature. Many of these ideas began in the classroom.

My greatest scholarly debt is to a student, Rory Scothorne, presently finishing doctoral research on devolution and the far left at the University of Edinburgh. His knowledge of the political magazines of the 1960s and 70s was indispensable, and at times he has been closer to an unpaid research assistant than a supportive friend. His enthusiasm for this project has been essential, and sometimes baffling.

This book is for Brigid, Nora, Georgina and Francis, and for my family in Canada.

Introduction

The Dream and The Grind

The shrinking, mouselike, shadowy figure of the goddess Devolution is not a Muse that would stir either a Burns or a MacDiarmid. So the idea tends to be itself devolved back into that unsatisfactory area of the mind where people mutter and grumble occasionally, and turn the thoughts over in a desultory way, and make half-hearted forecasts, but do not feel sufficiently moved or urged to apply the full powers of the brain to these things.
  – Edwin Morgan, 'The future of the antisyzygy' (1978)[1]

A few weeks before the 2014 referendum on Scottish independence, the novelist Alan Warner predicted that

> a No vote will create a profound and strange schism between the voters of Scotland and its literature; a new convulsion. It will be the death knell for the whole Scottish literature 'project' – a crushing denial of an identity that writers have been meticulously accumulating, trying to maintain and refine.[2]

Ironically, this rhetoric had much in common with Conservative unionist arguments of 2014, and dire warnings of the cultural legacy being jeopardised and recklessly endangered by those contemplating a Yes vote. Even more striking, for all its vaunted 'confidence' since the 1990s, Scottish literary identity here finds itself on public trial: a fragile construct pleading for its life. At the same time, writers were being credited with the dynamic cultural change which had made such a vote (and indeed such a polity) possible. What this scene manifests, I suggest, is the pervasive strength of 'cultural devolution' as an internalised folk belief, to which even shrewd and discerning Scottish writers intuitively reach in accounting for their social role. The submerged ironies of this narrative became fully visible in the wake of the No result. A year after the referendum, the novelist and playwright Alan Bissett – who had been highly active and visible as a Yes campaigner – reflected that 'the No vote, as Warner predicted, at first acted like the cancellation of a mandate, a "convulsion" in how I understood my own purpose. I'd presumed to give voice to a people, the majority of whom had turned out to be indifferent to the message.'[3] The trope of *giving voice* is central to my sense of how literary and political endeavours were brought into rhetorical and strategic alignment in the period at issue, and a considerable part of this study is spent tracing that process and its consequences. Its political efficacy is clear and impressive, but always carried certain hostages to fortune, typified by Warner's warning before the vote. It seems clear that his sense of democratic 'schism' embodies a malfunctioning sense of literature's representative role, where tallying with public opinion somehow becomes the paramount duty of the 'national' writer, and the people can be called upon to ratify the artist's sense of purpose. When public opinion shifts (or is formally tested at the ballot box), the artist's 'mandate' and representative function can be suddenly revoked. But note also the more reflective sense of disorientation on Bissett's part. Within the identitarian terms of the Dream, it is genuinely difficult to parse the popular rejection of a representative institution whose warrant, and meaning, is the validation of national identity. (Unaccountably, Scotland chose not to choose itself.)

In the years following the No result, a number of less circumspect writers followed Warner's logic through to its conclusion. In his poem digesting the outcome, 'Naw', Stuart A. Paterson takes the result as a self-cancellation of national honour, paradoxically ejecting the voting majority from any rightful claim to be 'Scotland's fowk':

The hail world's gan baith quair & peerie,
Heelster-gowdie, tapsalteerie.
Ah cannae jist jalousie at a
Hoo Scotland's fowk have votit Naw.
[...]
Yon whae wid chant the tribal sangs
O pride o whaur they maist belong
Maun wheesht & sing nae sange at a –
They have nae richt. They votit Naw.[4]

But who is 'they' in this bleak conclusion, and how is it related to
the Scotland on whose behalf the poet sings? In its performance
of vernacular presence and vitality, the poem evokes an earlier
condition of national health and pride, and a sense of 'we-ness'
(the poem argues) formally disavowed in 2014, but also anchored
'beyond' the fickle tides of public opinion. These quair unravell-
ings can easily be traced back to contradictions within the paradigm of 'cultural devolution' which emerged after 1979, which
has powerfully shaped how subsequent Scottish writers conceive
(and defend) their role. But we should not be too hasty in bust-
ing the vanities of a supposed literary vanguard, whose special
status as 'voices' and 'representatives' of Scotland was either cancelled by direct plebiscite in 2014, or revealed to rest on a 'higher'
conception of peoplehood un-testable by the electoral machinery.
The special authority of cultural 'we-ness', and its symbolic guarantors, did not come only from the writers themselves: this role
gained traction in a 1970s political context in which centralised
state authority was also invested in a story of Scottish *identitarian
empowerment* – arguably more so than the leading nationalist writers of the period.
      This book traces that history and its implications for Scottish
literary and cultural criticism. With the exception of Chapters
5 and 7 (on James Robertson's devolutionary epic *And the Land
Lay Still*, and 1990s fiction by Irvine Welsh, A. L. Kennedy and
James Kelman), it is not primarily concerned with detailed close
readings of literary texts, though the discussion is illustrated with
a number of key examples from novels and poems. It is equally
interested in the role adopted by Scottish writers and critics as

public intellectuals, cultural guarantors, and media mouthpieces of a national 'we-ness' no vote could overturn. We are concerned here with the political leveraging of 'Scottish literature' (considered as a critical project as much as a creative endeavour), operating beyond its own bookish sphere, and intervening in public affairs with a specific 'national' weight and social authority. This enquiry almost immediately reveals the *co-constitution* of a 'revitalised' Scottish literature and Scottish democracy since 1979, and clarifies a number of the interlocking claims sedimented in the imagery of the Canongate Wall. Casting a critical light on these connections, I do not set out to disprove the 'cultural devolution' thesis surveyed below, but to trace both its power and its limitations. Whatever its truth-value, this myth has been enormously influential and reality-shaping, continuing to undergird literary and critical production in Scotland, while functioning as the predominant discursive 'frame' in which the social value of Scottish writing is asserted and evaluated.

I have elsewhere questioned the tendency to locate (and often confine) the politics of contemporary Scottish writers within the relatively narrow horizons of the constitutional debate they are credited with re-energising.[5] Tropes of 'representation' are central to what is misleading and even mystificatory in this pattern. The key Scottish novelists of the past few decades largely reject the ambassadorial politics of 'representation' enshrined in parliamentary democracy, yet they are continually presented as the models and cultural guarantors of Scottish devolution understood as the (incomplete) recovery of national agency and identity via parliamentary representation. As we shall see, it is equally possible to understand devolution as a highly conservative process, defined by established state and party interests: one that openly figures 'cultural representation' as the containment and deferral of democratic empowerment. We should be wary of the limiting and distorting effects – both critically and politically – of reading Scottish literature by the terms of a self-congratulatory circuit of 'representation' (by which formally innovative literary novels act as catalysts to a political process held to delimit 'the political' in Scottish writing; most often by fixating on the display and recuperation of 'identity'). This study is an argument for recognising and exiting this cul-de-sac. To gain critical purchase on its contours, we must briefly revisit scholarly debates on the survival and reconstruction of Scottish political identity.

Chicken-and-egg nationhood

Alexander Smith has argued 'that the emergence of an apparently distinctive Scottish state at the turn of the twenty-first century is best understood as an outcome of the creation of a pro-devolution (Scottish) public in the 1990s'.[6] That devolution was democratically 'demand-led' is true enough, and yet only half the story. We should begin by acknowledging an important chicken-and-egg quality of the developments at issue. Atsuko Ichijo agrees with Smith in observing that the new parliament 'has secured a distinctively Scottish political discursive space'[7]: for both scholars, the state-like structures and national character of Scottish politics emerge as *outcomes* of legislative devolution. But they are equally the *ground* of the pro-devolution arguments surveyed in this book. Long before these national-political structures were achieved, key writers and thinkers spoke and behaved as though they already did – not least in the literary field – and this helped to bring them into being. As David McCrone observes, in the Scottish case 'substantial cultural capital is both the product and the driver of political change': 'having a parliament is both the outcome of a sense of identity, as well as reinforcing it in turn, bearing in mind that there is no simple relationship between preferred constitutional option and either party preference or self identity'.[8] The messy and inconclusive alignment between national self-identification and political preference – writing in 2005, McCrone cites social attitude research by Ross Bond and Michael Rosie showing that 'only about 1 person in 6 who say that they are Scottish and *not* British [. . .] support *both* Independence *and* vote SNP' – suggests that 'the density of cultural capital is such that it has no single political or social carrier', and is not 'reducible to "straightforward" cultural markers such as language, religion and ethnicity'.[9] This being acknowledged, the 'carrying-capacity' of markers such as language, in seeming to de-sublimate the very substance of nationality, should not be underestimated.

The 'vernacular' politics of devolution have far-reaching implications for Scottish culture (including academic criticism), which this study attempts to survey both historically and theoretically.

Elie Kedourie writes that 'language is the external and visible badge of those differences which distinguish one nation from another; it is the most important criterion by which a nation is recognized to exist, and to have the right to form a state on its own'.[10] However unfashionable these investments might now seem, they are baked into the most carefully post-romantic arguments for national self-determination. Arash Abizadeh insists 'the nation has a *concreteness* that cannot be done away with', and a putatively earthy, emotive, hyper-physical language is ideally positioned to realise the 'affective mobilization' which remains necessary even to the most strenuously civic post-nationalism.[11] Indeed, appeals to the vernacular as the paradigm of authentically grounded interpersonal community have largely cast aside their ethnic-cultural accretions and been assimilated to the vocabulary of liberal multiculturalism. 'Put simply', writes the political philosopher Will Kymlicka, 'democratic politics is politics in the vernacular'. In modern societies 'we can expect – as a general rule – that the more political debate is conducted in the vernacular, the more participatory it will be'.[12] The common language of a people is an emblem not of its ethno-traditional rootedness but of its accessible civic space, apparently rinsed clean of exclusivist claims to belonging. This post-nationalist recuperation of 'Herderian' rhetoric on language and political community – explored in Chapter 6 – begins to explain why tropes of vernacular nationhood and authenticity are so prominent in the metaphorical currency of Scottish devolution and the independence debate. In announcing to the Scottish Parliament the date of the 2014 independence referendum, First Minister Alex Salmond described it as 'the day when we take responsibility for our country, when we are able to speak with our own voice, choose our own direction and contribute in our own distinct way'.[13] Grant Farred observes that the vernacular, 'though it emerges from below is considerably more than a language of subalternity. It is not a language in itself, but a form [of] public discourse.'[14] This an important context for grasping how the 'real literary renaissance' of 1980s–90s Scottish writing, and its 'radical' politics of vocal equality, resistance and liberation, became eligible for incorporation into mainstream constitutional discourse.

Constituting devolution

In order to capture some of the complexities of the pro-devolution consensus which emerged in the late 1980s and early 1990s, and the intersection of cultural and political debates leading up to that period, I argue that a national Scottish political system, and its representative forms and discursive boundaries, were not caused by but *constituted in* devolution: called into being to give substance and reality to what pro-devolution politics assumed in advance. The features of 'an apparently distinctive Scottish state' in the early twenty-first century can reasonably be understood as the fulfilment of pro-devolutionary politics (that is, as the effectual mechanisms for 'delivering' the renewal of Scottish democracy demanded by the electorate), but this tends to obscure the most creative and interesting phase of their development. Two processes reinforced each other throughout the period at issue: the emphasis (and gradual naturalisation) of the Scottish national frame, 'dimension' or habitus (first in culture, then in politics), and the demand that Scottish political structures should evolve to a position of 'congruence', in Ernest Gellner's terms, with the palpable reality (and appealing difference) of Scottish cultural identity. (In Bourdieu's sense, habitus describes 'a set of *dispositions* which incline agents to act and react in certain ways': a repertoire of practices, perceptions and attitudes which 'are "regular" without being consciously co-ordinated or governed', and which constitute the normative structures of everyday social life.[15] For Gellner, 'nationalism is primarily a political principle, which holds that the political and the national unit should be congruent'.[16]) Thus the growing distinctiveness and 'solidity' of Scottish discursive space during the 1980s and 1990s might be understood as the 'form' of national politics crystallising out of its tacit 'content', in turn stimulating further demands for representative structuration.

As James Kellas and Lindsay Paterson (among others) argued decades ago, Scotland had many features of a distinctive political system, and qualities of (elitist, unaccountable) semi-sovereignty, long before the upsurge of nationalism beginning in the 1960s. Strikingly, Kellas dismisses the importance of culture even in the fourth edition of his influential study *The Scottish Political System* (published in 1989):

> Cultural nationalists make a small but vociferous contribution to Scottish nationalism. They encourage the use of a Scottish means of expression in literature, and cultivate Scottishness in the other arts. A few support the SNP, or political devolution, but most are uninterested in politics, preferring to change Scottish society through education and cultural activities. The SNP, for its part, takes little interest in cultural matters.[17]

If this were broadly true at the time of the book's first edition in 1973, it seems an eccentric reading of events in the pivotal decades that followed. One reason Kellas's model is so unhelpful for understanding the cultural dimension of devolution is that it makes 'national consciousness' a primary criterion for identifying Scotland (or any nation) as a distinct 'political system', while theorising national identity in a manner that nullifies its potential to be mobilised and managed within overlapping political systems – that is, one of the predominant historic patterns we describe *as* nationalism. In framing his general argument (against a homogenously British vision of a unitary UK state), Kellas notes that:

> the criteria for nationhood are never easy to determine, and vary from nation to nation. But they ought to satisfy two broad requirements: that the members of the nation think of themselves primarily as such, and not primarily as members of another nation; and that the nation should have some objective characteristics of its own, such as language, 'complementary habits and facilities of communication', religion, territory, previous statehood, a history of common action, and so on. The first requirement is well fulfilled in the case of Scotland.[18]

Kellas appeals to a tacit sense of nationhood as a kind of genealogical proof of political distinctiveness – other-than-British national consciousness, he writes, 'came to the surface during the late 1960s with the rise of political nationalism in Scotland, Wales and Northern Ireland (the last a quite separate variety). But in reality it was always there.' It is the anterior and 'inert' quality of this national consciousness – 'always there', scarcely noticed, gathering dust – which seems to consign questions of cultural identity to the background, in precisely the period they are moving swiftly to the political foreground. For Kellas 'national identification' is essentially banal in Michael Billig's sense: something children pick up at school and in the playground (in 'games of the "Scots versus the English" type'),[19] more or less unconsciously and by osmosis.[20] It is not something with any active political force or potential to alter the 'reality' of political systems and structures; seemingly it can only affirm and anchor what already obtains. Note also the disjunction between 'subjective nationality' in this scheme and the corresponding 'objective characteristics' of nationhood.[21] It seems clear in the passage cited above that national identity can exist separately from the sociological requirements of true nationhood, and in developing this model Kellas sharply distinguishes between 'subjective identification with Scotland' and its political expression. The fact that people who identity as Scots do not automatically vote Scottish nationalist (nor 'disdain cooperation with the "English" political parties') leads Kellas to conclude that 'most of the time [. . .] the political nationalism lies dormant, and the "British" pattern of political behaviour prevails'.[22] This model conflates in advance 'identity' and 'political behaviour': you are what you vote, and only wholesale electoral rejection of the British order would manifest national identity 'activated' from its default dormancy. In this model identity authenticates established political structures, but cannot really figure in their gradual transformation.

Followers of Kellas and Paterson may justly argue, *pace* Smith and Ichijo, that there was nothing truly new about the national political space constructed in the 1980s. But the active and mobilised role of cultural identity in *challenging* the existing (Scottish) political system is a signature development of that decade, which their models render illegible. Ray Ryan describes the post-1979

period as 'an obsessive quest for cultural self-definition as claims
for national distinctiveness were mediated through culture rather
than politics';[23] but this mediation cut both ways, with new
political weight attached to matters of 'identity' in ways that belie
airy 1970s gestures, both in Kellas and in the 1973 Report of the
Royal Commission on the Constitution, to 'national feeling'.
In most 1970s discourse national-cultural attachment operates as
an anchoring residue, or as a diffuse source of potential disruption, but seldom as a *structuring principle* for the re-constitution
of national political space. This is precisely what changed, and
Scottish writers really did play a significant and catalysing role
in the process; though not always pointed in the same direction
as the political actors who stood to gain most from reinstating a
Scottish politics.

David McCrone captures the complexity of this structural
shift, as well as the need to grasp its 'cultural' dimension without
simplifying or inflating it. Writing in 2005, he draws on Pierre
Bourdieu in tracing the pivotal importance of the 'Scottish frame
of reference' in the broader political shift toward devolution:

> The point is not that suddenly Scots changed their values
> and attitudes, but that the political prism through which
> they expressed these altered. [. . .] 'Scotland' rather than
> Britain was construed as the unit of political and economic
> management from the 1970s. [. . .] The emerging Scottish
> frame of reference fixed a new dimension to politics north
> of the Tweed, reflected in but by no means coterminous
> with the rise of the Scottish National Party. This is per-
> haps how one should understand Scottish-English differ-
> ences, not as the result of some deep differences in social
> and economic structures (because there are no significant
> structural ones), nor because there are separate 'Scottish'
> and 'English' values (again, because there are few), but
> because the cultural prism for translating social change into
> political meaning and action is different, always has been,
> and if anything, has become more so.[24]

Thus the creeping differentiation of the Scottish 'cultural
prism' since the 1970s – or in other terms, McCrone writes,

'what we mean by cultural capital [. . .] neither essentialized nor contingent, but dependent upon *habitus*'[25] – cannot simply be attributed to developments within 'culture' of the kind we might corroborate with references to literary texts; but neither can they be separated or disentangled from the growing sense of national-cultural difference and legitimacy. In the period this book explores, Scottish cultural otherness (within the UK) is overtly mobilised at the electoral level, and becomes a functional basis on which to solidify and democratise the Scottish political system, while also installing notions of cultural difference and representation at the heart of devolved common sense. It is for this reason I focus on the unusually close interplay of literary-cultural debate and hard-nosed party politics after 1979, when efforts to re-construct *national political space* were symbiotic with efforts to re-conjure *national literary space*.

These processes gave impetus to one another, and often flattered each other's claims. In 1988, a landmark achievement in Scottish criticism – the publication of Cairns Craig's four-volume *History of Scottish Literature* – was greeted by James Robertson in the pages of *Radical Scotland* as a political coming-of-age. Craig's *History*, Robertson notes, is

> informed by that great spirit of reassessment and serious self-appraisal which succeeded the Devolution disaster. Maybe future generations will decide that 1979 was *not* a disaster, that it was, for a people stripped in the industrial age of their political and cultural self-respect, yet one more necessary stagger before a firmer step. Could this unpretentious and sober, yet at the same time wide-ranging and unapologetic compilation have been produced ten years ago? I suspect not, and this is also partly why its overall political tenor – left nationalist – has also the air of intellectual maturity. There is no bowing and scraping to a Greater Lit., nor any knee-jerking in philabegs.[26]

The unapologetic assertion of a Scottish literary tradition – one liberated from the shadow of a 'Greater' (English) Lit. – is coeval with the achievement of 'mature' left-nationalism in politics.

Three areas

In the remainder of this introduction, I will foreground three areas of critical focus. The first is general and theoretical, and concerns the self-thwarting tendencies of (essentially liberal) identitarian political projects premised on 'recognition', of which Scottish 'cultural devolution' is one. The prominence and energy of contemporary debates concerning 'identity politics' is both suggestive and somewhat disheartening, when we consider that thoughtful recent critiques of identitarian social movements and leftist strategy[27] do not (it seems to me) advance significantly beyond their predecessors in the 1990s, the period in which the Scottish developments I am most concerned with reached their maturity. In 1997 Judith Butler argued that 'what we call identity politics is produced by a state which can only allocate recognition and rights to subjects totalized by the particularity that constitutes their plaintiff status'.[28] 'If we can claim to be somehow injured on the basis of our identity', explains Asad Haider,

> as though presenting a grievance in a court of law, we can demand recognition from the state on that basis [. . .] Our political agency through identity is exactly what locks us into the state, what ensures our continued subjection. The pressing task, then, as Butler puts it, is to come up with ways of 'refusing the type of individuality correlated with the disciplinary apparatus of the modern state'.[29]

This is a dense but powerful formulation of the critique I will outline (and partly 'problematise') below, and applies even more forcefully to movements centred on collective rather than individual identity. For more than two decades, the American political theorist Wendy Brown has argued that such projects inevitably end up essentialising and 're-subordinating' the very identities they understand themselves to be emancipating, particularly as they seek legitimation in some kind of secure institutional form (sanctioned by the state, or credentialing structures such as the university). This argument has much to offer a critical orientation to the project of Scottish literature, but I also mean to highlight key factors which fall largely outside of Brown's framing, namely the special features of liberal nationalism as a statist ideology. As Kennedy and Suny have it, 'the nation as representative of the people has become in the twentieth century the principal form of legitimation of the state'.[30] This renders key elements of Brown's critique beside the present point, while (more importantly) revealing specific limits and problems that attend the instatement of a literary nationalism centred on the recuperation of identity.

This observation forms a second strand of the book: how literary nationalism actively seeks out the 'pitfalls' of identitarian politics identified by theorists such as Wendy Brown and Nancy Fraser. In Pascale Casanova's helpful terms, the formation and reproduction of 'national literary space' in the post-romantic west involves the essentialisation and totalisation of difference/identity – above all, linguistic difference/identity – in the very logic of its instatement. National literary fingerprints and *qualia* are reified in the statist forms by which they are to be socially reproduced and institutionally anchored, a pattern readily observed in the Scottish case.

The third area of my discussion I will summarise is historical, and pervades the entire study. This revisits the cultural and political developments which guided many Scottish writers into their position of post-indyref bewilderment after 2014: the parallel stories of Scottish devolution understood as *vernacular cultural empowerment*, granting political authority to Scotland's authentic (neo-populist) voices and representatives ('The Dream'); and/or a *state-nationalist identitarian strategy* defined by electoral interests and the self-preservation of the UK constitutional order ('The Grind').

Devolution, recognition and logics of pain

Beginning in her 1995 study *States of Injury*, Wendy Brown poses the following question: 'what kind of political recognition can identity-based claims seek [. . .] that will not re-subordinate a subject historically subjugated through identity, through categories of race or gender that emerged and circulated as terms of power to enact subordination?'[31] This line of critique sharpens in *Politics*

Out of History (2001), where Brown cautions against a moralistic politics of social difference which ignores its disciplinary and historical production, thus 'mak[ing] a cultural or political fetish out of subordinated identities, out of the *effects* of subordination'.[32] 'Having lost our faith in history', she continues, 'we reify and prosecute its *effects* in one another, even as we reduce our own complexity and agency to those misnamed effects.'[33] Thus, we naturalise the 'wounds' of our historically produced identities – as gendered, raced and national subjects – in the course of constituting a politics of 'recognition' premised on their affirmation.

Pierre Bourdieu hits upon the same problem in exploring the register of difference/identity most relevant to this study, namely that of subordinated language. 'Those who rebel against the effects of domination that are exercised through the use of the legitimate language [e.g. Standard English] arrive at a sort of inversion of the relation of symbolic force and think they are doing the right thing by consecrating as such the dominated language [e.g. working-class demotic, vernacular Scots].'[34] Echoing Brown, Bourdieu insists this project of 'reversing' linguistic disesteem 'is still an effect of domination', because it can only ever affirm a condition and 'identity' of domination, popular language being recognised solely by its subordinated status. Thus, 'those who, out of a need for rehabilitation, talk about popular language or culture are victims of the logic which leads stigmatized groups to claim the stigma as a sign of their identity'.[35] ('Popular' here connotes working-class.) As Adorno puts the same point, 'glorification of splendid underdogs is nothing other than glorification of the splendid system that makes them so'; therefore 'to play off workers' dialects against the written language is reactionary'.[36] Bourdieu is less categorical, and leaves space for paradox and uncertainty in assessing the political valence of the 'quest for distinction' in which disempowered language lays claim to cultural value and representative legitimacy – a central theme, as we shall see, of the 'vernacular' cultural politics of Scottish devolution. Bourdieu is pessimistic about the forms of rebellion that may arise through identification with subjection, and relatively accepting of what in the post-Kelman Scottish literary context might be thought of as 'assimilation' to the language of domination:

When the dominated quest for distinction leads the dominated to affirm what distinguishes them, that is, in the name of which they are dominated and constituted as vulgar, do we have to talk of resistance? [. . .] Second question: when, on the other hand, the dominated work at destroying what marks them out as 'vulgar' and at appropriating that in relation to which they appear as vulgar (for instance, in France, the Parisian accent), is this submission? I think this is an insoluble contradiction [. . .] Resistance may be alienating and submission may be liberating. Such is the paradox of the dominated, and there is no way out of it.[37]

If Bourdieu's conclusion here seems pat, even reductive, the reason lies in the rather narrow way in which 'popular' and 'vulgar' language have been constructed within his argument: solely in the matrix of disempowerment, with no autonomous basis or 'content' that does not immediately reduce to a mark of oppression. Bourdieu himself notes this circularity: 'it is indeed paradoxical to define the dominated language by relation to the dominant language which itself can be defined only by relation to the dominated language'.[38] Here is another crucial difference: in the Scottish case explored in this study, the dominated language is aligned with a cultural politics of ethnonational difference, which opens a whole other field of political contestation, and access to 'cultural capital'. We shall return at length to the class/nation valence of vernacular language in the Scottish context (both literary and political), one of the richest but most complex topics this study attempts to illuminate. Here it is enough to acknowledge, with Brown and Bourdieu, that affirmations of identity are a limiting strategy with which to challenge the power structures from which we seek 'recognition' (on some uncertain *reciprocal* basis) as a distinct group, namely one whose *historical injury* grounds and defines its *social identity,* which is in turn essentialised into its *political interest.*

Such readings overlap with Nancy Fraser's influential critique of social and cultural movements driven by 'claims for the recognition of difference', which, she argues, tend to 'drastically simplify and reify group identities'.[39] 'Stressing the need to elaborate and display an authentic, self-affirming and self-generated collective identity', Fraser writes, such projects exert a moralising pressure 'for individual members to conform to a given group culture':

> Ironically, then, the identity model serves as a vehicle for misrecognition: in reifying group identity, it ends by obscuring the politics of cultural identification, the struggles *within* the group for the authority – and the power – to represent it. By shielding such struggles from view, this approach masks the power of dominant fractions and reinforces intragroup domination.[40]

Though not centred on projects of liberal nationalism (or 'post-nationalism'), this critique is highly pertinent to Scottish cultural and political movements. Both as a campaigning rubric and a critical heuristic, Fraser argues, the identitarian politics of recognition risks 'freezing the very antagonisms it purports to mediate'.[41] The second key term of Fraser's critique is 'displacement', whereby struggles for 'identity' both mask and de-centre 'redistributive' struggles for power and economic justice, while radically over-simplifying their imbrication. To treat identity as the product of 'free-floating cultural representations or discourses', she argues, is to neglect the '*institutionalized* significations and norms' in which unjust social divisions and exclusions are sedimented, and through which power produces and delimits 'identity' as available roles, subject positions and modes of participation.[42] The crucial error, Fraser argues, is to 'abstract misrecognition from its institutional matrix and obscure its entwinement with distributive injustice'.[43] Her proposed solution is a 'status model' that aims 'not at valorizing group identity but rather at overcoming subordination': struggling against that 'institutionalized pattern of cultural value [which] constitutes some social actors as less than full members of society and prevents them from participating as peers'.[44] 'Focused on culture in its socially grounded (as opposed to free-floating) forms', this model 'does not stop at identity but seeks institutional remedies for institutionalized harms'.[45]

The horizon of Fraser's critique, however, does not extend to the key 'institutional matrix' which grounds and governs claims to belonging, identity, participation and legitimacy in the modern west: the democratic nation-state. In an earlier version of her critique, Fraser concedes its limited application to struggles and mobilisations premised on ethnicity or nationality, noting that 'national struggles are peculiar [. . .] in that the form of recognition they seek is political autonomy, whether in the form of a sovereign state of their own (e.g. the Palestinians) or in the form of more limited provincial sovereignty within a multinational state (e.g. the majority of Québecois)'.[46] Where the claim of 'recognition' is less for status and standing in the eyes of a consolidated institutional matrix (such as the dominant or central state) but extends to the demand for 'our own' such matrix and powers of *self-institutionalisation*, Fraser's distinction seems to run aground. Where (as with liberal nationalism) the assertion of identity is not so much 'socially grounded' as constitutive of the very arena in which representative claims can be politically legitimated, we need a slightly different vocabulary. It is less that liberal nationalism has ways of avoiding the identitarian pitfalls identified by Brown and Fraser, but that it actively cultivates and exploits them. As with Fraser, there is a nation-shaped hole in Brown's observation that 'the problem with a politics of "difference" is that it lacks a vision of the future that overcomes the political significance of such differences, and thus lacks an affirmative political collective project'.[47] Brown does attend to the 'naturalistic legitimating narratives of collective identity known as nationalism',[48] but does not dwell on its difference from minoritarian identitarian projects in that nationalism *wants* to be essentialised and reified: precisely because it seeks the solid, durable and naturalised condition of statehood.[49]

Effectively invisible within most discourse on recognition (centred on the claims of groups and subjects minoritised by virtue of their race, gender or sexuality), modern struggles for statehood are a curious omission from this school of critique, because liberal nationalism would seem to represent the quintessential paradigm of 'displacement' and 'reification'. Wendy Brown has a telling illustration from the George W. Bush administration, dismissing commentators' 'moralizing condemnation of the National Endowment for the Arts for not funding politically radical art, of the US military or the White House for not embracing open homosexuality or sanctioning gay marriage', and other cosmopolitan disappointments. Such protest, she writes, conveys at best naïve political expectations and at worst, patently confused ones. For this condemnation implicitly figures the state (and other mainstream institutions) as if it did not have specific political and economic investments, as if it were rather, a momentarily misguided parent who forgot her promise to treat all her children the same way. These expressions of moralistic outrage implicitly cast the state as if it were or could be a deeply democratic and nonviolent institution; conversely, it renders radical art, radical social movements, and various fringe populations as if they were not potentially subversive, representing a significant political challenge to the norms of the regime, but rather were benign entities and populations entirely appropriate for the state to equally protect, fund, and promote.[50]

For my purposes, the final irony is central: the 'radical' demand for inclusion and recognition within the 'institutional matrix' of the nation-state is ultimately premised on a profound abnegation, a kind of promise by 'radical art' to be worthy of orderly admission into the ruling logic of state power. (The conferred prestige of the Canongate Wall begins to take on a slightly different complexion.)

To apply these insights to recent Scottish developments, the politics of identitarian empowerment and inclusion – so central to the rhetoric of devolution – only reinforce the power of a centralised UK state to 'grant' recognition of a subject polity asserting its national difference. This paternalist paradigm is, accordingly, highly amenable to the deeper logics of British constitutional governance, shifting the focus of nationalist contestation to accommodation and *incorporation* within state institutions, rather than challenging the legitimacy of UK state sovereignty. In the oft-cited words of Enoch Powell, power devolved is power retained.

Scottish injury and nationalist imaginaries

Profoundly naturalised as the legitimating basis for modern political authority, it is difficult to maintain a critical view of nationality as a *subjected* condition. Whether affirmed or suppressed (or both) by state power, nationhood is clearly not synonymous with freedom, for it enjoins particular duties, responsibilities and limits on the individual *as well* as securing various forms of belonging, community and protected rights. I highlight this elementary observation only because it becomes highly elusive when we enter the terrain of injured or subjugated nationhood. For Wendy Brown, the self-subverting qualities of identitarian politics follow directly from their 'logics of pain': identities premised on states of injury and suffering 'do not adequately articulate their own condition' because they figure 'suffering lived as identity rather than as general injustice or domination – but suffering that cannot be resolved at the identitarian level'.[51] Instead of seeking (with Fraser) 'institutional remedies for institutional harms', Brown writes, 'such political formations at times appear more invested in amassing and citing continued evidence of the injury justifying their existence than in figuring alternatives to these conditions'.[52] Viewed in the nationalist frame, however, this criticism overlooks the special value of injury as birthright and inheritance, the indispensable starting point of the nationalist 'salvation drama' – whether or not 'awakened' nationhood is restored to some lost wholeness.[53] The articulation of pain, loss and grief can be a nationalist end in itself, the re-animation of inherited postures of anguish and defiance which are *themselves* experienced as a condition of affective solidarity (injured nationhood), irrespective of the success, or even the conception, of some ameliorative path toward national redemption. To what extent can we understand Scottish literary nationalism within this paradigm? Allow me to cite the first page of the first issue of the first journal in the field, *Studies in Scottish Literature*, published in 1963, in which Tom Scott is admirably candid about the final vocabulary of the Scottish Literature project as he conceives it:

> Perhaps I had better make it clear from the outset that I have no pretensions to academic detachment in this matter [of Scottish Literature]. I am as disinterested as a husband who sees his wife slowly flogged to death under his captive eyes. Since the late 13th century, Scotland has been oppressed by a neighbour, England, whose amiable intentions towards Scotland have been, and are consistently, those of cultural and political genocide.[54]

The 'Scotland' produced in this tellingly gendered construction of national suffering is an absolute victim, devoid of agency except in the act of bearing emasculated witness to its own dishonour and degradation. Whether vengeful, restorative or otherwise, any national 'awakening' founded on this state of 'genocidal' injury will figure identity as a lurid scar, and conceive the national past as a record of humiliation. A political movement seeking not to valorise but to 'de-subordinate' this identity is not pleasant to contemplate. Scott, to be sure, is a provocative figure in the truculent MacDiarmid mould; surely this victimology went out with 'tartan terror'?

Not according to Andrew O'Hagan, writing in 2002. The intervening period – 1963–2002 – is roughly the period of salutary Scottish renewal familiar from many respected histories: so, having regained a measure of its democratic agency and self-respect, has Scotland managed to heal its old injuries? For O'Hagan, reviewing Neal Ascherson's *Stone Voices: The Search for Scotland*, the answer is a resounding no: the 'new', semi-autonomous Scotland has simply incorporated new, politically specific wounds (not England but Thatcher) into the Auld Enemy folkways frequented by Tom Scott and his unfortunate bride. A 'proud country mired up to the fiery eyes in blame and nostalgia', writes O'Hagan, devolved Scotland continues to articulate and understand itself via logics of pain – a pain that lies *beyond* any possible democratic recovery:

> A half-hearted nation will want to hold fast to its grievances, and in that sense Scotland has done well. [. . .] Scotland is a place where cultural artefacts and past battles – the Stone of Destiny, Robert Burns, *Braveheart*, Bannockburn – have more impact on people's sense of moral action than politics does. The people have no real commitment to the public sphere, and are not helped toward any such commitment by the dead rhetoric of the young parliament. Yet the problem is not the parliament, it's the people, and the people's drowsy addiction to imagined injury – their belief in a paralysing historical distress – which makes the country assert itself not as a modern nation open to progress on all fronts, but as a delinquent, spoiled, bawling child, tight in its tartan Babygro, addled with punitive needs and false-memory syndrome.[55]

O'Hagan recanted this view in 2017, declaring at the Edinburgh International Book Festival that 'Scotland itself, these last 15 years, has moved on from the old stasis I used to criticise', and reverted to 1990s devolutionary rhetoric in stressing the power of literary imagination to endow 'an open space of fresh possibility' in which Scottish writers can help 'constitute the nation' anew.[56] What had changed between these interventions? Politics more than culture: the Yes campaign of 2014 awakened O'Hagan to weaknesses in his own sceptical view of nationalism (given full rein in his 2002 article), and attuned him to the extent to which Scotland had already moved beyond the moth-eaten cultural Union articulated by the No campaign: 'It hardly matters whether or not I wanted the Nationalists to win, it was more that I felt they already had. [. . .] As I drove away from the count in Glasgow in the middle of the night I felt the Union wasn't saved, it was in fact over.'[57]

It is a sense of living injury that seals O'Hagan's reversal: outrageously casual disrespect for Scottish opinion displayed by both Labour and Tory leaders in 2014 – David Cameron's pledge to introduce 'English Votes for English Laws' the morning after the indyref result – followed by the unfolding disaster of England's Brexit in 2016–17, leave an utterly blighted future for Britishness, 'a black hole of impertinence and impossibility' for the unionist imagination. 'Now that the picture is clearing, we are left with an image of a belated Little England posing an existential threat to a Scotland that has seen itself for years as European. [. . .] Britain has mismanaged itself out of existence, and Scotland may not be the beneficiary, but it can certainly be the escapee, free to succeed or to fail in its own ways.'[58] The sense of intolerable captivity, and urgency of the 'existential threat', are not entirely different to Tom Scott's grisly fable from 1963. Viewed from a certain angle, O'Hagan's trajectory arcs back to the traditional folkways of mobilising grievance, though actuated by painful direct experience (of UK 'democratic deficit') rather than medieval victimology. The personal freshness of the wound alters all. These are indeed 'live' debates, which have continually shifted and evolved during the period I have studied them; but key features of the terrain remain fixed in place.

Pitfalls and parliamentarism

The cultural re-making and re-production of Scottish nationhood operates within a British constitutional order of a very specific character. Here I turn to the work of Tom Nairn, who observes of the post-devolution UK that 'the habits and instinctive assumptions of sovereignty' endure, but what they manifest 'has been a state-way rather than a folk-way [. . .] there has never been a British nation underpinning the state'.[59] In the freakish 'Ukanian' polity this implies – Nairn's name for the ersatz state-nation which would correspond to British constitutional tradition – there has been no mechanism of 'state-sponsored acculturation' imposing British unity, or assimilation of competing sub-British nationalisms. There has been no need, because peoplehood counts for so little in a constitutional order where the sovereignty of *parliament* is sacrosanct, and any retro-fitting of the state armature (and its legitimising alibis) can be more or less painlessly fudged and finessed from within the ambit of parliament's supremacy, without troubling the folk and their ingrained commonalities.

Thus, spectacles of official Ukanian unity – such as the famous opening ceremony of the 2012 London Olympics, a condensed historical pageant of post-imperial diversity – are the exception and not the rule. There has been no cause to ratify changes in UK territorial governance via top-down meddling with the culture-fabric of local/provincial/national identities. The machinery of parliament is where real power and authority reside, so constitutional change (Nairn argues) has been managed via Westminster's established mechanisms and traditions of elite consent. From the early 1970s, devolution represents an important but superficial shift in this continuum. A weakened central government sought to preserve its parliamentary mandate by re-figuring the relationship between sub-British peoplehood ('national feeling' in Scotland and Wales) and state sovereignty, seemingly acknowledging the centrally-legitimating role of popular, identitarian consent in the British peripheries: the notion that London rule was in some general sense dependent on its acceptability to the Celtic fringe. But the *expression* of this concession took the convenient form of an extra layer of parliamentary apparatus, leaving the nucleus of

UK sovereignty undisturbed and indeed symbolically strengthened: precisely by 'modernising' the outward manifestation of
(pluralist, inclusive) parliamentary 'representation' had the elusive
core of the *ancien régime* (on Nairn's account) re-consecrated its
deeply undemocratic, crypto-feudal basis. Thus devolution as the
reinvention of provincialdom, in Nairn's terms: the granting of
a 'new' importance to expressions of sub-British identity within
constitutional governance ended by affirming – and reproducing –
the supreme, reality-making powers of central authority.

The ultimate problem in any de-centralising British scheme is,
Nairn has argued for five decades, England: 'over-identified with
a single but extruded institutional form' – that is, Anglo-Britain
and its imperial residues – 'English nationality has consequently
little political horizon beyond that.'

> When summoned to present its credentials at a deeper level
> it has normally resorted to literature: English literature has
> often been made the vehicle of a national *Geist*. The latter
> grew less accessible in the narrower terms of territory and
> institutions, after the overwhelming expansion of the 18th
> and 19th centuries. Such habituation to a wider – at one
> time almost global – mode of political expression led to a
> compensatory internalization, a falling back on the spirit.
> The animating nation, when required, could now most
> easily be evoked via culture – by the English Word rather
> than the old English state.[60]

Though Nairn does not pursue the parallel, with Scotland something like the opposite has transpired: the lopsided cultural solidity and political vacancy of Scottish nationhood gave a different
impetus to the presentation of those deeper credentials. Literature has been made to figure not as the animating 'soul' inside the
hyper-diffused institutional machinery (as in the English case),
but as a means of collapsing this very dualism: both as cause and
folk-way, 'Scottish literature' operates as a direct analogue for
statehood, a cultural bone marrow seeking to calcify into a sturdy
institutional skeleton in which nationhood would be affirmed,
concretised and secured.

And what of the political scaffolding that would guide and support this structuration of Scottish sovereignty? The cultural importance of the *parliamentary form* remains to be fully interrogated in the Scottish context, and indeed broader political and sociological study of devolving Britain. The ideological significance of parliamentarism extends well beyond its own ceremonies and procedures, securing a much broader societal fiction well captured by Perry Anderson:

> Parliament, elected every four or five years as the sovereign expression of popular will, reflects the fictive unity of the nation back to the masses as if it were their own self-government. The economic divisions within the 'citizenry' are masked by the juridical parity between exploiters and exploited, and with them the complete *separation* and *non-participation* of the masses in the work of parliament. This separation is then constantly presented and represented to the masses as the ultimate incarnation of liberty: 'democracy' as the terminal point of history.[61]

This teleology is a frequent presence in devolutionary discourse of the 1980s and 1990s, where the prospect of 'self-determination' does double-duty in signifying both the reality of a 'deliverable' devolutionary settlement (a directly elected Scottish parliament with limited powers, explicitly framed as a subset of those exercised by the British state) and a more exhilarating ideal which combines a sense of cultural liberation with notions of existential self-realisation. The hegemonic importance of the parliamentary form extends well beyond the politics of culture and identity. As Anderson argues, 'the existence of the parliamentary State thus constitutes the formal framework of all other ideological mechanisms of the ruling class. It provides the general code in which every specific message elsewhere is transmitted.'[62] Thus, forcing the ethical and aesthetic specificities of Scottish literary texts into the mould of parliamentarism deeply limits their potential autonomy and counter-hegemonic force.[63]

A voice of our own

A recurring focus of the present study is the symbolic importance of distinctively Scottish language and 'voice' in the rhetoric of cultural empowerment and national self-representation. David McCrone cites Bourdieu in specifying the special value of language in claiming national space: 'cultural capital in its objectified state presents itself with all the appearances of an autonomous, coherent universe which, although the product of historical action, has its own laws, transcending individual wills'.[64] Thus, writes McCrone,

> cultural products objectify difference, both reflecting and reifying it in turn. One does not require the existence of a state in order to have this level of cultural objectification, although it is most obvious where a language maps on to a national discourse. As the Yiddish linguist Max Weinreich put it in 1945: 'a language is a dialect with an army and a navy' (Weinreich 1945: 13). One is Irish because the language is 'Irish' (once called simply Gaelic) even though English is the *lingua franca* of everyday life. One does not question that 'the Irish' are a distinct people; they have a state to prove it. Scotland is another matter. At best, it is an understated nation. There is debate north of the border about language, not about Gaelic, now confined to the North West and spoken by less than 2 per cent of the Scottish population, so much as whether 'Scots' is sufficiently distinctive from 'English' (language), which, ironically, is no longer the property of the English (people).[65]

Chapters 6 and 7 attend to linguistic nationalism and rhetorics of 'voice' in devolutionary discourse, exploring the shifting political context in which urban Scots took over the symbolic capital of Gaelic in earlier cultural nationalism. Throughout this study, we find that questions of 'voice' are central to very different strategic framings of devolution – whether viewed as a containment measure by central government, or as a channel of liberated vernacular

identity – and 'voice' serves as the key trope by which these contrary meanings became fully compatible and mutually reinforcing.

In recent work exploring the politics of the 'Scottish Literary
Field', the sociologist Bridget Fowler locates the class trajectories
of individual writers within a broader reading of language, habitus
and state culture. Rehearsing Bourdieu, she writes:

> The state devalues 'regional' or popular languages and cul-
> tures [. . .] [and] canonises as 'legitimate' certain arts and
> sports, classifying some forms through Royal or National
> Academies, national anthems, national ballet companies,
> etc. Further, the State is present at the genesis of a *national*
> habitus, thus forging certain points of social identifica-
> tion. Shakespeare becomes key for creating 'Englishness'
> rather than Renaissance humanism, Racine and Molière
> for 'Frenchness'.[66]

For Fowler, the political valence of 'Scottish Literature' in post-
devolution culture is a proof of how Bourdieu's model does not
insist on a strictly reproductive role for the State; that it can also
harbour and support energies against itself, including the work
of social critics, prophets and revolutionaries. She examines the
work of several major figures of the 'new renaissance' in this vein,
suggesting that recent Scottish writing has astutely managed to
invert the terms of official State culture, successfully penetrating
the regulated and regulating terrain of official art and establishing
a Scottish national habitus coded in the reverse terms (valorising
non-standard and popular language, celebrating working-class
and marginal identities, articulating cultural Scottishness as dig-
nified moral resistance to illegitimate authority). Thus, Fowler
traces the class experience of the most politically consequential
west of Scotland writers born in the 1930s and 40s (Alasdair Gray,
Tom Leonard, James Kelman, Liz Lochhead), noting that 'these
members of the restricted literary field came chiefly from working-class origins, specifically, from the unfashionable districts of
Paisley, Glasgow and Motherwell'.[67] While a sense of exclusion
from 'the linguistic hegemony of the standardised language'[68]
is another area of common ground, each of these writers was

able to secure a degree of cultural capital (such as subsidised university education, other small and irregular grants of public arts funding) via the 'distinct enabling conditions' of the post-war welfare state.[69] In this perspective, the rising children of clerks, train-drivers, picture-restorers and clerical workers are the product of a specific historical niche in the social formation, and the success of their work partly expresses the structural conditions which made it possible (a grant-assisted pathway from Riddrie or Motherwell to the Glasgow School of Art). Their prominence and political importance during the period of welfare-state retrenchment is at once more complex than a heroic outsiders' narrative – involving the potential for 'split habitus', that is, estrangement from their earlier social background and its cultural codes – and inseparable from this specific history, which is sedimented in many of their characteristic aesthetic tendencies. As Fowler observes,

> They are more experimental [than the Renaissance of MacDiarmid and Grassic Gibbon] in their use of modernist devices, sometimes alternating these with realist narratives (as in Gray's *Lanark*). In particular, they have reappropriated Kafka's and Beckett's worlds through the prism of Scotland's housing schemes, job-centres and Council bureaucracy. If, given the flight of shipbuilding, car manufacture, iron and steel, Caterpillar tractors and mining, the collective heterodoxy of these writers' socialist fathers and mothers can no longer be taken for granted, it has not stemmed the abundant representations of the subtle structures through which economic power and gender divisions continue to be renewed, written indelibly onto the body.[70]

Ironically, the enabling social structures which made possible the success and impact of these writers' work – and with it, Fowler argues, made Scottish independence politically possible – are those signature 'British' achievements of the post-war welfare state. Nonetheless, the claims to *Scottish* national representation attributed to these writers and their linguistic and aesthetic strategies

is the key element of their social impact, the factor which secured
political 'traction' for the rest of what they were saying and doing,
even while delimiting its political meaning to national space.
Their rebellious street-cred vis-à-vis British state culture could
be comfortably incorporated into the preferred self-image of the
devolved semi-state, affirming the moral authority of a 'restricted'
local institution.

We now turn to the dominant critical narrative in Scottish
literary politics to examine these claims, their influence, and their
limitations. This final section of the introduction establishes the
literary-historical context for much of the critique that follows.

'A parliament of novels': The Dream

In a *Scottish Educational Journal* essay published in August 1925,
Hugh MacDiarmid remarks that 'it may be that effective cultural
devolution will precede rather than follow political devolution.
If so, the latter will, of course, inevitably follow, and not until it
does will the former be freed of very serious and otherwise insur-
mountable handicaps.'[71] A prescient forecast, to be sure, but from
a rather fickle prophet. In 1923 MacDiarmid had argued 'mere
parliamentary devolution is useless [. . .] *the only thing that will preserve our distinct national culture*' is a Fascist programme adapted to
'Scottish national purposes'.[72] We are concerned here not with
schemes and predictions, but 'cultural devolution' as an historical
explanation of a particular kind: this holds that the path-breaking
work of Scottish writers and artists after 1979 helped to recover
national cultural confidence, stimulating a renewed appetite for
democratic agency. By this story, writers, artists and cultural
activists undertook the task of national self-representation (and,
by some accounts, national re-invention) for which the political institutions proved inadequate, operating as trail-blazers and
place-holders for the later parliament. 'If Scotland voted for *political* devolution in 1997', Cairns Craig argued in 2003,

> it had much earlier declared *cultural* devolution, both in
> the radical voices of new Scottish writing – from James
> Kelman to Matthew Fitt, from Janice Galloway to Ali

Smith – and in the rewriting of Scottish cultural history
that produced, in the 1980s and 1990s, a new sense of
the richness and the autonomy of Scotland's past cultural
achievements.[73]

'It is tempting', wrote Douglas Gifford in 1990, to see the
affirming 'confidence' of recent Scottish fiction 'as somehow
related to the 1979 Devolution referendum and the growing
assertion of Scottish identity and its varieties that emerged almost
in defiance of that quasi-democratic debacle'.[74] The temptation
quickly proves overwhelming as Gifford asserts a transformative,
quasi-constitutional role for Scottish fiction:

> With this new confidence, Scottish fiction approached the
> millennium as a standard bearer for Scottish culture, argu-
> ably even supplying the most successful explorations of
> changing Scottish identities, in a rich variety of voices and
> genres. The new complexities in novelistic vision relate
> dynamically to the changes taking place in Scottish soci-
> ety at large, not only reacting to them, but influencing the
> framework of thought in which they took place.[75]

But the dynamic character of this pattern – responding 'reflexively'
to ongoing developments – is so marked it begins to dissolve the
historical specificity of the 'new renaissance' Gifford described and
consolidated in another 1990 essay:

> There's no mistaking the present revival of hopes in the
> political and cultural scene. There's much of the heady
> atmosphere of the thirties [. . .] when our poetry and fic-
> tion offered folk epics and Scottish mythology to remind
> us of our roots and ancient separateness. And before that
> there was a revival of a different kind, of Celtic aware-
> ness, in the eighteen-nineties [. . .] Perhaps we should read
> all our 'revivals' as progressions; necessary stages of self-
> therapy which pull our introspective intensity out towards
> a wider light.[76]

Conceived as the latest instalment in Scotland's perpetual revival, the 'political and cultural scene' both reflected and shaped by 'new renaissance' writing is swiftly incorporated into 'our' innate psychic conditions, effectively de-historicised.

Parliamentary metaphors for literary representation pervade the discourse of the Dream. A 1999 issue of *Edinburgh Review* entitled 'New Writing for the New Parliament' carries an indicative quotation on its cover, as Duncan McLean declares: 'There's been a parliament of novels for years. This parliament of politicians is years behind.'[77] Reflecting on his pre-devolution anthology *Dream State: The New Scottish Poets* (1994), Donny O'Rourke declares that 'Scotland's artists did more than its politicians to dream up a new Scotland.'[78] In 1996 Keith Dixon heralded a 'radical cultural *neo-populism*' centred on 'authentic new representations of the people':

> It is now generally agreed that since the early seventies, Scotland has been experiencing something of a cultural revolution. A revolution which, perhaps unsurprisingly, has accompanied the remapping of Scottish political space resulting from the rise of political nationalism, the rearticulation of Scottish politics around the issues of political autonomy or independence, and the corresponding decline and more recent marginalization of the only party to actively promote the idea of continuing and unchanging union, i.e. the Conservative Party. [. . .] this movement has been about exploring new senses of community in the Scottish context after the general post-imperial breakdown of Britishness. It has since been to such an extent preoccupied with the need to provide authentic new representations of the people, that, were it not for the pejorative connotations that the term sometimes evokes, one is tempted to talk in terms of the emergence of a radical cultural *neo-populism*.[79]

This account leaves the class character and composition of the 'cultural revolution' somewhat ambiguous, and the present study engages this question only tangentially. But it is worth noting the prominence of class in the *rhetoric* of cultural devolution, particularly in concert with claims to 'cultural representation'. Beyond gestures and bromides in this direction, the class orientation of 'cultural devolution' and its protagonists is seldom foregrounded in its self-talk, except in broad and mythic terms treating Thatcherism as alien to Scottish cultural and political values.

For Robert Crawford, writing in 2000, 'devolution and a reassertion of Scottish nationhood were imagined by poets and writers long before being enacted by politicians'.[80] Michael Gardiner's 2005 primer on *Modern Scottish Culture* installs the post-Kelman novel at the heart of this process: 'dissatisfied with being politically silenced in the 1980s and 1990s, [Scots] had to find a creative solution [. . .] Kelman's rise came at a time when Scots were literally finding a political "voice" in the form of the new Parliament.'[81] Literature functioning as a 'vocal' surrogate for democracy has become a commonplace of Scottish literary studies. In 1998 Christopher Whyte argued that 'in the absence of elected political authority, the task of representing the nation has been repeatedly devolved to its writers'.[82] So effective were these unelected and far-from-unacknowledged legislators, when the new parliament finally opened Liam McIlvanney was struck by 'how little it now seemed to matter'.

> Its coming was welcome, certainly, but hardly seemed critical to the nation's cultural health. Above all, it was belated: by the time the Parliament arrived, a revival in Scottish fiction had been long underway [. . .] Without waiting for the politicians, Scottish novelists had written themselves out of despair.[83]

In an April 1999 item for television news, the broadcast journalist Sarah Smith interviewed Scottish writers and intellectuals on this very phenomenon. Pictured in a colourful Edinburgh wine bar, Smith claims that 'the huge change in Scottish attitudes towards self-government since the failed referendum of 1979 has largely been brought about by cultural changes – it's an artistic movement, one which politicians will find very difficult to control or to contain'.[84] An interview with A. L. Kennedy corroborates the 'enormous cultural explosion' since the 1970s, 'and that's meant that people on the ground will go with the idea of Scotland being a feasible identity. Because you've had Scottish television, Scottish models of success in visual art, in film, in books, and when you see yourself portrayed as a real place you begin to get confidence in a wider identity.'[85]

Perhaps the earliest articulation of this view is George Kerevan's contribution to a 1983 *Chapman* roundtable on 'The Predicament of the Scottish Writer'. The left-wing economist – then a Labour councillor, much later (2015–17) an SNP MP – observed that 'an explosion of cultural activity in Scotland in the Seventies and Eighties' represented 'a declaration of cultural independence'.[86] Consolidated as a grand narrative of cultural vanguardism, Alex Thomson traces its emergence to Cairns Craig's editorial foreword to the *Determinations* series published by Polygon beginning in 1989 ('the 1980s proved to be one of the most productive and creative decades in Scotland this century – as though the energy that had failed to be harnessed by the politicians flowed into other channels'). On close inspection, Thomson argues, this narrative of devolution as 'the metaphorical sublimation of political energy into literary production' appears 'not so much an argument as an immense rumour'.[87] Pointing out that 'circulation of the claim itself [is held to supply] evidence of the cultural revival to which it purports to attest', Thomson charts the repetition and (more cagy) corroboration of this narrative by critics such as Douglas Gifford, Duncan Petrie and Berthold Schoene, before emerging in its fullest articulation in Robert Crawford's *Scotland's Books* (2007). By Thomson's reading:

> [Crawford] links the international recognition by which he judges the success of Scottish writing to the decentralization of legislative control over a limited range of policy areas by Westminster to an elected body at Holyrood: 'there are connections between the recovery of a Parliament in Edinburgh and the ambitious course of modern Scottish literature [. . .] Though the word is a slippery one, a "democratic" urge within Scottish writing has grown in strength, going

beyond the boundaries of conventional politics, and beyond Scotland itself'. Indeed, 'literature has operated in advance of political structures'. It's an uplifting story. The vitality of contemporary Scottish writing, stemming from its concern 'to give voice to those apparently sidelined', has helped Scotland overcome alienation and disenfranchisement, and foster a positive 'reassertion of national identity' whose outcome is a 'people's Parliament' which was 'long imagined throughout the twentieth century'.[88]

The Dream attains semi-official status in James Robertson's *Voyage of Intent: Sonnets and Essays from the Scottish Parliament*. Published by the Scottish Book Trust 'to mark the first ever writer's residency at the Scottish Parliament', this project seems to enact the symbolic centrality of Scottish literature to the new institution. Enric Miralles' first architectural sketches are included alongside poems about the parliament building by Robertson, Kathleen Jamie and Edwin Morgan (appointed Scots Makar by First Minister Jack McConnell in 2004). The included text of a 'masterclass' Robertson delivered to MSPs and parliamentary staff figures devolution as a fundamentally artistic and imaginative project:

> In the 1980s and 1990s, partly in response to the immense sense of political failure and cultural insecurity felt around the 1979 devolution referendum, a wave of writers – far too many even to list here – began to do what those characters in Alasdair Gray's *Lanark* discuss: to use Scotland imaginatively, to reassess and repossess it imaginatively.[89]

These developments are understood to anticipate and even spearhead the political process that ultimately resulted in the parliament itself. Indeed, on being appointed the first culture minister of the new Scottish Executive in 1999, Sam Galbraith MSP – a Labour MSP and a confirmed unionist – told a meeting of senior arts figures that 'in his view, the artists had made devolution possible'.[90] In just these terms, Robertson explains to MSPs the backstory of the parliament in which they serve, and subtly claims, on behalf of

Scottish writing, prior authorship over their democratic warrant. After 1979 there was

> a resurgence of interest in the Scottish literature of the past, a renewed commitment to writing in Gaelic and Scots, and a wave of new writers, most of whom wanted some change in Scotland's political status. Much of the cultural regeneration of Scotland that preceded the referendum vote of 1997 – which made it quite clear that, in John Buchan's words, a substantial majority of the Scottish people desired their own parliament – was instigated by writers.[91]

The primacy of literary activism here positions the people as receptive *readers* moved by their true representatives, the poets and novelists. As Aaron Kelly argues, this 'standard critical narrative positions the post-1979 cultural realm as the space wherein authority and identity are devolved in a manner that actually anticipates the institutional devolution of power through the Scotland Act'.[92] It should be noted that evidence of Scottish writers embracing their new political burdens is highly variable, both in this period and later. Indeed, editing a 1979 issue of *Aquarius* dedicated to Hugh MacDiarmid, the poet Douglas Dunn argues the contrary, observing that 'as political nationalism has moved into realms of reality and possibility, literary nationalism, at one time more conspicuous than any other, has declined in force'.[93] In the same article Liz Lochhead comments: 'I'm scared to say I don't give a damn about whether or not I'm a Scottish poet [. . .] I don't feel that being Scottish has been nearly as important as being urban, working-class, or a woman.'[94] Exactly two decades later, Janice Galloway responded to a similar state-of-literary-nationhood prompt in a number of the *Edinburgh Review* marking the arrival of the new parliament. 'I don't think of myself as enmeshed in questions of national consciousness', she wrote, while hoping the parliament might provide practical help for writers (such as tax rebates on the Irish model, which would mean 'more women with talent *and* children could write'), and support for cross-cultural activity that might 'get us off some of the rather tedious single-track roads this country's writers are often expected to go down. Who wants to write about *nation* all the bloody time?'[95]

But such voices have been largely drowned out by the general chorus tendency traced above. For Douglas Gifford, writing in 1999, the Scottish Parliament arrived in tandem with

> a clear sense of bold new possibilities of Scottish identities [. . .] a sense of constant experimentation and rising confidence, devoid of political reticence. The reasons for this are many and complex, ranging, I believe, from the belated fruiting of the Welfare State to the singular success of the Scottish Arts Council, as well as the dawning recognition by Scots that they are in danger of being left behind, economically, culturally and historically, if they don't at last speak out.[96]

There is a problem with the Dream narrative, and not only, as Aaron Kelly demonstrates, its suppression of class politics. Paradoxically, the literary nationalism imagined to blaze the trail for political devolution aims not at a political outcome (constitutional change), but the 'curing' of the abnormal cultural condition of which it is a symptom. This *nationalist culturalism* reaches its fulfilment not in home rule or independence, but in the attainment of a 'healthy' (imaginative) condition of Scottish nationality – one relieved of the burdens of self-assertion and agonised self-examination, and embracing new expressive possibilities for 'identity'.[97] This exactly mirrors the conception of 'national feeling' evident in the 1970s governmental discourse responding to rising votes for the SNP and Plaid Cymru: electoral behaviour is regarded as a barometer of 'discontent' that betokens anything but a serious desire to contest UK state sovereignty. Instead, the growth of sub-British nationalism is understood as a circular pathology, where nationalist success at key by-elections is interpreted as a symptom of pent-up national consciousness, but of a deeply limited character spent by its own expression, and seeking no more than recognition and visibility. To neutralise the potential threat of 'national feeling', it was argued, central government need only witness and acknowledge it. On just these terms, the existence of the post-1999 parliament is held to end national malaise, and the venting of the cultural-political pressures which created it. Figured as the expressive release and 'resolution' of the problem of Scottishness, devolution is locked into a 'representative' orientation to culture limited in advance to *display and recognition*, and the channelled release of 'national feeling' away from political agency and toward the play and display of 'identity'.

Michael Gardiner's 2004 study *The Cultural Roots of British Devolution* argues 'that devolution represents the endgame of a growing ambivalence deep in the British management of culture'[98]; his *Modern Scottish Culture* presents the 1997 devolution referendum as 'the conclusion of a long period of mixed, and often vague, cultural demands for increased democracy'.[99] As we shall see, there is significant merit in this thesis – at the governmental level, devolution really is about the management of cultural difference – but surely 'increased democracy' is a *political* demand. Eliding culture and politics is a recurring feature in the Dream discourse, and a more recent Gardiner essay surveys the post-1979 era as follows:

> A new 'Britishing' period emerged, but without the cohesive pride of Blitz, the Welfare State, or industrial expansion. The new [Thatcher] administration faced a downturn while maintaining a combination of monetarist control over public finances and a popularising of social-Darwinist metaphors in business; unemployment more than doubled between 1979 and 1983, and social inequalities became broadly acceptable for the first time since before the war. Not only Wales and Scotland, but England's industrial north and rural edges felt disenfranchised, and even Londoners protested through the Greater London Council, and more than ever the UK state seemed less a form of representation than an oligarchy of financial management. National contexts became increasingly distinct from, and *opposed to*, those of the UK. As Scottish literature enjoyed a revival, Britain as an idea was collapsing more rapidly than at any time since the eighteenth century. Culture was behind this process.[100]

I cite this passage at length in order to highlight its notable avoidance of the *electoral* context and party politics which incontestably prompted and defined devolution. No reason is given why Wales, Scotland and the industrial north of England 'felt disenfranchised'; election results and patterns of party allegiance go without saying. It is not that Gardiner is unaware of these factors, or wishes to minimise them, but even the tacit understanding at work here – the common knowledge that Labour-voting areas of Scotland and Wales 'felt disenfranchised' by Tory rule – seems to figure elections as a simple mechanism of representation and protest. Electoral politics are a kind of second-order 'process' which merely reflects what lies 'behind' it, namely the primary realities of 'culture'. But this is to overlook the profoundly mediating role of party politics on that substrate of cultural allegiance and discontent, in two senses: the constitutive role of electoralism in *making* and *reproducing* those primary lines of affiliation, and the significant *autonomy* of parliamentary politics in the UK system – the sense in which party (and intra-party) jockeying is a realm unto itself, only vaguely and sporadically determined by 'outside' forces such as public opinion, let alone feats of literary dissidence.

Marie Hologa partly addresses this issue in her recent study of nationalism in contemporary Scottish novels, where she acknowledges that 'a literary text with its ambiguous meanings and functions both reflects *and* affects its historical and political contexts'.[101] Her view that contemporary Scottish literature 'serves as a discursive space that allows for alternative constructions of devolution' is easy to accept, though (like many such studies) a degree of circularity attends critical readings of novels held to contest political phenomena for which they are also the primary evidence; that is, artefacts of *literary nationalism* whose relationship to 'extra-literary' politics are not – and perhaps cannot – adequately be articulated.[102] Seemingly mindful of just this difficulty, Hologa cites Cairns Craig's influential argument that the 'tradition of the Scottish novel is [. . .] an index of the continuity of the nation' but adds that 'the very literary tradition also *produces* and *re-produces* these forms of national imagining in the first place'.[103] And yet, to conceive the Scotland of *Scotland the Brave* not 'as the actual, devolved political entity within the multinational state of the UK, but more as a discursive construction, a national "imagining" and historical narrative itself imposes significant limits on what this approach can reveal about the ultimate 'product' or political/sociological outcome of these literary imaginings. In setting aside the political and electoral context *in which* the reproduction if 'ImagiNation' takes place, we are somewhat stranded in the domain of Nancy Fraser's 'free-floating cultural representations'.

It is simply impossible to make an intelligible explanation of Scottish devolution without attending to these electoral factors and their profoundly mediating role. To a very large extent, 'devolution' names a process constituted within the horizon of government, responding to unexpected but ambiguous electoral signals with the potential to disrupt the UK party duopoly, which parties, politicians and officials interpret, ventriloquise and 'manage' according to an established nexus of interests. Accordingly, this book attempts to integrate historical awareness of the party politics of devolution with critical attention to the self-image of Scottish literary nationalism. Writing on the cusp of the Dream's fruition in 1999, Douglas Gifford poses 'one of modern Scotland's outstanding paradoxes':

> Why was it that, in the 1920s and 1930s with the Scottish Renaissance in full flight, and Scottish culture vigorous in assertion of ancient identity and political rights, no political gains resulted in terms of membership of parliament? Yet, in the 1970s, when Scottish writers from McIlvanney to Mackay Brown were repudiating Scottish literary traditions and insisting on the non-Scottish and international roots of their work, nigh a dozen Scottish nationalist members of parliament resulted?[104]

At one level, this book is an attempt to answer this question, extending the story beyond the 1970s to the establishment of the Scottish Parliament. At another, it rejects the premise of this 'paradox'. The key word in Gifford's formulation is 'resulted', as though there is some direct causal relationship between literary production and electoral behaviour. Even to 'surface' this assumption is to expose it; this implied equation can only hold

within a wider identitarian discourse of national representation, in which the *voicing* of Scottishness is the tacit meaning
of writing and voting alike. The apparent 'paradox' of opposed
elements held in tension is itself the product of assuming their
prior unity. Gifford continues: 'is it perhaps the case that Scottish culture and Scottish politics are doomed forever to be at
loggerheads, or – at last – are we witnessing the reintegration
of all the many split and divided traditions of our cultural and
social life?'[105] But looking 'beyond' this illusory divide between
culture and politics, and towards their 'reintegration', is to name
not the hopeful future made possible by Scottish devolution, but
the logic of its historical emergence.

Contradictory directions

Though emphasising electoral interests largely ignored in the literary field surveyed above, I do not suggest a tidy determinism
between party strategies of the 1960s–90s. In a recent essay Cairns
Craig makes the striking observation that in 1990 'no political
party in Scotland was in favour of the Parliament that actually
came into existence in 1999'.[106]

> Despite that oft-quoted appeal to the 'settled will of the
> Scottish people', there had been, in fact, no Scottish politi-
> cal consensus on the form that devolution should take. The
> Parliament happened, if not quite by chance, then through
> a series of apparently accidental and certainly unpredictable
> intersections of trains of events running in often contradic-
> tory directions.[107]

We begin to sense the challenge of imposing a narrative teleology on these developments, key episodes having been driven
(quite nakedly) by short-term electoral calculation. Thus, Craig
argues, an historical account centred on political parties and
positioning will take us only so far. After a precis of the Campaign for a Scottish Assembly (from 1980) and its successor the
Scottish Constitutional Convention (from 1989), and the emergence of a pro-devolution consensus in Scotland during the

Major government, Craig draws a clear and even provocative conclusion: 'if politics and votes were the means of bringing the parliament into existence, they were not its direct cause'; the parliament 'has been built on the foundations of a revolution in the nation's culture'.[108] This is the culturalist case at its strongest, and accords a position of tremendous influence to the artists and intellectuals who led this 'revolution'. Why should this be, and what can it tell us about the longer trajectory of Scottish nationalism? In his classic study *The Break-Up of Britain*, Tom Nairn observes that Scotland departs from the modern norm of the 'age of nationalism' in which 'the standard function of an intellectual class' was to construct and valorise (while seeming to 'recover' or awaken) 'the distinctively modern consciousness of nationality'.[109] 'A "national culture", in the sense which had become newly important' in the nineteenth century, Nairn writes, 'entailed an intellectual class able to express the particular realities of a country, in a romantic manner accessible to growing numbers of the reading public – a class operating actively in the zone of general and literary culture (rather than the specializations Scots became celebrated for)'.[110] This group (and class) typically 'became vital elements in the cohesion of society as a whole', except in Scotland: because 'the relationship between civil society and the State in Scotland precluded a fully national culture',[111] the intelligentsia were left 'unemployed on their home terrain'.[112]

Why, then, were Scottish intellectuals able to successfully assume (approximately) this role in the 1970s and 1980s? This is an introduction and not a conclusion, but the answer has more to do with British than Scottish political dynamics. Quite simply, the demands of nationalist intellectuals in the post–1967 period were politically aligned not with a disruptive, still less a 'revolutionary' movement seeking to overthrow the established order, but with a strategy to re-secure UK sovereignty in an upgraded, 'modernised' form. The Dream played out within the political logic and electoral boundaries of the Grind, and would not otherwise have passed from the terrain of imaginative literature to the affable stones of the Canongate Wall.

Chapter summaries

The first two chapters of the book survey competing narratives of developments prior to 1979. Chapter 1 explores the backstory of 'cultural devolution' – the Dream – through small magazines of the post-Hamilton scene, where *Scottish International* and its literary-nationalist rivals tussle over the mantle of Scottish renewal. In Chapter 2 a very different process is traced through the 'machine politics' of 1970s devolution, dominated by state and party interests. This is the Grind at its most grinding, as successive proposals, White Papers and Bills are debated, supplemented, 'fixed', abandoned, filibustered, guillotined and sabotaged. The ultimate failure of this governmental process created the vacuum into which Scottish writers and critics were able to offer 'vision', feeling and afflatus after 1979; but on terms largely continuous with the cultural logic of devolution established by the Royal Commission on the Constitution (1969–73), namely the *management of national feeling*.

After 1979, these divergent stories (the Dream, the Grind) were strategically yoked together in the re-construction of national political space. In Chapters 3 and 4 we trace the legacies of this paradigm in the 1980s and 1990s, notably in the burgeoning print culture of the Edinburgh intelligentsia (including *Radical Scotland*, *Cencrastus* and *Edinburgh Review*). In the emergence of a vanguard cultural elite ready to claim national moral and political leadership, the valorisation of Scottish 'voice', difference, injury and authenticity take increasingly solid form: the tactical promotion of 'the Scottish dimension' (grounded in culture, unrepresented in government) swiftly blossoms into a 'claim of right', a self-limiting demand for *distinctive government* phrased in the logic of popular sovereignty. Chapter 5 examines the most significant literary realisation – and self-portrait – of 'cultural devolution', James Robertson's epic historical novel *And the Land Lay Still*. Here we consider a series of narrative dilemmas in the conjunction of journalistic reportage and nationalist teleology, as Robertson assembles a Story of Scotland commensurate with the higher, unifying meanings of constitutional change. Drawing on the work of Pascale Casanova, Chapter 6 examines the constitution of 'national literary space' in the logic of vernacular Scottishness, a claim to limited autonomy in which the 'social-and-national' valence of Scots is inseparable from English, but required to signify the condition of ethno-cultural separateness traditionally evoked by Gaelic. Left-nationalist debates of the 1970s–80s clearly show the shifting strategic value of urban Scots, and the refashioning of *class speech* into a quasi-ethnic signifier of suppressed nationality. The final chapter returns to the parliamentary form, and the prominence of vernacular literary politics in Holyrood's own ceremonies and spectacles of representation, with direct resonances in some of the most influential Scottish literary texts of the 1990s. In the writing of Irvine Welsh, A. L. Kennedy and James Kelman, the liberation and commodification of Scottish 'voice' highlights a range of social contradictions entailed by the 'cultural devolution' thesis, and the limits of an identitarian politics of 'representation'. None of these chapters is as long or demanding as this Introduction.

A note on historical coverage

This study is focused almost entirely on literary and political developments leading to the implementation of legislative devolution in 1999, the key strategic and rhetorical bridgeheads having been secured in the 1970s and 1980s. Thus I do not closely examine the 1999–2014 period between the establishment of Holyrood and the referendum on Scottish independence.[113] The parameters of this study are more limited partly for reasons of space, but mainly because the pivotal debates which enabled, delimited and shaped Scottish devolution must be traced to this earlier period.

Notes

1. Edwin Morgan, 'The future of the antisyzygy', *Bulletin of Scottish Politics*, 1.1 (1980), pp. 7–29 (p. 17). From a conference speech delivered in June 1978.
2. Warner, 'Scottish writers on the referendum – independence day?', *The Guardian*, 19 July 2014.
3. Bissett, 'Scotland's no vote has forced its artists to rediscover ambiguity', *The Guardian*, 15 October 2015.

4. Paterson, 'Naw', *The Poets' Republic*, 1 (May 2015).
5. See Hames, 'The new Scottish renaissance?'
6. Smith, *Devolution and the Scottish Conservatives*, p. 4.
7. Ichijo, 'Entrenchment of unionist nationalism: devolution and the discourse of national identity in Scotland', p. 25.
8. McCrone, 'Cultural capital in an understated nation', p. 80.
9. Ibid. p. 80.
10. Kedourie, *Nationalism*, p. 58.
11. Abizadeh, 'Liberal nationalist versus postnational social integration', p. 240.
12. Kymlicka, *Politics in the Vernacular*, pp. 213–14.
13. Salmond, Official Report (Scottish Parliament), 21 March 2013.
14. Farred quoted by Hart, *Nations of Nothing But Poetry*, p. 12.
15. Bourdieu, *Language and Symbolic Power*, p. 12.
16. Gellner, *Nations and Nationalism*, p. 1.
17. Kellas, *The Scottish Political System*, p. 129.
18. Ibid. p. 5.
19. Ibid. p. 5.
20. Billig, *Banal Nationalism*.
21. Kellas, *The Scottish Political System*, p. 6.
22. Ibid. p. 6.
23. Ryan, *Ireland and Scotland*, p. 39.
24. McCrone, 'Cultural capital in an understated nation', pp. 78–9.
25. Ibid. p. 79
26. James Robertson, 'A culture of diversity', *Radical Scotland*, 31 (February–March 1988), p. 32.
27. See Michaels, *The Trouble with Diversity* and Haider, *Mistaken Identity*.
28. Quoted in Haider, *Mistaken Identity*, p. 10, citing Butler, *The Psychic Life of Power* (1997).
29. Haider, *Mistaken Identity*, pp. 10–11.
30. Kennedy and Suny, *Intellectuals and the Articulation of the Nation*, p. 1.
31. Brown, *States of Injury*, p. 55.
32. Brown, *Politics Out of History*, p. 26.
33. Ibid. p. 30.
34. Bourdieu, *In Other Words*, p. 154.
35. Ibid. p. 155.
36. Adorno, *Minima Moralia*, pp. 28, 102.
37. Bourdieu, *In Other Words*, p. 155.
38. Ibid. p. 154.
39. Fraser, 'Rethinking recognition', p. 108.
40. Ibid. p. 112.

41. Ibid. p. 108.

42. Ibid. pp. 114, 110.

43. Ibid. p. 110.

44. Ibid. p. 114.

45. Ibid. p. 116.

46. Fraser, 'From redistribution to recognition?', p. 69.

47. Brown, *Politics Out of History*, p. 40.

48. Brown, *States of Injury*, p. 53.

49. But note also that 'nationalism was precisely the epistemological obstacle' early proponents of 'identity politics', such as the Combahee River Collective, were seeking to navigate; with mixed results. See Haider, *Mistaken Identity*, pp. 24–5.

50. Brown, *States of Injury*, p. 36.

51. Ibid. p. 39.

52. Ibid. p. 40.

53. Smith, *National Identity*, pp. 19–20.

54. Tom Scott, 'Observations on Scottish Studies', *Studies in Scottish Literature*, 1.1 (1963), pp. 5–13 (p. 5).

55. O'Hagan, 'Scotland's old injury', p. 21.

56. O'Hagan, 'Scotland your Scotland'.

57. Ibid.

58. Ibid.

59. Nairn, *After Britain*, p. 177.

60. Ibid. pp. 177–8.

61. Anderson, 'The antinomies of Antonio Gramsci', p. 28.

62. Ibid. p. 28.

63. Of course, this problem attends national literary history as such, and is not particular to the Scottish case. See Thomson, '"You can't get there from here"'.

64. McCrone cites Bourdieu, 'The forms of capital', p. 50.

65. McCrone, 'Cultural capital in an understated nation', p. 73.

66. Fowler, 'Pierre Bourdieu', p. 74.

67. Ibid. p. 83.

68. Ibid. p. 73.

69. Ibid. p. 72.

70. Ibid. p. 79.

71. MacDiarmid, *Contemporary Scottish Studies*, p. 68.

72. MacDiarmid, 'Programme for a Scottish Fascism', p. 38.

73. Craig, 'Scotland: culture after devolution', p. 39.

74. Gifford, 'Breaking boundaries', p. 237.

75. Ibid. p. 237.

76. Gifford, 'At last – the real Scottish literary renaissance?', *Books in Scotland*, 34 (1990), pp. 1–4 (pp. 1, 3).
77. The cover shows a pull-quote from McLean's contribution to Various, 'Poet's Parliament', *Edinburgh Review*, 100 (1999), pp. 71–7.
78. O'Rourke, *Dream State*, p. 2.
79. Dixon, 'Notes from the underground', pp. 118–19.
80. Crawford, *Devolving English Literature*, p. 307.
81. Gardiner, *Modern Scottish Culture*, p. 155.
82. Whyte, 'Masculinities in contemporary Scottish fiction', p. 284.
83. McIlvanney, 'The politics of narrative in the post-war Scottish novel', p. 183.
84. Smith, ITN News broadcast, 29 April 1999.
85. Ibid.
86. Kerevan, 'Labourism revisited', *Chapman*, 35–6 (1983), pp. 25–31 (p. 26).
87. Thomson, '"You can't get there from here"'.
88. Ibid.
89. Robertson, *Voyage of Intent*, p. 55.
90. See Brown, 'Processes and interactive events' and Brown '"Arts first; politics later"'. Ian Brown adds: 'worth noting here that the claim is made by two very experienced and hard-nosed politicos [George Reid and Sam Galbraith], not artists claiming to be unacknowledged legislators!'
91. Robertson, *Voyage of Intent*, p. 33.
92. Kelly, 'James Kelman and the deterritorialisation of power', p. 175.
93. Douglas Dunn (and others), 'What it feels like to be a Scottish poet', *Aquarius*, 11 (1979), pp. 62–79 (p. 67).
94. Ibid. p. 71.
95. Various, 'Poet's Parliament', pp. 71–2.
96. Gifford, '"Out of the world and into Blawearie"', p. 300.
97. See Kelly, 'James Kelman and the deterritorialisation of power'.
98. Gardiner, *The Cultural Roots of British Devolution*, p. x.
99. Gardiner, *Modern Scottish Culture*, p. 133.
100. Gardiner, 'Arcades – the 1980s and 1990s', p. 181.
101. Hologa, *Scotland the Brave?*, p. 16.
102. To be sure, this problem is not confined to Hologa's study, but to the dearth of inter-disciplinary models in the field; Hologa's study is based on PhD research on Scottish literature and it would be churlish to insist her book incorporate a parallel study of Scottish politics, as the present volume nervously attempts.
103. Hologa, *Scotland the Brave?*, pp. 16–17.

104. Gifford, '"Out of the world and into Blawearie"', p. 300.
105. Ibid. p. 300.
106. Craig, 'Unsettled will', p. 10.
107. Ibid. p. 10.
108. Craig, 'Unsettled will', p. 12; Craig, *Intending Scotland*, p. 73.
109. Nairn, *The Break-Up of Britain*, pp. 153–4.
110. Ibid. p. 155.
111. Ibid. p. 155.
112. Ibid. p. 154.
113. See Pittin-Hedon, *The Space of Fiction*.

1

Chaps with Claymores to Grind

Literary and Political Nationalism 1967–79

In September 1967 Tom Nairn reported on the annual Edinburgh Festival for the *New Statesman*. At the height of his blistering disdain for 1960s Scotland – his 'Three Dreams of Scottish Nationalism' would be published a few months later – Nairn reflected on the 'sour anglicised whine' of Festival chatter.

> Behind the appalling artificial waterfall and a thousand care-fully poised teacups, a truly serious question is forced upon one: what *is* this Festival, after 21 years, what has it become? The answer is: it was Culture, it has become Scotland. It has not merely succeeded; it has turned fatally and permanently into another Scottish Thing, another structural element in the tiresome fantasy-life the Scots have been doping them-selves with for the past three centuries to avoid their real problem. Festival time in Edinburgh seems to have joined tartanry, militarism, Burns and Scott – those 'mummified housegods in their musty niches', as Edwin Muir put it – as a constituent of the Great Scottish Dream.[1]

The 'most important trait' of this dream, Nairn continued in *New Left Review* in May–June 1968, 'is a vast, impossible dissociation from the realities of history', a vision-quest driven by 'the hope for an identity' where none is possible.[2] Or not possible as the *real* identity of a living political nationhood: Scotland's wilful dream-ing is of a romantic 'substitute consciousness' which at the level of camp culture-nostalgia both admits and compensates for the 'unreality' of lived national experience.[3] Marked by a yearning

for 'identity' rather than political power, modern Scottish nationalism is a 'dream of redemption' that will make good the loss of
living collectivity: 'for the Scots, national existence must represent that magic, whole reality of which they have been cheated
by history – in it, their maimed past will be redeemed, in more
vivid colours than a history can ever provide'.[4] We are closer here
to imaginative compensation than historical recovery, and it is
notable that Nairn draws largely on novelists, poets and literary
scholars in developing this analysis. Indeed, the 'Scotland' which
has assimilated the Edinburgh Festival into its own 'tiresome
fantasy-life' stands revealed as a fundamentally *fictive* enterprise,
expressing latent cultural needs in 'crooked' and neurotic form.
'In Scotland the real must become unreal, and the unreal be seen
at all costs as real.'[5] Thus the cultural unit and topos 'Scotland'
generates a steady flow of signs, narratives and images to sustain
its formal 'identity', all the while knowing – and bracketing – the
placeholder function of this mask, a necessary stand-in for the
real, redeemed nationhood yet to come.

But tartanry and Burns-worship are only the most familiar
faces of the 'Great Scottish Dream'. At another level, the zom-
bie permanence of these phenomena serves as endless fodder for
strenuous debunking by the national intelligentsia, whose role is
to castigate the symptoms while affirming the reality of the underlying pathology, so validating the quest to supply 'Scotland' with a
viable political referent. The trouble, Nairn argues, is that the vigorous myth-busting of the cognoscenti coincides with their own
'intense romanticism', one which exceeds the sceptical impulse
and figures the actuality of modern Scotland as a craven disgrace
to the *ideal* nation. Pursuit of this seductive and elusive object is
the latent 'content' of the dream, whose caustic and romantic
elements are commingled in a volatile blend. This semi-Freud-
ianised Scotland is 'doubly dominated by her dead generations',
Nairn writes. 'At bottom there is the bedrock of Calvinism, the
iron, abstract moralism of a people that distrusts the world and
itself; then overlaying this, the sentimental, shadow-appropriation
of this world and itself through romantic fantasy.'[6] Sluicing the
tinsel 'house-gods' with anti-romantic acid only causes the lower
and meaner impulses to rise to the surface, releasing an implac-
able scepticism whose suspicion and self-contempt overflow

the conjuring trick of tartanry and spill onto the terrain of real experience. Thus, in the course of venerating MacDiarmid as a 'true bard' who unflinchingly 'presents the Scottish people with their own image', his raging protégé Tom Scott inveighs against 'Scotshire, a county in the north of England, an ex-country, an Esau land that has sold its birthright for a mess of English pottage'.[7] In this bleak but proudly undeceived vision, the real Scotland visible through the kitchen window is a *scar*, an embodiment of cultural damage which cannot be repaired at the level of image and 'identity'. Faced with these twin falsities – the infantile tartan fantasy, the living lie of Scotshire – Scotland as subject 'is rejected as travesty, and can only be rejected *totally*'.[8] The modernist-primitivist Scotland intended to take its place, in MacDiarmid's Renaissance project, is conceived as a blitzkrieg negation of this sham, but finds little purchase outside the clammy, circular debates of a vanguardist coterie. Thus the insularity and 'complacent narcissism' of an elect literary-nationalist milieu, in which the 'trash-image' of tartanry is forever being violently rejected by patriot-redeemers who find, like MacDiarmid, 'that the "real" Scotland which is worth while and has survived it all is—*oneself*'.[9] If there is the slightest doubt who Nairn is referring to, consider MacDiarmid's 1933 poem 'Conception', of which this line would serve as a jibing paraphrase, with the speaker's

> strange, mysterious, awful finding
> Of my people's very life within my own
> – This terrible blinding discovery
> Of Scotland in me, and I in Scotland.[10]

Scottish writers and intellectuals are, then, both central to the nation's ongoing neurotic self-construction (and surviving currency at the level of image and 'fantasy-life'), and the chief obstacle to waking from the half-life of the Great Dream. 'The really ugly truth of the spectacle lies less in its hideous content than in its semantic relationship to reality', Nairn insists, and the credence it commands from the national public whose possibility it both sustains and degrades in advance. Those intellectuals equipped to see past or through the dream are not excluded from this cycle, but central to it. Their extravagant derision for the most prevalent mirage – the lies about Scotland actually countenanced by really-existing Scotland – secures for the 'advanced' thinkers and visionaries a distinction wholly confined to their own enlightened refuge from populist escapism: a literature of their own.

> In Milne's Bar, the crowds of poets come and go among the portraits of MacDiarmid, Goodsir Smith, MacCaig and the other heroes. The prominent part of alcohol in the National spiritual life is well-known. The function of the mental whisky that also flows at Milne's is less appreciated: poetry. Next to tartan and soldiers, poetry is the greatest curse of contemporary Scotland. It is the intellectuals' special form of dope, which they can indulge in with a good conscience while the crowds go mad up on the Castle esplanade.[11]

The corny spectacle of the Royal Military Tattoo is the travesty-image of Scotland scorned by the bibulous literati, who condemn the romantic pabulum on offer at Edinburgh Castle not as a distraction from their tortured meditations on Celtic revival and spiritual wholeness, but as their founding premise: the extirpation of a false religion. Murdering to create, small wonder that the revolutionary energies of MacDiarmid's Renaissance found issue in 'almost entirely poetical' form, Nairn observes: 'poetry in this sense is a kind of magic: it conjures up the dead and the non-existent into a semblance of the desired object'.[12] But this third-choice alternative – an elite substitute-for-the-substitute for living nationhood – is doomed to failure, both aesthetic and political. Poetry of MacDiarmid's tradition 'has to conjure up the national culture, as well as the nation itself, through an impossible, encyclopedic lyricism. Devoted to this false task, the poets actually fail to disturb the real, terrible silence of Scotland.'[13] The mistaken need to speak 'for' the nation – and the deep contempt for the existing residues of national community which underpins this need – ensures the nationalist writer can never be *heard* by the collectivity in whose name he speaks.

The 'only possible sane reaction to the dilemma', Nairn concludes, is a 'Socialist Nationalism' which seeks 'cultural liberation from Scotland's pervasive myths as a precondition of political action and [which] must utterly condemn the kind of garrulous, narcissistic windbaggery to which the intelligentsia has so often resorted – in the absence of anything better – as its special contribution to the problem'.[14] Only the negation of that 'Scotland' constructed by neurotic literary nationalism – liberation from the poetical dreams of liberation imbibed in Milne's Bar – holds any hope for a genuine project of national *realisation*, one that might confront the nation's 'living contemporary history' rather than evading it, and take steps toward 'a wholeness expressing its life instead of hiding it, a three-dimensional being freeing the national will and tongue from their secular inhibitions, a realness to startle itself and the watching world'.[15]

Nairn's extended 'diagnosis' of a malformed, crooked, schizophrenic and castrated Scottishness develops along these lines over the next decade and more, and often traffics in essentialist, masculinist and ableist imagery of national 'paralysis' which, as Eleanor Bell has shown, tends to re-affirm the logic of romantic nationalism even as it castigates individual nationalist romantics.[16] In this study I am less concerned with Nairn's view of the 'national will' (and its stunting), than his critique of political devolution as a state process. His writing of this period claims two profound ruptures: one between substantive political nationhood and degraded cultural 'identity' – the loss of the former compelling the neurotic fantasies of the latter – and a second between the sleepy self-regard of an introverted nationalist intelligentsia and the dismal reality of the heedless Scottish public. Only a few months later, the landscape would look rather different; even Nairn would cease to dismiss 'the utter feebleness of Scottish political Nationalism' after the Hamilton by-election of 2 November 1967.[17] But the cultural and political developments that immediately followed Hamilton largely confirmed Nairn's sense of the twin gulfs separating, on one hand, cultural and political nationalism, and, on the other, the nationalist literati from the grain of prosaic national life. The political conditions in which these gaps could be finessed and elided would not arise until the 1980s, when the literary intelligentsia arranged for its special appointment as pathfinders for a restored national polity and cultural public. A real 'Scotland', they would claim, had been brought back from the dead by 'Culture', released from its vaporous and neurotic diffusion in Lallans poetry to become a solid, de-sublimated 'Scottish Thing', governed and affirmed by a discourse of 'identity' and self-representation, authenticated by a liberated national speech.

This book is a critical history of this shift, and the role of writers and critics in stimulating, strategising, popularising and institutionalising it. It is not quite a history of Scottish devolution – I have almost nothing to say about the relevant economic and sociological factors – but it is an effort to make sense of how 'Scottish Literature' positions itself within cultural, political and constitutional developments since 1967, often as both cause and effect. Nairn evokes an unchanging torpor in his Edinburgh vignette, but rapid and dramatic change was afoot. Four years later, two bombs were detonated in a cellar of Edinburgh Castle during the Royal Military Tattoo, causing extensive damage but no injuries.[18] Initial speculation linked the attack to Irish republicans but suspicion would later fall on the rag-tag 'tartan terror' groups which were sporadically active in the 1970s. Whatever the sensational plots and intrigues associated with the Scottish Liberation Army – fully exploited in Douglas Hurd and Andrew Osmond's novel *Scotch on the Rocks* (1971) – direct action groups were a sideshow to the electoral shift which stimulated so much reflection and re-assessment in the 1970s. The context of rising political nationalism would give a different complexion to 'dream-nationhood', altering its stakes and the place of writers and intellectuals within it. The distance between cultural and political nationhood did not suddenly close, however; it is not until after 1979 that their integration acquires a strong electoral expedience (guided by the interests of the Labour Party, rather than the SNP), and from the mid-1980s literary-cultural and electoral movements for a renewed Scotland begin to sing from the same strategic songbook. That story is examined in Chapters 3 and 4 of this study. Before we can grasp it, we need to examine what happened before the post-1979 'new renaissance', and how residues of the 'old' Scottish Renaissance responded to the altered political dynamic of the post-Hamilton world. For much of the 1970s, the standard-bearers of literary nationalism were deeply ambivalent about the rising SNP, and sceptical of the conventional electoral politics heralded by Winnie Ewing's victory. Exploring the discontinuity between these rival national movements is key to understanding the political logic of their integration after 1979.

Political nationalism

As SNP historian Peter Lynch observes, 'Scottish nationalism is not primarily concerned with language or cultural issues but with political and economic self-government.'[19] Christopher Harvie recalled the 'a-cultural quality of Scottish nationalism in the 1970s':

> Meetings of the SNP lacked both kilts and literary figures, in contrast to the apparent situation before World War II. Writers and artists, however nationalist in sympathy, shied from a party so explicitly 'modernising' in its ethos and, despite the literary enthusiasm of the chairman, William Wolfe, this distrust was reciprocated by many leading figures in the party.[20]

Indeed, the SNP's earliest modernising impulses ran counter to cultural traditionalism. Two important histories from this period date the 'fall of literary nationalism' within the SNP to the 1930s or 40s. H. J. Hanham's 1969 study showed that sidelining (and where necessary, purging) 'the wild young literary men' of the National Party of Scotland had been pivotal in the formation of the Scottish National Party as a credible electoral vehicle, effected via the merger of NPS with the right-wing Scottish Party. Romantic nationalists such as Compton Mackenzie, R. B. Cunningham Graham and Lewis Spence had been prominent in the National Party, but the architect of the merger, NPS secretary John MacCormick, sought 'respectability' for the movement and felt growing impatience with 'the more Radical literary men of the party, whom he regarded as little better than saboteurs'.[21] Hugh MacDiarmid's expulsion from the NPS in May 1933 – a party he had co-founded in 1928 – was a sign of the new pragmatism. 'While his communism was bad enough', notes Scott Lyall, for MacCormick 'MacDiarmid's endorsement of a nationalist paramilitary organisation hopelessly compromised the image the NPS was trying to sell to mainstream voters.'[22] After Edwin Muir's

1936 attack on the Lallans movement in *Scott and Scotland*, Hanham writes, the early SNP turned the page on the literary Renaissance and even 'MacDiarmid could now be excommunicated with a good conscience.'[23] 'Apart from MacDiarmid', argued Michael Keating and David Bleiman in 1978, 'the connection between literature and political nationalism is often tenuous': 'Scottish political nationalism has long been distinguished by the absence of a literary dimension, and a vernacular writer such as Lewis Grassic Gibbon, in his *Scots Quair*, which deals in political and socialist as well as Scots themes, could make clear his view of Scottish nationalism as a mere refuge for disillusioned Tories.'[24]

For SNP scholar Jack Brand, it was in the post-war period that 'the paths of the poets and the nationalists of whatever kind diverged'. Quite simply, there was little to fire the poetic imagination in the period of electoral wilderness and rebuilding: 'the battles of the 1920s and 1930s about the use of Scots and the importance of literature for the new nation were fought and over. [. . .] the small, defensive, post-war SNP was in no sense an attractive environment' for literary intellectuals.[25] The SNP's slow rise to mass electoral appeal only underscored this effect. Writing in 1978 Brand argued that 'we are now dealing with a mass party and the masses are seldom interested in poetry. [. . .] Despite the obvious quality of the modern writers, they seem to have ignored the questions of national identity which have come to be an interest of the Scottish people.'[26] This was a mistaken view, as we shall see, but it has political and historiographic importance: the surging SNP of the mid-1970s did not perceive itself to have a significant literary wing, and was certainly not relying on the afflatus of poets, thinkers and Lallans activists to chart the course.

Hamilton and its discontents

'The single political event which marked Scottish politics of the 1960s as colourful, vibrant and apparently distinctive was the Hamilton byelection of 1967', writes Ewen A. Cameron.[27] On 2 November, Winnie Ewing took Labour's safest Scottish seat, and famously 'travelled to London in triumph by train, accompanied by large numbers of enthusiastic SNP supporters, before being driven to Westminster in a scarlet Hillman Imp built at the Linwood car plant'.[28] Perhaps surprisingly, the faithful camp-followers of MacDiarmid's Renaissance deeply distrusted the surge of electoral nationalism. John Herdman spoke for many in declaring 'that the SNP is for the most part a crassly philistine body whose obsessive worship of economics is only a little less nauseating than that of the unionist parties'.[29] At best, Herdman argued in 1971, the apparent 'revival of national consciousness' manifested in the rising Nationalist vote might 'through the SNP express itself sufficiently in political action to effect a change in the constitutional position of Scotland, which in its turn would stimulate a genuine spiritual development in the Scottish people'.[30] It is that higher plane of spiritual development and redemption – the airy realm of Nairn's 'Great Scottish Dream' – which remained paramount to literary nationalists such as Herdman, Tom Scott, Duncan Glen, Alan Bold, Alexander Scott and David Morrison. The reformist SNP and its vulgar propaganda comparing food prices in Scotland and England – its tendency 'to appeal to everything that is basest and most inert and complacent in the public mind'[31] – can only grudgingly be accepted as a means to those loftier ends. In his regular column in Morrison's nationalist poetry newsletter *Scotia*, John L. Broom argued:

> A government of Scotland consisting of most of the present officials of the SNP would be a national disaster. Their outlook seems to be almost wholly materialistic – as long as we persuade 'the industrial companies, the research institutions, the commercial businesses' to locate themselves in Scotland all will be well (*Scots Independent*, leader 27/12/69). Their sights are aimed at the common man whose desire is primarily for a bigger wage, a larger house and a flashier car, and who cares nothing for culture, the arts, and the spiritual values. As a result, of course, the SNP has alienated most of Scotland's intellectuals and creative artists.[32]

To be sure, this was a view that treated committed nationalists in the Renaissance tradition as the only 'truly' Scottish artists and thinkers. However, writers falling outside that camp were also troubled by the sudden popularity of the SNP, fearing that the worst tendencies of the romantic nationalists grouped around outlets such as Duncan Glen's *Akros* and David Morrison's *Scotia* would be strengthened and exploited. Writing to Bob Tait – editor of the embryonic *Scottish International* – the day after the Hamilton result, the poet D. M. Black (then living in London) was quick to see potential danger:

> Well, I says to myself, if the Nationalists win at Hamilton, I'll come North to live in Scotland. My God, they have. Did I mean it? Who knows . . . There're going to be dangers in this movement if it bears up – dangers as well as exhilarations, I mean. The main one is the obvious, that the tartan-and-Lallans clan will begin to advertise themselves as the only true Scots, & the traditional good-humoured contempt for such claims, by the populace at large, may get swept away in the current of fanaticism. I think this may be a real danger: a quiet, unimaginative but frustrated people, as the Scots have been since 1745, is not going to have much discretion if it's imaginatively aroused. A main cultural duty may become the mere assertion of the badness of most of Scotland's contributions. [. . .] I am thinking of the trouble Yeats had in the '90s, in convincing the patriots that it was possible for Irishmen to write bad verse.[33]

In the immediate aftermath of Hamilton, different political orientations within the Scottish literati expressed real ambivalence about the rise of the SNP, each seeing in Ewing's triumph different portents of national degradation. For the Renaissance stalwarts, the growing strength of the SNP threatened to reduce the cause of freedom to 'an attractive proposition for self-satisfied and stupid materialists'[34]; for younger writers allergic to that Renaissance, the pipes-and-whisky fanfare that followed Hamilton augured a regression to uncritical tartanry.

It is notable that MacDiarmid's Renaissance, then approaching fifty years of sporadic activity (in several semi-distinct waves of poetic development), should be the prism through which the sudden dynamism of electoral nationalism was viewed. Even more surprising is how little the Hamilton shock registers in the key magazines of the Renaissance movement, which carry on their claustrophobic debates, self-laceration and hero worship almost without interruption. As we have seen, seasoned literary national-ists mistrusted the SNP's message and ideology while welcom-ing the excitement and possibility Hamilton seemed to herald. In more optimistic moments, this ambiguity was skirted by a redoubled romanticism that simply ignored the prosaic nature of Ewing's campaign and the social and historical conditions of 1960s Lanarkshire. In a birthday praise-poem for MacDiarmid published just after the by-election in the leading Scottish poetry magazine of the period, *Lines Review*, Sydney Goodsir Smith resorts to allegory in narrating this moment of hope and prophetic vindication.

> The braith ye breathed, the sang ye
> Sung for Scotland's nou
> In tens and tens of thousand mouths—
> The word has spreid, the music's on;
> Aa ye said's come true at last—or comin sune—
> [. . .]
> Nou at last, thae that fired it aa
> Can maybe see a howp, a glimmer growan
> And ken it's no juist 'mair snaw'
> —But maybe truly Spring at last
> For this benighted philistine land
> Eer it's owre late and dune.
>
> Let's hope, auld Chris, auld fechter, you,
> This is nae fause dawn but a right yin—
>   Gif it is, it's you
> Were pair o' the makkin o't,
> And nou ye're pair o' the winnin . . . [35]

('Chris' is, of course, Christopher Grieve, MacDiarmid's given name.) The realities of 'this benighted and philistine land' are acknowledged only as the grounds for a radical national revival, a dead-hearted condition which is spiritual rather than historical, and which warrants the resort to pastoral imagery of waste and renewal. If the dawn may be 'fause' – it is too soon to tell – it will be no fault of the nationalist visionaries whose influence is located on the plane of soulful inspiration. But MacDiarmid was not, even in his seventies and eighties, a figure grandly detached from the latest spats and spasms of Scottish literary culture. He took an active part in a key controversy of the period, in which we see writers and intellectuals mount competing claims for the mantle of national revival.

Scottish International v. the indigenists

'The critical change' in this period, wrote Christopher Harvie in 1975, 'is one of consciousness': the growing 'interest' in Scotland – both scholarly and moral-political – by its native intelligentsia. The conditions of this shift were negative, dramatic and took shape in the 1960s. 'The complacent conservatism which characterised middle-class Scottish culture seems almost completely to have disappeared', Harvie observed.

> The old Scottish institutions are admitted to be in dissolution; the hold of the churches has been broken; law is seen more as a restrictive practice than a national ornament; education is badly in need of reform. Political nationalism is no more prepossessing as an ideology than it was, but there is no longer a British or imperial alternative. The intelligentsia can only now create a tolerable, convivial community in its own country.[36]

Inverting the story of rising confidence, it is cultural breakdown and crisis which precipitate the formation of a national politics; and the later 'hardening' of that national politics in the 1980s which forms an arena of representative power the writers and intelligentsia can claim as their own. This pattern of intellectuals *re-instituting* national consciousness is most visible in the small magazines of the post-Hamilton period. This was 'a golden age of small magazine publication in Scotland', John Herdman notes: 'in the pages of the few long-standing journals and of those new ones which sprang up in the late sixties and early seventies the ideological wars of that era were fought out'.[37] The battle-lines of these literary magazines were partly inherited from the inter-war Renaissance, and partly organised around the patronage of the Scottish Arts Council, effectively autonomous from 1947 (as the Scottish Committee of the Arts Council of Great Britain) and formally devolved in 1967. The SAC set up *Scottish International (Review)* (1968–73) under the editorship of Bob Tait, with advisory assistance from the established poets Edwin Morgan and Robert Garioch. Generously funded and guaranteed against loss by the SAC, *Scottish International* also benefitted from office space and mentorship by Father Anthony Ross of the Catholic Chaplaincy at the University of Edinburgh, and additional funding from the English Department at the University of Stirling. It was a magazine of vital importance to both the literary and political developments of the pre-devolutionary period prior to 1979: the first venue to publish extracts of Alasdair Gray's *Lanark* and the dialect poetry of Tom Leonard, a key venue for political debate among figures such as Tom Nairn and Stephen Maxwell, and key in the dissemination of Gramscian perspectives on Scottish cultural politics.[38]

The story of *Scottish International* exemplifies the shifting 'predicament of the Scottish writer' during the period of rising political nationalism. Paradoxically, the electoral success of the modern, fresh-faced SNP was a cause of hope laced with despair. For Renaissance stalwarts, it represented an awakening of the wrong kind, led by philistine prophets, tarnishing the faith; for anti-nationalist and sceptic writers, the welcome excitement also represented the stirring of double-edged popular energies. The anxieties expressed in D. M. Black's letter to Bob Tait were a constant presence in the magazine's milieu, both in its published output and (especially) its tense relations with various nationalist writers and periodicals. As David Robb notes, *Scottish International* 'polarised Scotland's literary community and brought to the surface the deep divisions amongst those concerned with contemporary writing'.[39] The advance publicity and Arts Council rationale for the magazine emphasised its forward-looking qualities – a tagline used in *Scottish International* advertising heralded its aim to 'spearhead awareness of new cultural patterns for old'[40] – and a sense that shifting times called for new perspectives. Interviewed by Robb, Bob Tait admitted

> that while he and his colleagues had no trace of an anti-Renaissance agenda (MacDiarmid was the first person invited to join the board, though his refusal was not unexpected), they desired to create a new voice, expressing a wider vision for the future, rather than a narrow reinforcement and justification of the past.[41]

Whether out of courtesy or as a pre-emptive move (to neutralise complaints of exclusion), *Scottish International* had written to a number of prominent Renaissance figures seeking support for the magazine and inviting contributions and reviews. Tom Scott replied 'I shall not be able to support this magazine, in which I have no confidence whatsoever', objecting specifically to the twenty-four-year-old Tait's position as editor given his past advocacy (in *Feedback* magazine) for the concrete poetry of Ian Hamilton Finlay (a bête noire of the Renaissance school since the *ugly birds without wings* contretemps of 1962, in which MacDiarmid denounced the new poetic idioms and sensibility of the 'beatnik cosmopolitans'). Scott would later dismiss 'the Establishment rag, Scottish Antinational' in letters to David Morrison laced with sectarian hostility, as he blasted Arts Council support for an 'abomination' of a magazine 'run by the Catholic Tait from the Catholic Chaplaincy centre under the priestly eye of Anthony Ross and Anglican John MacQueen'.[42] His initial rebuff of October 1967 complains that even 'the title of the magazine is ludicrous – Scottish International'.

> What is it – a football match? The word 'international' in a Scottish context usually is a euphemism for 'English', or 'Anglo-Yank', now that the U.S. increasingly dominate English policy. [. . .] In any case, it is most likely to mean in practice 'anti-Scottish' in the case of this magazine, merely another manifestation of the Scottish national death-wish to immolate the nation on an English altar labelled 'international'. [. . .] I note that the name of Alexander Scott has

been dropped from the board, and that confirms my worst fears that this magazine is another Anglo-Scots Establishment manoeuvre against the best interests and writers of Scottish literature.[43]

Thus the magazine had a range of passionate enemies before it came properly into existence. As Robb notes, 'an "establishment"-maintained cultural organ, not conspicuously supportive of Mac-Diarmid's "Renaissance" project',[44] appeared highly suspect to the literary community most invested in the national-cultural terrain the magazine staked out for re-development. Navigating and soothing these conflicts was a constant distraction to the editors, but also forms a key element of the magazine's impact: loosening the grip of MacDiarmid's acolytes on 'Scotland' as a topic and possibility was arguably *the* crucial legacy of *Scottish International*.

Though the magazine is widely heralded for marking a fresh start in cultural and intellectual discussion, it is striking how swiftly and peremptorily it was swept into the grooves of prior literary-political alignments. In another letter to Tait prior to the first issue, D. M. Black commented:

Horrifying to think that Scott wasn't so far from being one of the editors of the mag. It might be a good idea to print something of his, merely to shut his mouth when the mag comes out. Or if he goes on attacking you, it'll at least be clear you've not been entirely unreasonable. [. . .] As you say, chaps with claymores to grind.[45]

Though Tom Scott had been most outspoken in attacking the magazine, the 'Scott' Black refers to is probably the poet-academic Alexander Scott, who had not been 'dropped' but withdrew himself from the advisory board in October 1967. In a rather cagey letter, he gave as his reason the acute divisions *Scottish International* had already stimulated in the Lallans poetry community, owing to the Renaissance poets' distrust of Tait and Edwin Morgan (Scott's colleague at the University of Glasgow, who not only celebrated concrete poetry but dabbled in writing it). Referring to the third member of the editorial team, Scott reported that 'the general feeling is that [Robert] Garioch isn't strong enough to see that the indigenists get a fair crack of the whip'; and so, guided by his steadfast loyalty to the Renaissance movement, he withdrew from the project.[46] MacDiarmid's own polite but firm snub was sent the next day, and followed by an article in *Catalyst* denouncing the still-unpublished magazine in December.[47] These skirmishes preceded the first issue, and any clear indication of what the magazine was likely to do or become. Writing to Ian Hamilton Finlay a week after Scott and MacDiarmid's letters, Edwin Morgan reported that

> the new magazine is running through squalls of a well-known Scottish type. It really is extraordinarily difficult getting anything started in Scotland. At any rate we start without the grace and favour of the 'only lecturer in Scottish literature in a Scottish university [Alexander Scott] and also of the "greatest living Scottish poet" [MacDiarmid]'. Well – [48]

It seems paradoxical that the key project articulating Scottish cultural and political dynamism in this period of rising electoral nationalism should be dismissed in advance by established literary patriots (and their younger successors, such as Alan Bold). In fact, these figures correctly perceived that *Scottish International* represented a rival claim to their effective ownership of Scottish cultural difference as a political cause.

The January 1968 launch issue of *Scottish International* is of particular interest in tracing the magazine's intended shift in cultural debate. The editorial clearly responds to the Hamilton shock of November 1967, and establishes clear parameters for the magazine's political engagement, expressing a serious interest in Scottish self-knowledge but wariness of cultural nationalism per se. The editorial begins prominently on the front cover, placing its own 'occasional' bearings and inspiration front and centre:

> SCOTLAND 1968. Mainly urban population, sharing with the rest of Britain a Government, mass media, and much of the available Press and publishing – among many other things. There is discontent with the consequences of

this situation for Scotland. As witness Hamilton and other
SNP successes. One must neither underrate nor exaggerate
what this unease means. [. . .] independence from a large
centre of power and influence is necessary for any people who have their own ways and want to communicate
among themselves and to the outside world their particular
image and likeness. This can be a problem for those north
of Hampstead as for the people north of the Tweed. Creative and critical energies, time for the development of talent, and the means of giving the energy and talent proper
outlets are all first essentials in ensuring such independence. We believe that people need their own publications
through which they can create a presence for themselves
and, perhaps, some influence too.[49]

The need for 'independence' is voiced at the level of expression
and self-identity, while carefully skirting an exceptionalist Scottish
orientation to these problems. Elsewhere, we see clearly the aim
to secure 'influence' by asserting and securing a national-cultural
'presence': affirming without narrowing the reality and interest of
Scotland as a topic:

Nor should one forget that the Scottish arts don't exist in
a Scottish world of their own. A colourless or promiscu-
ous internationalism is to nobody's advantage. But a self-
conscious cultural nationalism can lead to bad habits of
stereotyped thinking and unwillingness to look at the situation as it really is. [. . .] Everyone is aware, to a greater
or lesser extent, of how cultures other than Scottish
impinge upon us, through publishing and the mass media.
It is important that this awareness should be sharpened and
extended critically, so that more opportunity can be given
to compare Scottish work with work done elsewhere.[50]

The magazine thus adopts a comparative approach to avoid the
hazards of 'self-conscious' cultural nationalism, while walking a
tightrope between introspection and 'colourless internationalism'.
Though the Hamilton thunderbolt is highlighted in its first issue,

Scottish International largely steers clear of party politics, and comments only rarely on the saga of devolution and the Royal Commission on the Constitution established in 1969 (examined in Chapter 2). In his memoir of the literary scene in this period, John Herdman notes that 'the long-term significance of *Scottish International* was that for all its flaws it was an early part of the nascent movement towards a mature political, social, economic and cultural debate about the future of Scotland, which had been virtually forced upon a generation of intellectuals by the successes of the SNP'.[51]

But as we have seen, the magazine's wariness of cultural nationalism – and generous support from the Scottish Arts Council – stimulated acute envy and suspicion among committed literary nationalists in Herdman's circles, who saw *Scottish International* as 'establishment', staid and anti-nationalist. Their sense of political antipathy was perhaps not entirely groundless. A 1970 article on 'Scottish Writing and The Individual Writer' profiles the playwright Tom Wright and poets Alan Jackson and Robin Fulton (editor of *Lines Review*). Each of the writers expresses criticism of the Scottish literary scene and the unsigned commentary is tacitly aligned with the sense (attributed to Wright) of 'feeling really put off by a scene where a lot of blokes who fancied themselves as writers would enjoy great get-togethers in pubs and indulge themselves with sterile arguments about the rights and wrongs of using English or Scots and that kind of thing'.[52] A year later, Alan Jackson wrote a provocative attack on literary nationalism entitled 'The Knitted Claymore', published as an entire issue of Fulton's *Lines Review*, which was answered with denunciations in Renaissance-oriented magazines such as David Morrison's *Scotia* (after 1972, *Scotia Review*).[53] By the end of the magazine's short but influential run, a deep rift had opened between *Scottish International* and *Lines Review* (which moved away from the post-MacDiarmid Renaissance in the late 1960s, under Fulton's editorship) in one camp, and the more firmly, fiery nationalist grouping gathered around the Renaissance vehicle *Akros* (founded by Duncan Glen in 1965) and *Scotia/Scotia Review* (1970/2), leaving aside the journal of the (radical, nationalist) 1320 Club *Catalyst*.[54] The flavour of the latter reviews owes much to the example of MacDiarmid's macho polemicism, combining harsh denunciation, wilful extremity, quixotic leaps of logic and strategy, and ceaseless demands for radical action.

These are 'outsider' intellectuals fiercely self-conscious of their renegade status, who understand their role not as grappling with present realities (compare 'SCOTLAND 1968. Mainly urban population . . .'), but as visionary shock-troops of a country yet to come. These outlaws are devoted less to the real country their letters and scribblings pass through, transiting from one hub of poetic zeal to another, but to that ideal, 're-Scoticised' nation which figures in their writing as both imaginative playground and religious icon. This heady mix is captured in a column from issue 2 of *Scotia*, in which John L. Broom warns that 'all this talk of a Celtic "race" is very dangerous, and may easily lead to racialism of the Nazi Rosenberg type', before conceding that 'logically', the language of a (culturally) Celtic nation such as Scotland should be Gaelic; 'the alternative, of course, is Scots, but it would surely be a gross anomaly to have the people of a Celtic nation speaking a non-Celtic tongue!' He then considers Fionn MacColla's putative view – denied and disowned by an angry MacColla in the next issue – that 'the only hope for Scotland lies in a mass reconversion of her people to Roman Catholicism'.[55] Broom casts doubt on this latter scheme (noting that the recent description of St Giles Church as a 'Cathedral' was sufficient to raise the ire of the nationalist readership of *Catalyst*), before applauding the 'courage' of a recent article suggesting 'that the SNP should seriously consider violent means to achieve freedom for Scotland if the method of parliamentary representation fails' (another suggestion he rejects, this time on Christian grounds).[56] This all occurs on a single page of a closely printed newsletter: the milieu of committed literary nationalism in this period is full of wild fighting-talk consciously remote from journalistic discussion or 'academic' contemplation, proudly brandishing its sense of danger and un-compromise.

A Scottish cultural public?

D. M. Black's sense of 'the badness of most of Scotland's contributions' was not confined to sceptics of rising nationalism. A striking feature of this period is the profound pessimism expressed about Scottish culture and society even by its most committed advocates. This finds its parallel in political commentary allied to the SNP's first wave of youthful energy at the end of the 1960s. The second issue of *Scottish International* includes a short feature on 'SNP and the Arts' by party leader William Wolfe. He pledges 'direct government spending' to support expanded cultural production, and claims 'a free and independent Scotland will not be impelled to follow the tastes of England, as at present'.[57] But only a few lines later, the expected policy offer gives way to personal reflection:

> The ignorance of the people of Scotland of literature and the visual arts is abysmal. Many of us have been taught to love Scotland and honour her heroes, but how rare it is to find an adult Scot who has a basic knowledge and appreciation of creative poetry, literature, painting, sculpture and design. [. . .] As far as the artists are concerned, their creative talents are being mis-directed either because of lack of guidance or lack of confidence or lack of appreciation of their potential. As far as the consumers are concerned, most of them just don't know and don't want to know.[58]

Note that Wolfe is here decrying the people's ignorance not of distinctively *Scottish* literature and art – of their specific national traditions – but of 'culture' in general. In which case, it is difficult to know who the policy of improved government support for the arts is meant to entice; presumably Scotland's voters and potential cultural consumers – who 'just don't know and don't want to know' – are the same group of people. This assumed absence of a Scottish cultural public opens the way for the literary intelligentsia to speak and act on its behalf; an aspect of *Scottish International*'s influence emulated by cultural vanguardists in the following decades.

Electoral behaviour often seems to be the only legible form of 'Scottishness' of interest in this period, whereby votes for self-government are cast in the role of redeeming a people with no other, extra-political means of life or recovery. The profound disconnection between these two Scotlands – between the dream of a flourishing national polity and the doltish reality of the existing

Scottish public – is the gap the 'cultural devolution' thesis will later seek to fill, by making the very fixity of the tastes and loyalties of the Scottish electorate the basis of new claims to political voice. In the debates of the 1970s, the disparity between really-existing Scotland and the glowing ideal of cultural renewal is more painful and discouraging. Notional champions of Scottish Literature often express deep bitterness with the reality of literary and intellectual life, which is routinely castigated for its moral smallness and enervation. 'Let's face it', Alan Bold declares in 1973, 'the Lowland Literati are Crawlers and Toadies to a Prat. [. . .] I can't stand Scottish Writers by and large. [. . .] Their conversation is claustrophobic. They fret over the state of the Barclaycard. Their paws drip with the sweat of petty ambitions realised.'[59] Before Scotland could embrace the 'new', it must clear away the old and rotten. Tait's successor as editor of *Scottish International*, the poet Tom Buchan, commanded:

> let us exorcise once and for all
> the dead god of Scotland
> a god without tears
> for a country without joy.[60]

In the more militant nationalist reviews, the impression was not that a growing national movement was reaching political maturity, but that a pitiless *kulturkampf* was necessary to sweep away Scotland's diseased excuse for a cultural establishment. For figures such as Bold, 'Scottish literature' evokes a panorama of fushionless quislings, dilettantes and mediocrities: not a potential intelligentsia for an independent state but the chief *obstacle* to Scottish cultural advance. Perhaps surprisingly, the very grimness and abjection of Scotland was held to be part of its intellectual appeal. A 1971 advertisement for *Scottish International* makes the darkness and danger of the nation its edgy selling point: 'From one of the world's trouble spots . . . The worst housing in Western Europe, steep rise in violent crime, high suicide rates, high unemployment *and* new industries creating new social patterns . . . True or False?'[61]

A more open-ended question was explored at the 'What Kind of Scotland?' conference organised by *Scottish International* in April

1973, the peak of its influence on the emergent Scottish public sphere. This was a major three-day event featuring a who's who of culture and politics, and best remembered for the exhilarating debut of John McGrath and the 7:84 Theatre Company's *The Cheviot, the Stag, and the Black, Black Oil*. The conference was addressed by literary historians such as David Daiches, political scientists such as J. G. Kellas and politicians such as the SNP's Isobel Lindsay and Stephen Maxwell, and Labour's Norman Buchan MP and his wife Janey Buchan (later an MEP), well known as socialist sceptics of devolution. In his write-up for *Scottish International* John Herdman reports broad agreement on the principle of devolution: 'everyone agreed that the democratisation of politics and bureaucratic processes in Scotland was a development which had scarcely begun, and that this was a matter of how political power could be put back into the hands of the people'.[62] But, Herdman continued,

> as soon as the issue was raised as to where the concept of the national community came into this process, gaping divisions revealed themselves with irritating predictability. Everyone was up tight. It was not just that they were up tight about the idea of a Scottish nation, they were up tight about the idea of Scottishness too. An interesting phenomenon was the constant tendency of people on both sides of this debate to attribute any abuse which happens to exist in Scotland [. . .] to 'the Scottish character': 'There's your Scottish character for you!' This kind of self-deprecating self-regard was often used, of course, to suggest that Scots are inherently incapable of any kind of political responsibility, and no one seemed to realise that such an attitude approximates to self-hatred. It was very clear certainly that while self-hatred is an aid to quasi-political bombast, it is counter-productive for the chances of effective political action.[63]

There is a great deal of 'quasi-political bombast' in this vein, inveighing against the dismal condition of the Scots and their pathetic chances at self-reformation. This tone of 'pessimism' has come to be associated with Tom Nairn and his caustic influence, but was much more widespread in the period. Herdman's own contribution to Duncan Glen's 1971 collection *Whither Scotland?* expresses baleful 'reservations' about the prospect of the SNP stimulating a genuine national revival:

> These reservations refer particularly to the impenetrable stupidity and desperate fickleness of the electorate, to their apparently total inability to cope with any idea not directly related to their pockets, and the consequent hopelessness of any thinking about the future which turns upon an appeal to the electorate or a pandering to their will. If the people expect their will to be respected for much longer, then they must set about getting themselves a will which merits respect (and before anyone starts calling me a fascist for saying this, I think they should ponder how far they themselves think the will of the people should be respected on problems such as capital punishment, coloured immigration, and 'law and order').[64]

If we set aside the flirtation with Brecht's satirical suggestion (in 'The Solution') about dissolving the people and electing another, we can see here a genuine attempt to square the high claims of national revivalists – both literary and political – with the attitudes and mentality of really-existing Scots, evidently a people scarcely worthy of liberation. (*Whither Scotland?* is partly a response to the 1970 election, in which the SNP advance badly stalled.)

In a letter to *Scottish International* sent in lieu of his participation in the 'What Kind of Scotland?' conference, Nairn congratulates the editors for the magazine's opposition to 'a self-conscious cultural nationalism', so combatting the tendency of Scots to be 'defensive, exclusive and inward-looking mythologisers in their cultural life'.

> It's not quite enough to say I feel agreement with this stance. [. . .] In this sense I cannot help viewing each instalment of the magazine as a sort of battlefield. Reading through it the heart alternately rises and falls; triumphs of the spirit overlap with sloughs of inward-looking mythology; its bagpipe punctured by a stern look on page 1, self-conscious cultural nationalism is back again panting away by page 20.[65]

Stephen Maxwell replies in the next number, acknowledging the partial truth of Nairn's diagnosis but arguing that the very deformities of the national psyche can serve as the basis for renewal, no 'reason for abandoning the ambition to create a responsive Scottish culture, but as potentially the raw material of that culture'. Responding to Nairn's charge that Scotland has been a scene of nationalist failure, Maxwell adds 'yes, but [. . .] a scene of almost complete socialist failure also. Part of the reason for that failure lies in the unwillingness of the Left in Scotland to accept Scotland as a significant focus of intellectual and political activity.'[66] This was a counterblast insisting on the socialist value and perhaps necessity of national consciousness, anticipating Nairn's own insight that 'the theory of nationalism represents Marxism's great historical failure'.[67] This logic would come to electoral fruition only in the 1980s, by a pattern in which (as Ben Jackson has argued) nationalist thinkers successfully presented 'independence as the most effective way to promote the political agenda of the left in a neoliberal era'.[68] This worked out rather differently to the pattern Nairn had anticipated in a revised version of 'The Three Dreams of Scottish Nationalism' published in 1970. This time acknowledging valuable currents in Scottish culture other than those of Calvinism and tartanry – 'the Kirk and our miserable tartan-waistcoated bourgeoisie have never had things *all* their own way' – Nairn nonetheless warned that 'minor, subordinate traditions of protest' such as Clydeside radicalism and the folk movement were especially imperilled by the rise of popular nationalism:

> Populism unites the whole 'people' behind the image of the nation, which is everyone's birthright, everyone's property. But in fact, where it does this on the basis of a social and cultural structure like Scotland's, it really conscripts the rebels and the dissenting classes behind their old enemies. The Edinburgh baillie and the shipyard worker can both be joined in praise of nationalism; but the nation and its culture belong to the former, not to the latter, and the triumph of a merely populist nationalism will signify a greatly strengthened grip of the real ruling class.[69]

In this prophecy the ruling elite maintain their cultural domi-nance in the move toward statehood, are strengthened in their own romantic delusions, and cement their hegemony over mar-ginal currents of dissent. The tartan waistcoat is let out to cover an expanded, truly national body which 'includes' (by overwriting) all of Scotland's internal conflicts and distinctions. But something different happened, to similar ends. The specific cultural signi-fiers – above all, the vocal signature – of the Scottish working class emerged as privileged emblems of national difference and autonomy, and were not suppressed or marginalised by the 'real ruling class'. On the contrary, they were borne aloft like a ver-nacular talisman, as proof of the culturally grounded and inclusive nature of an elite political project centred on representation rather than sovereignty, emphasising national difference and deformation rather than deep historic continuities. This pattern becomes clear in the 1980s, but we can see its logic and electoral appeal begin-ning to crystallise in the post-Hamilton period. It emerged first in the left-nationalist milieu of the political and cultural magazines, which defined their various outlooks as much within the cultural traditions of the Scottish Renaissance, and established Marxist orthodoxies, as with reference to contemporaneous developments.

Rise of a betrayed, degradit nation

For much of the 1970s, a significant proportion of the left-nationalist activist milieu genuinely believed that independence was just around the corner. But for MacDiarmid's inheritors, this was a profoundly ambiguous hope. In the camp of *Scottish International*'s refuseniks, the gloom was deep indeed: not only was the nation in a degraded state, but its literature was increasingly under the con-trol of false prophets and cultural traitors. For the 1972 inaugural issue of *Scotia Review* – the Scottish Arts Council-backed expansion of *Scotia*, with the mission to 'be an even greater thorn in the flesh of those who wish to deny Scotland her independence on both a political and cultural level'[70] – Tom Scott penned an 'Epistle to David Morrison', the journal's editor. Far from a leading role in the national revival, the truly Scottish writer is positioned as a despised outsider to a philistine culture: 'ridden hard / By puirtith, ostracism

and isolation, / To entertain a betrayed, degradit nation'.[71] Bleaker
still, the people themselves are lost and barren, de-nationalised
beyond any possible cultural salvation:

> For we Scots the problem's deeper still,
> For the people hae lost theirsels – greater ill
> That stems frae the Union Treaties, the deceit
> Betrayed our state, tongues and arts, a defeat
> Neer bocht by enemy bluid on the battlefield,
> But a rulin-class sell-out, signed and sealed.
> [. . .]
> Whit a Scottish poet wants the-day's
> No genius, but the strength o Herakles –
> Tho even that could never integrate
> A nation desertit by its ain state.
> Nocht can end the chaos and the worry
> But oor ain government here in Edinburgh,
> For only wi oor ain governin centre
> Can oor house flourish, the Muses enter
> And be at hame, their bards hae peace to think,
> Nae mair to wander like ony ootcast tink.
> The so-called 'problem o identitie'
> Is this – a government to identify *wi*:
> For that nae London government ever can
> Be for a born and bred Scottish man.[72]

'A nation desertit by its ain state' is incapable of cultural revival,
and only full political empowerment can advance the project of
national literary reconstruction. A strengthened Scottish identity
will not lead, but *follow*, the establishment of 'oor ain governin
centre', and thus the focus of any hope is 'a government to identify *wi*': not the Scottish nation, but the redeeming machinery of
its representation.

   In summer 1973 Bob Tait announced his resignation as editor and wrote a retrospective article on his time at the helm of
Scottish International. Here he reflected on the political tides of the
time, and compared his endeavour to 'the making of a cultural

map (which has included the registering of quite conservative impulses)'.

> It involves a critique of extant theories and attitudes, in and for a Scottish context; and the quite obvious concern for the future of Scotland as such has involved beginning a new critique of 'cultural' and 'political' nationalism.[73]

Refusing to uncritically promote 'the Scottish dimension' is a key point of contrast with the magazine's more politically engaged successors in the 1980s. *Scottish International* was more interested in changing and interrogating Scottishness than renewing and strengthening it, an approach signalled by the second word of the title. As Rory Scothorne argues:

> *Scottish International* sought to place Scottish culture in an international context and set international cultural trends – such as 'concrete' poetry – in a Scottish one. It was clearly national, and represented an effort to create a distinctly national public for an intelligentsia whose cosmopolitan interests were already assumed. An increasingly radical, cosmopolitan intelligentsia, rooted in the universities, were thus identifying with the Scottish nation, and claiming it for themselves.[74]

The resistance of the Renaissance stalwarts stemmed largely from their own prior claim, via MacDiarmid, to a 'revolutionary' man-tle of nationalist intellectualism, and their established animus (also via MacDiarmid) against 'cosmopolitan' deviation. As Tom Scott wrote in his brusque refusal of the magazine's overtures, 'no nations, no international: so we begin with nations, and for us, with the Scottish nation'.[75] In the eyes of literary nationalists, accustomed to treating the idea of Scotland as their own spiritual property and artistic *donnée*, *Scottish International* represented not only a betrayal of the Renaissance, but an intolerable *re-coding* of Scottish difference and specificity within a cultural-political rubric which cancelled and devalued their own contribution.

This shift was not planned as a usurpation, but the loosening of the indigenists' grip – on 'Scotland' as 'Thing' and theme – was a key and necessary precursor to the post-1979 pattern in which literary intellectuals dropped the baggage of revivalist cultural nationalism and fully entered the political space *Scottish International* had helped to carve open. Once this space and argument had been fully opened – by writers more than politicians – a new 'vernacular' politics of voice and class emerge as central to 'cultural devolution'. These forces and opportunities were not entirely lost on the SNP, who did belatedly explore a populist culturalism in the collected essays of *The Radical Approach* (1976). There, we find Isobel Lindsay exploring the nexus of class oppression and national marginalisation within the Union:

> If there is something of a class stereotype in the attitudes of the Scots to the English, then it is because the Scots as a nation – middle as well as working class – have experienced something akin to what the lower classes experience as a sub-group in the larger society. Our language or dialect was rejected as inferior and the centres of power and influence increasingly moved outwith the country. With the growth of centralised media the people who dominated entertainment and current affairs were certainly not Scots. [. . .] Scotland was the poor relation, the dependent, the small and weak partner. The cumulative effect of this has been to produce in the Scots a sense of being, in Norman MacCaig's words, 'a failed nation'.[76]

The socialist and nationalist 'failures' anatomised by Nairn and Maxwell, with their echoes in the mordant soul-searching of Tom Scott, could be re-centred on questions of language, representation and marginality. We will return to these debates in exploring 'vernacular' nationalism in Chapter 6, but the Dream has held sway too long; we must now attend to the very different 1970s story of the Grind.

Notes

1. Nairn, 'Festival of the Dead', p. 265.
2. Nairn, 'The three dreams of Scottish nationalism' [1968], p. 4.

3. Ibid. p. 7.
4. Ibid. p. 8.
5. Nairn, 'Festival of the Dead', p. 265.
6. Nairn, 'The three dreams of Scottish nationalism', p. 8.
7. Quoted by Nairn, ibid. p. 10.
8. Ibid. p. 10.
9. Ibid. pp. 9–10
10. MacDiarmid, *Selected Poetry*, p. 142.
11. Nairn, 'Festival of the Dead', p. 265.
12. Nairn, 'The three dreams of Scottish nationalism', pp. 9–10.
13. Nairn, 'Festival of the Dead', pp. 265–6.
14. Nairn, 'The three dreams of Scottish nationalism', p. 17.
15. Ibid. p. 17.
16. See Bell, *Questioning Scotland* and Introna, 'Avoiding disability in Scottish literary studies?'
17. Nairn, 'Festival of the Dead', p. 265.
18. Kerr, 'Bomb attack during Tattoo', *The Guardian,* 30 August 1971.
19. Lynch, 'The Scottish National Party', p. 229.
20. Harvie: 'Nationalism, journalism and cultural politics', p. 30.
21. Hanham, *Scottish Nationalism*, pp. 158–9.
22. Lyall, '"The man is a menace"', p. 39.
23. Hanham, *Scottish Nationalism*, p. 162. Note that MacDiarmid returned to the post-war fold and ran a disastrous campaign as the SNP candidate in Glasgow Kelvingrove in 1945; Lynch, *SNP: The History of the Scottish National Party*, pp. 75–6.
24. Keating and Bleiman, *Labour and Scottish Nationalism*, p. 118.
25. Brand, *The National Movement in Scotland*, p. 104.
26. Ibid. p. 105.
27. Cameron, *Impaled Upon a Thistle*, p. 281.
28. Devine, *The Scottish Nation 1700–2000*, p. 574.
29. Herdman, 'Politics III', p. 104.
30. Ibid. p. 105.
31. Ibid. p. 108.
32. John L. Broom, 'Candid commentary', *Scotia*, 1 (January 1970), pp. 5–6 (pp. 5–6).
33. David M. Black, Letter to Robert Tait, 3 November 1967.
34. Herdman, 'Politics III', p. 108.
35. Sydney Goodsir Smith, 'Millennial Ode to Hugh MacDiarmid on yet another Birthday Occasion', *Lines Review*, 25 (Winter 1967–8), pp. 20–5 (pp. 22–3).
36. Harvie, 'The devolution of the intellectuals', p. 91.
37. Herdman, *Another Country*, p. 82.

38. Ray Burnett, 'Scotland and Antonio Gramsci', *Scottish International*, 5.9 (November 1972), p. 12. See Davidson, 'Antonio Gramsci's reception in Scotland', pp. 253–86.

39. Robb, *Auld Campaigner*, p. 126.

40. Scottish International, Draft advertisements for *Scottish International*.

41. Robb, *Auld Campaigner*, pp. 127–8.

42. Tom Scott, Letter to David Morrison, 18 August 1971.

43. Tom Scott, Letter to *Scottish International*, 11 October 1967.

44. Robb, *Auld Campaigner*, p. 127.

45. David M. Black, Letter to Bob Tait, undated.

46. Alexander Scott, Letter to *Scottish International*, 8 October 1967. On Scott's sense of personal and literary commitment to the Scottish Renaissance, see Robb, *Auld Campaigner*, p. 131.

47. Hugh MacDiarmid [C. M. Grieve], Letter to *Scottish International*, 9 October 1967. Tom Scott cites MacDiarmid's *Catalyst* letter in his crowing notice of *Scottish International*'s imminent collapse in Supplement to No. 4, *Scotia Review*, 4 (August 1973). *Catalyst* was the organ of the militant nationalist pressure group the 1320 Club, founded June 1967; see Herdman (briefly its editor), *Another Country*, p. 97.

48. Morgan, Letter to Ian Hamilton Finlay, 17 October 1967, in *The Midnight Letterbox*, pp. 206–7.

49. Editorial, *Scottish International*, 1 (January 1968), cover to p. 3.

50. Ibid. p. 3.

51. Herdman, *Another Country*, p. 102.

52. Scottish International, 'Commentary: Scottish writing and the individual writer', *Scottish International*, 9 (February 1970), pp. 18–27 (p. 18).

53. Alan Jackson, 'The knitted claymore', *Lines Review*, 37 (1971), pp. 2–38.

54. This is no attempt at a comprehensive survey of key literary magazines of the period. *Chapman* (founded 1970), *Tocher* (journal of the School of Scottish Studies Archive at the University of Edinburgh, founded 1971) and *Lallans* (journal of the Scots Language Society, founded 1972) are also important, though less overtly aligned within the nationalist/anti-nationalist battles of interest here.

55. John L. Broom, 'Candid commentary', *Scotia*, 2 (February 1970), pp. 5–6 (p. 6).

56. Ibid. p. 6.

57. William Wolfe, 'SNP and the Arts', *Scottish International*, 2 (April 1968), pp. 5–6 (p. 5).

58. Ibid. p. 5.

59. Alan Bold, 'Two interviews with Alan Bold', *Scotia Review*, 4 (August 1973), pp. 39–45.
60. Buchan, *Exorcism*, p. 4.
61. Scottish International, Draft advertisements for *Scottish International*.
62. John Herdman, 'What Kind of Scotland? A view of the conference', *Scottish International*, 6.5 (May–June–July 1973), pp. 10–15, 31 (p. 11).
63. Ibid. pp. 11–13.
64. Herdman, 'Politics III', pp. 105–6.
65. Tom Nairn, 'Culture and nationalism: an open letter', *Scottish International*, 6.4 (April 1973), pp. 7–9 (p. 7).
66. Stephen Maxwell, Letter, *Scottish International*, 6.5 (May–June–July 1973), p. 9.
67. Nairn, 'The modern Janus', p. 3.
68. Jackson, 'The political thought of Scottish nationalism', p. 50.
69. Nairn, 'The three dreams of Scottish nationalism' (1970), p. 52.
70. 'Editorial', *Scotia Review*, 1 (August 1972), p. 1.
71. Tom Scott, 'Epistle to David Morrison', *Scotia Review*, 1 (August 1972), pp. 3–9 (p. 6).
72. Ibid. p. 9.
73. Bob Tait, 'Facts sacred, comment free, and art for everybody's sake', *Scottish International*, 6.5 (May–June–July 1973), p. 33.
74. Rory Scothorne, unpublished doctoral research, University of Edinburgh, 2016–19. Used with permission.
75. Tom Scott, Letter to *Scottish International*, 11 October 1967.
76. Lindsay, 'Nationalism, community and democracy', p. 23.

2

Machine Politics of British Devolution 1967–79

On the eve of the 1979 referendum, the poet and playwright Donald Campbell anticipated a dramatic realignment of Scottish literary culture following the establishment of a Scottish Assembly. Writing in *New Edinburgh Review*, he observed that

> For a great deal of its history, the Scottish Literary Tradition has operated more or less underground, acting (in Alexander Scott's phrase) as a 'guerrilla movement' and, as such, has always been radical and anti-establishment in nature. The Assembly will change this, since its coming will inevitably lead to the creation of a new Literary Establishment. Some Scottish writers will inevitably become identified with this, while others will (just as inevitably) be in bitter opposition to it. This will, in all probability, lead to a literary war which will make the petty squabbles of recent decades look like child's play – but which will prove to be much healthier, since it will have its foundation in real issues and principles, rather than the vanities of small-minded jealousy and personal resentment.[1]

In the event, there was no Assembly and thus no occasion for 'literary war'. But Campbell correctly perceived some of the pressures and divisions which attend the institutionalisation of Scottish Literature, already present in the saga of *Scottish International*, and clearly evident in the protracted struggle to establish a Department of Scottish Literature at the University of Glasgow in 1971.[2] What he could not have foreseen were the political conditions in which champions of Scottish Literature relinquished their underdog marginality and claimed a place at the forefront of an elite national-political project. The Assembly-shaped hole in post-1979 Scotland created the conditions for a rather different re-alignment, in which the inveterate spats and hostility of the Scottish literary community – and indeed Scottish society at large – were forgotten or suppressed, the better to present a united front in an identitarian battle against Thatcherism. In place of a literary civil war, what emerged was a semi-organised common front which turned its rhetorical artillery on the perceived cultural invader. The disputatious energies of the literati moved from the guerrilla 'underground' to the mainstream of electoral politics, with the defiant assertion of national difference gradually incorporated into the rhetoric of Scotland's increasingly dominant party – Labour, rather than the SNP.

To make critical sense of the post-1979 Dream, and the extent to which literary figures and debates shaped the pro-devolution movement, it is essential to grasp its continuities with the prior Grind (of UK machine politics). Unusual in a work of literary and cultural history, this chapter reconstructs British constitutional change at the level of electoral politics and intra-party struggle, seeking to remedy (and clarify) what is missing from the story of 'cultural devolution'. Here we find that Scottish devolution can be explained quite adequately without reference to artistic or intellectual developments, by attending to the (far from simple) governing interests and parliamentary pressures of the period. This is not to dismiss or relegate the role of 'culture' in these processes, but to foreground the party-dominated electoral context in which claims to Scottish difference accrued a particular symbolic and strategic value. We return to the changeable salience of Scottish 'identity' in the electoral field at the end of this narrative survey, which adds archival detail to a synthesis of earlier work in Scottish history.

The most charitable perspective

Catriona M. M. Macdonald observes that 'constitutional change, by its very gravity, encourages analyses more rooted in high-sounding principles than party. Yet, even taking the most charitable perspective, constitutional motivations tend to be more pedestrian (and less principled) than one would suppose.'[3] This is certainly true in the Scottish case, and at times eye-wateringly so. Richard Finlay writes that 'the appearance of nationalism in the late 1960s caused some, but not much, consternation in the British political parties'.

> It was no great secret that problems with the economy were fuelling a sense of grievance and frustration that the SNP had been able to capitalise on. Some degree of tokenism was required to appease the electorate and show that the main parties were taking the issue of Scotland seriously.[4]

Up to this point, efforts at appeasement were as paltry as the electoral threat posed by Scottish nationalism. After the Second World War, Labour quietly but effectively abandoned its notional backing for home rule, a pledge which had decayed even from the 'token support' it enjoyed throughout the 1920s (during which period 'the party moved ever further from it in practice').[5] In a recurring pattern, different territorial publics were given different impressions of Labour's commitment to the principle. The SNP's wartime leader Douglas Young was fond of recalling that home rule 'was not mentioned in the UK Labour manifesto in 1945 but a manifesto put out by the party's Scottish office gave a Scottish parliament a priority second only to the defeat of Japan'.[6] Apart from tinkering with parliamentary procedure – slightly enlarging, in 1948, the powers of the Scottish Grand Committee – Labour in government did little to respond to pressure for home rule. This was organised on an all-party basis by John MacCormick, who had left the SNP in 1942 to establish Scottish Convention, 'more a rallying organisation than one offering a detailed scheme'.[7] Nationalist electoral stagnation removed any prospect of change in the following few years, notwithstanding Robert McIntyre's victory in the Motherwell and Wishaw by-election in April 1945, shortly before the end of the wartime electoral pact which largely suspended Labour-Tory competition. The SNP saved only two deposits in the general election of July 1945 and 'the sweeping overall Labour victory directed attention firmly in the direction of Westminster and Whitehall', thus relieving the pressure on Scottish Labour MPs to emphasise their home rule credentials.[8] Only a few years later, the success of the Convention's 1949–50 national petition, the Scottish Covenant, showed there was significant traction in home rule: the campaign secured up to 2 million signatures – the figure is contested – pledging support for a Scottish Parliament. But as Arnold Kemp notes, the Covenant and its moral force quickly 'disappeared, almost like a puff of smoke, because it had no significant location in parliamentary politics'.[9] Labour's disengagement in this period left the way clear for Unionists (after 1965, Scottish Conservatives) to exploit the patriotic mood stirred by the Covenant and especially 'the Convention's attacks on centralisation', playing the Scottish card to damage the Attlee government's energetic expansion and nationalisations.[10] Winston Churchill endorsed this classic unionist-nationalist tactic in 1950:

> The principle of centralization of government in Whitehall and Westminster is emphasized in a manner not hitherto experienced or contemplated in the Act of Union. [. . .] If England became an absolute Socialist State, owning all the means of production, distribution and exchange, ruled only by politicians and their officials in the London offices, I personally cannot feel Scotland would be bound to accept such a dispensation.[11]

While the starting pistol for devolution is usually fired in 1967, it is worth noting the presence of home rule pressure in UK party politics before the true emergence of the SNP as an electoral force. The post-war period shows a very different composition of electoral forces than are familiar from the 1980s–90s, reminding us that Scottish national identity is available for mobilisation from different ideological quarters, and that the logic of devolution shifts and evolves substantially with the tides of electoral interest.

Hamilton 1967

The Labour government's initial response to Hamilton was stunned caution: the result was a shock, but it was unclear what signal was being sent. In his study of *Hamilton 1967*, James Mitchell highlights the complexity of the political background, and several leading explanations – a protest vote in adverse economic conditions, signs of a Scottish 'cultural base' moving to the electoral surface, dissatisfaction with Scottish Labour traditionalism exploited by the SNP's 'modern, carnivalesque, upbeat and positive' campaign – but concludes that a sense of 'relative *political* deprivation' is the key to the SNP's 1960s advance: 'the demand was for an effective political voice'.[12] The Conservatives were first to announce, in 1968, an obviously tactical, internally divisive and ideologically muddled commitment to the principle of devolution (in Edward Heath's 'Declaration of Perth'), but it was Harold Wilson's Labour government who set the process in deliberately retarded motion following the emergence of the SNP threat at Hamilton.

The decision to appoint a Royal Commission on the Constitution was a gradual and contentious one. Wilson's initial response had been to establish a Cabinet subcommittee under Richard Crossman, whose first intention was to propose a 'Scottish Stormont' on the (pre-Troubles) Northern Irish model. When news of this emerging plan was leaked to the *Glasgow Herald* and published on 25 November 1967 – Crossman's diaries show that he was not displeased that his 'trial balloon' made the front page – a wave of hostility from Labour MPs resenting special treatment for Scotland quashed the idea.[13] The key obstacle within Cabinet was the powerful Secretary of State for Scotland, Willie Ross, 'who saw his role in the aftermath of Hamilton as a bulwark against unwarranted capitulation to nationalism'.[14] A patriotic unionist, Kirk elder and Burns enthusiast, Ross considered himself Scotland's man in the Cabinet. As a 'dogged opponent of anglocentricity' in government,[15] he considered his own formidable powers of leverage and patronage to be superior to any workable scheme for devolution, and a method with the notable advantage of being securely under Labour's control. Ross's opposition stymied initial efforts to formulate a proposal on devolution, and persuaded Crossman that the answer lay in economic revival rather than constitutional tinkering. Writing to Wilson in June 1968, Crossman reported that

> Willie Ross ended the discussion yesterday by stating his view that we should concentrate on 'bashing the nationalists' for their 'separatism'. I agree (and I think everyone

on the Ministerial Committee agrees) that since we are
not prepared to consider self-government to Scotland, this
should be a central theme of our propaganda from now to
the election. [. . .] [N]othing will win back votes except an
economic revival.[16]

The proposals which did emerge from the Cabinet subcommittee 'amounted to little more than the usual ideas for keeping
the Scots quiet', such as 'Edinburgh meetings of the Scottish
Grand Committee'.[17] But the problem remained, and James
Callaghan's flatfooted response to pointed questions on devolution at Labour's 1969 autumn conference moved the government towards the more decisive form of procrastination offered
by a Royal Commission. Wary of offering any sops to the Nats,
Willie Ross agreed 'only if its terms of reference extended to
England and Wales as well',[18] and Wilson announced in October
1968 the government's intention to appoint a Royal Commission on the Constitution. Publicly, this move must not give
any succour to Scottish or Welsh nationalism, and so a polite
formula was evolved citing 'a greater desire for participation
in the process of decision-making, nearer – wherever this is
possible – to the places where people live'.[19] The shift into a
spatialised rhetoric of place and proximity would emerge as a
common strategy in masking devolutionary concessions for the
next three decades. Wilson's statement claimed that nationalist parties in Scotland and Wales had 'aroused and, as some
would feel, unscrupulously played upon' legitimate desires
for greater 'nearness' in democratic involvement, their leaders
irresponsibly making 'extreme demands' that risked the economic strength of a unified Britain.[20] It would have been tacitly
understood that ventilating and exposing the arguments (both
cultural and economic) of separatist adventurers was central to
the Commission's task. In early 1969 Wilson appointed a Royal
Commission on the Constitution headed by Lord (Geoffrey)
Crowther. As Richard Finlay writes:

The idea behind this was to give the appearance of doing
something, which would avoid the need for real action for
as long as the commission was deliberating. According to

Wilson, the commission was designed to spend years taking minutes, but in public it gave the appearance that the
government was taking the issue seriously. It was hoped
that, by the time the commission reported, the SNP would
have gone away.[21]

The official remit of the Royal Commission upheld Wilson's
rubric of proximity and participation, centring its enquiry on
problems attendant to the massive expansion and centralisation
of the UK state since 1945 – in the words of its final report,
'there has been a decline this century in the extent to which we
as a people govern ourselves'.[22] Its internal documents, however,
show that the Commission clearly understood its role as tackling the problem of sub-British nationalism. Crowther's initial
memo on 'The task of the Commission' dutifully notes questions
of democratic 'participation' and administrative 'efficiency', but
the first of three 'purposes for which devolution (of any degree)
may be advocated' is 'Nationalism. It is alleged by the Nationalists
in Scotland and Wales [. . .] that the Scottish and Welsh peoples
are, or should be, separate nations, whose national interests are
not adequately represented within the present constitution of the
United Kingdom.'[23] The Commission's task was thus to assess
the nature and seriousness of the threat posed by rising votes for
nationalist parties, and the best means of managing – and if possible, harnessing – the problem of 'national feeling' within the
institutions of the UK state. In its final report, devolution itself
is neatly defined as 'the delegation of central government powers
without the relinquishment of sovereignty'.[24]

Taking minutes and wasting years

In a 1964 TUC speech, Harold Wilson opposed calls for a Royal
Commission on industrial relations by arguing that it would only
'take minutes, and waste years'.[25] Post-Hamilton, a stalling device
became highly appealing. Christopher Harvie suggests the Royal
Commission on the Constitution was premised on the assumption 'that no unanimity was required because no action would be
taken', and by the time the Commissioners reported, the threat

posed by the rising SNP vote did seem to have abated.[26] The local elections of May 1969 saw only modest gains for the party, and signalled a loss of momentum. Jim Sillars trounced the SNP for Labour (by 34 per cent) in the South Ayrshire by-election of March 1970,[27] and while the nationalists doubled their vote in the general election of 18 June (from 5 per cent to 11.4 per cent), the result 'was regarded by the party as a disaster [. . .] The SNP had got itself into another classic nationalist scenario, that of heightened expectations punctured by reality.'[28] The loss of Hamilton was balanced by gaining the Western Isles seat, but a single MP was a fragile base from which to rebuild electoral momentum under the incoming Heath government. The SNP's weak performance seemed to indicate that the nationalist threat had passed, and the leader of the Royal Commission, Lord Crowther, 'intimated to the new Conservative Prime Minister that there would be "no ill feelings" if Heath decided to bring the Commission's deliberations to an end'.[29] Heath allowed them to continue. Labour, for its part, 'might now have been expected to feign disinterest' in the Commission's recommendations, notes Peter Dorey: 'after all, those Labour politicians who had believed that the nationalist tide north of the border would recede appeared to have been vindicated'.[30] When Lord Crowther – 'no supporter of devolution', in James Mitchell's estimation – died of a heart attack at Heathrow airport in February 1972 he was replaced by Lord Kilbrandon, a 'reformist Scots lawyer' who 'would end up a supporter of the Scottish Patriots, a nationalist group'.[31]

Heath's new government was pledged only to a 'Scottish Convention' scheme recommended by a Tory committee chaired by Sir Alex Douglas-Home just prior to the 1970 election. This advocated a directly elected Scottish Assembly of 125 members, 'to deal with Second Reading, Committee and Report stages of Scottish Bills, leaving only the Third Reading and House of Lords at Westminster. [. . .] Legislative power was therefore not devolved, but the scheme did provide explicit recognition of Scotland's right to a political forum.'[32] This approach was viewed as a necessary dilution of Heath's 1968 'Declaration of Perth', which proposed 'the creation of an elected Scottish Assembly'.[33] Arnold Kemp notes that 'many Unionists felt that devolution had been foisted upon them quite against their traditions, instincts and judgement', and that about two-thirds of Unionist (Scottish Conservative) MPs 'opposed Mr Heath's declaration [of 1968], believing him to have been excessively frightened by the SNP'.[34] With the slide in nationalist support since Hamilton, devolution was a peripheral issue for a government battling more pressing economic problems. The launch of the 'It's Scotland's Oil' campaign in September 1972 generated significant publicity for the SNP, but Labour held Dundee East in a by-election of March 1973, narrowly defeating Gordon Wilson.

The Hamilton tide was clearly in spate. An item in *Scottish International* from April 1973 previews the completion of the Royal Commission's work, predicting that it 'may well turn out to be [. . .] an embarrassing boomerang from the bad, old days of 1967'.

> Labour set up the Kilbrandon (then the Crowther) Commission when they reckoned that the Scottish and Welsh Nationalist Parties were about to become the dominant forces in these countries, and that something had better be done to prevent 'separatist' movements from threatening the whole of the UK structure. But now they are confident that the nationalist bubble has burst. And though a group of Labour MPs is flirting with 'devolution', the leadership obviously wants to keep the options open – and, like the Tories, is unlikely to opt for radical change.[35]

By the time the Royal Commission issued its report on 31 October 1973, Heath's government was locked in the escalating industrial conflict by which it was ultimately overwhelmed; Britain was only two months from the Three-Day Week. The Kilbrandon recommendations were divided and unclear, as several attempts at summary tend to confirm. Vernon Bogdanor describes the report as 'a diffuse and long-winded document in which it is difficult to disentangle the essential arguments',[36] even before we consider the 225-page Memorandum of Dissent, a minority report contesting the Commission's terms of reference and resenting the concession implied by framing Scotland and Wales as 'separate nations with distinctive values and ways of life "struggling to be free"'.[37] (The Dissent argued for 'a scheme of executive devolution throughout the United Kingdom, on the principle that no part of the UK should be given privileges which were not enjoyed by other parts'.[38]) Scottish historians differ in their assessment of what the Royal Commission ultimately recommends. For Richard Finlay, Kilbrandon 'conclu[ded] that devolution was not necessary'[39]; for Peter Lynch, it 'supported the establishment of a Scottish parliament [sic] and gave a semi-official seal of approval to self-government'.[40] For Michael Lynch, the report 'agreed on the need for change but its members disagreed on the form devolution should take'.[41] The latter view seems closest to the meagre cross-party consensus around which the devolution debate was initially structured (insofar as it took place at all; Bogdanor notes that 'most MPs greeted [the report's] publication with bafflement and even mirth'[42]). *Scottish Marxist* magazine took advantage of the unsettled picture to claim credit for the report and recommendations, noting that 'it may be said, and not immodestly [. . .] that the findings of Kilbrandon and the main proposals contained in the report, are more closely akin to the proposals submitted by the Communist Party than to those of any other political party, including the Scottish National Party'.[43] Jim Phillips notes that in the Communist Party's oral evidence to the Royal Commission, Jimmy Reid

> emphasized that support for a devolved Scottish parliament was a logical extension of the CPGB's commitment to decentralized and pluralist democratic politics. This position had roots in the Popular Front politics of the 1930s, when Communists sought alliances with all 'progressive' anti-fascist political forces, and a footing too in the post-Second World War Communist platform, *The British Road to Socialism*, which avowed that Britain's revolution would flower through pluralist electoral politics.[44]

These arguments cut little ice with the Commission, whose chair at the time, Lord Crowther, voiced 'his assumption that the CPGB was a revolutionary organisation, which envisaged governing Scotland as a one-party state'. Reid rejected this as 'facetious' and centred the case for self-government on economic imperatives, arguing that 'the loss of industrial activity, arising partly from remote administration of economic and political power, and the consequent trend to outward economic migration from Scotland, were an affront to Scottish "national identity"'.[45] Thus, even the most economistic advocates for devolution grounded their arguments within the discourse of patriotic self-respect.[46]

However hostile it proved to the Communist case, this talk of 'identity' was much closer to the Royal Commission's preferred rhetorical terrain. The Commission was probably never intended to provide a clear impetus for government action, but does effectively define the problem it is asked to remedy as one of national *affect* and *attachment*: 'the question for us is whether in [Scotland and Wales] the existence of national feeling gives rise to a need for change in political institutions'.[47] Indeed, an entire chapter of the Kilbrandon Report is devoted to the nature, strength and implications of 'National Feeling'. The Commission is continually exercised by whether votes for the SNP – 'on any impartial assessment [. . .] a small minority party which has so far failed to consolidate its political position' – reflect a desire for constitutional change, or mere recognition of distinct national identity:

> While Scottish nationalism provides no evidence that the Scottish people as a whole wish to be separated from the rest of the United Kingdom, the nature and strength of the support it has attracted over the years suggest that a substantial body of people in Scotland would be likely to take a favourable view of a change to a system of government which did more than the present system to recognise their separate Scottish identity.[48]

Devolution is thus conceived as the management of 'national feeling' and its channelling into territorial forms of recognition within structures of British government. In the languid prose of the Royal Commission report, the question of 'attachment' is carefully separated from that of democratic legitimacy:

> the general impression we have formed is that, while the people of Great Britain as a whole cannot be said to be seriously dissatisfied with their system of government, they have less attachment to it than in the past and there are some substantial and persistent causes of discontent which may contain the seeds of more serious trouble. We think devolution could do much to reduce the discontent. It would counter over-centralisation and, to a lesser extent, strengthen democracy. It would be a response to national feeling in Scotland and Wales. In so far as the discontent is not regional in character, but arises from unsatisfactory aspects of the relationship between government and the people at large, devolution would probably be of limited value.[49]

As Tom Gallagher notes, the Royal Commission 'discerned the role of the SNP to be that of a barometer of discontent rather than a mass movement inexorably leading the country towards some form of self-government'.[50] The task was therefore to evolve a structure which could successfully contain 'feeling', 'discontent' and non-attachment otherwise capable of threatening the functional unity of UK governance. Devolution in this perspective is not about 'the relationship between government and the people at large' – that is to say, democracy – but about enregistering sub-national difference within UK government structures, so neutralising any 'serious trouble' it might pose to them.[51]

The victory of Margo MacDonald in the Govan by-election eight days after the publication of Kilbrandon – another shock SNP gain from Labour – forced devolution back to the top of the UK political agenda. Labour's response over the next ten months transformed the debate, in rash but enduring ways. In the February 1974 general election, Tom Devine writes, 'the SNP broke through as a real parliamentary force in Scotland, gaining seven seats and 22 per cent of the vote. Within a week, the incoming Labour [minority] government embraced devolution despite having fought the election on a platform opposed to it.'[52] This sudden conversion, Michael Lynch observes, 'rather like Mr Heath's Declaration of 1968 [. . .] involved obedience to instructions from London rather than repentance in the grass roots in Scotland for past errors'.[53]

Though the February election saw MacDonald's Govan seat return to Labour, and while four of the six SNP gains came at the expense of the Conservatives, the increasing vote share of the SNP was regarded as a major threat to Labour's fortunes UK-wide. 'There now developed an acute fear among the national leadership that, with Labour in government, it could become the main victim in the next election, which was inevitable within the year.'[54] The party's conversion to the cause of a Scottish Assembly was hasty and acrimonious. In June 1974 Wilson's minority government published a Green Paper entitled 'Devolution in the UK – Some Alternatives for Discussion' which 'set out five options for change. Even though many in the Labour Party in Scotland were opposed to this appeasement of the hated nationalists the Cabinet was determined to press for some form of change, not in order to improve the UK constitution, but to end the threat of separatism.'[55]

With some understatement, Vernon Bogdanor describes the 'decisions of principle' expressing Labour's U-turn on devolution during the summer of 1974 as 'hurriedly formulated'.

They were determined more by the fear of electoral losses to the SNP than by any particular conviction of the merits of devolution. Senior ministers were either sceptical or definitely opposed. At a ministerial meeting in July 1974, Roy Jenkins, the Home Secretary, despairing of the levity with which the issue was being treated, burst out, 'You cannot break up the United Kingdom in order to win a few seats in an election'. After the last draft of the White Paper had been agreed in Cabinet, Harold Wilson issued his benediction 'And God help all who sail in her'. Civil servants were, according to Barbara Castle, 'deeply alarmed at the whole exercise'.[56]

Wilson had great difficulty placating and eventually simply bypassing acute distrust of devolution within the Labour Party in Scotland. In its evidence to the Kilbrandon Commission, James Mitchell records, the Scottish Council of the Labour Party 'had been unequivocal in its opposition', telling the Commissioners 'they would prefer a Tory government at Westminster to a Labour-controlled Scottish Assembly'.[57] Fear of the 'slippery slope to nationalism' proved extremely difficult to quell. Labour's Scottish Council Executive met to debate the proposals of 3 June on 23 June 1974, which infamously clashed with a televised World Cup match between Scotland and Yugoslavia. As Colin Kidd records,

> Although the meeting was quorate, only 11 members of the Council Executive – there were more than thirty – turned up, and voted by six to five to reject a devolution platform. Wilson was appalled. Labour in London decided that Home Rule would have to be imposed on the Scots whether they liked it or not.[58]

Arnold Kemp noted that 'there was no doubting the sincerity of devolutionaries like [Donald] Dewar but the party came to heel with unhappy reluctance'.[59] Labour's (UK) National Executive Committee 'had that spring established a separate committee on devolution under their permanent Home Policy committee' headed by Alex Kitson of the Transport and General Workers' Union, 'who repeatedly argued strongly in favour of assemblies to Scotland and Wales'.[60] On 24 July the NEC 'without a vote, towards the end of a meeting attended by fifteen of its twenty-eight members, called for the establishment of a legislative assembly in Scotland' moved by Kitson.[61] 'As described in the *Glasgow Herald*; "in a matter of minutes [. . .] the Labour Party executive declared its voice on an issue that had been undecided for years, and had split the party in Scotland"'.[62]

A special devolution conference of Scottish Labour was called to decide the issue. Nothing left to chance, and 'a secret MORI poll carried out in Scotland for the British leadership was leaked to the press along with the conclusion that Labour could lose thirteen seats to the SNP if it failed to accept devolution'.[63]

A few weeks later, 'on 17 August, a special meeting of the Scottish Council of the Labour Party was held at the Dalintober Street Co-operative Halls in Glasgow. This is still remembered in the folklore of Scottish politics as the Dalintober Street fix.'[64]

This well-attended meeting – of 354 present, William L. Miller counted 183 trade union delegates and forty-two MPs and candidates – was called at short notice and with minimal time to discuss the issue within branches, leading to a form-less but essentially pre-ordained debate. Helen Linné Eriksen records that 'the Conference began with a Scottish Executive opposed to devolution, a government pledge to legislate on it, a NEC who favoured a Scottish Assembly with legislative powers and a split Party membership'.[65]

> Brian Wilson advocated that the Party should square up to the challenge of the SNP instead of hiding under the umbrella of a Scottish Assembly, something that could lead to nothing less than the wholesale destruction of the Labour Movement. It was also argued that it would be impossible to keep all the Scottish MPs, with the obvious consequences this would have. Jim Sillars was still a Labour Party member at the time and made a fervent pro-devolu-tion speech, advocating decentralisation and, therefore, as a logical implication, devolution.[66]

The leading anti-devolutionist Tam Dalyell MP realised swiftly that the debate was a fait accompli: 'Alex Kitson coolly told us that the NEC at Transport House were expected to give a lead, and this they had done in declaring their support for an Assembly. All too obviously it *had* been fixed [. . .] we never had a chance.'[67] Effectively lobbied and marshalled by Kitson and other union leaders, the meeting finally passed a resolution

> That this conference recognizing the desire of the Scottish people for a greater say in the running of their own affairs calls for the setting up of a directly elected Assembly with legislative powers within the context of the political and economic unity of the UK.[68]

In Neal Ascherson's recollection, 'the hall stank of humiliation and forced consciences, and the trauma of Dalintober Street lasted for many years'.[69] In his contemporaneous reflections Dalyell bitterly observed 'I bet the SNP chances have been greatly helped by the Labour Party in Scotland having to dance to the SNP tune. Devolution is little more than a political life jacket – and a life jacket, what's more, that will not inflate at the right time.'[70] Timing was indeed paramount. Wilson's minority government rushed out a White Paper in September 1974 entitled 'Democracy and Devolution. Proposals for Scotland and Wales', which proposed a Scottish legislative Assembly without revenue-raising powers and with the Secretary of State retaining a veto power.

The Labour leadership's frail commitment to devolution in the mid-1970s was conservative and centralist in nature, driven largely by anti-nationalist electoral calculation piloted from London. 'Essentially,' Tom Devine concludes, Labour's 'public support for Home Rule was founded on the paramount importance of halting the progress of the SNP'.[71] One of the more striking contradictions of this hasty process is the image of English MPs and government officials such as Michael Foot and Norman Crowther-Hunt imposing pro-devolution policies on Scottish MPs, driven by strategic imperatives impossible to square with the spirit of local empowerment. At the Dalintober Street meeting Tam Dalyell met Crowther-Hunt, a former (and dissenting) member of the Royal Commission on the Constitution brought into Wilson's government as a constitutional adviser, and found him 'very charming'.

> But I am far from convinced that he has his feet on the ground. I am conscious that for all his soothing words that all will be well, and that we should not worry, he neither knows us Scots, nor our history of faction; in fact, I sense that he regards us as interesting guinea-pigs on which to practise his constitutional experiments. He is obviously close to Harold Wilson, and will play a vital part in the coming months and years, in shaping these ideas. The real trouble is that he thinks the SNP exists because people want a different constitutional set-up; Ronnie [O'Byrne] and I know the SNP flourishes on account of the greed

of the people for North Sea oil revenues, disgust at local council corruption scandals, stirring up Rangers supporters' clubs by Orangemen because there are too many Catholics in the Labour Party, and a host of other matters, which are well known to those of us who struggle along in the gutter of political life, but which are somewhat novel, if known at all, in Oxford University Common rooms frequented by Norman.[72]

For Dalyell – a hereditary baronet who had himself been to Eton and Cambridge – the scheme for bringing political power closer to Scottish voters suggests a foolish distance from the grim realities of Scottish society and the national character. Whatever the prejudices reflected in his characterisation of rising SNP support, it is notable that an opponent of devolution grounds his opposition on 'cultural' arguments very much closer to the blighted image of Scotland entertained by literary nationalists such as Tom Scott.

In the second (October) general election of 1974 Wilson retained office and Labour gained an overall majority of three, but the SNP broke through to win eleven seats and over 30 per cent of the Scottish vote, taking four Tory seats. While Labour avoided any further Scottish losses, the SNP finished second in thirty-five of its forty-one Scottish seats, a dramatic upswing from the February poll (eleven of forty).[73] This underscored the importance and urgency of the issue. The new Wilson government pressed ahead with devolution, though Willie Ross played 'the reluctant convert, diluting and delaying wherever he could', encouraging Whitehall departments in their foot-dragging resistance to yielding power to a Scottish Assembly, and ensuring that the proposed body 'would have no economic teeth'.[74] Labour's hasty conversion came home to roost almost immediately, as various figures realised the gravity of what had been promised – and conceded – in the summer of 1974. While only a few Labour anti-devolutionists (led by Dalyell) went public with their opposition, 'other MPs were known to be uneasy, but went along with the majority feeling, which was that the issue should be disposed of as quickly as possible and that it was impossible in any case to escape from such a public and painfully adopted commitment'.[75] Barbara Castle wrote in her diaries that 'if devolution was inevitable we had better relax and at least look as if we enjoyed it', but both pro- and anti-devolution factions were dissatisfied with the rushed proposal of the previous summer.[76]

These divisions became increasingly public, and Helle Linné Eriksen captures their main contours:

> In the adjournment debate on devolution in February 1975, Neil Kinnock argued in the centralist, socialist tradition of his party, asserting that the aims of the class he represented could 'best be achieved in a single nation and in a single economic unit'. Norman Buchan, Robin Cook and Dennis Canavan, all Scottish MPs and Tribune Group members, issued a statement which accepted devolution, but also stated that 'this is no time to create a division of the working class movement in Scotland. We must unite to fight those whose real aim is to break up the UK and with it the British Labour Movement.'[77]

March brought continuing headwinds as Scottish Labour Conference narrowly voted to oppose substantial economic powers for the proposed Assembly.[78] Fractious internal debate, both parliamentary and within trade unions, delayed the emergence of a second White Paper, 'Our Changing Democracy', until November 1975. 'Its perceived inadequacy, in particular its omission of economic powers from the assembly's responsibilities, propelled [Jim] Sillars out of the party along with John Robertson. They led the breakaway Scottish Labour Party that caused an enormous but ephemeral excitement' in 1976.[79] Such was the reception of 'Our Changing Democracy', write Michael Keating and David Bleiman, 'the Government was obliged to issue a *Supplementary Statement*, virtually another White Paper, in August 1976', which still 'made no concession on the issue of revenue-raising powers'.[80] By this point the government itself had again changed. Harold Wilson's sudden resignation in March 1976 and replacement by Callaghan removed Willie Ross from the equation, who was succeeded as Scottish Secretary by Bruce Millan. The government was too fragile to re-open the hotly disputed decisions of 1974 – and now

reliant on SNP and Plaid Cymru votes in matters of confidence –
but at Labour's 1976 party conference, future leader Neil Kinnock

> spoke fervently against devolution, together with the
> delegate from Blaydon Constituency Labour Party who
> commented 'it seems to me that eleven SNP MPs some-
> times have more influence than the whole of the Northern
> Labour Group'. Michael Foot attempted to prolong the
> myth of uninterrupted Labour support for devolution by
> invoking the ghost of Keir Hardie in his reply to Neil
> Kinnock's charge of the Government's 'indecent haste':
> 'He [Hardie] would have asked us why we had not got on
> with it before.'[81]

While most internal debate focused on the scope and powers of
the proposed Assembly, the principle itself remained unsettled.
In the same year 'a "scrap the assembly" group of Labour Party
members briefly appeared', led by a Glasgow district councillor
and a former MP for Maryhill, as well as an 'all-party "Scotland
is British" campaign' financed by industrialists and attracting figures on the Labour right (including Tam Dalyell MP).[82]

Left-nationalist bewilderment and disgust at these developments are conspicuous in *The Red Paper on Scotland* (1975), edited
by future PM Gordon Brown. Though he omits to mention Dalintober, Brown's introduction pours scorn on the 'electoral calcu-
lations, nationalist and anti-nationalist passions and crude bribery'
which have precluded serious debate. In his essay on 'Devolution
and democracy' the journalist David Gow summarises Labour's
1973–4 volte-face on devolution before adding that 'as a socialist
and a Labour supporter, I should insist that the preceding report
makes clear that I consider the debate to have been undertaken
overwhelmingly in self-interested, narrow, cosmetic terms that
mask the heart of the matter: who shall control the lives of the people, who shall exercise power, who shall run the economy?'[83] The
cause of Gow's frustration is apparent in a 1976 Scottish Labour
pamphlet entitled *Why Devolution*, circulated to promote the more
detailed proposals for devolution published by the Callaghan government in the August *Supplementary Statement*. Although 'aimed at

the general public in Scotland', notes Eriksen, the rhetorical question of this pamphlet 'seems to be directed also at Labour Party voters, members and groups in England', insisting that 'the Government's proposals were firmly within the essential framework of the political and economic unity of the UK, and also stressed that the Labour Party in Scotland "would never endorse any form of devolution that carried the least danger politically, socially or economically to the rest of Britain"'.[84]

Reactionary state-nationalism

Unable to acknowledge the leadership's strategy of supporting a Scottish Assembly in order to triangulate the SNP and protect the Labour vote in Scotland – 'dishing' as well as 'bashing' the Nats – the *Why Devolution* pamphlet exhibits a high degree of cognitive dissonance in supporting its title. It studiously ignores the fundamental questions raised by Gow, and is shot through with nervous hostility to Scottish autonomy or national difference:

> The devolution of power to a directly elected legislature in Scotland is part of a long, natural and developing process begun after the Treaty of Union in 1707. Far from representing a move to fragment the United Kingdom it will further strengthen and consolidate the Union.[85]

This precis is followed by a rationale for devolution which emphasises the 'regional' rather than 'cultural' basis for this new democratic dispensation. Straining to dodge the party's internal tensions, in this vision of devolution questions of nationhood and sovereignty are everywhere absent: 'the creation of a legislature in Scotland will be an advantage open to any other identifiable part of the nation and, in satisfying and channelling the obvious national feeling in Scotland it will consolidate the functioning of the government of Britain'.[86] The real existence of a specifically Scottish polity, nation or culture is nowhere acknowledged; the state shall remain unitary, and its constitutional legitimacy remains beyond question. This repeats the defensive hedging of Wilson's post-Dalintober White Paper 'Democracy and Devolution: Proposals

for Scotland and Wales' (September 1974) in which the language
of *patrie*, heritage and unity is reserved for the defence of the British
state. Maintaining the economic and political unity of the United
Kingdom, the first White Paper declares,

> is not just a matter of tradition and sentiment, important
> though they are. The unity of the country and the econ-
> omy is essential both to the strength of our international
> position and to the growth of our industry and national
> wealth. [. . .] the Government are firmly convinced, as was
> the Royal Commission, that the United Kingdom must
> remain one country and one economy and that constitu-
> tional change must be undertaken with the clear objective
> of strengthening rather than weakening this unity.[87]

Finessing its internal opponents (quick to anger at signs of Scottish
exceptionalism) compelled Labour to adopt a vision of devolution
which laid the greater emphasis on strengthening and affirming
the *state-nation*. This tallies with the Kilbrandon Report's frequent
and jarring shift into a romantic idiom of national community
when defending, as beyond question, the 'essential unity' of the
United Kingdom. Its chapter on 'Core Principles' begins with
a subsection headed 'History and tradition', which declares that
'the geographical separation of the United Kingdom from the
continental mainland and its achievement of world prominence
as one people have had a strong unifying effect which we regard
as irreversible'.[88] This nervous tic pervades 1970s devolutionary
discourse, pledged to modernisation and reform but compelled
to couch its proposals in a vision of indivisible Britishness which
harkens back to the nineteenth century. Indeed, somewhat earlier: James Mitchell credits 'Victorian willingness to accede to
demands for pluralist styles and structures' for the foundation of
the Scottish Office in 1885.[89] While the ultimate proposals of
Kilbrandon continue in this flexible vein, they are closely chap-
eroned by a rhetoric of prickly reaction on the unchangeable
nature of Britain. As the Commission prepared its final report,
drafts were revised to downplay the extent and importance of
sub-national difference. The minutes of a meeting in November

1972 note discussion of chapters 'on the Scottish and Welsh peoples', agreeing 'that more emphasis should be laid on the fact that the differences described were historical and had been narrowing over time [. . .] To achieve better balance, there should be more reference to the common characteristics of the British people.'[90] An earlier proposed revision is even more forthright:

> Although the chapter attempted to assess objectively the dissatisfaction which arose from national feeling, it ought, to complete the picture, to lay more emphasis upon the considerable body of opposition, especially in Scotland, to further devolution (other than purely administrative). The extreme nationalists were a small minority in both countries [Scotland and Wales]; while there was a more widespread feeling that something should be done to recognise the distinctive status of Scotland and Wales, there were large numbers of people, including many of the most articulate, who were in favour of the status quo.[91]

In the end, the main Commission report presses beyond the status quo, but in largely 'expressive' and identitarian terms: 'we all see the establishment of an assembly [. . .] as being an appropriate means of recognising Scotland's national identity and of giving expression to its national consciousness'.[92] The 'national feeling' of the UK's constituent sub-peoples duly finds its proper outlet in arrangements which satisfy populist yearnings for identity without calling into question the 'essential unity' of the UK polity, formed by history, geography and tradition. 'National feeling' would be successfully canalised into affective and symbolic forms, without jeopardising the bedrock of the UK constitution and social contract.

The final throes of legislating for devolution in 1976–8 are too tedious and cynical to examine in detail, though I will give the main points of chronology. After three White Papers and incessant internal squabbling and horse-trading, Callaghan's government tabled the Scotland and Wales Bill in November 1976. It gained a second reading only when the government conceded to referendums, after Neil Kinnock tabled a motion signed by

seventy-six anti-devolution Labour MPs insisting on this condition.[93] Anti-devolution MPs won another tactical battle in defeating, on the first day of debate, a clause declaring 'that changes
proposed in the bill did not affect the unity of the UK or supreme
authority of Parliament'. James Mitchell notes that 'Nationalist
MPs had, of course, voted for this but it was anti-devolution MPs
voting with an eye to the referendum who wanted the removal
of this clause as it would make it easier to sustain the argument
that devolution was the "slippery slope to separatism".'[94] When
on 1 December 1976 the Shadow Cabinet opposed the second reading, the Conservatives' distinct cooling on devolution
under Thatcher reached freezing-point. Though Thatcher's official position right up to the 1979 referendum was that it was
Labour's specific scheme she was opposed to rather than devolution in principle, pro-devolution Scottish Conservatives viewed
the three-line whip as writing on the wall. The Shadow Secretary
of State for Scotland, Alick Buchanan-Smith, along with Mal-
colm Rifkind, resigned from the Tory front bench. The Bill met
stiff resistance at committee stage from both sides of the House,
with 350 amendments proposed on the first day. By such tactics,
and extensive filibuster, Dalyell and his fellow backbench refuseniks successfully inflicted a famous government defeat on a guil-
lotine motion of 22 February 1977. *The Scotsman* reported that
'the Bill was [. . .] backed by two-thirds of the Scottish MPs but
this handsome majority was nullified by the votes of English MPs
who have, in effect, exercised a veto on devolution'.[95] '"Now
Banquo's ghost came back to haunt the Labour government",
recalled Margaret Thatcher in her memoirs. '"Devolution, which
they had embraced solely as a means of staying in power with support from the Scottish and Welsh nationalists, turned to grimace
and gibber with Jim Callaghan at his lowest point".'[96] When Callaghan lost his parliamentary majority a few weeks later, 'Labour
backbenchers began to press his government to ditch the whole
devolutionary experiment.'[97] The SNP withdrew its informal
support for Callaghan's sickly government, which held on via a
parliamentary pact with the Liberal Party agreed on 23 March. As
part of the Lib-Lab deal, the Scotland and Wales Bill was 'split'
into two separate bills and re-tabled in November 1977.

On Burns Night 1978 the infamous Cunningham amendment was passed, requiring not only a majority of voters, but 40 per cent of the total electorate, to endorse a Scottish Assembly without revenue-raising powers, in the forthcoming referendum. By the Garscadden by-election of April 1978, the motive force of devolution had waned again. James Mitchell argues that 'devolution died in the 1974–79 Parliament on the day Donald Dewar, one of Labour's most consistent and sincere home rulers, entered Parliament as Labour MP for Garscadden. Labour was no longer frightened of the SNP and its anti-devolutionist wing gained strength commensurate with the SNP's loss of influence.'[98] But the irony of Scotland's first First Minister dealing the death-blow to the Scottish Assembly would not be realised until 1999. As the tepid referendum campaign reached its climax, the exhausted Callaghan government spoke with several voices in advocating for a Scottish Assembly:

> Michael Foot and James Callaghan argued along the left-ist, democratic line; that devolution would bring government closer to people. In choosing this argument, they tried to give the impression that the demand for devolution had more to do with resentment towards an over-centralised government than with the revival of a Scottish national feeling. Still, on 25 January at a Labour Party Political Broadcast the 'hammer of the Nats' Willie Ross talked about Robert Burns, about Scotland's chance for democracy, about how the Scottish people had been working for devolution for a hundred years. According to [Neal] Ascherson, the whole tone of the broadcast was one of 'noble nationalism'. The Labour Party leaders might argue that devolution was an old Labour policy, but the tone had certainly changed.[99]

The result

No reader of this book is likely to be ignorant of the referendum's outcome, a narrow majority in favour of a Scottish Assembly falling well short of the 40 per cent rule (32.9 per cent). 'It should

not be forgotten', Arnold Kemp argues, that '51.6 per cent of
those who voted did so in the affirmative.'

> Nor is it fanciful to assert that had there been a clear politi-
> cal consensus in favour of devolution Scotland would have
> endorsed it convincingly. In fact the result was not so sur-
> prising. It was Labour's measure and the rest of Unionist,
> Conservative or Liberal Scotland viewed it with suspicion
> as a formula for Labour dominance. [. . .] The abstention
> rate of 36.4 per cent of the official electorate testified to a
> nation's confusion.[100]

The most energetic critical response to this confusion was that of
Tom Nairn, who found vindication in the burial of 'an unloved,
undersized, consumptive, hypochondriac orphan on whom the
whole future of the family had been inexplicably pinned'.[101]
Central to his critique is the 'state-principle' underlying the pro-
spective 'gift' of an Assembly, and left unmolested by it. In keeping with his argument in *The Break-Up of Britain*, first published
in 1977, Nairn argued that devolution was merely the latest ploy
to retain and retrench the quasi-feudal essence of the British constitutional order. Such institutional tinkering, for Nairn, could
do nothing to exorcise 'the ghost of absolutism' retained within
the British system, 'in essence a decaffeinated version of the pre-
revolutionary monarchy'.[102] In this view the highly limited
form of constitutional change on offer in 1979 was something
of a joke. Its democratic and reformist credentials were a sham,
premised on 'almost religious faith in the state, in a political system so much at one with and so much in charge of society that
the latter offers no resistance to its plans'.[103] As we have seen, the
devolutionary policy of the Wilson and Callaghan governments
established an 'identitarian' logic of territorial governance, carefully separating questions of (sub-British) nationhood from sovereignty, in order to manage immediate electoral pressures. For
Nairn, these rhetorical games are only window dressing on the
part of a confident and 'utterly entrenched constitutional conservatism so secure that it feels instinctively able to negotiate and

compromise away almost any difficulty. [. . .] Any conflict can be institutionalised and defused in the same way.'[104]

While the unlimited plasticity of these arrangements is central to the 'absolutist' character of the UK constitutional order – what was made and remade in the 1970s can be un-made and changed by later governments – the precedents and concessions of the post-Hamilton process continued to exert considerable influence into the 1980s and 1990s, in various waypoints and debates on the road to Holyrood. Most notable, as we shall see, is the framing of devolution as the *management of national feeling,* on terms which offer 'recognition' of identitarian claims to difference and auton-omy by directly incorporating these claims into the structures of the 'modernising' union-state, strengthening its own claims to representative pluralism.

Thus was the ground prepared for 'cultural devolution'. Less a cause than a stratagem, the cynical and formalistic vision of devolution which ground its way painfully through British poli-tics in the 1970s was so far removed from a stirring affirmation of 'national feeling' that the very emptiness of the assembly half-chosen in March 1979 created a vacuum in which the intel-ligentsia could claim its kingdom, as inheritors of a thwarted popular mandate. The thwarting itself gave cause for concern among political scholars who viewed sub-British nationalism as unfinished business. In 1981 William L. Miller implored the dominant parties to restore some credibility to devolution, or face 'the possibility of a darker future':

There is, at present, a remarkably low level of popular sup-port in Scotland for political violence over devolution or indeed over other special Scots interests. But while low it is not negligible and attitudes to violence are coherently linked to other political attitudes. [. . .] the Kirk's Church and Nation Committee have considered 'why all attempts to obtain self-government have failed and reasoned arguments [been] brushed aside. Looking back to the past it sometimes seems as though British Governments will yield only to vio-lence, or at least to non-violent disobedience to the law.'[105]

The clean-handed 'civic' and constitutional basis of Scottish devolution is so firmly entrenched today, it can be difficult to grasp how 1970s commentators could associate the cause of self-government with threats of violence. Miller's real point was that the disruptive forces devolution was intended to manage and appease might find dangerous purchase outside the civic institutions which had failed to assimilate them. If Miller worried about shadowy figures seizing their moment, James Kellas maintained his faith in the established patterns of the Scottish political system, and the resilience of elite rule. Reviewing the 'referendum experience' in 1981, Kellas concluded that the weak and ambiguous democratic mandate which a Scottish Assembly had commanded in March 1979 was by no means the end of the matter. On the contrary this could prove to be the making of the policy, for

> it is much more usual for constitutional change to come about through 'elite' initiative; in particular, from party leaders and civil servants working through Parliament and the Whitehall machine. Until now, this elite has been most suspicious of devolution and has taken action only when forced to do so through the apparent pressure of the masses and the SNP. But now that that pressure has been removed, a section of the elite may feel more secure in moving toward devolution, this time as an elite demand and not as a concession to the irrational masses.[106]

And so, to an extent, it proved. By 1980, Kellas noted, 'the members of the Scottish Executive of the Labour Party were now predominantly devolutionists, and also demanded greater autonomy for the party organisation'.[107] But the policy was a much tougher sell in the Westminster party. Devolution was entirely omitted from Labour's 'draft manifesto' of 1980, and was not debated at the annual party conference of that year.[108] As chair of the Labour Campaign for a Scottish Assembly formed in 1980, George Foulkes MP corresponded with various strategists on means of reviving the policy within the Parliamentary Labour Party. A 1981 letter to Foulkes by the young political scientist Michael Keating, at that time a member of the cross-party

Campaign for a Scottish Assembly, recommends that interest be rekindled among English Labour MPs by framing devolution not as a matter of democratic 'voice' but as a functional upgrade of the machinery of state:

> Other points which it may be worth making to English MPs: Devolution is part of a necessary and long-overdue reappraisal of the institutions of the state and is to be seen in the same context as concern about the power and composition of the civil service and secrecy in government. It is a means of ensuring that (Labour) governments can get more control over the administration and more effective government. This ought to strike a chord ... [109]

Here 'elite demand' joins party self-interest; devolution will strengthen the organs of state Labour will command when it is eventually returned to power at Westminster. Party interests were seldom far from Labour's internal debate on devolution. A decade later, as the cross-party Scottish Constitutional Convention considered various proposals for voting methods in the projected new assembly, Foulkes pressed his party colleagues to remember the necessary limits of co-operation:

> We should not be ashamed about considering the interests of the Labour Party in any system we support. The advocacy of PR by the Liberals is not an act of magnanimity, but of pure self-interest. The Tories are able to exercise other levers of power in our society, while the power of Parliament is the only one which the Labour Party has the opportunity to have direct control of. [110]

This is a suitable note on which to conclude this digest. Politically speaking, the purpose and function of devolution is to re-legitimise rather than reform the inherited Westminster system – 'a policy of a strikingly conservative character', notes Vernon Bogdanor, concerned chiefly to 'renegotiate the terms of the Union so as to make them more palatable to Scottish opinion in the conditions of the late twentieth century'. [111] If 'the mainspring of the case for devolution was a democratic one', it conceived democracy almost entirely in governmental terms: as the question of ensuring existing administrative structures and channels of executive power were seen to 'reflect Scottish interests and needs more effectively', rather than acknowledging a distinct Scottish polity or political culture 'outside' the machinery of public administration.[112] On the contrary, as we have seen it was the immediate internal needs of the British political 'machine' which drove a limited re-formulation of the national polity/polities it notionally represents. This process was both plurinational and reactionary, premised on unshakeable unities (of the UK state-nation, of the Labour movement) to be mysteriously enhanced through an addition of new and flexible governing structure.

Devolution was a process devised and implemented within the sphere, and according to the interests, of established structures of power and governance. It is very difficult to regard this saga as a transformation of political structure by some external 'civic' or popular agency, let alone a 'cultural' expression or demand. Indeed, being positioned as a merely 'expressive' demand – an outlet of 'national feeling' – was the main strategy by which the political and constitutional threat represented by (sporadic) SNP electoral success was rhetorically contained. Where does this leave 'cultural devolution'? As has often been observed, Scotland does not fit the normative model of cultural nationalism established by Czech sociologist Miroslav Hroch, whereby 'distinctive national culture drives national identity, and [. . .] together they drive politics such that "a people" express that national identity in the quest for self-government'.[113] David McCrone points up a range of incongruities between this model and Scottish social and economic history, but acknowledges 'an influential strain of writing about the relationship between culture and politics' in modern Scotland, one which seeks 'culturalist' explanations for Scotland's unusual development.[114] This writing has an influence out of all proportion to its historical value, McCrone argues.

> Such culturalist accounts for (the lack of) political and economic development have powerful appeal despite (or perhaps because of) their lack of systematic and rigorous evidence to back them. They are predispositions

of considerable cultural power which set the frame for economic and political agendas. They may be wrong, in sociological terms, but they are powerfully wrong in setting the frame for debate.[115]

But it is too simplistic to dismiss such narratives as powerfully wrong. 'Culture' plays almost no role in the brazen machine politics outlined above, but of course these developments and strategic responses were ultimately actuated by electoral behaviour which cannot be severed from cultural assertion and affiliation. Explaining *The Growth of Nationalism in Scotland* in 1978, Keith Webb noted 'that national feeling is a permanent feature of Scottish culture':

> It is not possible, therefore, to explain the rise of a nationalist movement by referring to a sudden spread of nationalist sentiment. What is needed is an explanation of why the nationalist feelings already held by many Scots became politicized when they did. [. . .] What seems to have happened is that the Scottish identity has become relevant to politics, whereas previously politics was only seen in British terms.[116]

This is an important insight, touching both the question of timing and the 'extra-Scottish' factors which promoted national sentiment to political salience. This reading suggests the UK electoral context as a key determining factor; though this line of interpretation becomes circular, as Webb realises, after the SNP have achieved lift-off in the late 1960s: 'due to the great success of the SNP in the two general elections of 1974, and their now central position in Scottish political life, they may have had the effect of heightening and intensifying this self-image of Scotland. This would of course be an effect of their success, rather than a cause.'[117] We are close here to the 'double aspect' of modern Scottish nationalism, as described by James Kellas:

> The fortunes of the SNP have of course affected the intensity of national consciousness, but such consciousness is greater than the number of votes won by that party at

elections. It is not necessarily concerned, as is the SNP, with 'national self-determinism', or with political devolution. It is rather an assertion of Scottishness on the part of an amorphous group of interests and individuals, whose identity is caught up with that of Scotland.[118]

In one respect, this view bolsters the 'cultural devolution' thesis: a growth in confident national identity was a major factor in the political realignment of the post-1967 period. But in another, the very looseness of the ties between politics and identity is also key – their elision in the narrative of The Dream, where expressions of cultural Scottishness directly equate to support for political self-determination, badly distorts the factors at issue. For the critic or historian, the challenge is to recognise and respect this difference (or 'doubleness') without falsely isolating one factor from the other. John Caughie put it well in a 1978 issue of *New Edinburgh Review*: 'far from devaluing culture, I would want to give it a political specificity by inscribing within it the necessary political concept of struggle; and it's in this sense that the movement is made from "political culture" to "cultural politics"'.[119] This is essentially the pattern of Scottish national literary politics in the post-1967 period, with the important caveat that the inscription of 'struggle' was often made to appear like its opposite: constitutional change as the *prevention* of discord and division, a means of forestalling conflict between settled national and electoral loyalties.

Vanguardist assimilation?

As Donald Campbell pondered what impact devolution might have on Scottish literature, another curious doubleness emerged in his picture of the nationalist literati:

it would seem that we *are* going to have an Assembly, sooner or later, and this will have its effects on our literature as in other departments of Scottish life. In the short term, of course, the Assembly will change nothing as far as Scottish writing is concerned. As a matter of fact, a good argument could be made to the effect that the Assembly will make matters worse! The most serious threat to an indigenous Scottish Literature can be seen in the difficulty that many Scottish writers experience in resisting the temptation to become absorbed in the mainstream of contemporary English writing. It could therefore be argued that the Scottish Assembly, by virtue of the fact that it is largely an English creation, designed with the prime intention of solving an English problem (*viz.* maintaining the English-dominated unity of Britain), will lead to an inevitable increase in the process of anglicisation, thereby increasing the temptation of the Scottish writer to identify his work with the English tradition.[120]

Devolution will both 'change nothing' and pose a 'serious threat'; by affirming 'Scottish Literature' within a political paradigm concerned to maintain English-dominated Britishness, thus *cementing*, rather than eroding, its provincial status and value. This irony begets another as Campbell continues:

Some years ago, I had a conversation with an Austrian academic who was engaged in a study of Scottish literature. He was an intelligent, perceptive and knowledgeable man, but he asked one question which could not help but make me smile. 'To what extent is the present vigour of Scottish writing due to the growth of nationalism and the proposals for legislative devolution?' I lost no time in telling him that he had put the question exactly the wrong way round, that there would have been no national movement and no devolution proposals without the vigorous propaganda of Scottish literature over the last eighty years. Writers are always ahead of their time and, in the new situation that the Scottish Assembly will create, can be relied upon to impose a significant (if long-term) influence on the future. As its opponents have not been slow to point out, the provisions of the Scotland Act ensure that our assembly, in terms of the powers at its disposal, will be a soul-less, ineffective institution. However, if it does not have a soul for us to save, it will certainly have a backside for us to kick – and, when it comes to kicking, it will be up to the Scottish writer to put some education into the boots of Scottish opinion. He will not fail to do so.[121]

A true cultural vanguard 'ahead of their time', the Renaissance literati have, in this view, quietly occupied the commanding heights of Scottish politics for decades, wearing down their opponents and inspiring a national movement now poised to secure an Assembly. After devolution, the role of Scottish writers will change to supervising the Assembly's dismal work, using their cultural authority to keep the politicians in touch with Scottish opinion, while enlightening the national-popular mentality whose empowerment it has secured.

Because the 1979 referendum did not deliver a Scottish Assembly, the prophecy is moot. But this remains a highly suggestive reading of the relationship between culture and politics, literature and parliaments. When devolution re-surfaced as a serious political possibility in the 1980s, Scottish writers and artists took on a very different role than either of those Campbell had predicted. The general tenor of their response was to act as though the cause of a Scottish Parliament was much closer to contesting *cultural sovereignty* than any of the administrative or legislative proposals in the 1970s, effectively ignoring the deep limits, compromises – and Britishness – of devolution as a constitutional project.

Conclusion: before the watershed

Whatever the truth of the 'cultural devolution' story, there is a lengthy prelude to its official starting point in 1979. The accumulated pressure for a Scottish Assembly, and its established political logic, clearly passed from one side of the referendum watershed to the other. In truth, the Scottish elite took over a half-constructed, semi-derelict project whose developers – the Labour Party – had exhausted their resources, and lost all incentive to complete the job. When Scottish 'civic society' took rhetorical possession of the project, they did not – and could not – demolish the foundations already laid in the 1974–9 period, the most important being Labour's grudging and hard-won commitment to devolution as a strategy of nationalist containment and state 'modernisation'. Indeed, the core proposition of the early 1980s movement, beginning with the Campaign for a Scottish Assembly, was to revive mothballed commitments dating from 1974. CSA and its successors added to and modified the project, to be sure, but there are deep continuities between the Thatcher-era vision of devolution, in which writers and artists played an important role bridging and 'articulating' cultural and political mobilisation, and the core electoral logic and constitutional rhetoric of the earlier process (dominated by interests of state and party); we turn to this story in the next two chapters.

It should first be underscored that the Grind (of British machine-politics) precedes the Dream (of cultural devolution) and delimits its constitutional possibilities: just as no Labour government could fully disown tortuously secured support for devolution in the 1970s – especially as the context of Thatcherism gave it new electoral importance in Scotland – neither could Labour risk re-opening the strategic compromises baked into the 1970s version, with its emphasis on 'recognition' rather than power, and its hypersensitivity to the charge of undermining Britishness. Indeed, the over-development of defensive reflexes on this point, stimulated by the prospect of devolution, probably delayed the re-imagining of British identity and multiculturality often associated with 1990s British writing, and aligned with the impact of New Labour.[122]

To conclude with the Scottish scene, in 1982 Christopher Harvie observed that 'our consciousness of [national] distinctiveness has spread from poetry and politics to society as a whole'.[123] But the reverse pattern was even stronger, as Scottish literature set about *ingesting* constitutional politics in the 1980s. As David Leishman highlights, the debacle of 1979 became a touchstone of 'new renaissance' fiction into the 1990s.

> Evocations of the referendum stand out in these novels for their use of the language of trickery and deceit, seeking to portray the moment as a key instance of anti-Scottish conspiracy at the hands of the British Establishment. In [Alasdair Gray's] *1982 Janine*, as the narrator berates

the famous 40 per cent rule which changed 'the usual sporting rules for electing a new government' and saw a slight majority equated with a 'no' vote, his reasoned tone degenerates into vituperations about 'fucking politics', thus reiterating the novel's key sexual metaphor: 'Scotland has been fucked. I mean that word in the vulgar sense of *misused to give satisfaction or advantage to another*'. In [Iain Banks'] *The Bridge*, the tone is one of mock ebullience: 'The Fabulous Make-Your-Mind-Up Referendum was, effectively, pochled – rigged, in English'. As if to hint at the backlash to come, the use of a rare dialectal borrowing underlines Scotland's cultural distance from the metropolitan centre. In *Electric Brae*, Andrew Greig's dysfunctional micro-community of friends and lovers begins in March 1979 with the first cigarette smoked since the referendum, just as a Party Political Broadcast is symbolically switched off from a pub television.[124]

The set-piece mechanics of elections and referendums are prominent as convenient newsreel 'episodes' in devolutionary fiction, important not only for asserting reductive narratives of treachery or cowardice, but reifying ideas of democracy, 'Scotland' and 'the political', rendering them co-equal with these representative templates. This pattern is exactly mirrored in promotion of the 'Scottish dimension' in the pre-figurative devolutionary politics of the 1980s.

Notes

1. Donald Campbell, 'A focus of discontent: Scottish literature and the Scottish Assembly', *New Edinburgh Review*, 45 (Spring 1979), pp. 3–5 (p. 5).
2. See Robb, *Auld Campaigner*.
3. Macdonald, *Whaur Extremes Meet*, p. 261.
4. Finlay, *Modern Scotland 1914–2000*, p. 321.
5. Keating and Bleiman, *Labour and Scottish Nationalism*, p. 101.
6. Kemp, *The Hollow Drum*, p. 91.
7. Mitchell, *Strategies for Self-Government*, p. 85.

8. Keating and Bleiman, *Labour and Scottish Nationalism*, p. 134.
9. Kemp, *The Hollow Drum*, p. 93.
10. Ibid. p. 135.
11. Quoted in Keating and Bleiman, *Labour and Scottish Nationalism*, pp. 135–6.
12. Mitchell, *Hamilton 1967*, pp. 136, 137.
13. Quoted in Dalyell, *Devolution*, p. 88.
14. Cameron, *Impaled Upon a Thistle*, p. 286.
15. Ibid. p. 287.
16. Richard Crossman, Letter to Harold Wilson, 25 June 1968. National Archives.
17. Cameron, *Impaled Upon a Thistle*, p. 287.
18. Kemp, *The Hollow Drum*, p. 115.
19. 'Queen's Speech – Debate on the Address', 30 October 1968.
20. Ibid.
21. Finlay, *Modern Scotland*, p. 322.
22. *Report of the Royal Commission*, I, p. xii.
23. Geoffrey (Lord) Crowther, 'The Task of the Commission – Note by the Chairman', 13 May 1969. Emphasis in original.
24. *Report of the Royal Commission*, I, p. 165.
25. Quoted in Cartwright, *Royal Commissions and Departmental Committees in Britain*, p. 211. Wilson would appoint ten Royal Commissions in his period as Prime Minister.
26. Harvie, *Scotland and Nationalism*, p. 179.
27. Sillars would leave Labour to found the breakaway Scottish Labour Party in 1976; he joined the SNP in 1980, and would later serve as Deputy Leader of the party.
28. Kemp, *The Hollow Drum*, p. 103.
29. Mitchell, 'Devolution', p. 182.
30. Dorey, *The Labour Party and Constitutional Reform*, p. 217.
31. Mitchell, 'Devolution', p. 183.
32. Gay, 'Scotland and Devolution Research Paper 97/92'.
33. Heath, 'The Declaration of Perth', p. 29.
34. Kemp, *The Hollow Drum*, p. 112.
35. Possum, 'Who will kill the Commission?', *Scottish International*, 6.4 (April 1973), pp. 3–4 (p. 4).
36. Bogdanor, *Devolution in the United Kingdom*, p. 173.
37. *Report of the Royal Commission*, II, p. vii.
38. Keating and Bleiman, *Labour and Scottish Nationalism*, p. 163.
39. Finlay, *Modern Scotland*, p. 331
40. Lynch, *SNP: The History of the Scottish National Party*, p. 135.

41. Lynch, *Scotland: A New History*, p. 445.
42. Bogdanor, *Devolution in the United Kingdom*, p. 175.
43. Alex Murray, 'Whither Kilbrandon?', *Scottish Marxist*, 6 (April 1974), pp. 56–68 (p. 57).
44. Phillips, *The Industrial Politics of Devolution*, p. 101.
45. Ibid. p. 101.
46. Like Jim Sillars and George Kerevan, Reid moved steadily in the direction of political nationalism in later years, leaving the CPGB for Labour in the mid-1970s, and finally joining the SNP in 2005.
47. *Report of the Royal Commission*, I, p. 102.
48. Ibid. pp. 107–8.
49. Ibid. p. 331.
50. Gallagher, 'The SNP faces the 1990s', p. 10.
51. The paragraph here cited from the Kilbrandon Report was excerpted in a House of Commons Research Division 'Background Paper' assembled for MPs debating concrete devolution proposals in November 1976, suggesting this formulation played a continuing role in the framing of pro-Assembly arguments. Devolution Proposals 1973–6, 'Background Paper 54', p. 4.
52. Devine, *The Scottish Nation 1700–2000*, p. 575.
53. Lynch, *Scotland: A New History*, p. 445.
54. Keating and Bleiman, *Labour and Scottish Nationalism*, p. 165.
55. Devine, *The Scottish Nation 1700–2000*, p. 576.
56. Bogdanor, *Devolution in the United Kingdom*, pp. 178–9.
57. Mitchell, *The Scottish Question*, p. 165.
58. Kidd, 'The end of Labour?', p. 4.
59. Kemp, *The Hollow Drum*, p. 116.
60. Eriksen, 'Walking the tartan tightrope', p. 30.
61. Keating and Bleiman, *Labour and Scottish Nationalism*, p. 166.
62. Eriksen, 'Walking the tartan tightrope', pp. 30–1.
63. Miller, *The End of British Politics?*, p. 69.
64. Kidd, 'The end of Labour?', p. 4.
65. Eriksen, 'Walking the tartan tightrope', p. 31.
66. Ibid. p. 31.
67. Dalyell, *Devolution*, p. 106.
68. Miller, *The End of British Politics?*, p. 68.
69. Ascherson, 'Seven days that exposed the black hole at the heart of Scottish politics'.
70. Dalyell, *Devolution*, p. 107.
71. Devine, *The Scottish Nation 1700–2000*, p. 586.
72. Dalyell, *Devolution*, pp. 107–8.

73. Based on figures from Drucker and Drucker (eds), *Scottish Government Yearbook 1979*, pp. 261–7. See also Mitchell, *The Scottish Question*, p. 156 (who counts thirty-six of forty-one Scottish seats).
74. Kemp, *The Hollow Drum*, p. 139.
75. Keating and Bleiman, *Labour and Scottish Nationalism*, p. 181.
76. Castle, *The Castle Diaries 1974–76*, p. 173.
77. Eriksen, 'Walking the tartan tightrope', p. 46.
78. Hassan and Lynch, *The Almanac of Scottish Politics*, p. 421.
79. Kemp, *The Hollow Drum*, p. 140.
80. Keating and Bleiman, *Labour and Scottish Nationalism*, p. 176.
81. Eriksen, 'Walking the tartan tightrope', p. 51.
82. Keating and Bleiman, *Labour and Scottish Nationalism*, p. 186.
83. Gow, 'Devolution and democracy', p. 60.
84. Eriksen, 'Walking the tartan tightrope', p. 44.
85. Labour Party in Scotland, *Why Devolution*, p. 1.
86. Ibid. p. 1.
87. Cited in Devolution Proposals 1973–6, 'Background Paper 54', pp. 8–9.
88. *Report of the Royal Commission*, I, p. 122.
89. Mitchell, *Strategies for Self-Government*, p. 41.
90. Royal Commission on the Constitution – Papers. Minutes of 16 November 1972 meeting.
91. Royal Commission on the Constitution – Papers. Minutes of 9 December 1971 meeting.
92. *Report of the Royal Commission*, I, p. 335.
93. Mitchell, *Strategies for Self-Government*, pp. 161–2; Eriksen, 'Walking the tartan tightrope', pp. 52–4.
94. Mitchell, *Strategies for Self-Government*, p. 161.
95. Quoted by Eriksen, 'Walking the tartan tightrope', p. 55.
96. Quoted by Torrance, *'We in Scotland'*, p. 28.
97. Torrance, *'We in Scotland'*, pp. 28–9.
98. Mitchell, *Strategies for Self-Government*, p. 216.
99. Eriksen, 'Walking the tartan tightrope', p. 93.
100. Kemp, *The Hollow Drum*, p. 152.
101. Tom Nairn, 'After the referendum', *New Edinburgh Review*, 46 (Summer 1979), pp. 3–10 (p. 3).
102. Ibid. p. 3.
103. Ibid. p. 4.
104. Ibid. p. 4.
105. Miller, *The End of British Politics?*, p. 263.
106. Kellas, 'On to an assembly?', p. 151.

107. Ibid. p. 150.
108. Ibid. p. 151.
109. Michael Keating, Letter to George Foulkes MP, 30 June 1981.
110. George Foulkes, Submission to Labour Party Discussions (on Proportional Representation), 22 April 1991.
111. Bogdanor, *Devolution in the United Kingdom*, p. 119.
112. Ibid. p. 118.
113. McCrone, 'National identity and culture in a cold climate', p. 53.
114. Ibid. p. 54.
115. Ibid. p. 56.
116. Webb, *The Growth of Nationalism in Scotland*, p. 102.
117. Ibid. p. 102.
118. Kellas, *The Scottish Political System*, p. 119.
119. John Caughie, 'Political culture/cultural politics', *New Edinburgh Review*, 40 (Spring 1978), pp. 4–7 (p. 4).
120. Campbell, 'A focus of discontent', p. 3.
121. Ibid. p. 5.
122. See Marks, *Literature of the 1990s*.
123. Christopher Harvie, 'Beyond bairns' play: a new agenda for Scottish politics', *Cencrastus*, 10 (Autumn 1982), pp. 11–14 (p. 13).
124. Leishman, 'A parliament of novels', pp. 131–2.

3

The Scottish Dimension

Cultural and Constitutional Politics 1979–87

If literary devolution has a Hollywood moment, it is William McIlvanney's speech at the 'Scotland Demands Democracy' demonstration on 12 December 1992. Held in Edinburgh to coincide with a European Heads of Government summit, the event was charged with the defiant energy of new pro-devolution groups formed after John Major's victory that April. Three such groups – Scotland United, Democracy for Scotland, Common Cause – were formed within 48 hours of the surprise result.[1] If in 1981 William Miller felt the need to gloss 'demand for devolution' as a phrase 'that should not conjure up visions of street parades', three consecutive Tory election victories had transformed the atmosphere.[2] Neal Ascherson sets the scene in *Stone Voices: The Search for Scotland*:

> The procession was immense. Some 30,000 people, touched by the sense that Scotland was under the eyes of Europe, made their way to the Meadows and asked for their country back. Out of many speeches, I remember only one, and snatches of it are still quoted by many others who remember. The novelist William McIlvanney [. . .] looked out over the faces stretching away towards Salisbury Crags in the distance and he said: 'Let's not be mealy-mouthed about all this. The Scottish parliament starts here, today!' When the clapping died down, he went on: 'We gather here like refugees in the capital of our own country. We are almost seven hundred years old, and we are still wondering what we want to be when we grow up. Scotland is in an intolerable position.

We must never acclimatize to it – never!' And then, in a tone of tremendous pride, he said this. 'Scottishness is not some pedigree lineage. This is a mongrel tradition!' At those words, for reasons which perhaps neither he nor they ever quite understood, the crowd broke into cheers and applause which lasted on and on. After that December mobilization, the game was up. The Tories knew that they were doomed; Labour knew that they must deliver Scottish self-government as soon as they came to power. McIlvanney was right: the parliament had started that day.[3]

It is a powerful tableau – the charismatic cultural leader rebuilding democracy in the streets – but too much is missing from this crowning moment of the Dream. As we shall see, the key players and interests who strategised this moment into existence – and whose later authority and legitimacy were grounded by it – are cropped out of the frame in Ascherson's triumphal vista, and must be restored to the narrative.

The emotional release of the 1992 speech may be traced back to McIlvanney's equally famous response to the failure of the March 1979 referendum on a Scottish Assembly. This date marks the nadir of national failure and malaise against which the flowering of the 'new Scottish renaissance' is usually measured: a 'democratic debacle', according to Gavin Wallace, seeming to stifle all 'hopes for an autonomous Scottish political culture, and cultural politics'.[4] In fact, 1979 marks a new beginning in Scottish cultural politics, and the inception of a devolutionary movement whose agitation against *non-representation* travelled freely across the membrane that usually separates cultural and constitutional debate. To put it simply, in the early and mid-1980s the 'Scottish card' was played in ways that changed and expanded the game in which it featured. Pervasively in this period, tacit claims to national-cultural difference are the bedrock of key arguments within the constitutional debate. But the specific features and traditions of national culture were largely immaterial to the political leveraging of 'Scotland' as a civic-political unit, a 'counter' whose legitimacy – and marginalisation – was quite separable from its 'content'. This chapter documents the emergence of key discursive frames concerning Scottish cultural and political difference between 1979 and 1987, while Chapter 4 reviews their full deployment and institutionalisation in the period between Thatcher's third electoral victory ('Doomsday', or near enough) and the catharsis of the 'Scotland Demands Democracy' moment of 1992.

Back to 1979

But first the nadir. SNP leader William Wolfe had pitched the 1979 referendum on a Scottish Assembly as nothing less than 'a struggle for the soul of our country'.[5] The struggle aroused remarkably little interest. The first public meeting held in Dundee's Marryat Hall, a heavyweight clash between Jim Sillars (pro) and Tam Dalyell (anti), attracted an audience of just six, 'one of whom was George Cunningham MP', the Labour backbencher who had fathered the 40 per cent rule.[6] Burdened with expository longeurs on the financing and powers of the Assembly, key Yes arguments died in the throat. A crib-sheet for speakers in the Labour Movement Yes Campaign devotes fully sixteen pages to the long gestation of the Scotland Act 1978 before making 'Labour's Case For A Scottish Assembly' on less than two pages.[7] A further five pages offer guidance on 'Dealing with Doubts', reserving 'People are just not interested in an Assembly' to the end.

McIlvanney's essay 'Before: February 1979' traces this shrugging ambience to the tepid qualities of nationality itself: 'if the indifference with which most of us seem to approach the impending referendum on devolution is an accurate gauge of our sense of national identity, the flag of Scotland might be a lion dormant, with mange'.[8] Leading up to the vote, McIlvanney frames 'Scottishness' as an elusive and somewhat perilous question, almost incapable of formulation (still less resolution): 'if the Scotland Act has less the aspect of Moses leading us dramatically to a new sense of identity than that of a confused policeman vaguely pointing us toward a place he has never heard of, it is still all we have at the moment'.[9] The chanciness of Scottish nationhood is not yet a matter of defiant mongrel pride, and is shot through with confusion and self-reproach. But voting Yes (as McIlvanney gently advocates) would signal a willingness to confront the limits and evasions of Scottishness, providing 'the

means for us to confront ourselves a little more honestly' and
'a way of relating fresh to reality as opposed to hiding from it
behind archaic masks'.[10]

A few months after the result, squandering this modest opportunity for growth has shifted McIlvanney's sense of what was
at stake. In place of muttered self-accusation before the vote,
his poetic response 'The Cowardly Lion' positively roars with
self-disgust. Here the No result represents a national failure of
nerve, laced with moral cowardice and self-abasement. In this
allegory, the restive lion is offered the additional elbow room of
an 'extended compound' in order to forestall its outright escape.
Its keepers are divided between those who 'would pretend to free
it but still keep / it as their pet' (devolution as safety valve) and
others secretly hoping for its emancipation (a stepping stone to
independence), who, 'in their cunning':

> thought they understood
> The lion would escape this half-way house.
> This was a lion. It was not a mouse
> To be content with just a little room.[11]

Finally, the new compound is constructed and the lion approaches
the threshold of its cage:

> The day of 'freedom' came. The cage-door creaked
> Out on its ancient hinges and swung open.
> In awe the keepers waited. What would happen?
> Would the lion attack and had they been too bold
> In their decisions? Would the compound hold?
> The lion approached the door. Its head emerged
> Noble and proud, its snout raised to the wind.
> It smelt the terrible distances of freedom
> It felt the risk of being not confined,
> It knew the pain of hunger unassuaged,
> It sensed the emptiness where self is found,
> It heard the bitterness where life is waged.
> Slowly the keepers relaxed into a smile
> And giggled and nodded again, were winking while

Those who loved the lion had nothing to say.
For the lion had turned to its cage and slunk away.
And lives still among stinking straw today.[12]

The image of devolution as enlarged captivity is a telling one, but even this roomier confinement is ultimately needless: the lion prefers the familiar cage of old. Why? Because of a failure of identity – it 'sensed the emptiness where self is found'. Not only freedom but lionhood itself has been renounced: shirking the struggle with 'Scottishness' effectively abolishes it. This very condition of nullity becomes the identity to rally around in one strand of 1980s cultural politics, the wounded attachment through which a new quest for self-realisation is articulated: one that ultimately exchanges lionhood for mongrelism, pride for injury, and freedom for representation. In another, intersecting strand, it is the solidity of the cage itself – the established category and container 'Scotland' – which seals the argument for self-government. The health and condition of its inhabitant (mangy, cowardly or otherwise) is beside the civic-institutional point.

McIlvanney's disgust was widely shared in nationalist and pro-devolution circles. An editorial in *Crann-Tàra* declared: 'The '79 is over. You can add it to the '15, the '19, the '45, if you like, but that's all just so much vainglory.'[13] The mood was not for elegy or excuse-making but pitiless self-recrimination, an indictment of Scotland's historic identity as 'a drowning nationality clutching at a straw, a peasant culture wallowing in its own defeat, enjoying the attention of other people's scorn'.[14] It had been foolish to expect courage from a mythical creature. The purpose and powers of the Assembly were emptied out by the unreality of the Scotland it would claim to represent: 'no amount of last-minute socio-economic presentation of the self-government case could save us from the weaknesses of the nationalist image'.[15] Thus, the SNP surge over the prior decade is retroactively invalidated: 'Our patriotism was misplaced. It was rooted not in the spirit of equality, but in guilt and inferiority. All tootle-tattle and nae substance, that's our nationalism.'[16]

As in *Crann-Tàra*, the self-laceration of 'The Cowardly Lion' moves on the moral-psychological plane, quite removed from the 'civic-republican' discourse Ray Ryan identifies as a key element of McIlvanney's warmly humanist fiction and essays.[17] In *Surviving the Shipwreck* (1991) McIlvanney sets out the exceptionalist quality of his left-nationalism in the following terms:

> Scotland has existed for almost 300 years in a uniquely arrived at limbo in which a strongly shared sense of social and cultural values persists without the political means to express itself effectively. [. . .] Here is held in embryo the possibility of some kind of socialism, a more just way of living with one another.[18]

This essentially Nairnite rhetoric is subtle but important. Here Scotland's special problems and potential concern the disjunction between a settled but impotent sense of 'us-ness': the thwarting of tacit bonds which can gain no purchase 'out there' in the civic space where functional togetherness is fashioned and governed. But in 'The Cowardly Lion' the national troubles are markedly internal, revealed by outer circumstance but not their product, seemingly fateful. Commenting on the potency of 'The Cowardly Lion' in August 1992, Jim Sillars in his '90-minute patriot' phase (lamenting the lack of an SNP breakthrough in that year's election) was moved to ask 'why is the author not a raging revolutionary leading 50,000 into Glasgow's George Square?'[19] But this is to misread the flow of scornful rage in the 1979 moment, which draws in from without. All the poem's energies are directed toward inner self-contempt, not action in the public square. McIlvanney's lambasting of the lion re-orients his whole diagnosis to the clammy terrain of self-identity – what Scotland *is*, and will remain, lacking the guts or means to transform its nature – in a register markedly different to the later emphasis on the failure and inadequacy of the constitutional machinery ('no mandate'). In that later phase, the empty shells and hollow claims of Scottish democracy self-condemn the unionist order purely on the basis of electoral divergence, without any need for tortured national soul-searching. Through mass rejection of Thatcherism, the voting system itself yields an image of 'Scotland' which salves the wound opened by the 1979 referendum, and the burden of nullity and self-justification shifts decisively from the lion to the unionist keepers. By 1992 there was less sonorous talk of Scotland-the-Patient changing, confronting or redeeming itself through constitutional change, and a much stronger emphasis on how Scotland-the-Category had been failed and eclipsed by a system of British governance. If the embrace of McIlvanney's 'mongrel tradition' by devolutionary intellectuals signals an acceptance that the forms of nineteenth-century nationhood (or lionhood) were never really available to them, it is also an acceptance that Scotland's arrested political development will not be rectified from 'inside' its own cultural problematic, but will require the transformation of the containing structures by those (in London) ultimately responsible. Thus the nation's stalled maturity, in the 1992 speech, is both 'intolerable' and the essential condition of Scottish nationality, marrying a thrawn refusal to 'acclimatize' to its own (impure, comfortless) nature, and an impulse to claw at the scab of non-congruence between this 'identity' and the structures which govern it. The burden of action and courage shifts from the people to politicians and technocrats, in a process notionally driven by an impatient neo-popular consensus, voiced and grounded in the streets.

Healthy polarisation

A different emphasis is marked in Nairn's own response to the disaster of 1979. Writing in *New Edinburgh Review*, Nairn was both mordant and chipper about the future prospects of devolution, insisting that 'what the referendum experience destroyed was not the movement for self-government – as some enemies of nationalism hope – but a number of false and uncertain assumptions clinging to this movement'.[20] Despite the general depression which followed the vote – a leading Scottish journalist noted that 'devolution is now a topic for discussion only among consenting adults in private'[21] – it could also be said that 'a great deal of spineless self-affirmation was blown away in the result'. For Nairn, clearing the cobwebs and tootle-tattle was an advance in its own right:

> The simple polarisation of the referendum dissipated a good deal of Scotch middle-class mist. [. . .] We had lived in Sandy Mutch's windy, sleekit, after-dinner 'Patriotism' for

a century and a half, to the point of being often uncertain whether any real backbone sustained it. [During the referendum campaign] people were made to line up in some sort of vague battle-order, and Scotland was made to see more clearly that the growth of real national consciousness is a difficult conflict, a civil war within the nation as much as a struggle between it and the metropolis.[22]

Thus Nairn reaches a rather different conclusion from McIlvanney, despite the clear echoes of his cultural diagnosis: the 1979 referendum has been a clarifying experience, but not one that 'lays to rest' any pernicious myths, or which cures or resolves any of Scotland's inner pathologies. Instead, the No result draws bracingly into the open the necessary conflict at issue, as well as its political character. Devolution will not be a process of healing or redemption, a cure for national schizophrenia, but a healthy outdoor confrontation between opposed interests – both within Scotland and with the UK establishment – in which sides must be taken and battle joined.

But the drawn-bayonets conflict Nairn had welcomed would never arrive. On the contrary, the 1980s see the cultural politics of Scottishness elided with a constitutional project proud of its own urbane consensualism, keen to parade its suspension of intra-nation hostilities as a model for civic renewal. Indeed, Nairn's own project (with Neal Ascherson, Christopher Harvie, Jack Brand and others) to launch a short-lived *Bulletin of Scottish Politics* in 1980 is suffused with the new co-operative idealism:

There is a broader, more progressive national movement not yet born. Its elements surround us, and the will towards it can be felt on every hand: in the devolutionist wing of the Labour Party, in the new Campaign for a Scottish Assembly, in the women's movement and on the left of the Scottish National Party, among the Liberals and many Scottish marxists, and in the ranks of Scottish trade-unionism. There lie the seeds of the new democratic-popular identity which the Scottish people needs. In the 1980s we must learn how to nurse them into growth, and avoid self-destructive conflict. The point of such an identity is that through it, and through it alone, our old egalitarianism will seek and find its only possible contemporary form: a Scottish socialism uniting the image of ourselves with that of the age.[23]

The intellectual insurgents of home rule would come dressed as peacekeepers, keen to figure devolution as a movement from 'outside' and 'below' narrow party politics, renewing 'identity' while avoiding conflict, and squared in advance with the electoral interests of the big battalions. In place of a 'civil war within the nation', Scottish politics skipped straight to the ceasefire and declared victory all round for 'representation' – of a nationhood identified directly with procedures of self-governance.

Alliance-building of this kind was a hallmark of developments throughout the 1979–97 period. The Campaign for a Scottish Assembly (forerunner and laboratory of the Scottish Constitutional Convention) was established on the first anniversary of the failed referendum, on 1 March 1980. Its founding declaration aims to create 'a National Convention representative of Scottish life and society to consider detailed proposals for the constitution and powers of a Scottish Assembly', a project pursued by an initial National Committee carefully balanced across party interests (seven members associated with Labour, seven with the SNP and four Liberals, in addition to a former Moderator of the Church of Scotland).[24] 'The favourite theme was unity', records Keith Aitken, 'and the need to heal the divisions that had levied such a grievous price the previous year.'[25] Cross-party ecumenism was felt to be so important, attacks on the Tories – shortly to become the very watchword and motor of devolution – drew groans, and were frowned upon in the presence of a lone representative from the Scottish Conservatives (Helen Millar).[26] Inter-party organising was central to the work and identity of CSA from this first meeting. The initial chair, Jack Brand, was an SNP 79 Group academic who worked closely with leading Labour devolutionists such as George Foulkes MP and Dennis Canavan MP. Foulkes' letters record detailed discussion with Brand on tactics and strategy, with particular focus on extra-parliamentary means of reviving the Assembly cause. In an August 1980 letter to Foulkes, Brand is highly conscious of the limits of mass mobilisation:

The terrible example of the Scottish Convention [of 1942–50] must be remembered. They got enormous support for home rule but they did not get home rule. We need to build more than a majority of Scottish voters. It is possible that a government in the future might decide to ride out even a large SNP vote on the grounds that, if you ignore it for long enough it will go away. They could be right.[27]

Thus it was necessary to bind into the cause of devolution the power brokers capable of delivering it, ensuring they recognised their own interest in doing so.

In addition to mass support the campaign should try to persuade important institutions in Scotland. Trade Unions seem to be convinced, but we must work to 'firm up' this support. We should work with other organisations starting from the specific benefits which an Assembly could bring them. To businessmen we could point out that home rule would make it easier to represent Scottish business abroad. In a nutshell we must be sure of 'elite' as well as mass backing. [. . .] I am sure that many members of the Campaign will object but we have to lobby members of the British elite if we are to improve the chances of having an Assembly. Major figures in the Labour Party should be primary targets as should civil servants and leaders of industry.[28]

Against Foulkes' enthusiasm for extra-parliamentary agitation (largely to revive the issue at Westminster), Brand was highly aware that non-party bodies such as the CSA could only achieve so much, and favoured a strategy continuous with the proposed Assembly (via the Scotland Act 1978), and 'opposed fundamental revisions that might frighten Labour off'. Bob McLean records that 'as far as Brand was concerned, the Labour Party was key. It was the serious contender for power at Westminster and most likely to deliver constitutional change.'[29]

Thus it was tactical developments in the sphere of party politics which prepared the ground for home rule in the years following the 1979 disaster, a 'war of position' in which elite, electoral and identitarian interests were brought into alignment behind the cause of a Scottish parliament. The internal agonies of cultural Scottishness would feature in these developments, but as a 'given' and irremediable factor effectively closed off from the dynamic changes visible elsewhere. Indeed, the rhetorical *fixity* of Scotland's intolerable identity became the firm ground on which it was levered into a new kind of political currency (as chronically disenfranchised subjects of Conservative governments with no Scottish mandate). It was in the sphere of party politics, not culture, that the 'given-ness' and solidity of Scottish identity was effectively weaponised. Electorally speaking, the 'content' and reality of that identity was largely beside the point. Primary was Scottish difference as a recognised frame and political attachment, a card available to play; indeed, a card which could be made to play itself. In an October 1980 strategy letter (advising the newly formed Labour Campaign for a Scottish Assembly) Neal Ascherson urges Foulkes to 'be on the lookout for every chance of emphasising the Scottish dimension':

Anything which heightens the profile of Scottish politics is almost bound to have spin-off effects creating a climate of opinion more favourable to an Assembly. The substantial support for an Assembly in 1974/78 was built largely on the sheer publicity level of Scottish, as distinct from British, politics in those years.[30]

While LCSA were keen to make a fresh start in pro-devolution campaigning – figuring the 1970s Labour commitment as a pork-barrel regionalism 'revolving around the Secretary of State and the Scottish Office, a bureaucratic decentralization of administration existing mainly for the convenience of Scottish local authorities, businessmen and other community notables including, up to a point, trade unionists'[31] – its leaders took Ascherson's advice fully on board in leveraging 'the national dimension'.

Playing the nationalist card

James Mitchell puts it simply: 'Labour adopted an increasingly nationalist agenda in Scottish politics in the 1980s.'[32] Almost irrespective of pressure-groups such as the CSA and Labour Campaign for a Scottish Assembly, the electoral appeal of supporting devolution was as obvious as it was uncomfortable. In July 1982, with Margaret Thatcher's government riding high in the post-Falklands polls, Mitchell cites 'a former Labour cabinet minister' quoted in the *Scotsman*:

> We are certain to lose the next election in England. We will return even more MPs from Scotland, but we will be out of office down here for another ten years. We will have to play the nationalist card in Scotland. We will have to go for an Assembly with substantial economic powers short of independence, but not much short.[33]

In the aftermath of Thatcher's victory in June 1983, elements of Scottish Labour (including the MPs Dennis Canavan and George Galloway) advanced the 'no mandate' argument as a means of resisting Tory rule in Scotland. In the 'Foulkes Memorandum', strategically leaked to the press and later published in *Radical Scotland*, the MP for Carrick, Cumnock and Doon Valley suggested an escalating Labour campaign of parliamentary disruption 'to provoke the constitutional crisis necessary to get change'.[34] Foulkes' 'suggestions' extended as far as 'tax revenue disruption' and a 'nationwide plebiscite on Devolution/Home Rule organised by the Labour movement'.[35] But it was not the content of these fanciful proposals that 'caused a serious panic in the Scottish Labour leadership'[36] so much as the logic on which they were premised: 'challenging the legitimacy of administrative directives and circulars which the majority of Scottish MPs have not endorsed'.[37] In other words, Foulkes threatened to treat the body of Scottish MPs as one conferring 'national' assent, distinct from the Westminster calculus (or indeed that of the Parliamentary Labour Party). Campaigners were bullish about the risks and rewards of this approach, insisting that Labour's own electoral and ideological interests were best served in the national(ist) frame. Had the Assembly proposed in 1978 come into being, an LCSA strategy document argues,

> its importance would have been to provide a more power-ful and public platform for anti-Thatcherite ideology and policy than any other existing in Britain at the moment. The Labour Party must stop being frightened of Scottish nationalism. As a force detached from political ideology it is no threat to anyone. As a card for socialists to play it has considerable possibilities in some circumstances.[38]

Here 'Scottish nationalism' is simply an electoral tactic, 'detached from political ideology', whose effects are confined to the Labour-dominated institution it will bring into being (the Assembly). This logic may raise a smile through post-devolution eyes (certainly after 2007, and Labour's loss of power at Holyrood), and remained controversial in the Labour movement throughout the interven-ing period; but arguments on these premises were crucial to the development of a pro-devolution consensus, establishing the rhe-torical space in which various interested parties from both SNP and Labour could find common ground.

'Scottish Resistance'

In the most obvious sense, these arguments were a tactical reac-tion to the failure of devolution in 1979, but they were also continuous with the logic of the plebiscite itself. Reflecting on Labour's extended flirtation with nationalist rhetoric in the 1980s, Jack Geekie and Roger Levy note that

> the precedent is to be found in the very expedient that was supposed to 'dish' the nationalists in the first place – the referendum on the Scotland Act of March 1979. Undoubt-edly effective as the final coup which demoralised the SNP, it also reinforced, indeed legitimised, the idea of the sov-ereign Scottish mandate. Labour politicians evidently feel increasingly comfortable with this idea despite its nationalist origins and its profound constitutional implications.[39]

The SNP made their own arguments in this line, but the party was weakened and divided by the 1979 result. In its aftermath left-wing members of the SNP did adopt a 'Scottish Resistance' campaign effectively tartanising working-class opposition to Thatcher, but there was little appetite in the party (or in the country) for nationalist civil disobedience. The radicalism of the May 1981 conference motion establishing the 'Scottish Resistance' initiative – expressing 'outrage at the destruction of Scotland's industrial base by the policies of an English Tory government' and 'recognis[ing] that a real Scottish resistance and defence of jobs demands direct action up to and including political strikes and civil disobedience on a mass scale'[40] – was not matched by wide support within the SNP leadership. The campaign's most memorable stunt was to end in farce, with Jim Sillars and five other members of the nominally socialist and republican 79 Group arrested for vandalism in October 1981, after breaking into the Royal High School on Calton Hill, the building intended to host the abortive Scottish Assembly. Less than a year later the 79 Group was forced to disband and its members were briefly expelled from the SNP, which, distrustful of devolutionary alliance-building, reverted to a 'fundamentalist' orientation under Gordon Wilson. The decisive shift occurred within the Labour Party, with the help of pro-devolution nationalists – many of them 79 Groupers – who focused their activism on establishing a new strategic frame for left-nationalism, strongly mediated by party competition but not bound by it.

Appeals to Scottish difference were key to these developments, and brought usually tacit dimensions of cultural politics to the electoral surface. This closely followed the trajectory implied in Jack Brand's 1978 study of *The National Movement in Scotland*. Brand downplayed the importance of North Sea oil or specific policy positions in accounting for the SNP surge of the 1970s, instead focusing on class de-alignment and the politicisation of Scottish nationality:

> The crucial connection seems to have been forged by a gradual restructuring of the political consciousness of the Scottish electorate in such a way that they began to perceive themselves as Scots in terms of their political interests

rather than as, for example, members of the working class. Thus the party which stood for Scotland was the one which began to get their support. [. . .] More important than anything else was [the electorate's] identification of their own position in political terms. The growth of Scottish identification in this sense grew out of the earlier non-political consciousness and led to the SNP breakthrough.[41]

These 'non-political' substrates of nationalism bring us into the terrain of cultural and indeed literary identity, to which Brand pays specific attention in charting the SNP's early development. But to what extent did 'cultural' developments shape this restructuring of political consciousness, and, once established, how was it mobilised to secure elite support for home rule? Again, the mediating role of party politics is key. It is striking to note that even the most damning 1979 post-mortems of cultural failure and identity-death could prescribe *electoral-strategic* remedies to this condition. The hyperbolic 'After the 79' editorial in *Crann-Tàra* cited above moves swiftly from excoriating a hollow patriotism rooted in 'guilt and inferiority' to asking 'where do we go from here?' in the cause of devolution. The Scots have shown themselves to be scarcely a people, but this humiliation itself mandates a renewed push for their democratic rights. The goal of self-government is both separate from the tragicomedy of cultural Scottishness and the means of surpassing it, a substitute for what nationalism has been shown to lack. Even before the more expansive question of what Scotland wants to do and be can be posed, the focus narrows to party-political strategy centred on this goal:

> What we've all been waiting for has finally happened. A left-wing has emerged within the SNP – an organized left with platforms and policies of its own. But where is the Labour equivalent? [. . .] If Scotland is ever to move again, we need to see a '79 Group' on the Labour side. Sufficient credibility can not be gathered by one side of the equation alone. We have now a nationalist faction for socialism. Do we have a socialist faction for self-government?[42]

This is precisely the terrain in which *Crann-Tàra*'s successor title, *Radical Scotland*, would establish the cultural politics of devolution. On the Labour side of this project, appeals to the cultural givens of Scottishness were leveraged to argue for self-government – Scotland is self-evidently a nation, with a distinctive political culture, and therefore it deserves its own democracy. On the nationalist side, the prize of self-government promised to redeem what was missing from (or degraded within) Scottishness itself: devolved institutions would manifest a latent, viable nationhood capable of independence, tangible proof of lion-ness without the need to test lionhood in any deep or sustained way. The frame of Scottish difference and representation was a key structuring motif of these debates, and effectively established the discursive space (and electoral logic) of devolution for both parties. To trace the emergence of this frame – of the constitutive importance of 'the Scottish dimension' – we must look just below the electoral surface of Scottish politics, to the pivotal influence of cultural and political magazines in the full development of left-nationalist strategy and identity.

A second front: cultural and political magazines

The early 1980s was a period of intense exchange between the cultural and political spheres in Scotland. Writing in *Radical Scotland* in 1983, George Kerevan observed that 'politics is no longer confined to the Establishment and Labourist agenda of economic tinkering. Cultural values represent a new Second Front.'[43] There is a step change in the focus and urgency of these discussions, which lose their air of bohemian chatter around 1983. As we saw, British jingoism during and after the Falklands conflict, and the clear likelihood of Thatcher winning a second term, prompted demands for Scottish democracy that overtly played the national(ist) card. In the same period, Labour wrestled with the mandate question and how far to borrow nationalist clothes in arguing for devolution.

A crucial site of these exchanges, in which the 'Second Front' of culture was directly linked to electoral politics, were the Scottish political magazines and cultural reviews which blossomed in the wake of *Scottish International*. Loosely centred on the University of Edinburgh, overlapping literary and political circles produced a rich ecology of left-nationalist debate in the 1970s and 1980s, in cheaply printed periodicals that turned 'the Scottish dimension' into a living discursive formation visible in bookshops and newsagents. Though produced by a relatively narrow strata of the intelligentsia, primarily talking to itself, this body of writing had a wider political importance. Rory Scothorne writes:

> These publications are not only significant as a sign of renewed engagement with Scottish nationhood amongst elements of the radical left from the late 1960s onwards; they also constitute the vast bulk of writing about Scottish society and politics outside of academia and the daily print media during the 1970s. [. . .] The accumulated printed matter of this effort formed a bridge across which radical intellectuals were able to reach a secure sense of their place and role in a newly politicised Scottish nation.[44]

They were a crucial arena and testing ground in which the Scottish intelligentsia established a new habitus and role for itself. In selectively tracing the specifically literary and constitutional strand of these debates in the post-1979 period, our focus falls primarily on *Radical Scotland*, with cameo appearances from *(New) Edinburgh Review, Chapman* and *Cencrastus*. Linda Gunn and Alistair McCleery helpfully summarise themes shared by *(New) Edinburgh Review* and *Cencrastus*, which apply more generally to this Scottish periodical scene of the 1980s and 1990s: 'the identification of working-class with national identity', and growing belief on the part of cultural producers, critics and the wider intelligentsia

> that cultural change could effect political change – or at the very least that cultural confidence, in the sense of a flourishing and internationally recognised arts scene and 'positive' representations of Scottish identity, created political confidence that then translated into support for devolution.[45]

As we shall see, the 'agency' of the cultural sphere was profoundly mediated by electoral strategy and alliance building; it was political parties who mobilised cultural difference rather than cultural figures who pulled the levers of politics. But artists and writers did shape the contours of what emerged, both sharpening the 'cultural' arguments for self-government and identifying the limits of national-popular mobilisation.

Radical Scotland

First published (as a re-launch of *Crann-Tàra*) in summer 1982, *Radical Scotland* was highly focused on political strategy in its aim to construct an irresistible pro-devolution consensus in Scottish politics – and in so doing, constituting a firmly recognised 'Scottish politics' which would embody the nation's need and readiness for self-government. The magazine's signature openness to previously warring tribes, both party-based and ideological, is captured in James Robertson's thinly veiled description of the magazine's activist milieu in his epic novel of devolution, *And the Land Lay Still*: 'gradually it becomes possible for a kind of socialism and a kind of nationalism to exist in the same person, in the same room, in the same political party. And these locations, private and public, no longer have to be battle zones.'[46] The party focus is key, and its logic of mutual non-aggression had been forecast as a central feature of devolutionary expectancy by Nairn in 1976. Responding to the SNP essay-collection *The Radical Approach*, he observed:

> in so far as nationalists have become genuinely radical, and socialists have become Scottish, they have the most powerful common interests here. In the old quarrel the nationalists used to say: keep the ranks closed until independence. The socialists used to answer: what kind of independence? Independence for what? 'Independence' was an abstraction in that kind of argument. As it ceases to be so, the argument has to change, because all parties who accept the change seriously – however different their ideologies remain – acquire a mutual interest in the construction of a viable arena to conduct their affairs in. They will have to redefine their quarrels in the new Scottish context.[47]

This precisely captures the impetus and function of *Radical Scotland* in the wake of devolution's failure, and a chastened but determined effort to reconstruct national political space. The new magazine was itself re-launched in February/March 1983 after two issues, and taken up by an entirely new editorial team led by Kevin Dunion (who was himself succeeded by Alan Lawson in mid-1985). The first editorial of the new series refers back to these roots, and defines the aims and target audience of *Radical Scotland* in straightforward terms:

> The relaunch then is a time not for bravado but for justification and a statement of intent. *Radical Scotland* should appeal to devolutionists in the Labour Party, left-wing nationalists, and other elements of the radical left. It should also attract interested opponents and the merely inquisitive. [. . .] The first issue of our direct predecessor *Crann-Tàra* declared 'We want to summon together the radicals and nationalists of Scotland, and that can only be done by the reawakening of common roots'. Success in this summons is not a case of prodding the socialist/nationalist cusp into a sleepy awareness of amorphous need for a political magazine, but rather causing a jarring realization of want for *Radical Scotland*. And that is our intention.[48]

A second part of the editorial ('Getting it right now') manifests what can later be recognised as a distinguishing feature of the magazine, in its direct and detailed focus on electoral positioning. Referring to the SNP's collapse in the 1979 general election, it focuses its pressure on a Labour Party predicted to dominate Scottish seats in the June 1983 elections, and presses the case for Labour to take up the mantle of national representation:

> Untrammelled by any electoral threat from the SNP, [Scottish Labour] will have protected their minority with ease, only to be faced once more with five years of impotency. The time can be whiled away by rushing from the scene of one factory closure to the next like Dutch boys sticking

fingers into the dyke of the Scottish economy which is now grievously fractured. But to what purpose? [. . .] The Labour Party in Scotland must recognize that its majority is held in trust in return for true representation. This does not mean sterile contributions at Westminster but an obligation to carry through its popular mandate by providing a lead to the forces which oppose Tory policies outside Parliament. Previously they were afraid to employ this mandate for fear of giving strength to the nationalist case. With the SNP standing aloof and deserted, the Labour Party can now provide the lead on its own terms. What it cannot do is nothing.[49]

Thus the debate over the Tories' absent Scottish mandate stimulated new thinking about Labour's own national obligations – the duties incumbent on a party seeking to play the Scottish card. The questions of 'true representation' and legitimacy registered here would become key touchstones of literary and political debate in these magazines, and a key 'bridging' metaphor uniting parliamentary and literary-critical discourse over the next two decades.

Radical Scotland's emphasis on party strategy is exemplified by Christopher Harvie's wily article in the second issue. Harvie was much later an SNP MSP (from 2007 to 2011), but was at this time active in Labour politics: 'since 1979 co-operation within the Scottish devolutionist left has increased, despite the hostility of the Labour and SNP establishments. [. . .] Can such co-operation be continued until the General Election, with the goal of eliminating the Conservatives as a credible force in Scottish parliamentary politics?'[50] The level of debate is bare-knuckle electoral strategy (triangulation, exploiting press bias, effectively brandishing the 'nationalist threat'), not lofty constitutional principle. There are signs that the practical lessons of 1979 really have been learned, and energies are being devoted to battlefield manoeuvres (destroying the enemy) rather than fine sentiments. Most striking here is Harvie's prescience in advocating the key 'cultural' dynamic of the distinctly Scottish political space crystallising at this time – anti-Toryism as Scottish national resistance:

Between now and the election the left has to increase its information on the class and regional basis of Tory support, on the impact of Tory policies, present and future, and on the character and record of individual candidates. Hard, perhaps, on individuals who have done what they can to mitigate Mrs Thatcher's policies in Scotland, but we must see that the image of Scots Toryism is as right-wing, Thatcherite and English-nationalist as possible. The pay-off is a Scottish politics so dislocated from Westminster's norms that Scottish representatives are forced into a national role – a situation like that created by Parnell and his party in Ireland in 1884. Westminster will then be faced with the alternatives of repression or concessions in the direction of self-government.[51]

This argument largely repeats Harvie's observation in a *New Statesman* article of November 1975, and seeks to cement and institutionalise – to secure as a 'given', raised beyond party dispute – his sense then that 'Westminster alignments appear useless as guides to opinion in Scottish affairs [. . .] a specifically Scottish politics now exists whose preoccupations are steadily diverging from those of the body which will, in the last analysis, have to decide on home rule'.[52] The economically game-changing advent of North Sea oil, Harvie wrote, 'has not accomplished this: it has simply acted as a catalyst in the transformation of existing relationships and tendencies into a new national politics, not a movement but a range of preoccupations which absorb nationalist and home-ruler alike'.[53] It was the electoral and not the cultural or economic context which had decisively shifted.

And yet, the re-framing of Scottish politics was ultimately, implicitly premised on the established character of national-cultural difference. A key intervention highlighting this point came in Cairns Craig's article in the second issue of *Radical Scotland*, taking issue with Ian Hepburn's ribbing review of *Cencrastus* number 10 in the prior (inaugural) issue of the magazine. This had congratulated *Cencrastus* 'for coming off the editorial fence in support of the broader nationalist movement'. Craig rejects the charge, noting that Hepburn's review:

implies – consciously or otherwise – a significant disjunction between the 'cultural' and the 'political' as though those realms were entirely sundered from each other, or as though a political commitment was somehow more crucial than a cultural commitment. [. . .] Such an opposition between the cultural and the political is deeply embedded in the thinking of the Scottish Left: on the one hand 'high art', divorced from life, and on the other politics, identical with the very stuff of working-class experience. It is one of the oppositions that a truly radical Scotland ought to dissolve. The paradox of such an opposition between culture and politics, from a nationalist perspective, ought to be self-evident: it is precisely on the basis of the value of a *culture*, the culture of a people, that nationalist politics makes its claims. What distinguishes nationalisms from other ideologies is that the defence of cultural difference and cultural integrity is the basis of its claim to control over the economic and social powers within the society of that culture.[54]

Here Craig brings to the surface the tacit identitarian basis of the 'mandate' argument, insisting on the primacy of cultural difference not only within nationalism, but its imbrication with any leftist politics aiming to justify control over economic and government power in the interests of a defined 'people'. Orthodox left-wing thought (for which 'the only true path for the working class is the march towards an international revolution and entry into the non-national culture of the world-wide proletariat') overlooks this fact, Craig argues, and 'enjoins on the Scottish working classes a passivity towards the state structure which is the instrument of their suppression':

They must wait for the [UK] 'national' rise in working-class politics before they can get any relief from their present condition, and, if the working classes of the British nation never achieve that breakthrough they must wait on an international transformation of the capitalist economy. The result, however, is that the Scottish working class, like all elements of the Scottish populace, gets more and more

insistently drawn into the hegemony of an English culture which is an essential implement of the British state in
maintaining the status quo. [. . .] To treat the problems
of Scotland as a purely *political* problem, whether in terms
of class analysis or in terms of nationalist aspirations, is to
ignore entirely the ways in which culture operates as a
powerful force for the existing state within the fabric of
our total social experience. [. . .] It is on the cultural question that Scottish nationalism has failed.[55]

This is a clear and compelling statement of the 'culturalist' argument for Scottish left-nationalism, which frequently adopted and
elided the language of class politics: 'the Scottish working class,
like all elements of the Scottish populace', is subject to English
hegemony, which remains the fundamental injustice at issue. This
would become the key component in 'vernacular' arguments for
a Scottish self-determination premised as much on the release of
'identity' as joining battle against class oppression, and is the signature move in Scottish cultural politics of the 1980s. Thatcherism
was the occasion for its deployment (and reification) in mainstream politics, but it is not difficult to trace its pedigree in literary
debates of the inter-war Renaissance, being a key problematic
for both Lewis Grassic Gibbon and Hugh MacDiarmid. It is
more immediately anticipated in John Caughie's 1978 article in
New Edinburgh Review, which notes that

much of what is said about 'class culture' applies also to
'national culture', the one clarifying the other. The Scottish
nation cannot identify itself by its autonomous cultural
practices anymore than can a social class. Nations, perhaps
even more obviously than classes, define themselves in
struggle. The politics of Scottish culture are not separate
from Scottish politics, and both occur in the context of the
hegemony of the bourgeoisie, and the political and economic dominance of England within the British Isles. It is
this context which has to be understood since it provides
the ground on which the Scottish nation conducts its specific struggle, cultural *and* political.[56]

This 'struggle' could only really achieve its dynamism when political conditions provided a clear incentive for mobilising cultural difference and grievance. Language was a key marker and symbol. Writing in the 1978–9 period, Stein Rokkan observed that the SNP operates in a region with a distinctive identity,

> but where the language is that of the centre. In the case of Scotland, all but a handful of immigrants have a Scottish identity, which both limits and permits the use of the latter [i.e. the dominant language, English] as a basis for mobilization or partisan differentiation. The problem here [. . .] is not just to focus on identity, but also to turn the multiple identity with state and region [i.e. with Britain and Scotland] from a benign to an incompatible, even antagonistic, relationship.[57]

But little of this transpired, or was ever likely to (such as 'othering' the English language in ways analogous to the 'othering' of Tory and unionist identities). Instead, the *civic values* of Scotland and England were presented as incommensurable, and minoritised language was made to iconically represent the divergence: the contrast of chilly and formal Standard English and the demotic warmth of vernacular Scots. In 1996 Michael Keating noted that 'Scottish nationalist discourse has traditionally had a rather weak cultural dimension' and that 'little attention is paid to language or to ritual'.[58] But in the 1980s, in a zone of cultural debate external to traditional nationalism, language did become a powerful and valorised way of mapping precisely Keating's sense 'that national conflict in Scotland is closely tied to perceptions of class struggle and opposition to the Conservative government with its English base. Scottish identity is closely correlated with social class, with the upper classes least likely to identify themselves as Scottish.'[59]

Just as Thatcherism 'helped identify neo-liberalism with English values and restore the old association of nationalism with dissent',[60] the traditional demotic language held to embody Scotland's communitarian values was charged with new kinds of political representivity. This gave the familiar hobby horses of Scottish literary debate – 'the language question' central among them – a new edge and salience, and transformed the terms of cultural-nationalist debate (see Chapter 6).

'The way forward'

If there is a nakedly strategic quality to party-political manoeu-vring in the early 1980s, it is matched by the unusual directness of parallel debates in the literary sphere. The fifth issue of *Radical Scotland* reports a July 1982 event held in Edinburgh to discuss a special issue of *Chapman* magazine on 'The State of Scotland – A Predicament for the Scottish Writer?'. Christopher Whyte – later to become an important critic of literary nationalism[61] – reports that 'editor Joy Hendry set the tone of the proceedings when she underlined that one thing was now perfectly clear to everyone: the way forward for Scottish literature lies through political inde-pendence'.[62] There are hints of the literary politics of the follow-ing decade – Tessa Ransford 'urged on us new, non-hierarchical forms of collaboration and organization, some of which were already emerging in the Scottish Poetry Library Association' – later to emerge, with the support of the Scottish Arts Council, as the Scottish Poetry Library, and serving as an important platform for national literary community and a repository of its heritage. The pet debates of modern Scottish letters are all present in the *Chapman* issue – Muir, MacDiarmid and the language question; the hostility to Gaelic by the education authorities; questions of anglicisation and Europeanism – but posed with a new impa-tience, even anger. In her introduction to the special issue of *Chapman*, Hendry notes that 'each contribution here confirms that politics and culture are inseparable. That this issue should appear at a time when a party opposed to Scottish autonomy, and to the ideology of most people in Scotland, is returned to power, is crushingly ironic.'[63]

Hendry – who would later serve on the CSA's Constitutional Steering Committee – evokes a call to action, with an overt focus on politicising Scottish literature to achieve national self-determination. Until some form of autonomy is achieved, she concludes, 'we must sit back powerlessly and watch the progres-sive dilution and disintegration of our culture, and most psycho-logically damaging of all is that sense of powerlessness, which breeds nothing but apathy. [. . .] we can stop *talking* about the State of Scotland only when we are in a position to *do* something'.[64] Thus the priority is to take Scotland's existing cultural resources and fashion the tools necessary to effect change. However, the most incisive contributors to the special issue query both the diagnosis and the prescription, posing challenging questions of the social-national consensus evoked by Hendry's editorial. Three figures who would later be firmly associated with pro-independence politics – Alasdair Gray, Joyce McMillan and George Kerevan – expose key fault lines within the literary community being ushered toward the home rule barricades.

Gray ponders whether there truly is a 'predicament' worth bothering about, and – perhaps basking in the critical reception of *Lanark*, published in 1981 – moves to dis-identify the cultural and political issues. After all, the nation is in rude literary health:

> The fact that Scotland is governed from outside itself, governed against the advice of the three Parliamentary Commissions and against the wishes of most Scots who voted on the matter, cannot be used to explain our lack of talent because that lack is no longer evident. Scotland has as many first-rate writers as the USA had when Twain wrote *Huckleberry Finn* and a far greater crop of good second-raters, all surveying the universe across a Scottish foreground from the current of their particular Mississippi. There is no evidence that the local experience of Royal Home Counties writers gives them worthier subject matter or more intelligent dictions. Why should it? Does the proximity of a thing called government inspire a finer class of thought?[65]

George Kerevan offers more prescient analysis of the declining fortunes of Labourism in Scotland, grounded in shifting class alignment: 'Today the Scottish intelligentsia has defected from Labourism as a creed. In the Seventies and Eighties it has become overwhelmingly politically nationalist while retaining its old social radicalism.'[66] Kerevan went on to argue that changes in Scotland's class composition – above all, the expansion of university education and the social strata of the intellectuals – was a key factor behind cultural resurgence:

> The Sixties and early Seventies saw Scottish universities flooded with the sons and daughters of the working class, all imbued with the Labourist welfare state notion that education was a passport to the good life. This swollen mass of the new professional middle class rapidly became disenchanted with the realities of secondary school teaching in Drumchapel and Pilton. One side-effect was the wave of teachers' strikes throughout the Seventies, a telling break with the service ethos. The most significant result, however, has been the explosion of cultural activity in Scotland in the Seventies and Eighties, feeding off the psychic frustrations of this new and enlarged intelligentsia. The Sixties cosmopolitanism of [Richard] Demarco and the Traverse, part harbinger of these changes and part echo of the world youth revolt, has been overtaken by the creation of an indigenous performing theatre, an infant movie industry and an endless outpouring of local writing talent. In effect this has been a declaration of cultural independence.[67]

Taking shape here is the 'trans-class people-nation' which would emerge both as the subject and product of devolution, according to sociologists Gerry Mooney and Alex Law.[68] Note how directly a shift in the (class) composition of the intelligentsia results in a cultural appetite for (national) autonomy. If Scotland is conceived as a disenfranchised, dispossessed worker in many 1980s–90s debates, Kerevan highlights the active and generative role of culture in *constituting* Scottish nationality:

> A self-aware Scotland demands a popular culture which reaches out to the mass of the population. When the real Scottish cultural renaissance came in the Seventies, it was not a contrived exercise in Scottishness but the very fact of creating a popular local cultural life on stage, at the typewriter or on celluloid meant inexorably that it would by its own existence breathe independent life into the manufacturing

of ideas about Scotland, about being Scots, and about the predicament of a thinking Scotland without a state to turn its aspirations into reality. Where MacDiarmid failed gallantly, the Mayfest, Women Live and 'Gregory's Girl' have succeeded: almost to a person the Scots cultural intelligentsia support Home Rule and the Scottish Workers' Republic in place of London state socialism.[69]

But a chicken-and-egg problem attends the artistic reproduction of nationhood. In Kerevan's argument, the already marked pro-devolution consensus among the cultural intelligentsia becomes – at least rhetorically – a manifestation of their underlying closeness to popular-democratic energies. Being closely bound to the national public they help to consolidate, the views of Scottish artists serve as a barometer of Scottish opinion. For Kerevan, it is this class – the rising intelligentsia – who must form a 'Home Rule Alliance', rather than established campaign bodies such as the Campaign for a Scottish Assembly, 'cast too much in the mould of the apolitical Covenant movement of the Fifties: too middle class, too Protestant, too male, too middle-aged. In other words hardly representative of the real Scotland of the working people or the radical intelligentsia.'[70] Being special ciphers of the 'real Scotland', the dynamic cultural elite are ideally placed to lead the movement for representative empowerment.

The people's speech

Here we are very much in the terrain of Jacques Rancière's *The Intellectual and His People*, and his biting critique of a shift in the 'ideological function of representing the social to the political' in post-1968 France.[71] In a 1978 essay, 'Les révoltes logiques', co-written with Danielle Rancière, the authors unpick the doubleness of 'engaged' intellectuals renouncing academic detachment only to re-ground their claims to knowledge within the body of dissident popular energies, over which they swiftly achieve ideological mastery and new claims to power and responsibility. 'The liquidation of the old intellectual who had to keep silent in order to let the voice of the people be heard was succeeded by a new figure of the intellectual as spokesperson or protector of the people's speech.'[72] However sincerely such figures – the image of Sartre looms large – 'have acted to bring the ideological order into crisis and struggled to give speech back to those deprived of it', the dynamics of 'representation' in this shift remain profoundly ambiguous.[73] Self-endowed with 'the new power of filling the breach dividing the political class from the life of the social body', and flushed with the (Maoist) passion of 'rediscover[ing] [their] lost universality in the masses', the intellectuals' theatrical renunciation of class privilege in fact marks an expansive re-coding and 'socialization' of their authority.[74] ('As they proceed', the Rancières remark, 'their discourse slips from the first person into the third.[75]) It is a profitable disowning that trades academic aloofness for the 'restitution of a *role* for the intellectual, preparing new substitutions and new forms of representation'.[76]

What is striking in the Scottish 1980s is the general absence of critical reflection on such themes by intellectual voices claiming a deep affinity with popular energies. To be sure, it is a very different situation: there was no social revolt for devolution, and virtually all the political and cultural figures we will encounter are seeking to spur and mobilise a broad movement which would legitimate their political project from 'outside' the formal political system. It is nonetheless striking how readily intellectuals and cultural commentators speak on behalf of the silent masses, or assume the popular warrant of their own learned insights. Perhaps it is simply that the pebble-dashed homogeneity of post-war Scottish society – in which a very large segment of the population seems to be living broadly the same pattern of life – invites an over-identification between the intellectual and the noiseless many. We might note in passing the strong echoes of this pattern in the 2014 referendum on independence – where the trope of 'missing Scotland', that is, the non-engaged masses, Arianna Introna argues, 'was *made* missing in indyref imaginings, while Yes radicals became the icon to be repackaged and transmitted to posterity as representative of the new Scotland'.[77] Just this pattern of elite identification helped the Scottish middle classes to 'go native' in their growing support for devolution from the late 1980s. Tracing this development in *Radical Scotland* in 1990, Lindsay Paterson points to 'cultural resurgence' as a leading factor in the 'new willingness amongst some of the traditionally most influential segments of Scottish society to renegotiate Scotland's relationship with the rest of the world'.[78] Awareness of the growing 'confidence' of Scottish culture gradually opened the way to a stronger political identification with Scotland's interests as a 'trans-class people-nation', but this very narrative of civic-national renewal was powered by an earlier sense of class-coded grievance and victimhood (Scotland marginalised and dispossessed by Thatcherism). It is this proletarianised Scotland which has greatest currency within the story of cultural devolution. As Christopher Whyte observed in 1998, 'the task of embodying and transmitting Scottishness is, as it were, devolved to the unemployed, the socially underprivileged, in both actual and representational contexts'.[79] The national valorisation of these states of injury yields a crude division of symbolic labour: middle-class Scotland is tasked with speaking on behalf of 'the people' (via devolved politics), and 'the people' are tasked with embodying the condition of (injured) nationality that warrants a distinctive and inclusive political sphere.

The discomfort of this paradigm was already evident in 1983, and is touched upon in Joyce McMillan's article in the same special issue of *Chapman*. McMillan begins by querying Kerevan's class analysis, questioning where middle-class Scotland fits into this paradigm, and the perils of compulsory national self-consciousness, which often induces a 'guilt-ridden, sentimentalizing tendency' in ex-working-class writers straining after the popular rootedness Kerevan celebrates:

> The Scottish cultural establishment itself cherishes its hard-won consciousness of the ways in which Scottish culture has been discriminated against, and tends to demand that that consciousness never be let slip; and it is at this point the artistic rot set in. [. . .] When I read modern feminist novels, I can often sense, breathing down the writer's neck, a kind of internal group of prefects or cheer-leaders from the women's movement, whose predictable and insistent cries of 'right on' or 'sexist bullshit' can be seen influencing the progress of the novel at every turn. Likewise, a great many Scottish writers

seem to be accompanied by a mental band of Scotland supporters, an internal Ally's army who are liable to shout 'English poof', 'snob', 'traitor' or 'we wuz robbed' if any incorrect, English-looking or (god forbid) middle-class sentiments creep into the prose; and this situation is intensified by the fact that the west-of-Scotland working-class has come, in some circles, to be seen as the main repository of genuine Scottish language and culture, so that the self-righteousness of the oppressed working classes and the culturally-robbed Scot comes into play simultaneously.[80]

Here is a sharp premonition of the 'vernacular' mode of Scottish cultural politics, whereby the politics of national self-assertion draw on the emotional resonance of class dispossession, concretised in the demand for linguistic dignity. However McMillan accepts that this pattern is largely a matter of political circumstance. 'The destructive obsession with the need to emphasise and preserve the "Scottishness" of our writing far beyond what comes naturally and truthfully to writers will persist for as long as Scotland remains in political limbo; in other words, it will last until Scotland either becomes a full nation state, or loses its sense of nationhood altogether.'[81] McMillan rejects the assumption that cultural spokesmen and spokeswomen for Scottishness are a reliable guide to the popular appetites they serve:

These days, working people in Glasgow are much more con-cerned about the next episode of *Dallas* than about the survival of Scottish culture in any form, and the persistent preoccupation with Scottish forms of cultural expression and Scottish writing is one factor which, in itself, alienates many Scottish writers from the Scottish working class, who are fully as sophisticated, as up-to-date, as well-travelled and as internationally-connected as any modern Western proletariat.[82]

Thus, intellectuals distanced from those codes of living 'Scottishness' rooted in popular appetites feel a concomitant need to exaggerate the forms of difference to which they do have access; beginning with language.

'Beyond the pale'

Squarely in the political sphere, pro-devolution thinkers were taking similar analysis of the shifting class composition and political
alignments of the middle class, and translating them into a comprehensive strategy for achieving home rule. In an unpublished
essay, Douglas Robertson and James Smyth reflect on their experience in the group invited to take over *Radical Scotland* in 1983,
after its first two issues. 'At that point the magazine's collective
was composed entirely of SNP '79 Group members, who were
heading out of that party, following its decision to proscribe internal groups at its Ayr conference in 1982.'[83] It is clear that *Radical
Scotland* took its bearings primarily from party politics, and was
driven by a clear strategic vision:

> The magazine's prime role was to build up a political
> acceptance that self government could not be ignored,
> and the issue would not go away. [. . .] Our ambition was
> to make that assumption, the creation of a Parliament, a
> given for an entire generation of politicians and political
> activists – that was our audience. And those who did not
> agree with self government were to be rendered effec-
> tively beyond the pale.[84]

The frame-shifting influence of the magazine met with considerable success. This was partly a cultural and identitarian strategy: maximising the 'dislocation' between English and Scottish
politics (as Harvie had put it in issue two of the magazine), and
'exposing and encouraging the marginalisation of those activists hostile to self government'.[85] In this regard, Robertson and
Smyth persuasively argue that *Radical Scotland*'s real successes
'were in agenda setting' and in '[firming] up a set of political
assumptions and expectations which, in time, ensured that self
government was at the core of the Scottish political agenda, and
therefore a done deal'.[86]

The national-cultural resonance of Thatcherism played its
role in these developments, heightening the contrast *Radical
Scotland* intended to hegemonise. 'As long as the Scottish political

dimension remained latent', David McCrone reflected in 1992, 'it was perfectly possible for generalised Conservative rhetoric about the nation to coexist with the everyday reality of Scottishness'.[87] But in a period when 'Conservatism spoke overwhelmingly with a southern English voice', both Scottishness and Anglo-Tory Britishness were drawn to the electoral surface, and 'the populist, nationalist, anti-state appeal which sustained Thatcher in England for the whole of the 1980s had distinctively negative resonances north of the border'.[88] This enabled cultural and political identity to be elided in ways represented in the editorial to the famous 'Doomsday' issue of *Radical Scotland* ahead of the 1987 general election (contemplating a collapse of Conservative legitimacy north of the border): 'the stage has been reached in British political history where Scotland's rights must be respected, her culture – including her political culture – must be properly reflected, and her aspirations for some measure of self-determination must be enacted'.[89] Scotland's political culture – its distinct political values, as expressed at the ballot box – are here a subset of its deeper, 'given' and continuous national culture; it follows that 'self-determination' would be both cultural and political, a necessary salvaging of national self-respect. Working in these grooves, the twin mobilisation of Scottish cultural difference and Thatcher's British nationalism swiftly made 'Scotland as an ideological category incompatible with Conservative Anglo-British rhetoric'.[90]

Radical Scotland achieved its objectives not, primarily, by campaigning for self-government, but by *naturalising* the terms of that debate, gradually cementing the frame as though the arguments for self-government had already been placed beyond doubt. This followed the precedent set by the *Bulletin of Scottish Politics* in 1980, whose inaugural editorial declared that the journal 'will not be much concerned (except retrospectively) with the debate on whether or not self-government is desirable for Scotland. This occupied much of the last decade, and was settled at the referendum. Now there are new questions to be confronted, in a new situation.'[91] At times this strategy meant overtly acknowledging the cultural basis of the 'Scottish dimension', but without examining the specificities of Scottish culture or its distinctiveness. In issue four of *Radical Scotland*, the question is posed in the following terms:

> The problem for the Labour Party in Scotland is that it has been difficult to take a principled stance on devolution without having to give consideration to what it is to be Scottish. [. . .] Acceptance of Scottish nationality makes irresistible the demand for self-government maintained by the recognition that sovereignty remains with the people. The concept of popular sovereignty has never held many attractions for Labour who have, as [John] Maxton does, maintained the sovereignty of Parliament (presumably to demonstrate their fitness to govern, and to deny any resistance to the legitimacy of their government once installed). Further, the concept of *Scottish* popular sovereignty would entail the demarcation of the population on a historical and cultural basis, which gives too much ground to nationalism.[92]

Radical Scotland was highly effective in prying Scottish politics away from Westminster norms *via the Westminster electoral system*, in order to construct a national political space in which Tories (and principled unionists) would have no choice but to concede devolution or be seen to 'repress' Scottishness. This went as far as openly 'othering' Scottish Toryism as incompatible with the authentically national desire for self-determination.

In Alasdair Gray's *1982 Janine*, published in 1984, the alcoholic protagonist Jock is quite prepared to link his conservative politics to the abject servility of his national identity:

> The truth is that we are a nation of arselickers, though we disguise it with surfaces [. . .] Which is why, when England allowed us a referendum, I voted for Scottish self-government. Not for one minute did I think it would make us more prosperous, we are a poor little country, always have been, always will be, but it would be a luxury to blame ourselves for the mess we are in instead of the bloody old Westminster parliament. 'We see the problems

of Scotland in a totally different perspective when we get
to Westminster,' a Scottish MP once told me. Of course
they do, the arselickers.[93]

This vignette aside, it is notable that the key literary developments of the period make little impact in the pages of *Radical
Scotland*, which is firmly focused on the party politics of devolution. There is nothing on the pivotal influence in Scottish fiction
of this period, James Kelman, until a short review of *Greyhound for
Breakfast* in 1987. Over the page, more than twice as much space
is devoted to a review of the Proclaimers' debut album, headlined
'The Voice of Scotland'. It is the pop group and not the novelist
who are celebrated as champions of 'uncompromising Scottish
accents', and pioneers of 'what might be called vernacular rock n'
roll'. Simply by virtue of their medium, the Proclaimers and their
politicised lyrics and voices could be expected to have a much
larger impact in the left-nationalist milieu to which they were
clearly and visibly attached. The reviewer (the Scots translator and
theatre scholar Bill Findlay, a co-founder of *Cencrastus* magazine)
heralds their arrival in national-popular terms which update the
soft Gramscianism of *Calgacus*:

the appearance of the Proclaimers at this juncture further
testifies to this new-found confidence many young Scots
seem to have in the sustaining powers of their own country. It is a confidence, though, which is both evidence of
change and catalyst *for* change. In this last regard, after this
General Election Scotland will need the vernacular agency
and political cutting-edge of modern voices like The Proclaimers if young Scots generally are to be persuaded of the
need to determine our own priorities and forge our own
solutions here in Scotland.[94]

Clearly Kelman's writing does not press the same buttons, and is
difficult to incorporate into a narrative of recovered confidence;
the review of *Greyhound for Breakfast* focuses on the bleakness and
waste of the title story, which evokes a Scotland fit only to be
left behind through emigration. Thus the outstanding political

novelist of 1980s–90s Scotland, whose writing creates a radical new form of 'vernacular agency', is awkwardly positioned on the fringe of devolutionary culture. Some of the greatest achievements of Scottish literary culture in this period simply do not fit the frame-narrative of the Dream, whereby Scottish Literary Culture has a specific rhetorical function and social reach.

Right back to Burns

The strategic logic of mobilising Scottish 'voice' is even more clear in a 1987 interview with Billy Kay in *Radical Scotland*. 'Scottish' and 'working class' are openly conflated as Kay and his interviewer survey the political scene:

> Interestingly, although most people don't have the kind of knowledge of Scottish culture that would enable them to make choices about being Scottish, about what Scottishness is, it's the culture of that same majority which constitutes the important facets of the national culture, certainly of the literature. [Quoting Billy Kay:] 'Thank God there is a working-class identity, because without it there would be no identity. As Stephen Maxwell has pointed out, very little has been written about the Scottish middle-class experience – right back to Burns, and today with William McIlvanney or Tom Leonard, it's the working class that has written up its own experience.' The argument extends even to a writer like Walter Scott, whose most successful Scottish characters are not the upper-class ones but Davie Deans and Eddie Ochiltree – and they're why Scott is still read. It's as if Scott knew that this was where the strength of Scottish identity lay. One could also argue that the middle classes find their identity in their privilege, private property and prosperity, not in any sense of community, and that this is why their sense of Scottishness can be a source of embarrassment to them, not least in the matter of the way they speak.[95]

The middle classes who stand most to gain from devolution are excluded in advance from vernacular Scottishness; distinctly

Scottish speech cuts across the class divide, but only working-class Scots can benefit from the rising symbolic capital of their tongue. Thus the paradox that minor working-class characters symbolically dominate the realist national literature in which their voices are rendered as alien and without authority; that is, as marginal, 'subaltern' subjects valorised in accordance with modern identity politics. Viewed from this angle, the strategic question would be how to allow middle-class Scots to gain politically from their cultural distinctions. Such considerations are near the surface of the interview, as Kay remarks on the success of his TV series on Scots, *The Mither Tongue*:

> 'For me, the argument for Scottish culture is watertight, from any point of view – European, world, British – the culture produced in this part of the world should be up there being regarded with the same kind of prestige as the rest. But the Cringe gives Scots a fear of the cultural dimension because even though I don't think people need have that fear, I don't want to alienate them from their culture if they're Unionist by inclination, because getting them to realize what they have in their own cultural identity by its nature brings them closer to a more political version of that identity – to political nationalism.'[96]

Here the 'water-tightness' of Scottish cultural difference leads directly and automatically to political nationalism – because the former can only be realised via the latter, it is a 'done deal' to demand liberation from Anglocentric repression. As with electoral strategy in *Radical Scotland*, the exploitation of identity is discussed with disarming candour:

> 'Whereas, in a political sphere, the purely economic case for nationalism *is* arguable, the cultural case is not answerable in that way. Ultimately I don't think you'll have the culture achieving the status it should without the politics, but the reason I don't wave any particular party flag is that people could then say, "*That's* why he's doing all this!" I do it because I am a Scot, this is my culture and it's the

culture of a lot of people who don't realize what they've got. I'm trying to lift it to the status it deserves. If you tie that too closely to a political argument you can alienate a lot of people who should be going along with you' [. . .] The idea that 'This place has cultural expression, therefore it exists,' is now a fact of modern Scotland. The confidence feeds on itself, and encourages others who hear voices like their own, both literally and metaphorically. So the process goes on. 'Ultimately, how far it can go culturally without the final, political stamp of approval – who knows?'[97]

Here is the cultural devolution argument of the 1980s at its most direct: 'this place has cultural expression, therefore it exists'. And if it exists – Scotland 'demarcated' on a cultural and historic basis – it has political rights, and the mandate argument becomes unanswerable. Each phase of this strategy works by instrumentalising Scottish national difference – treating it as a 'given' from which other claims and demands follow logically – without any call for examining the 'content' or reality of Scottish national culture. No deep or tortured introspection was necessary to this political process, and there was no healthy outdoor confrontation of the kind Tom Nairn had once anticipated.[98] The broader alliance which took its place was largely the creature of those parties and representative forms of the Grind. There was no need to open the container-identity 'Scottish' in order to leverage its electoral value. To return to McIlvanney's enclosure, it was enough to see the designated sign – 'Lion' – in close proximity to stinking straw to make the case for recruiting new keepers.

While there is plenty of passionate soul-searching to be found in 1980s 'state of the nation' writing – we might think of Edwin Morgan's *Sonnets from Scotland* (1984), Iain Banks' *Lanark*-inspired novel *The Bridge* (1986), Liz Lochhead's drama *Mary Queen of Scots Got Her Head Chopped Off* (1987) – the actual 'content' of these works did not feature significantly in the devolutionary debates surveyed here, except to manifest the 'confidence' or 'vitality' of the Scottish *identity* whose political value was being inflated, reified and exploited at once. After Thatcher's third election victory in 1987, this 'Scottish Dimension' began to be formally institutionalised as the basis of a new civic order.

Notes

1. McLean, *Getting it Together*, p. 140.
2. Miller, *The End of British Politics?*, p. v.
3. Ascherson, *Stone Voices*, pp. 75–6.
4. Wallace, *The Scottish Novel Since the Seventies*, p. 3.
5. Sandbrook, *Seasons in the Sun*, p. 766.
6. Berridge and Clark, 'Dundee', p. 73.
7. Labour, Co-Op, STUC, 'Speaker's Notes', Labour Movement Yes Campaign [Labour, Co-Op, STUC].
8. McIlvanney, *Surviving the Shipwreck*, p. 17.
9. Ibid. p. 18.
10. Ibid. pp. 20, 21–2.
11. Ibid. p. 24.
12. Ibid. pp. 24–5.
13. 'After the 79' [Editorial], *Crann-Tàra*, 8 (Autumn 1979), p. 2.
14. Ibid. p. 2.
15. Ibid. p. 2.
16. Ibid. p. 2.
17. See Ryan, *Ireland and Scotland*, pp. 37–90.
18. McIlvanney, *Surviving the Shipwreck*, p. 13.
19. Cusick, 'How fearful Scotland stayed in its cage'.
20. Nairn, 'After the referendum', *New Edinburgh Review*, 45 (Summer 1979), pp. 3–10 (p. 3).
21. Quoted by Miller, *The End of British Politics?*, p. 259.
22. Nairn, 'After the referendum', p. 8.
23. 'Editorial: Presenting the *Bulletin*', *Bulletin of Scottish Politics*, 1.1 (Autumn 1980), pp. i–iv (p. iv). My thanks to Rory Scothorne for access to this source.
24. McLean, *Getting it Together*, pp. 48–9.
25. Aitken, *The Bairns O' Adam*, p. 269.
26. McLean, *Getting it Together*, pp. 48–9. McLean notes that the CSA took up a partisan anti-Tory posture from late 1982, with Jim Boyack as chair.
27. Jack Brand, Letter to George Foulkes, 15 August 1980.
28. Ibid.
29. McLean, *Getting it Together*, pp. 55–6.
30. Neal Ascherson, 'Next steps for the LCSA', 16 October [1980?].

31. 'Labour campaign for a Scottish assembly – a Scottish Socialist initiative'.
32. James Mitchell, 'The evolution of devolution: Labour's home rule strategy in opposition', p. 482.
33. Ibid. p. 482.
34. Hepburn, 'The Foulkes Memorandum', *Radical Scotland*, 4 (August–September 1983), p. 16.
35. Ibid. p. 16.
36. Hassan and Shaw, *The Strange Death of Labour Scotland*, p. 35.
37. Hepburn, 'The Foulkes Memorandum', p. 16.
38. 'Labour campaign for a Scottish Assembly – a Scottish Socialist initiative'.
39. Geekie and Levy, 'Devolution and the tartanisation of the Labour Party', p. 401.
40. Lynch, *SNP: The History of the Scottish National Party*, p. 177.
41. Brand, *The National Movement in Scotland*, p. 301.
42. Ibid. p. 301.
43. George Kerevan, 'The cultural consequences of Mr Keynes', *Radical Scotland*, 4 (August–September 1983), pp. 23–6 (p. 23).
44. Rory Scothorne, unpublished doctoral research, University of Edinburgh, 2016–19.
45. Gunn and McCleery, 'Wasps in a jam jar', p. 42.
46. Robertson, *And the Land Lay Still*, p. 535.
47. Nairn, 'The radical approach', p. 168.
48. 'Editorial: A hope and a prayer', *Radical Scotland*, 1 (February–March 1983), p. 3.
49. Ibid. p. 3.
50. Christopher Harvie, 'Tasks for self-governing socialists', *Radical Scotland*, 2 (April–May 1983), p. 16.
51. Ibid. p. 16.
52. Christopher Harvie, 'The devolution of the intellectuals', p. 88.
53. Ibid. p. 89.
54. Cairns Craig, 'Across the divide', *Radical Scotland*, 2 (April–May 1983), pp. 24–5 (p. 24).
55. Ibid. pp. 24–5.
56. John Caughie, 'Political culture/cultural politics', *New Edinburgh Review*, 40 (Spring 1978), pp. 4–7 (p. 4).
57. Rokkan and Urwin, *Economy, Territory, Identity*, p. 157.
58. Keating, *Nations Against the State*, p. 189.
59. Ibid. p. 173.
60. Ibid. p. 182.

61. See Whyte, 'Nationalism and its discontents'.
62. Christopher Whyte, 'Out of a predicament', *Radical Scotland*, 5 (October–November 1983), pp. 20–1 (p. 20).
63. Joy Hendry, 'Editorial', *Chapman*, 35–6 (1983), p. 1.
64. Ibid. p. 1.
65. Alasdair Gray, 'A modest proposal for by-passing a predicament', *Chapman*, 35–6 (1983), pp. 7–9 (p. 9).
66. George Kerevan, 'Labourism revisited', *Chapman*, 35–6 (1983), pp. 25–31 (p. 26).
67. Ibid. pp. 26–7.
68. Alex Law and Gerry Mooney, 'Devolution in a "stateless nation"', p. 172.
69. George Kerevan, 'Labourism revisited', p. 27.
70. Ibid. p. 30.
71. Rancière and Rancière, 'The philosopher's tale', p. 79.
72. Ibid. p. 85.
73. Ibid. p. 93.
74. Ibid. pp. 79, 90.
75. Ibid. p. 74.
76. Ibid. p. 93.
77. Introna, 'Reveries of a progressive past', p. 123.
78. Lindsay Paterson, 'Are the Scottish middle classes going native?', *Radical Scotland*, 45 (June–July 1990), pp. 10–11.
79. Whyte, 'Masculinities in contemporary Scottish fiction', p. 275.
80. Joyce McMillan, 'The predicament of the Scottish writer', *Chapman*, 35–6 (1983), pp. 68–71 (p. 69).
81. Ibid. p. 70.
82. Ibid. p. 70.
83. Robertson and Smyth, '*Radical Scotland*', p. 3.
84. Ibid. p. 2.
85. Ibid. p. 4.
86. Ibid. pp. 9, 4, 6.
87. McCrone, *Understanding Scotland*, p. 171.
88. Ibid. p. 173.
89. 'Hoping for the best . . . preparing for the worst' [Editorial], *Radical Scotland*, 25 (February–March 1987), pp. 9–11 (p. 11).
90. McCrone, *Understanding Scotland*, p. 171.
91. 'Editorial: Presenting the *Bulletin*', *Bulletin of Scottish Politics*, 1.1 (Autumn 1980), pp. i–iv (p. ii).
92. 'In the red corner' [Editorial], *Radical Scotland*, 4 (August–September 1983), pp. 7–8 (p. 7).

93. Gray, *1982 Janine*, pp. 65–6.
94. Bill Findlay, 'The voice of Scotland' [reviewing The Proclaimers, 'This is the Story'], *Radical Scotland*, 27 (June–July 1987), p. 33.
95. Billy Kay, 'Interview with Billy Kay', *Radical Scotland*, 25 (February–March 1987), pp. 33–5 (p. 34).
96. Ibid. p. 35.
97. Ibid. p. 35.
98. An important exception is Barbara and Murray Grigor's 'Scotch Myths' exhibition (1981), though I have no space to do it justice here.

4

Claims of Right

Self-Determination and Consensus 1987–92

In 1989 Cairns Craig reflected on a decade since the failed referendum on a Scottish Assembly: 'Ten years ago the talk was
all of emigration or of lying low for a generation and hoping
that someday it ("the independence movement", "nationalism",
"Scottish creativity") might pick up again.'[1] The conflation
sponsored by Billy Kay in his *Radical Scotland* interview two years
earlier was well on its way to being naturalised, with the prospects of independence and cultural vitality presented virtually as
synonyms. Craig is the key figure in the discourse of cultural
devolution, and his view of the 1980s is unsurprisingly upbeat,
emphasising the reassertion of Scottish difference as an impetus
to artistic exploration and political rebuilding:

> Instead of political defeat leading to quiescence, it led
> directly into an expression of cultural creativity, a creativ-
> ity coming to terms with the origins of the political defeat
> and redefining the nation's conception of itself. The '80s
> have been one of the most significant decades of Scottish
> cultural self-definition in the past two centuries. In part this
> was because the events leading up to and resulting in the
> '79 referendum, whatever their political outcome, focused
> attention on the fact that Scotland was profoundly different
> in social texture and values from England.[2]

Craig's view of the prevailing codes of Scottish distinctiveness is,
however, critical: the reconstruction of a Scottish cultural imaginary has traded largely in outdated and nostalgic imagery centred

on 'the archetype of modern Scotland – the urban working class'.[3]
Craig identifies the 1971 UCS work-in as a pivotal but ambiguous moment in this story: less an industrial dispute than a 'media
event' involving the re-performance of traditional roles and ideals.

> Jimmy Reid's famous 'no-bevvying' speech was a direc-
> tor's instruction to the actors, who were not actually work-
> ing in the yard building ships but performing the role for
> the international gathering of cameras that had come to see
> them building ships. And as a media event, UCS brought
> into conjunction many artists and performers, either here
> to provide the support of their media presence or to per-
> form in fundraising concerts. Those artists found, as it
> were, a new commonality of purpose in the reassertion of
> values, the values of Scottish socialism and of the Scot-
> tish proletariat, that seemed to have been made redundant
> by the 'never-had-it-so-good' era of the '50s. Of course,
> the fact was that those images *were* redundant – but their
> redundancy could only be accepted once they had been
> fully realised and lived through again.[4]

This response is striking in its acknowledgment of performative
(and often conservative) qualities of the 'vernacular' assertion of
Scottishness which characterised the Thatcher era. It is as though
the confidence-shattering failure of 1979 could only be overcome
through a mild form of cheating: push-starting the cultural system by coasting downhill toward familiar and nostalgic signifiers.
Craig is sceptical about the value of the re-heated workerism of
this period, but emphasises its value in re-legitimising the *language*
in which the performance is conducted. He continues:

> Lived over in story and song they have been throughout the
> '70s and '80s: plays about shipyard workers, novels about
> traditional working class hard men, comedy focused on the
> experiences of the factory and the slum. [. . .] the impor-
> tant thing throughout was that what was actually being
> recovered was the Scottish voice. Let us not forget that
> in the '50s and '60s the Scottish voice had no presence in

the media except when ring-fenced by those images – the kilted country dancers or the football terracings – which made Scotland an identifiable but unchallenging part of the fabric of the UK (the *Uniform* Kingdom).[5]

By 1989 Scotland has recovered a good deal of dignity and danger, via the revalidation of national voice in political conditions which made the assertion of cultural difference, class resistance and constitutional disquiet one and the same. 'Scottish voice' now becomes a key metaphor for unifying constituent elements of the national community, and the direct index of those 'social textures and values' which distinguish Scotland from England. The aesthetic qualities and political content of artworks read in this frame are immaterial – the expressive channel is all:

> Whatever the specific quality of the works of art of the '70s and '80s, they have all been explorations of and assertions of the vitality and validity of the Scottish voice. And that vitality has taken the Scottish voice through the gradations from identification with the core experience of the working class – let's say Billy Connolly – into a flexible instrument which can range across many different kinds of Scottish experience, each of which is voiced differently but still voiced as Scottish – 'Naked Radio' and Robbie Coltrane. The voicing of Scotland is what the '80s have been about in cultural terms, from Liz Lochhead's poetry to the Proclaimers' songs, from *Gregory's Girl* to *The Steamie*.[6]

The confidence and separateness accrued in the cultural sphere, argued Craig, had structural importance in other areas, as the recovery of national 'voice' fostered the re-development of Scottish social organisation:

> Essentially what happened after '79 was the declaration of autonomy by groups which gave up on the political scene as a whole and concentrated on creating a devolved, autonomous power base for their own activities within their own sphere of control. The creation of new institutions – in the

arts new magazines, new publishing houses and imprints, new archives for the past achievements of Scottish culture, new facilities for creation and promotion – took the business of independence into the very texture of creative life.[7]

The function of national civic bodies – from the Scottish Arts Council to the Confederation of Scottish Business – 'may be described as a "feedback mechanism" by which the "nationness" of the nation is reinforced. [. . .] It is through such channels that the people of the nation encounter the nation-in-action, and through which they can see their own intentions becoming elements of national action.'[8] It is this layer of active and autonomous national structure which holds such promise for both the normalisation of self-government (in lived experience) and the potential for large-scale re-institutionalisation of the national habitus:

> An undeclared independence was created at the level of organisations and institutions, and this is what gives real foundations to the current transformation of Scottish politics, a fundamental underpinning of political activity which just did not exist in the '70s. Not only are there now the institutions and organisations of an independent polity in Scotland; there are an enormous number of people who have got used to acting in that independent environment.[9]

'Authentic voice' has become a kind of liberatory structuring principle, yielding an empowered mode of civic self-organisation which is the direct analogue of home rule. As we shall see, 'self-determination' emerges as a key but ambivalent principle in this milieu, operating on multiple scales (personal, class, national). The pivotal shift over the preceding decade is not so much the retrieval of (untimely, self-conscious) popular imagery of collective experience, but the *reconstitution* of national structures – of expression, of organisation, of cultural and political reproduction:

> The institutionalisation of Scottishness in the '80s means that a far greater proportion of people in Scotland are now actively involved in specific forms of activity whose

rationale is based on Scottish decision-taking, or whose rationale is based on opposition to London decision-taking [. . .] all the cultural workers of the community are now in the situation where much that was fought over in the '70s can be taken for granted: Scotland exists, has a past, has a future, has VOICES that can be heard.[10]

We can see precisely these themes and emphases across the 1987–92 period. From 1987 the 'no-mandate' argument highlighted the hollowness of Scottish democracy within the UK, and representative legitimacy was claimed and contested in the field of 'culture', in both new and reactive ways. By 1989 organised popular defiance (of Thatcher, of industrial policy, of the poll tax) was incorporated into an elite consensus in favour of devolution, most importantly via the Scottish Constitutional Convention (a body with deep roots in *Radical Scotland*). The complex relationship between this quasi-representative body and the popular energies in whose name it made its *Claim of Right* brings into focus the shifting identity politics of class, nation and party in this period.

Neo-populism?

Keith Dixon writes of a 'radical cultural *neo-populism*' in the Scottish 1980s, motivated by 'the need to provide authentic new representations of the people' in conditions of democratic deficit.[11] While Dixon regards the key literary figures of this movement (Tom Leonard, James Kelman, Alasdair Gray) as 'underground' and dissident voices, the 'neo-populist' turn he traces clearly occurred within, and was shaped around, a *statist* constitutional paradigm derived from the Westminster system. Stephen Tierney locates this feature of Scottish devolution in a wider pattern of similitude and replication:

> The powerful normative claims to be found in the narratives of substate national societies are rooted [. . .] not in the politics of difference but, rather, in what we might call the politics of similarity. Hence the processes of nation building and consolidation that remain ongoing within substate nations parallel to the equivalent processes at the state level.[12]

These state-making and nation-building processes clearly inter-sect in the story of 'cultural devolution'. In essence, the discourse of national-popular representation in 'culture' gave majoritarian social substance to a devolutionary project premised on electoral interests and parliamentary forms. This project was formulated almost entirely in the image of established civic and state institu-tions, and gained its decisive power and influence by constituting itself *as* a national representative body: a parliament-in-waiting whose authority would be recognised tacitly and in advance, largely by reference to its 'extra-political' identitarian grounding.

That is not to suggest that all dissenting energies were com-pletely or successfully absorbed. In magazines such as *Edinburgh Review*, we can see the internal strains of a state-centred con-stitutional politics seeking validation and popular traction in the sphere of (recovered) 'national' cultural repertoires. This is espe-cially visible in the effort to align tropes of 'self-determination' in key schools and works of Scottish art with the priorities of devolution. Literary and cultural figures played a key role in dis-guising and managing these contradictions, often by eliding the *expressive liberation* of marginalised social groups with the cause of re-legitimating national political institutions. Thus, the no-mandate paradigm gave way to a cultural politics of 'voice' where the channels and forms of 'representation' were pre-given par-liamentary structures only waiting for the right accents to speak a new Scottish polity into existence *through* them. (We return to this motif in Chapters 6 and 7.) Shadowing this pattern were powerful critiques of the highly limited discourse of parliamentary 'mandate', and a caustic rejection of the 'cultural' regeneration of civic and political identities, by the very literary figures presented as their guarantors. Not all of the 'VOICES that can be heard' were keen to be enfolded into a state-identitarian project.

Doomsday: 1987

The single most influential issue of *Radical Scotland* carried the famous 'Doomsday' cover in February–March 1987, anticipating a collapse in the legitimacy of a Tory-led UK government after the June general election. The 'no mandate' argument had been part of devolutionary discourse since at least 1983, but lacked popular traction. Now, the prospect of a glaring electoral divergence between Scotland and England seemed to justify dramatic language. A *Radical Scotland* editorial cited opinion polls showing that 61 per cent of Scots believed that further loss of Tory seats north of the border would destroy their right to govern Scotland, and deliver a genuine crisis of legitimacy:

> The stage has been reached in British political history where Scotland's rights must be respected, her culture – including her political culture – must be properly reflected, and her aspirations for some measure of self-determination must be enacted. If these legitimate aspirations are further thwarted by the most reactionary forces in the UK, then we must – for reasons of self-respect if nothing else – be prepared to take a stand for democracy.[13]

The June 1987 election result made Doomsday real, or real enough. It was not a Tory wipeout, but Labour won fifty of seventy-two Scottish seats to the Conservatives' ten, doubling their advantage from twenty to forty. UK-wide the Tories lost twenty-one seats, but Thatcher was returned as Prime Minister by a comfortable majority of fifty on a very healthy 42 per cent of the UK vote. Roughly half of Tory losses (eleven of twenty-one – including two Scottish Office Ministers, the Scottish Whip and the Solicitor General for Scotland) and Labour gains (nine of twenty) came in Scotland, strengthening the impression that Scottish politics increasingly obeyed its own electoral counter-dynamic. (In 1983, Thatcher's landslide yielded only one additional seat in Scotland, while only three of Labour's fifty-two losses occurred north of the border.)

This result marked a key milestone in devolution. Within the Campaign for a Scottish Assembly (CSA), Bob McLean recalls the 'shock created by the reduction of [Scottish] Tory MPs from twenty two [sic] to ten. It bestowed credibility on the "No Mandate" argument, which challenged the legitimacy of this Tory rump to govern Scotland.'[14] A national consensus seemed to be emerging, and opponents of devolution were increasingly marginalised within the Labour Party. A *Radical Scotland* editorial insisted that anti-Tory tactical voting expressed 'a demand for Home Rule in some shape or form, a demand for a form of government in Scotland which would display a different set of values altogether from those represented so vividly by Mrs Thatcher herself'.[15] Political divergence was increasingly explained with reference to engrained national differences. Hearkening back to *The Radical Approach* (1976), the SNP's Isobel Lindsay found in the result clear evidence of 'a Scottish/ English ideological divide':

> The enthusiasm which many working-class as well as middle-class English feel for Margaret Thatcher is related to their perception of their national identity. She represents an assertive, aggressive, maudlinly sentimental English nationalism – fulfilling a yearning for renewed imperial glory. [. . .] This dominant strand of English nationalism strikes few chords in Scottish hearts. Scottish national sentiment has developed in different directions. We are David rather than Goliath; we are the underdogs, with considerable sympathy for other underdogs; we are less xenophobic (if for no other reason than that so many of our friends and relatives live abroad); we have no delusions of potential 'great power' status. [. . .] the lack of identification with the current brand of English nationalism combines with the rejection of the possessive individualism it also represents, to make it alien to three-quarters of Scotland.[16]

This 'alienation' from Thatcherism – strongly contested in later scholarship underscoring the popularity in Scotland of policies such as Right to Buy[17] – was the basis of an emergent Scottish political consensus which had the salutary effect of de-stigmatising national *cultural* identity. As Lindsay observed, 'the Scottish dimension has become more culturally acceptable than it was even in the mid-70s. It does not have to be defended to the same extent against the charges of being divisive, "anti-modern", parochial.'[18] The tweedy aura of nationalism itself followed suit. 'Standing for Scotland' against Thatcher, Jack Brand noted, effectively forced the SNP leftward: having earlier decoupled class identity from political interest, 'the Nationalists could not but identify with the working class if they wanted to appear to be against the government'.[19] In this shifting party terrain, devolution was increasingly identified with broader cultural renewal. In September the Scottish Trades Union Congress held a 'Festival of Democracy' on Glasgow Green, an event 'designed to bring together the pro-devolution and anti-government forces from Scottish political and public life in a celebration of Scottish culture and in demand of a change to Scotland's system of government'.[20] Inter-party squabbles caused the SNP and Liberals to pull out of the event, but the message of national unity survived – the CSA distributed stickers 'emblazoned with the figure 78 per cent, the overwhelming majority of Scottish people who had voted for parties advocating constitutional change'.[21] In a pattern repeated over the next decade, the 'national dimension' could be invoked strategically to disguise tensions within the undergirding party alliances supporting devolution, and to aggregate support for rival visions of home rule which were not strictly compatible. Liberal insistence on proportional representation in any proposed assembly, and SNP–Labour tussles over the need to frame constitutional change 'within the UK', were long-running battles, but within the domain of 'culture' and the affirmation of 'identity' the broad consensus could receive popular validation.

Questions of national grounding and belonging had always been key to the logic of devolution, but now shifted from latent to explicit political claims. This created real unease within the unionist parties. Iain Macwhirter noted that Scottish Labour's Doomsday success, and its accompanying crypto-nationalism, presented real difficulties for its leadership:

Donald Dewar was, and is, a supporter of devolution, but he is also a constitutionalist who did not endorse the growing clamour from within his party for some kind of extra-parliamentary action to expose the lack of a Government 'mandate' in Scotland. At the first Scottish Question Time of the new parliament, when Dennis Canavan the neo-nationalist Labour MP for Falkirk West, drew attention to the presence of 31 Tories from English constituencies on the Government benches by crying 'I spy strangers', his leader drew back.[22]

Despite such reservations, the rhetoric of national suppression and resistance moved increasingly to the fore. Jim Ross spelled out the logic: 'if the only elections held are on a British basis, and if those elections give power in Britain to a Party with derisory representation in Scotland, then the government of Scotland must grow steadily more like the government of Northumberland or Dorset, whatever Ministers may pretend'.[23] In this respect Doomsday's de-nationalising implications presented a golden opportunity for home-rulers: 'there is an excitement and a resentment in Scotland now on which action and advance can be founded'.[24]

This energy, Ross argued, should be invested in a strategy of pre-figurative devolution whereby a 'comprehensively representative body – let's call it a Constitutional Convention' would 'legitimise, promote and co-ordinate expressions of the demand for constitutional change in Scotland to the point at which it became irresistible'.[25] The lessons of 1979 made the case for building widespread and overwhelming public support, but note the elitist-outsider role assumed by a vanguard body obliged (in Ross's words) 'to *create itself in resistance to Government* instead of being set up by Government'.[26] Cairns Craig emphasises the 'haphazard' and unofficial character of this body, which was 'conjured up' between Ross (a former civil servant at the Scottish Office) and Alan Lawson, the editor of *Radical Scotland* from mid-1985, while meeting for coffee in the Grassmarket in 1987.[27] This constitutional convention would be instating itself with a 'provisional' representative authority drawn from outside the democratic process, in the name of the national community but without its electoral warrant.

In February 1988 the CSA duly established a 'Constitutional Steering Committee' chaired by Sir Robert Grieve, with Jim Ross as secretary, to formulate concrete plans for an assembly that could be used to mobilise public support. This committee – the precursor body for the Scottish Constitutional Convention – included key members of CSA (including the SNP's Isobel Lindsay and

Paul Scott), prominent home-ruler academics and trade unionists, church leaders, women's aid workers and literary/cultural figures such as Joy Hendry and Judy Steel. Andrew Marr notes that the CSA, 'lacking its own national organization and a large membership list, was using a certain amount of ventriloquism' to voice the demands of the nation – presenting its own longstanding agenda as matters of burning public concern – and to 'persuade the big parties to take its ideas seriously. But it worked.'[28]

Developments within the Labour Party were crucial to this success. Despite internal unease Labour gradually moved to embrace 'the Scottish card' and even the language of popular sovereignty (an SNP shibboleth). In a 1989 article for *Parliamentary Affairs*, two Labour supporters alarmed by this shift documented the 'Tartanisation' of Labour's message and warned of its potential pitfalls. James Geekie and Roger Levy highlighted the uncomfortable affinities of no-mandatery with nationalism *tout court*:

> The acceptance of nationalist arguments by Labour does not stop at the theory of the Scottish mandate. There is a range of ideological preconceptions, policies and strategies which Labour has inherited from the SNP and earlier nationalist Home Rule movements. For example, the case for devolution is often underpinned by Labour spokesmen by allusions to Scotland's loss of statehood in 1707. Writing in *Radical Scotland* (February/March 1987), Jack McConnell, a Stirling district councillor and Labour's prospective parliamentary candidate in Perth and Kinross in 1987, argued that Labour's devolution campaign should show voters 'that the control over their own lives, which Scots have been deprived of for almost three centuries, can be re-established'.[29]

James Mitchell cautions that Geekie and Levy 'offered an unsubtle caricature of what was happening', but it is not difficult to find Labour voices making unequivocal nationalist noises in this period.[30] McConnell and Canavan (along with Robin Cook, George Galloway, John McAllion, Ian Smart, Bob McLean and

Susan Deacon) were leading figures of Scottish Labour Action, formed in February 1988 by members of CSA dissatisfied with Labour's lukewarm attitude toward no-mandate rhetoric and 'inaction on the Poll Tax issue' (on which the SNP had stolen the initiative by endorsing non-payment, an approach rejected by Kinnock as 'fruitless' and a 'policy of despair').[31] The SLA – 'or "Scottish Liberation Army" as some activists dubbed it – leapt over the head of the Labour Co-ordinating Committee and other tendencies, to become the most influential grouping within Scottish Labour politics'.[32] It is often difficult to hear a meaningful difference between SLA and SNP rhetoric on the constitutional issue in this period. Even decades later, First Minister Jack McConnell characterises the internal Labour divide over no-mandate rhetoric as one 'between those who looked at that from a Scottish perspective and those who felt the retention of the Union was more important'.[33] This grouping did not shrink from 'othering' Tory government as English and foreign: in 1988 John McAllion argued that 'we need the interim assembly to focus anger and pressure on what is undoubtedly an alien and increasingly isolated form of rule'.[34]

Not only true believers adopted this rhetoric. Robin Cook had campaigned against a Scottish Assembly in 1979, but explained his reversal in terms of the altered stakes of national community: 'in the 1970s, devolution had been a "compromise with nationalism". A decade later, he maintained, it had become a means of protecting Scotland from Thatcherism.'[35] These were the conditions in which all-Scotland united fronts came to the fore of constitutional politics, with pro-devolutionists strongly promoting the 'national dimension' and its alignment with social democracy.

Edinburgh Review

After its re-launch by students of the University of Edinburgh in 1984, *Edinburgh Review* (formerly *New Edinburgh Review*) took a close interest in the unfolding politics of devolution, and the interplay of literary, cultural and constitutional debates.

Under the editorship of Peter Kravitz, an American-born student later to organise the (Glasgow-based) Free University, the magazine evinced a strong sense of engagement with ongoing cultural debates, adopting in the first editorial Alasdair Gray's slogan 'to gather all the rays of culture into one whole' and Tom Leonard's credo 'all livin language is sacred / fuck thi lohta thim'.[36] The 'rediscovery' of George E. Davie was an abiding interest of the magazine, which from this first editorial adopted a stance of Scottish 'democratic intellectualism'. Reviewers' names were excluded 'so that the not-so-famous can demand as much attention as the famous and so mix on equal terms for once', and the magazine's purview was defined to include 'culture as something that is not *either* Dostoevsky and Charles Rennie Mackintosh *or* a Guinness in your local and a football match, but BOTH'.[37]

A cultural review rather than a political magazine, *Edinburgh Review* had little to say about the electoral stratagems by which the Scottish Parliament was eventually delivered, but a great deal to say about *self-determination*, which was a touchstone of the magazine's moral-aesthetic agenda. The concept of self-determination effectively functioned as a relay between 'intellectual' themes of the magazine – an abiding interest in 'outsider' voices, cultural non-conformity, emancipated self-expression – and the salience of constitutional politics in Scottish culture. As Linda Gunn and Alistair McCleery note:

> 'Devolution' was referred to directly in *Edinburgh Review,* though support for more 'autonomy' and criticism of Westminster were presented as a stance against disenfranchisement in general. According to Kravitz, devolution was seen in Glasgow – certainly amongst writers – as 'a middle-class obsession that ignored class politics . . . actually only really interested in wresting power for the middle-class', specifically, middle-class intellectuals based in Edinburgh. At the time, he was editing the magazine from Glasgow, mixing with Libertarian Anarchists and writer James Kelman.[38]

Kravitz's own interest in anarchism, psychology and Kelman was important in shaping the magazine's agenda. A 1988 editorial captures the political space occupied by *Edinburgh Review*, as Kravitz insists that 'opposition must begin to crystallize around

"self-determination" as opposed to nationalism', casting a sceptical eye on the prospect of 'a centralized state with a parliament
in Edinburgh'.[39] The magazine consistently sets the question
of government in broader humanistic contexts, and grounds its
anger in the experience of individuals. A 1988 salvo is centred on
the mental anguish of 'stressed' citizens who suffer

> under the triple yoke of a one-party UK state, a one-party
> local state and a global market oscillating unaccountably
> from overdrive to free-fall. Total rule by the Conserva-
> tives in Britain and Labour in Scotland flourishes through
> a handshake between the political class and the permanent
> experts. Both use bureaucracy and appeals to profitability
> to suffocate difference.[40]

This emphasis on the liberation of 'difference' and anti-bureau-
cratic expression brought *Edinburgh Review* into the trajectory of
radical art magazines of the 1960s and 1970s (including *Scottish
International*). As such, Kravitz casts a wary eye on promises of
deliverance via new forms of state power (with an eye on late-
Soviet unfreedoms):

> It is hard to imagine voting out this global market authori-
> tarianism. What can be done is to appreciate areas hitherto
> ignored by the political class and to conceive games that
> do not play by the rule of the commodity. Needless to say,
> such initiatives cannot be entrusted to future governments
> of 'nations' however 'socialist' they may advertise them-
> selves to be.[41]

Both the national frame and its egalitarian character are in question
here. There is an enthusiasm for forms of cultural participation and
political association that will refute Thatcher's 'no such thing as
society', but a clear scepticism about centralised organisation:

> People have escaped into family and self because the
> State has claimed a monopoly on democratic activity.
> To organize outside institutions without being made to

feel marginal is the only way to prevent new ideas being absorbed and thereby defused by Party and State. One co-operator alone will wither away in alienation, but small clusters of co-operators can move into combination in the most hostile of environments. [. . .] Beginning with an assembly of individuals who rely on reciprocity, it may just be possible in this world of apparent egotists, for mutual co-operation to evolve without central control.[42]

The agenda here runs counter to the strategic blueprint of *Radical Scotland*, namely the achievement of new state institutions to channel and strengthen national politics. (A 1986 editorial puts it starkly: 'The goal must be to remain forever critical, constantly negating life as defined by the state.'[43]) The emergence of self-managed community projects and creative platforms noted by Cairns Craig in his 1989 retrospective need not precipitate neo-national governance. In the same month as *Radical Scotland*'s 'Doomsday' issue, we find *Edinburgh Review* contemplating very different responses and possibilities:

The British State has become increasingly absolutist and centralized since 1939. The question now is how to rekindle the remaining embers of democracy. One possibility is to return to the eighteenth and nineteenth centuries and have a look at the conditions which prefigured the rise of popular democratic movements: the tavern discussions and abstemious coffee-houses, the debating clubs and corresponding societies. Imagine: TOM PAINE IN THE AGE OF VIDEO. This is no backward-looking nostalgia, but a venturing into the future.[44]

In place of the demand for strong institutions to rectify the 'democratic deficit' whereby the nation is denied electoral representation, *Edinburgh Review* looks to dispersed and grassroots forms of connection, on a personal scale. At times *Edinburgh Review* aims squarely at the limits of devolutionary political debate – the editorial to issue 82 (1989) is titled 'Nations can't be beautiful, only people can'. In keeping with the person-centred and existential flavour of the magazine (embodied by regular appearances from R. D. Laing and Tom Leonard), the author underscores the psychic and personal dimension of essentially apersonal devolutionary arguments:

> 'Scotland should be governing itself.' To what extent does the reliance on this idea become a compensation for things lacking in ourselves? [. . .] The politico in Scotland today all too often looks like the person jockeying for position as one of the people who will be running the Scotland of the Future. Beyond cynicism such a failure to adapt displays lack of imagination. [. . .] It's no use getting rid of the big, obvious tyranny over a people if we do nothing about the hidden tyrannies of the soul.[45]

The issue of self-government is consistently thematised in *Edinburgh Review*, but generalised and relocated from the sphere of specific constitutional proposals to the ethical plane of personal growth and responsibility. While the magazine understands itself as providing friendly criticism of a movement defined above all by national anti-Thatcherism, its emphasis on inner and personal change chimes with 1980s discourses of self-reliance and self-help:

> It is no good wanting constantly to change the world for other people unless you are willing to meet the challenge: change yourself. Take on some personal responsibility for the way you run your world. Self-government is a contradiction in terms unless governors take a look inside, at who or what in reality governs them. Without this look, the world they are going to shape in a liberated Scotland will be a gnarled and twisted one.[46]

Here is a pathway for linking the question of personal (subjective) liberation – highly topical in Scottish fiction of the 1980s and 1990s, and exemplified in this very issue of *Edinburgh Review* by work from James Kelman, Tom Leonard and Janice Galloway – to the narrowly political focus on devolution. In just this way the bridging motif of 'self-determination' tends to blur the differences between psychological and (national) political autonomy.

In navigating questions of class representation and exclusion the magazine did not seriously break with the left-nationalism of *Radical Scotland*, whereby general, broadly humanist appeals for free expression and authentic personhood quietly slide into demands for national empowerment. Gunn and McCleery capture the sense in which the magazine could be heard to address and endorse devolution without doing so explicitly:

> even *Edinburgh Review* readers may not have been able to recognise that the magazine's use of the phrase 'the people' actually meant 'a homogeneous community comprising all manner of outsiders or disenfranchised individuals' as opposed to 'the Scottish people'. Under these circumstances, the magazine's preference for 'self' (individual) liberation or empowerment might easily be interpreted as a substitute for 'national' (collective) liberation or empowerment during a period when some proponents of devolution were using the need to create the former to justify the pursuit of the latter. A 'free' Scotland would be composed of individuals free to exercise their differences, whether of ethnicity, gender or religion.[47]

While strongly critical of the unaccountable elite who quietly and invisibly govern Scotland, the magazine – perhaps guided by its anti-statist tendencies – invests real hope in civil society, both as refuge and model, in ways that would be echoed (if not appropriated) in the elite discourse of 'Civic Scotland' during the 1990s.

> The autonomy and solidarity of civil society: writers' groups, noticeboards, flyposters, carnivals, credit-unions, home-made badges, fanzines, ai-kido clubs, chat-lines, indie-labels, essay clubs, Womens' Aid, bring-and-buy sales, joggers, pagan ritualists, coffee-mornings, co-operatively run dance clubs, toy libraries [. . .] can only survive if informal links are made laterally among them to offset control by state or

market. [. . .] Here is where democracy can be preserved and built in a nation where it is otherwise disappearing under the rule of law.[48]

The anarchist inflexion of Kravitz's statement is quite different to what the Scottish Constitutional Convention would claim to represent, but the emphasis on non-state bodies and their organic public character (and consequent quasi-democratic authority) does bolster a key element of the official story of devolution.

A Claim of Right for Scotland

At the same time as these alternative perspectives and parallels were being explored in *Edinburgh Review*, the organised movement for self-government was rapidly settling into hardened institutional forms. The arguments developed in *Radical Scotland* and the wider CSA were consolidated in *A Claim of Right for Scotland*, launched in July 1988, as the report of the CSA's aforementioned Constitutional Steering Committee. In the CSA's official history Bob McLean offers the following synopsis:

> The logic of the 'Claim' was as follows. Scots in 1707, and since, assumed that the Union with England guaranteed certain aspects of Scottish identity, including the church and the law. The 'Claim' concluded that, as old assumptions were no longer being fulfilled there was a need for a Constitutional Convention.[49]

This summary undersells the rhetorical force and dynamism of the document (drafted by Jim Ross), which frequently voices ideals well in excess of the modest aims of the Steering Committee. Framed as a practical intervention setting out 'what we consider must be done if the health of Scottish government is to be restored', the *Claim* mounts a bracingly radical critique of 'fundamental flaws in the British constitution', centred on questions of national distinctiveness: 'although the government of the United Kingdom rests nominally with a "British" Parliament, it is impossible to trace in the history or procedures of that Parliament any constitutional influence other than an English one'.[50] As for Scotland, the *Claim* begins with a clear and confident distinction between the basis of a political community and its forms of governance:

> Much ink is wasted on the question of whether the Scots are a nation. Of course they are. They were both a nation and a state until 1707. The state was wound up by a Treaty which clearly recognised the nation and its right to distinctive government in a fundamental range of home affairs.[51]

Distinctive government, then, is the living sinew and guarantor of continuing nationhood, now dramatically placed in doubt by the democratic deficit. Scotland's redundant civic organs underscore the sick and depleted condition of the nation within the English/British constitutional order; but (in a curious early swerve of argument),

> the fact that institutional forms, however empty, reflecting these distinctions have been preserved to the present day demonstrates that no-one in British government has dared to suggest openly that the nation no longer exists or that the case for distinctiveness has now disappeared.[52]

That the diseased organs have not been excised by London attests to the underlying durability of Scottish claims to national difference, which are grounded *beyond* government. Thus we begin in a curious double-move whereby the suspended animation of 'distinctive government' grounds the reality of Scottish nationhood in 'institutional forms' held to be null: empty shells akin to the Royal High School pointlessly renovated to host the Assembly aborted by the voters (and the 40 per cent rule) in 1979. The emptiness of these forms now becomes the problem to be addressed – that is, the need to restore their democratic lifeblood and activity – *without* querying the underlying realities of cultural or national separateness, on which 'distinctive government' is ultimately premised.

Thus Scottish cultural difference is once again central to, but effectively outside, the constitutional argument: figuring as an extragovernmental 'given' invested with fundamental importance.

The *Claim* does pay an unusual degree of attention to traditional culturalist arguments about nationhood and sovereignty, but as 'closed' issues whose real importance lies in the non-congruence between this fixed reality and its non-representation in constitutional governance:

> Scottish nationhood does not rest on constitutional history alone. It is supported by a culture reaching back over centuries and bearing European comparison in depth and quality, nourished from a relatively early stage by an education system once remarkable by European standards. Since the Union, the strength of that culture has fluctuated but there is no ground for any claim that, overall or even at any particular time, it has benefited from the Union. On the contrary the Union has always been, and remains, a threat to the survival of a distinctive culture in Scotland.[53]

In retrospect this seems an extraordinarily anti-unionist stance to be supported by parties arguing that devolution would strengthen and modernise Britishness. Reviewing the published version (with accompanying commentaries) in *Radical Scotland*, James Kellas noted its affinities with earlier 'Claims of Right' in 1689 and 1842, in its character of mounting 'a revolutionary challenge to the authority of Government and Parliament':

> The authors of the *Claim* (worthy Scots from the middle-class professions on the whole) do not baulk at civil disobedience, challenging the authority of Government, and decrying the 'English Constitution' as giving the Prime Minister 'a degree of arbitrary power few, if any, English and no Scottish monarchs have rivalled'. Even more surprising is that the [Scottish Constitutional] Convention [formed between the publication of the *Claim* in July 1988 and this review], meeting in the Church of Scotland General Assembly Hall in Edinburgh, and attended by

many of Her Majesty's Loyal Opposition, should sub-
scribe to such sedition – and get away with it (in 1793
the penalty was transportation to Botany Bay).[54]

The SNP 79 Grouper Stephen Maxwell welcomed 'a beam of
republican optimism', but noted that the *Claim*'s 'practical political purpose [. . .] appears to have blunted the subversive edge of
its argument', clearly establishing the illegitimacy of the British
constitution without spelling out 'the implications of the unrepre-
sentative character of Westminster government for the individual
citizen's obligation to obey the law of the land'.[55] But Maxwell
also admires the tactical canniness of this timidity, in a spirit of
common-front pragmatism: 'perhaps the caution which the
Claim demonstrates in extending its republican logic to the right
of individual resistance is a tribute to the bourgeois character of
the Committee which drafted the *Claim*': a sincere compliment
on enabling a potential breakthrough in middle-class support for
significant constitutional change.[56]

On issues of culture and identity, no special effort is made
to pacify the horses. The *Claim* goes out of its way to scotch
any 'unionist-nationalist' middle ground celebrating Scotland's
achievements within the British system, insisting that the 'zenith'
of Scottish culture in the late eighteenth-century is 'sometimes
facilely attributed to the Union, but that leaves for explanation the subsequent decline of the culture as the Union became
more established'.[57] (The Tory devolutionist Michael Fry – later
of the SNP – found the *Claim* a 'lamentable piece of work',
noting that 'at various times in the past the Scottish Conservative party has been more nationalist than its opponents'.[58])
More recent cultural developments are pressed into the narrative of neo-renaissance and vernacular empowerment familiar
from *Cencrastus* and *Radical Scotland*. Signs of linguistic revival
(the stirring of Scottish Voice) are taken as a direct index of
democratic awakening, noting that 'the indigenous languages of
Scotland, Gaelic and Scots, are being revived in education, the
arts and social life. We think it no accident that this trend has
accompanied an increasingly vigorous demand for a Scottish say
in Scotland's government.'[59]

Though largely occupied with civic-constitutional principles and structures, the *Claim* returns to matters of national identity and 'survival' in its final pages:

> Scotland faces a crisis of identity and survival. It is now being governed without consent and subject to the declared intention of having imposed upon it a radical change of outlook and behaviour pattern which it shows no sign of wanting. All questions as to whether consent should be a part of government are brushed aside. The comments of Adam Smith are put to uses which would have astonished him, Scottish history is selectively distorted and the Scots are told that their votes are lying; that they secretly love what they constantly vote against.[60]

This language draws on republican and nationalist notions of sovereignty, suggesting a programme of constitutional reform far more radical than any the *Claim* actually proposes (or than its key supporters would feel able to endorse). As James Mitchell points out, the Claim 'used the language of popular sovereignty [. . .] but in practice the proposals had no popular democratic component'.[61] Despite this, the logic of (limited, constitutional) devolution is presented as a radical demand for self-determination, scornful of monarchy and impatient of parliamentary ciphers:

> These questions [of consent and accountability] will not be adequately answered in the United Kingdom until the concentration of power that masquerades as 'the-Crown-in-Parliament' has been broken up. [. . .] Stripping away the power of politicians outside Whitehall (and incidentally increasing the powers of Ministers inside Whitehall) restores power not to the people but to the powerful. The choice we are promised in consequence will in practice be the choice the powerful choose to offer us. Through effectively answerable representative institutions we can edit the choices for ourselves.[62]

The doubleness and ambiguity of *A Claim of Right*, I suggest, stems from its need to present a limited constitutional change – centred on functions of established government – as a bold re-making of Scottish nationhood itself, a fresh new democracy where we 'ourselves' can fashion our own choices and freedoms.

The central issue of nationally distinctive governance returns to centre stage in the final sections of the *Claim*, as the problem is reframed around the urgent need to relieve the undemocratic effects of English constitutionalism: 'Scotland, if it is to remain Scotland, can no longer live with such a constitution and has nothing to hope from it. Scots have shown it more tolerance than it deserves. They must now show enterprise by starting the reform of their own government.'[63] The uncomplicated nationalism of this statement voices a radical logic before pulling back to demand the salvation of 'distinctive Scottish government' (within a reformed British constitution):

> Contesting the authority of established government is not a light matter. We would not recommend it if we did not feel that British government has so decayed that there is little hope of its being reformed within the framework of its traditional procedures. Setting up a Scottish Constitutional Convention and subsequently establishing a Scottish Assembly cannot by themselves achieve the essential reforms of British government, but they are essential if any remnant of distinctive Scottish government is to be saved.[64]

Its directness and clarity were important factors in the galvanising influence of the *Claim of Right*, but as we have seen the document speaks in several voices. Given its more stridently nationalist moments, it seems remarkable that the Labour leadership (under Donald Dewar) ultimately committed the party to the *Claim*'s key recommendation of establishing a Scottish Constitutional Convention. The potential dangers of this move were clear: Murray Elder recalls Donald Dewar 'saying that it would be like riding on the back of a tiger'.[65] Announcing Labour's support in a speech at the University of Stirling in October 1988 (shortly before the Govan by-election in November, a famous victory for Jim Sillars of the SNP), Dewar concluded 'the people must decide if they are prepared to live a little dangerously to achieve what they want'.[66] It is clear why the *Claim* and the strategy it prosecuted was distrusted by Labour unionists. The document flirts with classically nationalist arguments for popular sovereignty, but is governed by a strategic logic rather than a political ideal. It stops short and indeed veers away from the consequences of its central argument – which clearly point to an independent constitutional republic – in order to leverage its strongest 'culturalist' card, the salvation of distinctively Scottish *government*. This is not to deny the boldness of the *Claim*, and the strategy it embodies. One of its fundamental achievements was simply being accepted as a 'national' statement, issuing from a national-democratic mouth called into being by the utterance itself. (The SNP withdrew from the convention process early in 1989, fearing a Labour stitch-up in which they would be 'marginalised numerically but also politically, as the convention would discuss devolution but not independence'.[67]) As Tom Nairn notes in his commentary on *A Claim of Right*, the document

> presents itself as an 'articulation' of Scotland's need for political institutions: the voice of a common identity as yet unrepresented by institutions of its own. The task of the Constitutional Convention proposed by the *Claim* will be to design and legitimate these bodies before – 'in due course' – presenting the plan to a British government and negotiating with it. This of course assumes the Convention's right – its effective if *de facto* embodiment of the Scottish national sovereignty.[68]

In common with all constitutional starting points – we might recall Derrida's well-known exposition of 'We the people' as a performative leap of legitimation, the notional author of the American Declaration of Independence writing itself into existence[69] – there is an element of plunging ahead of accepted realities, and the Convention empowering itself to exercise 'representative' rights prior to any possible democratic endorsement. What anchors its self-legitimating gesture is precisely the central (but tacit) claim from culture and national distinctiveness, the terrain of the necessary broad-based mobilisation that will achieve real legitimation.

As we have seen, Scottish difference and distinctiveness are the 'final vocabulary' of this strategic logic: the 'givenness' and ungain-sayable qualities of Scottish cultural identity are what make the argument stick. Thus 'Scottishness', and its popular traction, is both what holds the strategy together and what it assumes in advance. We can now recognise that strategic logic as one of recognised *'identity' re-institutionalising itself*, within a larger (bruised and dis-enchanted, but not directly challenged) UK constitutional order, which retains its own traditional claims to legitimacy. The cultural and political climate had changed significantly, but this logic was essentially continuous with 1970s devolution. In 1989, Labour pro-devolutionists were pressing the newly formed Scottish Con-stitutional Convention to pursue a more substantive and ambitious scheme of self-government, arguing that 'events have bypassed the notion of devolution as conceived in the 70s',[70] and that Labour should 'seize the opportunity to [. . .] look more imaginatively at where sovereignty should reside'.[71] Scottish Labour Action went so far as to argue that a future Assembly be funded by sharing North Sea oil revenue 'with an agreed percentage going directly to the Assembly', thus directly grasping the thistle of the SNP's most memorable campaign of the early 1970s ('It's Scotland's Oil').[72] But neither revenue-sharing nor the re-imagining of UK sovereignty survived the internal compromises of the SCC itself, straining to maintain a consensus built upon the shaky Labour foundations of the 1970s.

A culture of devolution

In 1977 the SNP intellectual Stephen Maxwell partly conceded the charge (by the Labour devolutionist John P. Mackintosh) that Scottish nationalism 'lacks a foundation of cultural nationalism'.

> If [. . .] he intends to draw attention to the lack of a liter-ary-cultural base for contemporary Scottish nationalism of the sort which sustained the Nationalist movements of the nineteenth century; he is undoubtedly correct. [. . .] And in the absence of a vital literary nationalism, Mackintosh is right to refuse to be impressed by whatever claims might

be made for Scotland's traditional institutions as untapped reservoirs of cultural energy. Yet his implicit definitions of culture may be too restrictive. Cultural identity need not depend on literary culture alone. It can draw sustenance from other areas of culture, from social institutions or even, as the case of Switzerland demonstrates, from 'distinctive political ethos or institutions'.[73]

Precisely this formation was now emerging in the early 1990s: a distinctive Scottish political culture anchored by an 'ethos' of anti-Toryism, seeking institutional anchorage in a process directed by political parties and governing interests. James Mitchell notes 'the elite preoccupations' of the Constitutional Convention, reflected in the fact 'about 80% of Scotland's MPs and MEPs attended meetings and 59 of Scotland's 65 local authorities, including all Regional and Island Councils, nominated representatives to attend'.[74] Just beyond its own sphere – that is, within the inky milieu of left-nationalist periodicals and cultural reviews operating as a 'Second Front' – this activity was premised on the neo-popular mobilisation of abiding cultural 'givens' (latent national consciousness, beyond the reach of the government it legitimates). Just as importantly, this project of institutionalisation – seeking a parliamentary vehicle for the expression of 'Scotland's values' and 'Scotland's interests' – became central to the assertion of cultural difference, vitality and identity. Paradoxically, what lent Scottish literary and popular culture an aura of oppositional 'edge' in this period was precisely its symbiotic relation to a state-centred process of institutionalisation, a channel for 'dissent' endorsed by nearly all of the Scottish political establishment, and the emancipation of a 'Scottish Voice' whose political force was effectively captured in advance by the 'civic' elite.

Of particular interest is the role, both practical and symbolic, of the Scottish Trades Union Congress in binding this movement together. As 'a new form of civic politics began to gather force' in Scotland during the mid-1980s, writes Keith Aitken, the STUC served as a fulcrum of no-mandate agitation across a range of industrial and constitutional issues, 'in that what [these arguments] presented themselves as was Scotland against Thatcherism'.

In this guise, the STUC became 'the normal and the natural convenor of the assembly-in-waiting'.[75] A sort of scaffolding around which new forms of national politics took shape, the STUC's role extended to the cultural field, and served as an important vector of these arguments directly into Scottish popular culture.

'A Day for Scotland' 1990

With Scottish Arts Council backing, the STUC appointed an arts officer for the first time in 1985, 'and in the years that followed would become an enthusiastic supporter of theatre productions, exhibitions, music festivals and young talent'.[76] On Bastille Day 1990, the STUC organised a 'Day for Scotland' at Fallen Inch Field in Stirling, an outdoor pop concert and rally. 'More than 30,000 people flocked to hear the music of Runrig, Hue and Cry, and Dick Gaughan, but also to celebrate their nations hopes for itself.'[77] This was a larger and more successful version of the 1987 'Festival for Democracy' (also STUC backed), with posters advertising 'A POSITIVE CELEBRATION OF SCOTTISH LIFE – WHICH SAYS WE MUST DECIDE OUR FUTURE. NO-ONE ELSE'. A write-up in *Radical Scotland* reproduces statements by Elaine C. Smith and Pat Kane, key supporters of the event. Here we see the mainstreaming of nationalist identity politics within the common-front structures crystallising around STUC and the SCC. Smith's statement comes close to a feel-good credo for left-nationalism:

> To be Scottish, in my book, is to have a sense of enterprise coupled with an innate sense of justice, a sense of caring for our fellow man and woman and an ability to relate to others on a cultural and political level. These qualities have been demonstrated in our involvement in movements against the Poll Tax, unemployment and health and education cuts. [. . .] Our involvement with people in South Africa, Nicaragua and El Salvador has demonstrated our international abilities in helping those countries and people in the struggle for self-determination and sovereignty – it seems only right that we start that struggle for our own country now. Culturally,

there seems to be an amazing blossoming of talent – again in the face of Arts Council cuts, de-regulation of television and the influence of multinational recording companies. Yet out of that have come writers like Liz Lochhead, John Byrne, Tony Roper, Marcella Evaristi, and Dave Anderson, and theatre companies like Wildcat and the Tron.[78]

With these dubious parallels and arguments from 'innate' national qualities, Scottish demands for self-determination are re-routed via Third World liberation movements struggling against imperial aggression and apartheid.

Pat Kane's statement emphasises the diverse basis of this resurgence, arguing that a media-savvy and 'sophisticated sense of Scottishness has been developed over the Eighties: a voice both historical and contemporary, politically forthright and culturally stylish', and urging that 'the Nineties must continue the development of a plural and principled national identity'.[79] The real emotional heft of 'the rise of the Scottish Voice', however, expresses a nationhood anchored in the industrial past, positioned as the national 'truth' too long distorted by 'clouds of Scotch myth'. This emphasis is in keeping with a rock festival whose signature moment came as the STUC's president, Clive Lewis, 'stepped onto the spotlit stage in his son's leather jacket and set up a chant of "Ravenscraig, Ravenscraig" in which the crowd thunderously joined'.[80] Here is 'vernacular' Scottishness being amplified to a mass audience. Kane continues:

> The experiences of the urban working classes are a major part of this voicing of Scotland. Presaged in the Seventies by comedians like Billy Connolly and charismatic union leaders like Jimmy Reid, the Eighties saw a flourishing of proletarian and socialist images of Scotland – in the theatre, with Wildcat's propagandist musicals or 7:84's radical history; in literature, with such stylistically diverse writers as William McIlvanney, James Kelman and Liz Lochhead taking working-class experience as their natural subject; and in art, with painters like Ken Currie and Peter Howson simultaneously idealising and analysing the Scottish worker.[81]

The resulting 'elision between political and cultural representation', in Kane's terms, becomes a rubric for asserting national working-classness. This historic 'meeting of Scottish artists under a commitment to self-determination' encapsulates the success of the Scottish political elite in claiming a 'radical' national-popular warrant for its project of distinctive government; a key episode in the parallel struggle to supply 'intellectual patriots' with a 'validating Popular Culture', as Thom Cross had playfully argued in a *Radical Scotland* satire published a few months earlier.[82]

'Self-Determination and Power' 1990

Needless to say, not all Scottish artists could be aligned with this movement; indeed, several artists claimed *by* the movement were involved in cultural activism running counter to efforts to posit 'innate' Scottish values as the justification for new state structures. Six months prior to the 'Day for Scotland', a major event in radical circles was held at the Pearce Institute in Govan: 'Self-Determination and Power'. This was a two-day programme of workshops, discussion groups and lectures co-organised by *Edinburgh Review*, *Scottish Child* magazine and the Free University (an autonomous education project led by Peter Kravitz, editor of *Edinburgh Review*). James Kelman was heavily involved in planning and organising the event, whose star attractions were Noam Chomsky and George E. Davie.[83] A *Radical Scotland* report on the event several months later directly questions the 'common viewpoint that in Scotland something called self-determination is relevant and necessary'. The organisers' anarchist orientation comes swiftly to the fore as Lorna Waite highlights 'the inscribed power relations of a centralised State' maintaining an 'illusion of democracy'.[84] Here there is no fond embrace of civic bodies claiming to embody a heart-warming national identity:

> Institutional structures with many different functions indirectly collude with the State in sustaining forms of oppression whether it be education, party politics, a corporate press, or male-dominated trade unions. [. . .] Disillusionment with the real inadequacy of present oppositional

structures was one of the strong feelings that emerged from
the event as a whole. [. . .] Calls for everyone in Scotland
to fight together, achieve independence and freedom for
Scotland are all very well and good but not terribly helpful
to those who share a distaste for the alignment of s-d [self-
determination] with nationalism and the insidious prospect
of replacing one set of party bosses with another. It is even
more disastrous for those who are committed to an intellectual and practical distrust for any political party and associated parliamentary structures. [. . .] One could think of
the central point therefore being the debate around 's-d
[self-determination] against the State'.[85]

Thus, even within the pages of *Radical Scotland* and *Edinburgh
Review*, the ideal of 'self-determination' was being contested
between groups whose cultural politics were centred on embryonic state structures (with 'Scottish Voice' as their channel of
democratic legitimation) and those bringing independent critical,
political and aesthetic languages to bear on Scottish artwork and
experience in this period.

James Kelman became a familiar and pivotal figure in reviews
such as *Edinburgh Review*, uniting Kravitz's interest in class politics and anarchism with an abiding focus on matters of language and expression. That Kelman's fiction stages a politics of
personal authenticity within 'objective' social conflict becomes
an inviting peg on which to hang his wider relevance. Indeed,
Linda Gunn and Alistair McCleery note that 'Kelman could be
said to embody the identity that *Edinburgh Review* was striv-
ing for from 1984; he dominates, while retaining the status of
an outsider in many ways, the "burgeoning of the arts" of the
inter-referenda period (although Gray's *Lanark* is often cited as
its starting point)'.[86] But viewed from another angle, Kelman's
work jars with cultural nation-building, holding out for a more
radical and anti-statist form of 'self-determination'. His writing
demonstrates with especial clarity that reading Scottish literature
in the terms of the 'consensus' traced above tends to *release,
and lock*, Scottish cultural production into reified postures of
'representation'.

The dubious politics of national representation are the target of Kelman's satirical essay 'Let the wind blow high let the wind blow low', written in the aftermath of the 1992 general election. The re-elected Major government quickly restated its firm opposition to devolution despite the fact, in Kelman's words, that 'parties advocating Home Rule or independence had won the support of 75 per cent of the electorate and 85 per cent of the seats in Scotland'.[87] This directly echoes earlier CSA rhetoric, but Kelman is scathing about efforts to resolve such a blatant injustice from within the horizon of parliamentary representation, and mocks the 'pragmatism' counselled by the cross-party Scottish Constitutional Convention (CSA's successor body):

> The current debate on self determination has degenerated into one of these Bipartisan Issues that crop up every now and again on matters of National Importance, such as wars and acts of god. 'Pure' politics are forced to the sidelines. It becomes bad form to discuss one's differences. Unity is the watchword. It isn't a time for awkward questions. Those who persist are shown up as perverse, slightly bammy, crackpots – or occasionally as unpatriotic. What we discuss is what we are allowed to discuss.[88]

In other words, the 'debate' on self-determination requires its own disciplined negation. Kelman's parody of the polite constitutionalism of the SCC campaign highlights the shared emptiness of electoral 'solidarity' – the duty to maintain Labour's 'national' mandate – and theatrical displays of Scottish 'consensus'. Seeking recognition within the terms of established power, it is necessary to adopt its forms and norms:

> We shall be asked to retain our collective strength in a unified cross-party struggle, yielding not to easy options, nor to undignified posturing, nor to rash action, nor to impolite hectoring, nor to self righteous tubthumping; propriety will become the mark of the movement. When we march forward we shall march solidly, not breaking ranks; we shall comb our hair and wear smart leather shoes, dress

in suits and shirts and ties – formal highland attire will not
be frowned upon – this includes females and those from an
ethnic background, for this way forward will unite everybody regardless of gender, race, creed or culture and will
be led by a multifarious but patriotic group of notables:
various party leaders, media personalities and constitutional
experts; S.T.U.C. full-timers, representatives from the different religions – priests, ministers, mullahs, rabbis etc. – all
striding arm-in-arm with bright-new-dawns glistening on
our rubicund faces.[89]

As this vision develops, a sharp irony emerges between the unity
and diversity of the assembled representatives, and the highly
indirect and hyper-mediated character of democratic protest: 'We
shall march on Westminster itself, the entire voting population
of Scotland, and when we arrive we shall demand of U.K. ruling
authority that they pay heed to our unified cry for self determination. Our demand shall be carried by our appointed representatives, appointed by and from the patriotic group of notables.'[90]
The scenario gains in outlandish momentum, and the absurd
quality of (tactically, gradually) 'demanding' national democratic
recognition via proxies of proxies (a Constitutional Convention
consisting mainly of elected MPs) becomes un-ignorable:

> And if Her Majesty's Government does not listen why then
> our All-Scotland representation shall further remind her
> Majesty's Government that a mandate exists, and what's
> more they have it [. . .] And if they don't pay heed to us
> now then this is our very last word and we cannot vouch
> for our continued participation in the rules and proce-
> dures of state as laid down in 1707 by Their Forefathers in
> association with Our Forefathers, the then ruling author-
> ity of Scotland. And by the Gude Lord Jasus the entire
> voting population would just damn well carry on waiting
> right there on this pavement and see what Her Majesty's
> Government was going to do about that![91]

Despite the strength of their electoral mandate, those charged
with 'All-Scotland representation' are figured as incapable of

extra-procedural *action*; the height of their defiance is to 'carry on waiting until they give us an answer, that'll show them the measure of our resolve'.[92] All the democratic energies invested in this show of unity are seemingly exhausted by the humble request that it be acknowledged. In this fantasy, all the 'Scottish Voice' is capable of expressing – the 'mandate' of 'identity' itself – is a plea for recognition by the state apparatus in whose image it has been formed.

Conclusion: culture strikes and spectacle

In an essay of 1992 Pat Kane was upbeat about the influence of cultural figures in mobilising public support for Scottish self-government:

> one watched with interest, in the late eighties and nineties, as other interventions from musicians, writers, actors began to spread the issue of strong Scottish autonomy across different screens and surfaces, putting an unaccustomed nationalist grit into contexts of leisure consumption – TV shows, concerts, newspapers. In so far as polls measured anything, they registered over this period a burgeoning popular sense of the rights of Scotland as a nation, politically, economically and culturally. It seemed natural to assume that this nationalist mood had been partly fuelled by the acts of such Scottish 'cultural-politicians'.[93]

But there were other voices on the Scottish cultural scene who took sharp exception to this story. In a 1993 essay in *Edinburgh Review* Andrew O'Hagan takes aim at the feel-good communitarianism he associates with Kane's cultural politics, whose faults are partly those of the mass-media channels in which he operates, trading in specious claims to recover 'authentic' national language, memory and attitude:

> Something of a community of pop singers and bands has gathered around the issue of Scottish independence. Where English and American rockers have been singing about love, bubble-gum and urban life for years, these Scottish

popsters can't get away from their determination to overcome their linguistic expression problems and *say* something. Pat Kane, the singer with Hue and Cry, bends over
backwards trying to render the socio-linguistic contradictions of the here and now by lingering around the doorways
of old tenements and yodeling fairly juiceless 3-minute pop
songs, revelling in the ulterior glory of Glasgow's superior
reality. 'Ma home toon' and 'ma wee wean' run Kane's
show: he's as sentimental as a lollipop and his often quoted
negative dialectics sit oddly with his game of twisting modern Scottish experience into braids of cultural stereotype.[94]

This is hostile but not groundless criticism, focused on the non-
representative quality of nationalist popular culture devised for
'leisure consumption', trading on stereotype and false unities. The
very common-frontism that created a platform for the 'cultural-
politicians' of devolution generated a reified idiom of Scottishness
that severely restricted, rather than liberating, the scope of 'national'
political expression – evacuating 'Scottish culture' of all meaning
other than its own affirmation. In this vein O'Hagan argues that the
reliance of the neo-nationalist imaginary on familiar and romantic
urban iconography, gilding the wound of post-industrial want, is
in fact a betrayal of history by the shallow satisfactions of popular
nostalgia:

> Like the photographer Oscar Marzaroli (who, alongside
> Deacon Blue and William McIllvanney is praised by Pat
> Kane for bearing 'visual witness to industrial change'), he
> sees something wonderfully genuine and poetic in images
> of snottery-nosed Gorbals weans tottering around in their
> mothers' high-heels. [. . .] Those Glasgow kids look good
> on Athena postcards (and that's one type of modernity)
> but they were helplessly toddling on their way from over-
> crowded tenements to dangerous high-risers in a handful of
> years (and that's another).[95]

The problem is especially acute in the mass-media environment where this movement was most influential. In his 1992

essay, Kane recounts a disagreement with a BBC producer over his terms of reference in a TV arts documentary. Kane's script argued that 'the growing political nationalism of Scottish musicians (and Scottish culture in general) during the eighties was a reaction to Thatcher's explicit English nationalism', while the series producer insisted on 'Thatcherism' alone, for fear of 'annoying them down in Wimbledon'.[96] Kane draws a suggestive wider meaning from this experience:

> My distinction between 'Thatcher's English nationalism' and 'Thatcherism' precisely recognised the growing nationalist explicitness of Scottish popular opinion (corroborated by fistfuls of opinion polls at the time). To elide this distinction was to make Scottish musicians' attitudes diffusely anti-Establishment, rather than part of a growing, positive awareness of being socialist-through-Scottishness.[97]

The 'elision' Kane protests – the alleged de-nationalising of Scottish artistic dissent – is, in fact, an undoing of the prior conflation we have been tracing over the past two chapters, where Scottishness implies a political and ideological commitment (to self-government) premised on ersatz proletarian nationality. These very representational dynamics look different after the 1992 election result, viewed by Kane as a victory for the swallowing of democracy by consumer media. Kane writes of voters 'passively mesmerized by the spectacle, and taking their orders from it', and of Scotland lacking the critical mass necessary to generate arguments for independence 'genuinely "independent" of the messages coming from the media'.[98] Following the disappointing result, he argues, pro-devolution campaigns such as Scotland United must be re-focused on '"people power" and community mobilisation':

> For me, the election signalled the end of my over-estimation of the powers of cultural politics, and of attempts to use the media to bind together collectivities for radical change in Scotland. The 'imaginary community' of nationhood – that consensus of values which gives a majority endorsement to left-of-centre policies in

Scotland – is not enough on its own; either as something expressed infrequently and abstractly through parliamentary democracy, or as the background to our daily dealings with each other in Scottish life.[99]

Here Kane broadly accords with O'Hagan's critique, seeing the need to press beyond fine statements and the play of media representations to grapple with what lies beneath. But the solidity of that underlying 'consensus of values' is not truly in question: Kane seems not to query whether Scotland's leftish majority is a mirage *generated by* the electoral system – another, more respectable game of representations. Re-committing his energies to 'real', effective institutions in place of media spectacle – echoing the Foulkes Memorandum of 1983, Kane suggests 'we must begin to put our imaginings and ideals into some kind of practice – organising and holding a referendum, non-cooperation with Westminster laws and edicts, acting as if we were prepared to defend our values' – Kane posits a forum in which to *enact* 'Scottish values' which was not also the site of their constitution *as* 'Scottish values'.[100] Eliding the structures with the content of self-government – the parliament with national-societal ethos – condenses the broader conflation of democracy and identity we have traced to this point.

Many writers and artists directly identified with this project. In a 1992 *Chapman* essay Robert Alan Jamieson noted that 'in the edition of *Scotland on Sunday* immediately after the April 9th debacle, Cairns Craig was quoted as saying that Scotland had declared cultural independence ten years ago. I thought, yes, but who noticed?'[101] This is a symptomatic moment in the story of 'cultural devolution', in which the movement comes very close to voicing its inner paradox: an elite movement of literary intellectuals has declared itself so far in the vanguard, and yet so authentically representative of the nation, Scottish society at large has failed to register the momentous shift effected in the domain of 'culture'. But in a sense this position was always assumed: nothing the literary intellectuals could say, write or do would change the salience of 'Scottish' within the statist constitutional discourse, and thus there was no need or possibility to *transform* Scotland through cultural production. Thus, Jamieson continues, there is need for a more overt and disruptive political statement of the 'cultural' consensus, a gesture drawing on the tradition of nationalist pledges, petitions and – more tellingly – strategies drawn from industrial conflict:

> In the months since then, monitoring the attempts to win a referendum out of a government that clearly has no intention of providing one, the seed sown has germinated. Scotland, I believe, must make a *formal* declaration of cultural independence. Or rather:
> A FORMAL DECLARATION
> OF CULTURAL INDEPENDENCE.
> The date could not be better selected than 1996, to coincide with the bicentenary of the death of Burns and the centenary of Gladstone's aborted bill, which would have provided an assembly a century ago. [. . .] For the duration of that year, let Scotland's artists withdraw from London as an example to its MPs, in a kind of cultural strike. For the duration of that year, let us celebrate Scotland's diversity-in-unity.[102]

Here is the apogee of neo-popular cultural devolution, overtly conceiving 'creative' nationhood in class terms. Scotland's artists can be understood as a trade union bound by common interests, empowered to withdraw their labour (cultural representation) from an uncaring employer ('London') who ignores their demand for greater workers' control. Perhaps inevitably, the national-representative basis of this solidarity is devoid of specific content ('Scottishness is not the cause of Scottish culture nor indeed its effect. It is the free essence of humanity, but fixed in a particular form by a particular locality'[103]), and its distinctive qualia are swiftly ushered from the chancy domain of culture to the sturdier toeholds of geography:

> The land pre-exists human habitation. Essential Scottish-ness, as I have used the term above, is a deep feeling for that land and its situation in relation to the rest of the world, not rooted in the past but in the present moment, in our

individual perceptions of what this land is and has been to the peoples who have lived here over the centuries – and what it could be.[104]

Thus, the political claims of 'Scottish culture' in its mobilised and interventionist mode boil down to the insistence that *the national category has a referent*, from which follow certain rights to self-government:

> Scotland, the place, exists. Its culture grows out of the experience of living in that place and that experience is diverse, but can be unified in the word *Scotland*, if we can make it meaningful, so that all its constituent parts feel included. That meaning must depend to some degree on freedom to pursue its own political objectives. Without an assembly, the meaning of *Scotland* is indistinct.[105]

Scotland is a real 'place'; but not a meaningful nation while it lacks democratic institutions of self-determination. Thus the very ideal of Scottishness rings hollow until the representative functions of 'culture' have been superseded by the machinery of distinctive governance. Scotland is a Scottish Parliament or it is nothing.

Such was the logic of the identitarian movement of the late 1980s and early 1990s, when many 'cultural-politicians' grew increasingly assertive in their claims to representative power (while others grew increasingly sceptical). Viewed in these terms, there was no dramatic concession by 'the elite' in the face of 'radical' neo-popular pressure channelled by cultural figures and activist intellectuals. Devolution was effected by and through elite rule, as the institutionalisation of the all-Scotland civic ethic embodied by CSA, 'Scotland United' and other home rule campaigns. How could a truly 'national' story explaining this process, while grounding it in the lived experience of citizens, be told? This is the novelistic problem explored in the next chapter.

Notes

1. Cairns Craig, 'Scotland 10 years on (the changes that took place while Rip Mac Winkle slept)', *Radical Scotland*, 37 (February–March 1989), pp. 8–11 (p. 9).
2. Ibid. p. 9.
3. Ibid. p. 9.
4. Ibid. p. 9.
5. Ibid. p. 9.
6. Ibid. pp. 9–10.
7. Ibid. p. 10.
8. Craig, *Intending Scotland*, p. 69.
9. Craig, 'Scotland 10 years on', p. 10.
10. Ibid. p. 10.
11. Dixon, 'Notes from the underground', p. 119.
12. Tierney, 'Giving with one hand', p. 735.
13. 'Hoping for the best . . . preparing for the worst' [Editorial], *Radical Scotland*, 25 (February–March 1987), pp. 9–11 (p. 11).
14. McLean, *Getting it Together*, p. 98.
15. 'Responding to Doomsday' [Editorial], *Radical Scotland*, 28 (August–September 1987), p. 3.
16. Isobel Lindsay, 'Divergent trends', *Radical Scotland*, 29 (October–November 1987), pp. 14–15 (p. 14).
17. See Torrance, *'We in Scotland'*.
18. Lindsay, 'Divergent trends', p. 14.
19. Brand, 'Defeat and renewal: the Scottish National Party in the 1980s', p. 7.
20. Deacon, 'Adopting conventional wisdom', p. 64.
21. Ibid. p. 102.
22. Macwhirter, 'After Doomsday', p. 23.
23. Jim Ross, 'Grasping the Doomsday nettle – methodically', *Radical Scotland,* 30 (December 1987–January 1988), pp. 6-9 (p. 6).
24. Ibid. p. 6.
25. Ibid. pp. 6–7.
26. Ibid. p. 7. Emphasis in original.
27. Craig, 'Unsettled will', p. 31.
28. Marr, *The Battle for Scotland*, p. 198.
29. Geekie and Levy, 'Devolution and the tartanisation of the Labour Party', p. 403.
30. Mitchell, *The Scottish Question*, p. 228.

31. Deacon, 'Adopting conventional wisdom', p. 66. Kinnock quoted in Burns, *Poll Tax Rebellion*, p. 40.
32. Macwhirter, 'After Doomsday', p. 24.
33. Quoted by Torrance, *'We in Scotland'*, p. 189.
34. Geekie and Levy, 'Devolution and the tartanisation of the Labour Party', p. 404.
35. Mitchell, 'The evolution of devolution', p. 486.
36. 'Editorial', *Edinburgh Review*, 68–9 (1984), p. 3.
37. Ibid. p. 3.
38. Gunn and McCleery, 'Wasps in a jam jar', p. 45.
39. Peter Kravitz, 'It began slowly, with a distinct interval between each blow . . . or, Towards a parallel culture', *Edinburgh Review*, 80–1 (1988), pp. 3–8 (p. 8).
40. Ibid. p. 4.
41. Ibid. p. 8.
42. 'Editorial', *Edinburgh Review*, 76 (February 1987), pp. 3–4 (p. 4).
43. 'Editorial', *Edinburgh Review*, 75 (November 1986), pp. 3–5 (p. 5).
44. Ibid. p. 3.
45. Peter Kravitz, 'Nations can't be beautiful, only people can', *Edinburgh Review*, 82 (Winter 1989), pp. 5–8 (p. 5, p. 8).
46. Ibid. p. 5.
47. Gunn and McCleery, 'Wasps in a jam jar', pp. 47–8.
48. Kravitz, 'Nations can't be beautiful', p. 8.
49. McLean, *Getting it Together*, p. 107.
50. Edwards (ed.), *A Claim of Right for Scotland*, p. 13. Hereafter, references to the 1988 *Claim of Right* document will not be attributed to Edwards, who edited the published version with accompanying commentaries in 1989. The *Claim of Right* itself (pp. 1–53 of the edited book) is presented without an author, as the 'Report of the Constitutional Steering Committee, Presented to the Campaign for a Scottish Assembly, Edinburgh July 1988'.
51. *A Claim of Right*, pp. 13–14.
52. Ibid. p. 14.
53. Ibid. p. 14.
54. James G. Kellas, 'Restless natives' [reviewing *A Claim of Right for Scotland*], *Radical Scotland*, 39 (June–July 1989), p. 37 (p. 37).
55. Maxwell, 'Scotland's Claim of Right', p. 121.
56. Ibid. p. 122
57. *A Claim of Right*, p. 14.
58. Michael Fry, 'A claim of wrong', pp. 96, 93. See also Kidd, *Union and Unionisms*.

59. *A Claim of Right*, p. 14.
60. Ibid. p. 51.
61. Mitchell, 'Factions, tendencies and consensus in the SNP in the 1980s', p. 59.
62. *A Claim of Right*, p. 51.
63. Ibid, p. 52.
64. Ibid. pp. 52–3.
65. Elder, 'A Scottish Labour leader', p. 87.
66. Stewart, *The Path to Devolution and Change*, p. 212.
67. Lynch, *SNP: The History of the Scottish National Party*, pp. 195–6.
68. Nairn, 'The timeless girn', p. 164.
69. See Derrida, 'Declarations of independence'.
70. Scottish Labour, 'Devolution is dead: the constitutional status of the Assembly' [Scottish Labour Action report], undated, but shortly after the formation of the Scottish Constitutional Convention in spring 1989.
71. Scottish Labour, 'Labour and a Constitutional Convention' [Scottish Labour Action report], undated, but probably July 1989.
72. Scottish Labour, 'Devolution is dead'.
73. Maxwell, 'The trouble with John P. Mackintosh', p. 145.
74. Mitchell, *Strategies for Self-Government*, p. 130.
75. Aitken, *The Bairns O' Adam*, p. 292.
76. Ibid. p. 296.
77. Ibid. p. 296.
78. Elaine C. Smith, 'A Day for Scotland', *Radical Scotland*, 46 (August–September 1990), pp. 14–15 (p. 14).
79. Pat Kane, 'A Day for Scotland', *Radical Scotland*, 46 (August–September 1990), p. 15.
80. Aitken, *The Bairns O' Adam*, p. 296.
81. Kane, 'A Day for Scotland', p. 15.
82. Thom Cross, 'Another look at the thistle (a discussion worth a dram)', *Radical Scotland*, 41 (October–November 1989), pp. 28–9.
83. For much more on Kelman's involvement in the event, see Miller and Rodger, *The Red Cockatoo*.
84. Lorna Waite, 'Self-determination and power event', *Radical Scotland*, 44 (April–May 1990), pp. 26–7 (p. 26).
85. Ibid. pp. 26–7.
86. Gunn and McCleery, 'Wasps in a jam jar', p. 50.
87. Devine, *The Scottish Nation 1700–2000*, p. 613.
88. Kelman, 'Let the wind blow high let the wind blow low', p. 86.
89. Ibid. p. 86.

90. Ibid. p. 86.

91. Ibid. p. 86.

92. Ibid. p. 91.

93. Kane, 'Banality, solidarity, spectacle', p. 128.

94. Andrew O'Hagan, 'Homing: the anti-kailyard aesthetic of Bill Douglas', *Edinburgh Review*, 89 (Spring 1993), pp. 75–85 (p. 81).

95. Ibid. p. 81.

96. Kane, 'Banality, solidarity, spectacle', p. 126.

97. Ibid. pp. 126–7.

98. Ibid. p. 130.

99. Ibid. p. 130.

100. Ibid. pp. 130–1.

101. Robert Alan Jamieson, 'MacDiarmid's spirit burns on', *Chapman*, 69–70 (Autumn 1992), pp. 3–8 (pp. 6–7).

102. Ibid. p. 7.

103. Ibid. p. 7.

104. Ibid. p. 7.

105. Ibid. p. 8.

5

And the Land Lay Still

Curating Devolution with James Robertson

Radical Scotland published its final issue in the summer of 1991, with an editorial noting that 'the Scottish political situation has developed so much in the years of the magazine's existence that the uniqueness of RS and its line has been overtaken by events'.[1] Having largely achieved the strategic goals set out by Christopher Harvie in 1983 – cementing the discursive space and electoral logic of a 'Scottish devolutionist left', organising home rule politics as 'a "popular front" against the Tories', forging 'a Scottish politics so dislocated from Westminster's norms that Scottish representatives are forced into a national role'[2] – there was good reason to feel the argument had been won: 'the case for self-government – and for a separate Scottish political and cultural identity – has been accepted in all but the darkest corners of Scotland'.[3] Such confidence might seem premature given John Major's electoral victory in April 1992 (when the Scottish Tories arrested the Doomsday trajectory by re-gaining a seat from Labour), but, as Jonathan Hearn notes, 'there is substance to the general argument that the [pro-devolution] intelligentsia-media milieu had grown tremendously' in this period.[4]

This milieu was clearly conscious of its success, and the valedictory editorial of the final issue was preceded by an earlier toast to the magazine's historic achievement in August/September 1990. Its editor and fulcrum, Alan Lawson, reflected on the need to record for posterity the developments in which *Radical Scotland* had played a central role. Taking stock of the 1980s, Lawson worried that 'no-one has so far put pen to paper (or fingers to keys) to give us "the definitive story" of the past ten years in Scottish political life, setting it in the context of the great cultural changes which occurred during that decade'.[5] A great many political studies, memoirs and diaries had appeared, but none with the required scope and narrative drive. First-hand knowledge was a second problem: the need for such a writer to be intimately acquainted with the key developments and personalities, with ready access to documents and primary sources. But given the unreliable condition of Scottish party archives and newspaper indexing, Lawson argued, this effectively narrowed the field of potential chroniclers to the participants themselves: 'unless someone has been "amongst us taking notes", then the task of writing up what *really* happened in Scottish political life in the eighties will be made very much harder'.[6] The anticipated conclusion of this story – a self-governing Scotland – raises the stakes of this task, elevating it from the terrain of political history to national memory:

> If the next General Election does bring forward self-government for Scotland in some form, then the story of how, why, and by whom that came about will surely be a piece of our national experience which deserves, indeed *requires*, to be properly told. Yet as time passes, as memories grow fainter, as individuals depart the political stage, the more difficult it will be to tell the tale with real accuracy and with full understanding.[7]

As with a victory lap at the Olympic games, the addition of a flag transforms the achievement of a small group of the eccentrically committed into a matter of national honour and responsibility.

This chapter explores a range of narrative problems implicit to the 'story of devolution', and various approaches to addressing them in the writing of James Robertson (a member of the *Radical Scotland* editorial collective and a frequent contributor to the magazine). Lawson's piece of conjectural history in 1990 – a glance backward over ripening events yet to reach fruition – invites several observations relevant to Robertson's fiction of devolution. First, even for a figure at the heart of the home rule movement – party to its private and public faces, acutely conscious of its importance – there is an abiding lack of narrative satisfaction in the saga of

Scottish devolution. The story is missing something, Lawson admits: a galvanising moment, character or 'change of such significance as would encourage a potential writer to say "right, that's it," and set about writing, researching, analysing across the whole spectrum'.[8] Second, home rule activists recognise that their mission cannot be truly fulfilled without *entering national memory* and becoming part of Scotland's historical self-knowledge. It is one thing to refashion Scotland's political claims on the terms, and via the institutions, of the political class; it is another to securely lodge this achievement in the 'common knowledge' of the nation at large. This problem derives from another. As Lawson notes, a relatively small number of activists, intellectuals and political operators drove events and had the depth of personal experience necessary to write the inside story of devolution 'with real accuracy and understanding'. And yet the partisan intensity of their involvement – minute-takers at a hundred small meetings, trusted insiders party to gossip and hearsay – ill-equips them to tell this story on the broad national scale of its ultimate significance.

Each of these dilemmas will re-emerge as we consider the most ambitious and successful attempt to narrate Scottish devolution, James Robertson's epic 2010 novel *And the Land Lay Still*. Looking back on the fictionalised version of *Radical Scotland* in the novel, Robertson's central character (and in this scene, his alter ego) modestly notes that

> There were other, more visible, magazines with similar agendas that achieved much more in political terms, but Mike still feels a touch of pride when he looks at a copy of *Root & Branch*. And yet the argument that was conducted in its pages, as it was in the pages of those other journals, should not have been necessary. What was it again? It was, in the end, so convincingly won that it is hard to reconstruct it.[9]

This labour of reconstruction, and its complex narrative problems, are the subject of this chapter. Here we break from the chronological focus of the preceding chapters and turn our attention to the retrospective gaze: efforts to make a palatable, effective and democratically *involving* story from the political and cultural developments charted thus far.

James Robertson and the 'Republic of the Mind'

The figure 'among us, taking notes' was James Robertson, who became involved with the *Radical Scotland* collective during the late 1980s, while writing an Edinburgh PhD in history on 'The construction and expression of Scottish patriotism in the Works of Walter Scott'. This study – which argues that Scott's writings 'were always designed to enhance the accommodation of Scotland in the British present by locating the Scottish sense of identity in the past, where it could pose only a rhetorical threat [. . .] to political and social stability' – was an ideal preparation for his subsequent career as Scotland's leading historical novelist.[10] By the early 1990s Robertson was deeply engaged in pro-devolution politics and publishing rhetorically nuanced fiction about these events even as they unfolded. We can better grasp the aims and difficulties of *And the Land Lay Still* if we first examine an important precursor first published in Robertson's 1993 collection *The Ragged Man's Complaint*.

'Republic of the Mind' opens with a social gathering to mark the 1992 general election, and the mounting frustration of Robert and Kate as the results come in:

> There were seven or eight of them, and they had come to celebrate. It was understood that, even should the Tories get back in overall, they would be annihilated in Scotland. This would force a constitutional crisis. But only a few hours had passed since the polls had closed and already Scotland was snatching ifs and buts from the jaws of certainty.[11]

In a burst of frustration Kate hurls a wine bottle through the television set, where it remains implanted as 'a monument to the moment when they left the politicians behind; a regrettable but glorious moment to be forever relived'.[12] Going 'beyond the politicians' is the story's central motif, figured as the mental surpassing of failed systems and limiting beliefs. After the election, Robert increasingly withdraws himself from the world reported by television and transports himself 'to the republic of the mind. The politicians could follow when they were ready. Robert was there, and Kate a lot of the time, and also many of their friends, although they didn't always know it.'[13] This imaginative vanguard may be read as a condensation of the 'cultural devolution' thesis, but figured as escape rather than transformation. On his 'return' from one mental sojourn, Kate asks 'Where is it you go to?': 'Och, just away. I just think what a waste of time it is, having to wait to be a normal country, having to waste all this energy identifying ourselves. So I bugger off anyway. To the Scottish republic of the mind.'[14] This 'republic' is viable at the level of allegory or thought-experiment, but cannot be rendered as a shareable reality. Robertson does not attempt to convey the human texture of this transformed national condition, and largely for this reason there is a sense of the 'alternative' being only half-chosen, a mental possibility never fully entertained by either the character or the writer. In 1992 the commitment to that alternate reality remains conceptual, akin to Robert's 'accepting' and un-bigoted attitude to a homosexual overture he politely declines later in the story; something theoretically possible but not a realistic option.

Kate's own escape takes a different form: she is less inclined to inhabit a hazy future than to connect the present moment to fabled episodes in the national past. Grisly details of the execution of Mary, Queen of Scots both attract and repel a sense of identification: 'It was four centuries ago and these people were the most important people in the land. And yet that was all they were, just people. The game they played – treaties, alliances, invasions, marriages, plots, executions – was a game of chess with human beings for the pieces.'[15] Focusing on the severed head of Mary Stuart – 'she had learned to think of her by that name, it made her more human somehow' – generates one kind of gory empathy, but the Scotland in which Mary moved and ruled recedes ever further into a storybook realm: 'Queens, castles, clerics and knights, and, somewhere else, in a separate world again, cities full of pawns, a countryside dotted with pawn peasants'.[16] The national terrain that connects Kate to Mary, on whatever dubious terms (she 'wasn't into royalty'), is beyond imagining, and so is the rest of the dynastic chess-game belaboured in the history books.[17] We are left with the iconic image of the beheaded queen as an emblem of personal tragedy, a flash of horror effectively isolated from the broader national story. It seems impossible to connect to Mary on a human scale without tearing her from that larger fable, and impossible to integrate Kate's romantic-picturesque mode of national memory with the arid political chatter which defines Robert's imagined future republic.

Midway through the story, Robert receives news of his father's death, and tries to collect his thoughts in a local pub. He is joined by a quiet older man sitting nearby, and the talk falls instantly to plans for water privatisation, leading swiftly to constitutional politics:

> 'The trouble is', [the man] said, 'we're powerless because there's too many issues. If water was the only thing on the agenda they wouldn't have a chance. Or if it was just about having our own parliament – if that was the only issue we'd have it by now. But it's not, we keep having to try to get Labour in down there as well, to, like, minimise the damage. Ken what I mean?'
>
> 'Aye,' said Robert. He was thinking how nobody ever assumed their neighbour was a Tory in a public house in Scotland. 'But self-government is the one unifying issue. If we had the parliament we could deal with the other issues the way we wanted.'[18]

Not just one priority among others, a Scottish Parliament represents the very possibility of choosing what matters and demands attention. As the chat develops Robert is 'aware that his dad had come into the conversation. He should tell the guy he was dead', but steers the discussion away from his own emotional turmoil and toward the imaginative terrain of national consciousness. Confiding to the man that 'as far as possible I live life as if the republic's here already', Robert explains: 'I don't see what else to do. I mean, if your mind's already arrived there, if you're psychologically and emotionally and culturally in that other place, it's just tearing yourself apart getting frustrated about the fact that the actuality is different.'[19] His companion objects that 'there's folk out there with fungus on the walls and no job and their benefit getting cut and fuck knows what else – I don't think your wee nirvana's going to help them much', to which Robert retorts 'neither are the politicians. Politics has failed these people. [. . .] They can forget about politics because the political system as presently constituted has forgotten about them.'[20] It follows that re-constituting Scottish democracy will involve a national act of social remembrance: a re-founding of the political imaginary centred on the lives of 'these people' (the voiceless Scottish poor), and not the stolid fixations of party politics. Yet Robert, like Kate, cannot grapple with history as lived experience, or ground his anger and refusal in a social reality outside (or underlying) the electoral chess-board.

In this devolutionary fiction vast aggregates of private belief, rendered as textbook 'historical forces', must substitute for the texture of living community. The most mundane political hopes ('we keep having to try to get Labour in down there as well') are offered as the imaginative means of 'going beyond' this selfsame mentality. Instead of a fresh possible Scotland that achieves some distance from electoral self-thwarting, we visit instead a curiously idealised version of the existing order in which 'leaving the politicians behind' means *turning everyone into politicians*: a counter-escapist utopia where ordinary social life has been emptied of everything but the intractable banalities of political strategy.

Less than whole

After the funeral of Robert's father, Kate hopes to take him away for a few days, 'to be somewhere else'. As in a novelised history, the personal is supercharged with collective significance.

> And she thought of that curious limbo they were in, that place between what they had and what they sought. They were whole people but they were less than whole because of how their country was. Yet she felt a confidence in herself, that she had reached an understanding of the situation.

This was only a temporary lull. [. . .] What she recognised in the hopelessness of the politics was her own hope, her complete inability to give up. That's the thing we have, she thought, the unbeatable hand that we never play but that we always hold, the thing that they just don't understand. All we are doing is waiting.[21]

Robert is 'going beyond', but clinging fixedly to the rails of nationalist destiny; Kate is 'waiting' for the fruition of a will that cannot be lost or denied. The present situation cannot be met on its own terms, but can (and must) be referred to a higher plane of faith and belief. On these terms 'leaving the politicians behind' takes on a quasi-mystical air, where the mismatch between inward escape and collective liberation can be suitably finessed. Although the notion of a 'Scottish republic of the mind' flirts with reducing self-government to a pipe-dream, it also highlights the overarching importance – and chimerical slipperiness – of national consciousness:

It was more than some utopian fantasy about society. It filled the gap between actuality and possibilities of all kinds. [. . .] The novelist Neil Gunn had the concept – the atom of delight – a state of contentment and completeness – '*I came upon myself sitting there.*' The republic was something like that, except it was constant, and for everybody. It was a state of being in which all the people understood themselves, and what they were doing, and why they were where they were.[22]

This imagined plenitude of national being, flushed with Heideggerian 'rightness', is a condition of totalised community which suspends history and struggle. It is realised inside the individual, by an act of sovereign identification with the national mythos which effects a spiritual *deliverance* from politics:

The more often you got there, the longer you stayed. And this was the secret of it – it didn't depend on the politicians at all. It didn't need constitutions and laws, but simple self-determination. It was as if every individual made their own Declaration of Arbroath. It was like going up to the mountain, and coming down whole.[23]

Collective self-belief is what truly defines peoplehood, over and above the machinery of parties and parliaments; but this short story offers us no terrain of collective reality *in which* to believe, and figures the reproduction of nationhood as a personal attitudinal choice. The free blend of spiritual and national-historical vision here is significant, and we have already observed the flexibility of 'self-determination' as a term bridging personal self-empowerment and national democracy in the 1980s–90s. What was 'left behind' in Robert's initial refusal of 1992 Scotland, the 'curious limbo' of unsettled self-belief, is almost instantly repossessed as a soulful facet of the questing self. Scotland is not a thwarted polity but a pilgrim in search of faith, on terrain where the doings and happenings of realist fiction instead function as the signs and omens of a national parable. As the story ends, Kate models the corresponding readerly attitude to Scottish history:

> She went to the bookcase and picked out the book of Scottish history. She kept going back to it, to the famous passages, as if it were a Bible. Nearly always she went to the brief fame of Kate Douglas, who tried to save her king, James Stewart, first of that name, before his assassins had him cornered in the sewer and finished him with sixteen deadly wounds to the breast.[24]

Kate reads a passage of racy contemporaneous reportage, and finds her point of mystical identification, both flushed with significance and discreetly self-contained: 'such simple, desperate courage. One moment in a woman's life, and down the centuries all that was left of her was that moment. But what a moment! What it spoke of, and left unspoken!'[25] Only the moment, isolated, remains: the task is to weave a totalising story around and through it. But the national-societal canvas eludes Robertson when operating on this scale, unable to ground political developments in any area of common experience external to 'politics' itself.

Druidism

Kate's predicament is recognisably one discussed at length in Robertson's PhD thesis on Walter Scott, drawing on Neal Ascherson's 1985 John P. Mackintosh Memorial Lecture, 'Ancient Britons and the Republican Dream'. In Robertson's summary, 'Ascherson talked of English historiography, where "Druids", in order to justify the existence and form of British institutions, organized the historical perspective into a sacred landscaped garden, inviolable by change, and he contrasted it with the Scots' "chaotic" vision of the Scottish past.'[26] The lecture was later published in *Radical Scotland*. In Scottish historical writing, Ascherson argued,

> Time is not generally used to enforce perspective, and instead there is a scrap-book of highly-coloured, often bloody scenes or tableaux whose sequence or relation to one another is obscure. But there is a source of energy in this dislocation [. . .] What is more intense appears to be in some way nearer; its impact is not diminished by informed distancing. I take for example the tableau of the murder of Archbishop Sharp on Magusmuir which has so powerfully seized the imagination of Scottish writers. Innocent of context, stripped of explanation, this murder takes place always now, in our Scotland, the contorted face of Hackston who has bungled the killing and is now urging his horse to stamp on Sharp's head is your face and my face; when the screaming is finally over and they open Sharp's little snuffbox to find his familiar, we all hear distinctly the noise of the bumble-bee escaping from the box and spiralling away across the heather. Walter Scott tried to play the Druid, to organise scenes like these into a mere heritage and say that they were over. But he did not really succeed, and they are not over.[27]

Kate's point of emotional and imaginative contact with Kate Douglas or Mary, Queen of Scots, in brief moments of stand-alone drama, clearly hearken back to this Scottish school, to which Robertson, challenging Ascherson's charge of druidism, suggests Scott also partly belongs. (Taking only the Magusmuir assassination, he argues, 'it is hard to match Scott's descriptions of them for high colour and bloodiness, and it is only through Scott that many of them have come down to us at all'.[28]) We can see Robertson's later historical fiction as addressed to precisely the problem Ascherson identifies: seeking not a 'sacred landscaped garden' to flatter and vindicate Scottish history, but narrative forms that embrace the discontinuity and incompletion of the national story. These must include dramatic flashes of gore and glory, and the murky contradictions of the political chess-game, while also accommodating states of national consciousness grounded in humdrum realities of modern Scotland. Robertson's debut novel, *The Fanatic*, makes great strides in this direction, employing parallel historical narratives and traditional Hogg/Stevenson motifs of doubleness and psychological disturbance to bridge incommensurable realities and mentalities. By contrast, his flawed epic of Scottish devolution tackles the question of national consciousness on the scale of its own impossible totality, seeking to transmute an avalanche of newsprint explanation into the stuff of collective memory.

And the Land Lay Still

In 2012 Stephen Maxwell justly observed that 'while the novels of Alasdair Gray, James Kelman, Irvine Welsh and Andrew Greig reference political themes, James Robertson is the only contemporary Scottish writer to have put the dramas of Scotland's public life at the centre of a novel'.[29] *And the Land Lay Still* is a panoramic social novel which strives to dramatise and explain the reformation of national collectivity during the post-war era leading to devolution. In so doing, Robertson must somehow integrate the twin narratives I have been calling the Dream and the Grind.

The novel was named 2010 Scottish Book of the Year, and was also a political hit, described by Fiona Hyslop MSP, the SNP Government's Cabinet Secretary for Culture and External Affairs, as 'a must read for anyone wanting to learn about and understand the last five decades of Scottish life', and by First Minister Alex Salmond as 'an outstanding and important novel about Scotland, and what it means to be Scottish'.[30] As a literary endeavour, its achievement is major but incomplete, for Robertson's ambition to rig up a truly national historic perspective on these events brings a host of novelistic difficulties. Its aesthetic tensions are here read symptomatically, as indications of the difficulty – and perhaps the impossibility – of narrativising Scottish devolution on terms that satisfy its own preferred meaning: as the recovery of national consciousness, memory and agency.

Over 670 pages, Robertson spreads the narrow ground of constitutional debate to the full dimensions of the modern nation, cramming a formidable range of social realities and historical landmarks into the novel's six interlinked sections. Several of the major plotlines and milieus might easily have been central to distinct novels, and deeply immerse the reader in specific social-historic worlds spanning the period of the late 1940s to 2008. It is a novel that defies summary, but Robertson describes the main frame narrative in a 2010 interview:

'It begins with a son curating an exhibition of work by his father, who was a very successful photographer but has now died,' says Robertson. 'This leads him, in 2008, to examine aspects of his father's life and to re-examine aspects of his own. Then at the start of each of the six sections, you start again with a new character, all of whom have their own story to tell from over a period of 46 years, but as you progress you realise these stories actually overlap and intersect at various points.' The characters featured include a Conservative MP, Scottish Home Rule activists, a WWII veteran and an Asian shopkeeper, the possibilities for engagement with Scotland's recent political history strikingly apparent.[31]

All the legendary and picturesque moments find their way into the tale: the Stone of Destiny caper, the construction (and decommissioning) of Dounreay, Hamilton '67, It's Scotland's Oil, *The Cheviot* . . ., Allie's Army, the rise of Thatcher, the Falklands conflict, and the poll tax rebellion; but the novel also ranges beyond and 'beneath' the headlines to explore, for example, forgotten mining disasters, gay subcultures of the 1970s, and the inner workings of the Campaign for a Scottish Assembly.

The central character is Michael Pendreich, who we first encounter as he prepares an exhibition of his late father's celebrated photojournalism. This task entails a patient selection and curation of key images from the Angus Pendreich archive, to be arranged, displayed and contextualised for a general audience, accompanied by an exhibition catalogue written by Mike himself. (That Angus had an uncanny knack for witnessing and capturing key events in the national story is forgivably convenient to Robertson's purpose.) The exhibition frame allows Robertson to handle a vast array of striking fragments and isolated moments, while also portraying the active and value-laden process by which they are connected and narrativised. Robertson conducts this task in a mainly realist and journalistic register close to its primary materials, but also via recurring allegorical elements and forays into the folkloric, the paranoid-conspiratorial, and the alcoholically surreal.

The resulting tome attempts to weave every corner, faction and identity of the country into an intelligible Story of Scotland, one that makes political and emotional sense of quietly transformative times. But the scale of this ambition is matched by the depth of amnesia it must grapple with. Despite the novel dealing primarily with post-war events, Robertson cannot count on his readership – even his Scottish readership of the optimal vintage, born around 1950 – recognising the basic timeline and dramatis personae. Even the headlines and landmarks of the main narrative will seem obscure to readers unschooled in recent Scottish history, so that the novel must produce as it goes the 'memory' it seems to be recounting. Michael's task is to re-invest meaning in Angus's photographs as 'known' public artefacts already in circulation, but Robertson himself has no such luxury, and must patiently introduce and contextualise his raw materials as he goes. Thus, we have a novel forced to laboriously produce the basic story-stuff it wants to recover and recollect. In this sense the book carries within itself the problem of national historical recovery it sets out to represent, resulting in a vexed orientation to the narrative and emotional dynamics of popular memory.

This explanatory burden necessitates occasional 'info-dumping', as one reviewer has it,[32] and an abundance of symbolic minor characters whose intimate lives are tightly yoked to political events:

> Sir Malcolm Eddelstane, after a prolonged argument with Lady Patricia, succumbed to her advice and stood down prior to the 1964 General Election. The Profumo affair, the general disarray of Macmillan's government and a wider change of mood in the country, she said, signalled not only that the Conservatives were due for a spell in opposition but also that a more modern type of candidate would increasingly be required to counter the appeal of Labour. Sir Malcolm was only fifty-five, but looked much older, and was definitely on the traditional wing of the party. 'Choose the time and manner of your departure,' Lady Patricia said.[33]

We are very far from lived experience or natural speech here, and encounter characters like the Eddelstanes largely as historical ciphers. All too often, such characters arrive oversaturated with representative significance, tangibly functionaries of an explanatory schema which falsifies rather than authenticating the social substrate of political history.

We accept unbelievable dialogue in historical novels, but in the service of adding human texture and an aura of subjective aliveness. A more extreme effect is at work in *And the Land Lay Still*: frequently the novel simply reverts to journalism, employing a voice of marked externality and 'informed distancing', in Ascherson's terms, which profoundly muffles and deadens the inner reality of the scenes depicted. The effect is strongest in passages of historical sinew where the novel's expository needs defeat any sense of dramatic possibility. Take a passage from the world of *Radical Scotland*'s birth. It is July 1983, shortly after Thatcher's landslide re-election, and the Scottish Left have gathered to squabble and lick their wounds. A long section recounts a conference held in Glasgow to debate 'Which way now for the Scottish Left?'

> There was tension in the air: identity politics versus class consciousness. The one policy that offered some prospect of common ground, devolution, was once again being squeezed from all sides. Nobody loved it, and nobody had much of a good word to say for it. Only the representatives

of the Campaign for a Scottish Assembly, the cross-party, non-party organisation that had been doggedly reconstructing the case for devolution since the failed referendum of 1979, seemed genuine in their enthusiasm.[34]

This is followed by a detailed recollection of Robin Cook's defection to the pro-devolution cause during this event, a significant and compelling moment. But the quoted passage is preceded by considerable longeurs – much too long to cite – explaining the whole political prospectus in various parties (Labour, SNP, Communist), and the electoral traps and temptations which attend devolution. Historically, this technique is faithful to the clerkly character of alliance-building in this period, which was (as we have seen) the work of diligent grinders such as Jim Ross, Alan Lawson and forgotten functionaries operating in the background of the STUC quite as much as parliamentary orators such as Robin Cook. The novel makes this plain, as when it explains the post-*Radical Scotland* moment with which we began this chapter. Its fictional avatar *Root & Branch* comes to an end, but the movement it sustained continues to grow, as 'folk whose names and faces meant nothing to the general public' pursue the thankless work of 'steering negotiations around treacherous constitutional reefs, arguing tactical details and strategic principles'.[35] This is undoubtedly 'good history', and superior to several scholarly accounts I have cited in this study; but the 'matter' or (content) of this telling is hamstrung by its 'manner'. Hundreds of such passages issue from a lofty, encyclopedic narrative consciousness at odds with the humble toil described. In place of human contact with the world of 'the cause' – we can imagine plastic chairs, draughty halls and instant coffee – we hear a preterite voice briskly explaining The Cause as an achieved, over-and-done-with reality, drained of inner possibility. The former is an obscure and hopeful dream, the latter is historical trivia.

This is more a facet of Robertson's subject than a sign of clumsy writing. While most historical accounts of devolution are (quite naturally) absorbed in the stratagems of political parties and factions, Robertson needs to humanise and nationalise the story on a much broader scale. Centred on civic activism more than parliamentary jockeying, the book toils very hard to connect the bureaucratic, tactical grind to ordinary social life, but in so doing it is forced to thickly populate Scotland with hordes of journalists, radical teachers, MPs, folk revivalists, intelligence operatives, politics lecturers, shop stewards, nationalist poets, and other eccentrics. In other words, an heuristic, post-facto image of 'Scotland' must be generated to illustrate the political process by which Scotland was actually re-fashioned and democratised; a process impossible to dramatise without badly exposing the narrative sleight of hand implicit to national democracy itself.

This intractable problem is forced on Robertson by the goal of evoking a national experience which was never inscribed in common knowledge, except by a caste of operatives, experts and 'insiders'. The novel abounds in minor characters 'in the know' about matters opaque to the implied reader, who function largely as tour guides to their portfolios of special expertise. Take young Michael's lover, Adam Shaw, a kind of Swiss-army informant with a ready gloss and insight for every occasion:

> Adam was a busy man, steeped in politics. He'd been an official in the health workers' union before he was elected as district councillor for Borlanslogie, and he was a key figure in his local Labour party branch. [. . .] He seemed to know everything – in particular everything concerning the history, music, art and literature of Scotland that Mike's education had entirely omitted.[36]

Adam's superior knowledge is intimidating – he is eleven years older, and 'never disguised his greater experience of life' – but Mike also finds 'something comforting in the rough paternalism' of their teacher/pupil dynamic.[37] Is the reader tacitly encouraged to make peace with the same condition, of being endlessly edified by a more worldly voice? It is an uncomfortable dynamic Robertson's narrative style wishes to acknowledge and perhaps 'problematise', but which it cannot really do without. In another early scene at the very heart of the cultural and political action – in Jean Barbour's Edinburgh flat, surrounded by musicians and intense chatter on the 'Scottish question' – Mike seems almost to glance wryly at the camera when observing that he 'had never come across such enthusiasm for political debate, especially when it revolved around questions of national identity and self-determination'.[38] These pageants of small-scale collectivity – a somewhat narrow world of enthusiasts and obsessives who share the novel's own special interests – serve the larger needs of the narrative collage, and stand revealed as vehicles of a supervening narrative discourse operating far above and outside unfolding events.

Where the novel does achieve a credible and breathable ethos, it is often that of a clammy demi-monde or secretive club, in which 'insiders' can meet on their own special terms. The most effective passages of historical exposition are not in the open air of communal life but furtive spy-talk, intelligence briefings in which the factual, strategic-operational quality of the knowledge imparted requires no creaking pretext or camouflage. The novel's strongest section as 'straight history' is an interview of this kind. Peter Bond is an alcoholic ex-spy whose career in the security services involved infiltrating fringe 'tartan terror' groups of the 1970s. Being debriefed by his erstwhile handler Croick, he briskly telescopes developments from 1974 to 2007. There is little sense of human memory or recollection in this passage, but it is easy to see its merits as a frank factual recounting:

When I think about it now it's clear enough. Those months between the two General Elections that year [1974], that was when the whole direction of Scottish politics for the next three decades was laid down. The SNP won seven Westminster seats in the February poll and came second to Labour in thirty-four more. Bound to loosen the bowels a bit, eh, if you were a Labour MP? So the party machine clanked into reaction. Wilson told the Scottish leadership they were going to have to go down the devolution road, like it or not, in order to shunt the Nats into the ditch. Result? Five years of bluster and barter, a failed referendum, eighteen years of Tory rape and pillage, ten years of Labour-led devolution and, at the end-up, a Nationalist government in Edinburgh.[39]

Yet, it is precisely these passages which strike the reader as most thrillerish and unconvincing, as though bolted onto the novel to provide a kind of artificial excitement. This was the view of Allan Massie, referring to the Bond narrative and his task monitoring potential terrorists: 'simply because Scottish politics have been so lacking in drama, [Robertson] had to do this wildly exaggerated picture of extremist groups. If you try to write about Scottish political parties, you're not going to have anything very interesting to put in a novel.'[40] If the story of devolution gains a kind of ersatz raciness by being re-told as dime-novel pastiche, it is at the expense of its own genuine puzzles, which are not noir-ish personal struggles and mysterious roadside deaths (such as the Willie MacRae case), but the question of how to locate the lived experience of individuals against the horizon of public memory – a horizon formed by practices the novel teaches us to question and distrust.

Even the most privileged insiders are given reason to doubt the manner in which reality enters history. In the depths of a drunken reverie, Peter Bond recalls his glory days of espionage in a blended narrative voice straining to cloak crisp textbook insights in the casual-personal aura of lived experience:

And here's an interesting statistic. No, not a statistic, a graph. There are two lines on this graph. One represents the electoral performance of the SNP in the 1970s. The other represents the number and intensity of 'tartan ter-ror' events in the same period: pipeline explosions, pylons blown up, caches of guns and explosives found, letter-bombs sent to public figures or organisations, trials of sus-pected terrorists, conviction and imprisonment of same. [. . .] Surprisingly – no, not surprisingly – no, not fuck-ing surprisingly enough – the two lines rise and dip and rise like a flock of those wee birds you see at the seaside sometimes. [. . .] almost as if the graph is saying vote for Scotland's oil and you get bombed pipelines, vote for independence and you get bad guys in balaclavas. Weird, eh, how that repeats. A repetitive pattern. Spooky even. Like something is happening and you don't know what it is, Mr Jock, but maybe you'll just stick with the devil you know for another five years, eh?[41]

The suggestion here is that 'tartan terror' incidents were false flag operations either conducted or encouraged by the British security apparatus, in order to discredit the rising SNP. Peter entertains this theory mainly because of his distrust of the accepted intelligence, which hints darkly at links between the SNP and the bad guys in balaclavas. He discounts these 'links', but his superiors Croick and Canterbury 'made them exist, they put [Peter] in the chain and kept him there, adding more links'.[42] His own undercover observations are used to corroborate a smear his 'insider' experience tells him is false, but which his handlers and bosses in London cause to become 'real' within the closed protocols of state intelligence. Thus the 'truth' of Peter's own memories is determined elsewhere: the carefully gathered facts are powerless to challenge the impersonal narrative structure in which they are embedded (and distorted). This aspect of Bond's troubled memory invites critique of over-mighty British authority, but constructing a viable Story of Scotland from the disparate materials and voices handled in this novel will also involve the forced imposition of 'links', connections and narrative symmetries.

A benevolent spider at its heart

A different problem of narrative self-determination is centred on Jean Barbour's Edinburgh flat, a hub of whisky-soaked, folkie-nationalist bohemia that draws several strands and generations of the panorama into human proximity. Attracting a wide and unpredictable range of seekers, storytellers, subversives and informants, Jean's flat is the novel's main index of change and continuity, a stable 'vernacular' space through which shifting cultural and political energies flow. Here, patterns of gossip, intrigue and tradition produce memory as embodied social knowledge rather than expert advice. We first encounter Jean soon after the opening sequence of the novel, when Michael has grown frustrated with the draft text he is writing to accompany his father's exhibition: '*My father's contribution to that art form was not inconsiderable . . .* Such a pompous tone! It's not how he thinks, he hopes it's not how he speaks, so why does it come out like that? [. . .] he picks up the phone and calls Jean Barbour.'[43] From her entry to the story, Jean is figured as an authenticating influence whose intimate candour and personal experience will supply much-needed emotional heft to Michael's essentially third-order curatorial task, trying to adequately see and explain how his father pictured Scotland. In addition to her front-row seat to the unfolding 'event' of cultural devolution, Jean has a complex romantic history with Angus, and secrets beyond Michael's ken. He makes arrangements to visit her in Edinburgh, and conducts a lengthy whisky-fuelled interview in which Jean's life history is made to enliven and humanise the tale of postwar Scotland.

Reflecting on her 'mixed-up memories', Jean suggests 'chronology is just a regime to stop us going insane. Sensible, but not very . . . *imaginative*.' 'A story is a whole mass of details that come together and form a narrative', she continues, like a jigsaw puzzle, 'and there's no picture to guide you'.[44] In sharp contrast with the encyclopedic narration which dominates *And the Land Lay Still*, here is a trope for understanding 'story' at the level of its telling: a dynamic totality held together by acts of memory both analytic and creative, where the puzzle pieces have humanly pliable edges. Jean's own personal and political reminiscences are blended quite successfully on this basis. At the end of their lengthy interview, interspersed with numerous historical vignettes in the novel's more journalistic register, Jean urges Michael to 'trust the story' through which he is reconstructing the national mythos lodged in his father's archive.[45]

Here is a situation

In Jean's analogy of the jigsaw, the totality of the finished image is paramount: 'without that coming-together they're just a lot of wee pieces'.[46] *And the Land Lay Still* has its share of introverts and traumatised loners, but its narrative architecture insists on the piecing together of personal scraps and fragments into the larger mosaic of a national story, one whose structural movements are defined by aggregative public occasions such as elections and referendums. Such capital-E events lodge themselves securely in the journalistic archive, and can be retrieved and displayed as the very substance of collective memory. In this narrative economy the significance of the personal experience or novelistic detail will derive ultimately from the connections drawn upward through them – connections revealed and determined by the overarching totality of national historic consciousness. A key passage offers the following brisk synopsis of where devolution came from:

> Here is a situation: a country that is not fully a country, a nation that does not quite believe itself to be a nation, exists within, and as a small and distant part of, a greater state. The greater state was once a very great state, with its own empire. It is no longer great, but its leaders and many of its people like to believe it is. For the people of the less-than country, the not-quite nation, there are competing, con-flicting loyalties. They are confused.[47]

'They' might be confused, in their personal fumblings and smallness, but even their bafflement is clear and orderly from up 'here', viewed on the national scale – one not quite visible or inhabitable down at ground level. Reflecting in the novel's closing lines on his own efforts to trace an artful unifying thread through personal, sexual and political transformation, Michael Pendreich insists 'the connections will be made, and he under-stands that it has fallen to him to make them'.[48] But for all of the novel's preceding 670 pages the fully joined-up big picture is beyond the ken or experience of individual characters, vis-ible only to the talking-textbook narrator who possesses 'the situation' in advance. As Robert Alan Jamieson observes in his review, the novel's great slabs of historiography are 'sometimes offered to the reader by an authoritative, noncharacterised voice which doesn't appear to emanate from within the diegesis'.[49] The marked *externality* of this knowledgeable voice creates a deep tension with the need to authenticate national memory at the level of mundane lived experience (the novelistic). Whereas Walter Scott's historical fiction was celebrated by Lukács for 'portraying the totality of national life in its complex interaction

between "above" and "below"',[50] in this novel the very reality of the nation is constituted by perspectives available only
up 'here', and sustained by an encyclopedic knowledge of the
special rituals and routines of the political class. Only by making
these elite journalistic-academic-governmental strata stand in for
the nation at large can devolution be rendered explicable within
the required narrative parameters.[51]

To be sure, it is not that Robertson ignores or occludes the
vast un-organised, un-politicised majority of the population,
devoting as he does considerable attention to a host of prosaic
characters and lives (the Lennie and Imlach family sagas, the buses,
pubs and offices of Wharryburn and Borlanslogie, the tedious garden parties of the Perthshire gentry). If for Lukács 'the principal
figures in Scott's novels are [. . .] the decent and average, rather
than the eminent and all-embracing', this novel goes out of its
way to evoke a similar milieu of small-town post-war life.[52] In his
attention to miners, students, housewives and retired profession-
als Robertson shows 'society's un-interrupted self-reproduction
through the activity of these individuals', in Lukács' terms: 'in
and through this activity the socially general asserts itself'.[53] But
when it comes time to draw these local lives and realities into the
larger frame of the national tapestry, it becomes inescapably clear
that the unifying forces that make Robertson's novel work – both
politically and in narrative terms – are actuated elsewhere. The
resulting portrait of collective life we are offered arises not from
the reality in which these ordinary 'world-maintaining' characters move, but from the curatorial production of a second-order
national 'normality', a layer of representative *typicality* (like the
photojournalism of Angus) through which they can be integrated
into the aesthetic and political totality of nationhood.

In his recent re-working of Lukács' paradigm, Fredric Jameson
argues that 'the historical novel as a genre cannot exist without
[the] dimension of collectivity, which marks the drama of the
incorporation of individual characters into a greater totality, and
can alone certify the presence of History as such'.[54] Viewed from
this angle, what kind of history is being represented and valorised
in *And the Land Lay Still*? Whereas in Scott (for Lukács) '"below"

is seen as the material basis and artistic explanation for what happens "above"', in Robertson's epic we find the reverse: a totalised (if pluralistic) Story of Scotland that effectively brings into being the representative national subjects whose doings and happenings fill in the gaps between crucial by-elections.

Scrape and swoop

Stylistically, this panoramic social novel is characterised by a *scrape and swoop* pattern, akin to sweeping a floor with a brush and dustpan. We have passages of bird's-eye narration which range very freely across the surface of things, moving swiftly and lightly over large areas of social, political and industrial change, and then much fussier, more detailed sections of ground-level exposition, where the accumulated dust of history – 'wee pieces' – is collected, examined, and put in its correct place. It is sections of the latter type that are most characteristic of the novel as a whole: a kind of synoptic journalism which is spooling out facts and explanations seemingly as 'background' for the main drama, but whose empirical, expository impulse turns out to be primary. This dual approach is successful on various set-piece occasions, but the novel's real importance lies in the failure of this technique at points where the social-historical aperture is at its widest, where the tension between a large structural pattern (visible only from some non-characterised, metahistorical remove) and specific concrete detail tears asunder any credible sense of collective experience. The big, unifying picture can only be glimpsed from on high, an army of deadening details recruited to that commanding gaze as typical and typifying particulars. Marie-Odile Pittin-Hedon describes a 'highly anaphoric style' and a sense of ineluctable social and economic process, the narrator's 'emphatic tone' directly evoking state-of-the-nation Victorian fiction such as Benjamin Disraeli's *Sybil, or The Two Nations*.[55] Here is a fictive mode suited to a Prime Minister surveying the scope of his power and problems. Shifting media from print to screen, I read the same effect as akin to dusty newsreel footage, panning endlessly across a lifeless social body the chirrupy voice-over fails to humanly animate. The following inventory is loaded with Victorian superfluities, but also achieves a kind of melancholy cinematic grandeur:

> This was Scotland in 1950: coast to coast Jock Tamson's bairns stood or sat, lugs cocked to the wireless for news from home and abroad, from Borlanslogie, from Korea, or tuned in for *The McFlannels* on a Saturday night, or *It's All Yours* on a Monday with young Jimmy Logan doing the daft laddie Sammy Dreep, spluttering, 'Sausages is the boys!' This was Scotland in 1950: land of 250 pits and 80,000 colliers, 100,000 farmworkers and four universities; land of Singer sewing machines in Clydebank, the Saxone Shoe Company in Kilmarnock, Cox Brothers jute mills in Dundee and the North British Locomotive Company in Springburn, every town and city and every part of every city with its own industries and hard-won skills [. . .] This was the land of Leyland Tiger buses from Thurso to Dalbeattie, and double-deckers crowding the city trams towards oblivion, of grandiose department stores and miserable slums, tearooms and single-ends, savage sectarianism and gloomy gentility, no-quarter football and stultifying Sundays.[56]

Even drastically curtailed for reasons of length, the copiousness of this passage feels stylised, but never fully attains a shaping aesthetic distance from its materials, rendered as an inexhaustible freight of ghosts: social history as the oppressive, oceanic sum of what is 'real' but gone. The strain to cram in ever more names and details, as though trying to jog the reader's memory or hoard these facts against oblivion, only heightens the effect of acute externality. We are much closer, here, to the static terrain of *epic*: this inexhaustible catalogue of things and events 'are the form taken by the objective and extensive totality of the world', as Lukáks puts it, recollected by a heroic (and perhaps Prime Ministerial) narratorial consciousness who 'is only the luminous centre around which this unfolded totality revolves'.[57]

At one level, passages like the above seem to be aiming for nostalgic recollection: to spark some dormant memory of *The McFlannels* or a cousin who worked for British Leyland. But the patient completism of the telling also suggests a responsible authorial effort to record and inscribe what has *yet* to be caught and collected in public consciousness, so that we are torn between postures of witness and evocation. We are told – and with some elan – the 'big picture' of modern Scottish history and social change in Robertson's novel, but we *hear and feel* it as the rehearsal of collective knowledge we ought already to have, a professional secret in which we are only belatedly being included. This can only deepen our reliance on the newsreel-narrator and his squad of expert tour guides, who seem doomed to stockpile their endless facts for evermore, so incapable are we of receiving, digesting and reproducing them as 'story' on terms that would (as in Jean's boozy salon) knit the listener-student into collective self-knowledge.

In place of a societal narrative we can inhabit and carry around with us, we have set-piece events which force a unity between the personal and the national. Elections and related public ceremonies (political rallies, public debates) are figured as central to and constitutive of collective life, effectively shrinking 'the political' to the stomping grounds of journalists, MPs, campaigners and academics. It is the electoral system itself which generates an image of commonality and social simultaneity. As in 'Republic of the Mind', Robertson's device is a tradition whereby the full gamut of the Edinburgh cognoscenti – 'the left-leaning nationalists, the nationalist-inclined socialists' – gather in Jean Barbour's flat to watch the election results:

> They came, usually, more in fear than in hope. Mike doesn't recall it happening in 1979, but maybe that was because in 1979 everybody knew what was coming: the blessed Margaret, quoting Saint Francis. But he remembers the communal despair in 1983, when she wiped the floor with the opposition; likewise the briefly raised expectations of 1987, the so-called 'Doomsday Scenario' election, which was supposed to demonstrate that the Tories had no mandate to govern in Scotland – and it did, and they carried on regardless. There was 1992, when the gathering really believed the long, dark winter was about to end, and it

didn't; and 1997, when finally it was over, and things, for a moment, could only get better. Off on, off on, like a light, like a relationship. Like the relationship he had with Adam.[58]

As this final sentence hints, the personal and national-political are perfectly synchronised. Moments after the 1997 'Doomsday scenario' has been realised, Mike and Adam dissolve their relationship and sample the fresh dawn of a Tory-free Scotland:

> The enormity of what had happened between the two of them was worth looking at. But the distance between the two of them was also immense. Of course Mike knew exactly what he was talking about.
> 'It's over, isn't it?'
> 'Aye, I think so.' [. . .]
> It was the summer after the election. [. . .] [Adam and Mike] saw each other occasionally, and got on better than they had for years. They were still high from whatever had been in the air on that night in May. Life seemed hopeful: disillusion had not yet set in, despite the still-to-be-leaped-over hurdle of a two-question referendum, which the new government, headed by Tony Blair, insisted would have to precede the establishment of a Scottish parliament.[59]

What should we make of this pat, one-to-one equivalence? An abrupt recourse to allegory finds the personal love-story shifting abruptly into the terrain of Romance, suddenly drained of its extra-political dimensions. (This may in fact be a coded tribute to the endings of Scott novels.) This pattern applies to nearly all the 'ordinary' elements of societal life incorporated into the over-determined pattern, with none of the incidental everydayness that characterises the novelistic. In this sense we have an inversion of the Lukácsian paradigm, in which textures of 'the complex and involved character of popular life itself'[60] must come before their generalised representation in romantic-historic deeds: a totalisation of *electoral process* as the ambient sociohistorical world which determines individual experience. There is nothing that cannot be explained with reference to electoral-strategic forces, and nothing that exceeds those forces that is 'worth looking at' in this narrative frame.

Thus the devolutionary watershed ushers in a perfect synchronicity: 'everything from then on is another story. The new parliament, the new country, the personal and the political.'[61] This confirms the teleology driving the construction of this historical epic: full integration of the social, personal, cultural and political was assumed in advance, and the task of the novel has been – like Michael's selection of photographs for the exhibition – to supply the journalistic backfill to populate and corroborate that fixed schema. The landmark of this failed condensation in 'Republic of the Mind' – the hurled wine-bottle embedded in the shattered television – is supplanted by frictionless identity between the emotional inner state of the individual, and the condition of national consciousness.

The novel frankly admits and thematises this pre-ordainment in the final chapters. The moment finally arrives for Mike to introduce his father's exhibition, and to gather all the novel's threads and vignettes into a lasting whole. He speaks without notes:

> He's never been much good at forward planning. Let the moment dictate what you say, what you do. And now, this is the moment. He feels the density of it, he hefts it like a glass paperweight, or one of those perfectly smooth, tide-rolled stones from a particular bay on the north coast [. . .] and he wants to hold it out to this crowd of people and say, Look at this. This is what we have. Treasure it. Remember it.[62]

The contingency of the living moment subtly stiffens into the trans-historic symbolism of the tide-rolled stones, tokens of connection and destiny handed to young Mike by a wandering figure from another strand of the novel. Mike's speech is gradually depersonalised as he ventures a dusty lecture on 'that massive painting that David Octavius Hill, one of the fathers of Scottish photography, did of the Disruption of 1843':

> 'Over a period of years Hill and Robert Adamson made calotype portraits of most of the ministers who walked out of the General Assembly of the Church of Scotland that

day to found the Free Church. And then Hill recreated the scene in a painting, using the calotypes as the models for the people in it. [. . .] And some of the people in the painting weren't present on the day but were instrumental in setting up the Free Church, and many of those who *were* present were photographed years after the event, looking much older than they were in 1843, so the whole exercise is like a reverse of the process of airbrushing people *out* of history. Hill brushed them *in* to his painting. Yes, the Scots invented everything – including Stalinist methodology long before Stalin was even born.' A few knowing, appropriately grim chuckles. 'So. Not a historically accurate picture, but a representation of a moment, a movement, in history. And it took Hill, with his wife's assistance, twenty-three years to complete it. A long time in the making.'[63]

This is clearly an extended reference to the novel's own mechanics, the Disruption portrait a meta-textual vindication of its own didactic-documentary form. In such works, the selection and curation of details is always governed in advance by the requirements of national memory, which Mike now seems to directly voice. Like the Octavius Hill portrait, the truth and significance of all the individual portraits and fragments assembled in *And the Land Lay Still* derives from the totalised view in which they now click into position:

Years after the event, David Octavius Hill knew what the story was he wanted to tell with his great big painting, and he told it. But at the time it happened, who knew what the outcome of the Disruption would be? He didn't. Nobody did. When we're *in* the story, when we're part of it, we can't know the outcome. It's only later that we think we can see what the story was. But do we ever really know? And does anybody else, perhaps coming along a little later, does anybody else really care?[64]

At the novel's resolution we grasp that the 'caring' at issue is the affective *product* of the narrative so told, not its prior appetite.

Through the connections it forces and fosters, this is a novel that makes us care differently, and nationally, about the diverse worlds and creeds it struggles to hold together. Whether we align our gaze with that of Michael, and look back on the composite with the knowing generosity he extends to the Octavius Hill portrait, is a question of locating ourselves in the 'we' who are '*in* the story'; but it seems inescapable that 'trusting the story' will involve conscious loyalty to a higher narrative authority, a nationed subject accepting the determinations of national history.

'You are not alone'

It is through that higher vantage-point that the accumulated events the novel both spews forth and re-collects can be arranged into a drama of *recovered collectivity*, a sprawling but determinate mosaic in which the labours of obsessive insiders are scaled up to the remaking of national space, agency and belonging. Fittingly, the scribblers, activists and editors who render these events into text and story, churning out the printed matter in which both national politics and national memory can be reconstructed, find their place in the redeeming story:

> There were magazines recording and encouraging this process of self-exploration. They were small-scale, low-budget, sporadic affairs, and their sales were tiny – a few hundred, a very few thousand – but the people running them weren't doing it for the sales. They were doing it to address that pervasive sense of wrongness. And the people who read them – culturally aware, politically active people – were hungry for what they provided. More than anything, perhaps, the magazines said: *you are not alone*.[65]

And The Land Lay Still lacks grand heroes who embody history, and its average human plodders are really pawns of forces and connections beyond their ken. But it abounds in that minority stratum of minute-takers and the civically engaged whose interest and experience of devolution must stand for the whole. Since his 1992 story, Robertson has shifted from an idealist model where the individual simply makes his own Declaration of Arbroath, vacating the real and 'given' field of political contestation (in which he lacks democratic agency) to forge a new but imaginary Scottish republic. With *And The Land Lay Still* we encounter a model of historical recovery and production which nationalises the individual subject while figuring the nation both as spectral nobodies 'down there', and the very horizon of meaningful combination. In this narrative form, reliance on a higher curatorial knowledge to bind us together *is* the condition of national community. Like figures in the Octavius Hill portrait who are depending on the painter to fix, unify and if necessary airbrush them into the same place and event, rendering the scene for an implied viewer outside the flow of lived experience, our connectedness is a function of the *aesthetic totality* in which our common bonds have been arranged and articulated.

In that sense this novel is the crowning achievement of the 'new renaissance', in its sometimes vivid, sometimes authentically boring reconstruction of what the devolutionary vanguard helped to foster. In another strand of Scottish literary culture in the period of devolution, it is not narrative but *vocal* co-presence that grounds the national 'we'. The final part of this book explores the strengths and limits of 'vernacular' nationhood on these terms.

Notes

1. 'Why this is the last issue' [Editorial], *Radical Scotland*, 51 (June–July 1991), p. 3.
2. Christopher Harvie, 'Tasks for self-governing socialists', *Radical Scotland*, 2 (April–May 1983), p. 6.
3. 'Why this is the last issue' [Editorial], p. 3.
4. Hearn, *Claiming Scotland*, p. 81.
5. Alan Lawson, 'Has anybody been taking notes?', *Radical Scotland*, 46 (August–September 1990), pp. 24–5 (p. 25).
6. Ibid. p. 25.
7. Ibid. p. 25.
8. Ibid. p. 25.
9. Robertson, *And the Land Lay Still*, p. 537.
10. Robertson, 'The construction and expression of Scottish patriotism in the Works of Walter Scott', p. 325.

11. Robertson, 'The republic of the mind', p. 132.
12. Ibid. p. 132.
13. Ibid. p. 133.
14. Ibid. p. 133.
15. Ibid. p. 133.
16. Ibid. p. 133.
17. Ibid. p. 132.
18. Ibid. pp. 138–9.
19. Ibid. p. 140.
20. Ibid. p. 140.
21. Ibid. p. 150.
22. Ibid. p. 134.
23. Ibid. pp. 134–5.
24. Ibid. pp. 145–6.
25. Ibid. p. 146.
26. Robertson, 'The construction and expression of Scottish patriotism in the Works of Walter Scott', p. 13.
27. Ibid. pp. 13–14. Ascherson's lecture was published in in *Radical Scotland*, 18 (December–January 1986).
28. Robertson, 'The construction and expression of Scottish patriotism in the Works of Walter Scott', p. 14.
29. Maxwell, *Arguing for Independence*, p. 150.
30. Quoted in Scotland on Sunday, 'Books of 2010'.
31. David Pollock, '*And the Land Lay Still*' [Review].
32. White, 'Landscape for a decent bloke [review of *And the Land Lay Still*]'.
33. Robertson, *And the Land Lay Still*, p. 426.
34. Ibid. p. 532.
35. Ibid. p. 573.
36. Ibid. pp. 117–18.
37. Ibid. p. 117.
38. Ibid. p. 64.
39. Ibid. p. 319.
40. Campbell, 'A life in writing: James Robertson'.
41. Robertson, *And the Land Lay Still*, p. 311.
42. Ibid. p. 312.
43. Ibid. p. 28.
44. Ibid. pp. 40–1.
45. Ibid. p. 128.
46. Ibid. p. 40.
47. Ibid. p. 534.

48. Ibid. p. 671.
49. Jamieson, 'Review: *And the Land Lay Still*'.
50. Lukács, *The Historical Novel*, p. 49.
51. It is notable that Robertson's PhD almost entirely ignores Lukács, the most eminent theorist of the historical novel and a key twentieth-century interpreter of Scott. His only appearance is the slightly pedantic dismissal that 'Lukács' work suffers from a lack of understanding of the particular context of Scottish history (with unsettling observations like, "It is no accident that this new type of novel arose in England", and his confusion of chronology in the settings of *Waverley* and *Rob Roy*).' 'The construction and expression of Scottish patriotism in the Works of Walter Scott', p. 20.
52. Lukács, *The Historical Novel*, p. 36.
53. Ibid. p. 39.
54. Jameson, *The Antinomies of Realism*, p. 267.
55. Pittin-Hedon, *The Space of Fiction*, p. 61.
56. Robertson, *And the Land Lay Still*, pp. 199–200.
57. Lukács, *Theory of the Novel*, p. 89.
58. Robertson, *And the Land Lay Still*, p. 585.
59. Ibid. p. 616.
60. Lukács, *The Historical Novel*, p. 39.
61. Robertson, *And the Land Lay Still*, p. 619.
62. Ibid. pp. 639–40.
63. Ibid. pp. 640–1.
64. Ibid. pp. 641–2.
65. Ibid. p. 535.

6

Language Nationalism and Vernacular Literary Space

Tom Nairn's 1967 assault on 'subnational' half-life had linked the neurotic escape from history with vocal self-suppression: 'Society is language; Scotland is silence. The poet's wish is above all to burst through this heart of inarticulacy, to cry the Word which could restore all things whole. But the loss is far too deep for this. [. . .] Scotland has no voice, and no present.'[1] In the final part of this book, we shift our gaze from history to language, and the restoration of national voice. We begin by exploring 'vernacular' claims to social and national difference during the period of devolution, and the promotion of Scottish language(s) as a medium of national empowerment and display. 'The link between the state and literature', writes Pascale Casanova, 'depends on the fact that, through language, the one serves to establish and reinforce the other'.[2] But Scotland's uncertain claims both to statehood and a distinct national tongue force a departure from the 'Herderian' paradigm in which the valorisation of popular language drives the emergence of national literary space. Instead, the nebulous difference – and class valence – of Scots sponsors a canny 'vernacular' nationalism which is remarkably flexible in its claims. Centred on its marginality vis-à-vis English, this semi-separate tongue cherishes its social and aesthetic particularities, and essentialises (as a quasi-ethnic marker) its reproduction in class violence. On these terms Scottish vernacular writing is released, and locked, into postures of *resistant non-assimilation* rather than mobilising claims to an independent literary and cultural system. This chapter explores the appeal, and trade-offs, of 'vernacular' literary space instated in this ambiguous claim to 'social-and-national' difference, whose critical implications under a parliamentary rubric of 'representation' are examined in Chapter 7.

Nationalism and/in the vernacular

Joshua A. Fishman catalogues a wide range of modern nationalisms in which language operates as 'the authenticating device for finding, claiming and utilizing one's inheritance':

> The frequency with which vernaculars have become part and parcel of the authenticity message of nationalism [. . .] is certainly, in no small measure, due to the ease with which elites and masses alike could extrapolate from linguistic *differentiation* and literary *uniqueness* to sociocultural and political independence.[3]

The appeal of this model in the modern Scottish case – offering a kind of shortcut between claims to difference and autonomy – is obvious. The vernacular offers *empirical affirmation*: utterances and texts can be rendered up as solid artefacts of Scottishness – concrete embodiments of a 'settled' and achieved condition of national difference. It also assures *popular recognition*: distinctively Scottish forms, with their classed and demotic associations, have a strong social charisma and populist valence. Crucially, in both respects the Scottish vernacular operates on the boundary – not truly outside – of 'English', and is accessible not only to a minoritised or ghettoised population. (We will touch further on the Scots/English continuum; suffice to note that there are no speakers or readers of 'Scots' who are not also speakers or readers of 'English'.) Most Scots vernacular writing – and virtually all of Literary Scots – functions as an ethnicised para-English rather than a rival national language eligible to replace English as the medium of education, journalism, state bureaucracy, and so on. This distinction is important to the historical specificity I mean to capture by situating Scots language nationalism in the period and debates of devolution.

As Fishman suggests, the legitimacy, integrity and authenticity of the vernacular language becomes a metonym for the continuity of an autonomous Scottish cultural system. But the 'reality' of a distinctly Scottish lifeworld has, in the modern period, more usually been articulated from the opposite end: as sustained and reproduced by post-Union *institutions*. Various national bodies and infrastructures continue independent traditions in law, education and religion, alongside a range of discrete mechanisms for national self-administration. What place for language within an official devolutionary nationalism premised on these institutions, and wary of romantic appeals to pre-political, ethno-cultural collectivity?

Signposts and 'display-identity'

'The predominantly civic and constitutional mode of twentieth-century nationalism in Scotland', writes Nairn, 'was partly an accident: the fate of a population which had conserved institutional identity without statehood, and therefore never *had* to have a state for its national identity to survive'.[4] But with the 1970s emergence of 'the question of Scotland and its repoliticisation', the relationship between cultural and institutional identity assumed a new orientation. Discussing Lindsay Paterson's argument in *The Autonomy of Modern Scotland* (1994) – that substantial 'domestic sovereignty' was enjoyed by the key post-Union Scottish institutions – Nairn highlights Paterson's defence of an 'administrative' ethic which separates politics from culture as a matter of principle, positioning civic institutions as the sturdy locus of Scottishness.[5] While acknowledging the strength and nuance of this thesis, Nairn argues that 'since Walter Scott's time, the Scots have indulged in chest-beating display identities *because* the one [Paterson] singles out as real has been in certain important respects both deeply unpalatable and functionally useless'.[6] 'Nationality is not in the genes', he argues, 'but it is in the structure of the modern world', and it requires cultural anchorage in some particularism capable of symbolic expression:

> In the mainstream of modern nationalism, institutionally forged identity has almost by definition been unimportant: national movements normally have to demand 'their own'

civil institutions on the basis of their identity signposts. Hence politics is an ethnic-cultural, sometimes a religious, mobilisation foregrounding such signs.[7]

Whereas the official cultural politics of devolution trafficked in civic-institutional Scottishness – introducing the *Claim of Right for Scotland*, Owen Dudley Edwards notes the technical dryness of a document 'suggest[ing] the primacy of institutional consciousness around which a nucleus of national self-consciousness spins itself'[8] – this was never likely to be a sufficient basis to remake the stuff of nationhood. As Chimène Keitner observes, even the most strenuously civic nationalism 'involves allegiance to a nation: while the nation may coincide with state institutions, the focus of loyalty is the people conceived as internally cohesive and separate from state structures'.[9] It follows that efficacious signposts must evoke a substantial, pre-political basis for communal solidarity: something worth beating your chest over. No 'intellectual adhesion to abstract principles' – or in Nairn's sardonic Scottish example, fondness for 'the beauties of the sheriff system'[10] – can replace what Dominique Schnapper calls the 'emotional mobilization aroused by the internalization of the national tradition'.[11] It follows that the necessary identity signposts will index nationhood 'as a concrete social and political form', and not a set of hoary governing arrangements.[12]

Enter, once again, the vernacular. As Benedict Anderson observes, languages 'appear rooted beyond almost anything else in contemporary societies': thus their pivotal role in the spread of national consciousness via 'vernacular print-capitalism'.[13] Of course, Scots was not standardised and dispersed on this pattern, and is specifically excluded from Anderson's model: 'already in the early seventeenth century large parts of what would one day be imagined as Scotland were English-speaking and had immediate access to print-English', effectively eliminating, 'before the age of nationalism, any possibility of a European-style vernacular-specific nationalist movement'.[14] But this only intensifies the post-romantic valence of this minoritised, anti-institutional tongue and the '*particular solidarities*' it makes possible.[15] Excluded from the authority of print, the vernacular of the common people functions both as object and praxis of concrete national attachment. It is available for affective mobilisation by artists, politicians and advertisers alike, and signals affiliation to a folk *demos* tangibly un-integrated with the protocols of state power. In addition to its extravagant anchorage in a more authentically Scottish past, working-class Scots (and Scottish English) carry salient populist and democratic associations, affirming national difference in the grain of daily experience.[16]

But there are differences within this difference. Classically, Schnapper reminds us, 'the nation state took pains to arouse or impose markers that would be exclusively linked to the national entity. As part of this process, a national language is invented or employed which differs from that of each ethnie.'[17] But Scotland lacks a popular national language which clearly demarcates a separate ethno-cultural domain – the obvious candidate, Scottish Gaelic, is spoken by a small and often marginalised minority (approximately 1 per cent of the population). Scots is much more widely spoken, but both its legitimacy and distinctiveness vis-à-vis Standard English are socially contested, enjoying only partial and uneven recognition in the population at large. Several linguists and campaigners attribute the result of the 2011 Census, showing that 62.3 per cent of respondents self-reported 'no skills in Scots', to weak popular awareness of what 'Scots' refers to, linguistic insecurity, and related methodological quandaries (notably the fact 'there is no objective boundary between Scots and English, and no consensus about where the boundary should be placed').[18] Hence one departure from the Herderian nationalist paradigm: the 'difference' of Scots (and Scottish English) is uncertain and unofficial in character, certainly in the popular mind. This is a key problem in (increasingly bullish) commentary on Scots in the period covered by this study, during which this selfsame problem becomes a *solution* to a political dilemma. We will return to the political contexts of Scots activism in the devolving decades of the 1970s–90s, but need first to consider the broader stakes and logic of language nationalism. The specificity of Scotland's semi-nationalist language revival(s) can best be grasped in this light.

Unpicking the nationalisation of literature

Pascale Casanova's 1999 study *The World Republic of Letters* attempts to deconstruct 'the "nationalization" of literature and literary histories' by casting a critical light on the post-romantic reduction of literature 'to the political and linguistic boundaries of nations'.[19] In her model, national literary spaces emerge into competitive rivalry with one another on the analogy of Marxian 'uneven development', via Bourdieu's critique of cultural capital.[20] Independent 'capitals' of literary development (Paris, London) set the standard and canon of 'autonomous' literary achievement in the major world languages, establishing a transcendent, non-national 'Greenwich Mean Time' of artistic progress against which the laggard 'national' standards of their rivals may be measured. In turn, these competitors are stimulated to cultivate 'their own' forms of literary capital via the manufacture and reproduction of national difference, deepening the heteronomy of merely national writing and cementing its relative dependence on the international standards consecrated in the great capitals. Cairns Craig rejects this model, for Casanova's 'world republic of letters' is one 'hierarchically structured such that writers from the margins must submit themselves to the judgment of Paris before they can be accepted as citizens'; on these terms literary nationality can only be 'imprisoning', with liberation available only to those who 'recognize that their work should not be *about* their cultural homeland but should be "autonomous, purely literary"', and who successfully de-nationalise their art.[21] This is a powerful critique of the structural inequality of international literary space – of which Casanova had aimed to 'give an adequate description', rather than endorse – but it does not diminish the value of her insights into how literary nationality is claimed, constituted and reproduced; for the 'national' writer accesses a special role and social duty.[22] The pivotal figure here is Johann Gottfried Herder, who, Casanova writes,

> provided the theoretical basis for the attempt made in politically dominated territories, both in Europe and elsewhere, to invent their own solutions to the problem of cultural dependence. By establishing a necessary link

between nation and language, he encouraged all peoples who sought recognition on equal terms with the established nations of the world to stake their claim to literary and political existence.[23]

Instead of viewing German literature as 'backward' by international standards – notably the universalistic canons of French classicism – Herder argued that nations, like living organisms, 'needed time to develop their own peculiar "genius", embodied by their national vernaculars'.[24] In the 'world of diversity' bequeathed by Herder, writes Elie Kedourie, language becomes 'the external and visible badge of those differences which distinguish one nation from another; it is the most important criterion by which a nation is recognized to exist, and to have the right to form a state on its own'.[25] Authenticated 'popular' language is crucial in the resulting legitimation – and institutionalisation – of national literary space. 'Following the Herderian revolution', writes Casanova, 'the national character of a literature was fixed in terms of a series of traits declared to be peculiar to it', and this 'nationalization had tangible consequences for literary practice':

> Acquaintance with the texts of a particular national pantheon and knowledge of the major dates of a country's nationalized literary history had the effect of transforming an artificial construction into an object of shared learning and belief. Within the closed environment of the nation, the process of differentiation and essentialization created familiar and analysable cultural distinctions: national peculiarities were insisted upon and cultivated, chiefly through the schools, with the result that references, citations and allusions to the national literary past became the private property of native speakers. National peculiarities thus acquired a reality of their own, and helped in turn to produce a literature that was consistent with accepted national categories.[26]

This model is highly suggestive for grasping the constitution and reproduction of nationhood more broadly. It is crucial to note that Herderian nationalisation is as much about the *production* of difference, as the valorisation of common currency. 'The principal task pioneering writers face is to manufacture difference', Casanova writes, 'for no specifically national resource can be accumulated so long as literary works are entirely assimilable to the dominant space'.[27] Paradoxically, this model would appear to make 'English' readers the final arbiter of Scottish literary nationality: if vernacular texts can be recognised and embraced as 'our own' by the dominant transnational space called English Literature – one which already includes entire national literatures other than England's – they fail to be truly national *qua* Scotland. But it is precisely the vernacular's realisation of (productive, even pleasurable) friction *vis-à-vis English* that generates the aesthetic and sociographic effects of greatest interest to most Scottish writers employing it: the vernacular operates along the very boundary held to enshrine its cultural value (not in Herderian self-sufficiency), in a literary sphere with almost total 'autonomy' (and, often, a good measure of class alienation) from the national-popular culture whose living vitality it signifies. The resulting flexibility has a range of signifying potentials, linked to shifting perceptions of Scots as a distinct national tongue.

The half-blood prince

'In a way', writes James Costa, 'Scots is the half-blood Prince, the shameful cousin of English whose legitimacy constantly needs to be proven or reasserted.'[28] A history of Scots is beyond the scope of this study, but it will suffice to cite the pioneering scholar of Scots A. J. Aitken, who observed in 1964 that

> by the early eighteenth century, as a result of the Unions of the Crowns and the Parliaments and certain other factors, many of the functions that Scots had had in the older period were usurped by its near relative, standard English. Thereafter Scots remains chiefly as a group of mainly working-class and rural regional dialects, and also of course as the vehicle of a considerable vernacular literature.[29]

Note Aitken's acceptance that written Scots survives as a language suited to distinct and specialist purposes, such as the role of transmitting the national literary tradition. Up until the 1970s, even its most ardent champions acknowledge this reality – a few decades into his Scottish Renaissance, MacDiarmid admitted 'it is true that Scots is used in print for few purposes save poetry'[30] – and the weak differentiation of Scots from English. By comparison with Gaelic, J. Derrick McClure notes in 1979, it is not easy to say just what Scots is: 'however adulterated the Gaelic language may be in practice, the theoretical concept of Gaelic is well-defined. No such clarity exists in the concept of Scots: it is, on the contrary, extremely nebulous.'[31] In a 1981 paper on the question 'does Scots have an identity?', Aitken set out the case for 'maybe', adumbrating several reasons linguists such as Heinz Kloss would come to describe Scots as a dialectalised 'kin tongue',[32] rather than a language:

> according to the typology devised by [William A.] Stewart (1968), Scots qualifies as no more than a dialect and neither as a standard nor a classical language. Using Stewart's terminology, its functions are marginal to the patterns of communication within the polity: in fact it has unquestionably only one of the functions (*literary*) which Stewart takes into his reckoning, unless we consider it has the *group* function within the working class. As a spoken language it lacks *standardisation*; it is heteronomous with – bound up in a sociolinguistic continuum with and constantly influenced by – Standard English, and therefore conspicuously lacking in the crucial attribute of *autonomy*.[33]

Caroline Macafee contextualises the gloomy outlook of Aitken's view – certainly viewed in comparison with the plucky confidence of more recent Scots advocacy – by noting that 'the 1970s was probably the nadir of Scots in education, when middle-class Scots were ceasing to speak the language or participate in its culture'.[34] For the next generation (and growing numbers of left-nationalists in the 1970s), precisely the 'nebulous' and 'heteronomous' qualities of Scots made it eligible for a new and more optimistic valuation, centred on its 'group function' and evocation of working-class identity. This shift altered (or perhaps masked) the clash between literary value and popular currency in earlier revitalisation discourse. In 1979, McClure's conception of the Scots literary tradition seems forearmed against urban dialect, dismissing in advance the whole explosion of Glasgow literary demotic then emerging (encouraged by 'non-literary' developments in Scottish music and stand-up comedy, noted by Cairns Craig in his 1989 *Radical Scotland* essay reflecting on the intervening decade – see Chapter 4):

> It is impossible to express the highest and most sublime thoughts in the everyday tongue of a group of people. If this appears to be an elitist stance, the fact requires no apology. It is true almost by definition that the capacity for experiencing real exaltation of thought and feeling *and* of conveying it in words is a capacity which very few people have. [. . .] No poet (not even Wordsworth, despite his theories) has expressed sublime thought in commonplace language: it is simply not possible to do so.[35]

However, what McClure regards as a disqualifying impediment to vernacular literary value – the linkage between dialect and 'commonplace' people and experience – would emerge as its trump card in the period of devolution, where precisely the ordinary, marginal and class-laden qualities of urban Scots acquired a new political value. This shift begins within the left-nationalist milieu of the 1970s, where 'the language question' was swiftly transformed by the rise of the SNP, and the new strategic priorities of a mass electoral project.

Shifting constructions of 'Scottish speaking Scotland' in the 1970s

The politics of language were almost nowhere in the SNP's official priorities in this period, Nairn writing that 'few Scots easily understand or sympathize with the anguishing dilemmas of the language-problem; on the other hand, Welshmen are often puzzled by the very existence of a nationalist movement without a language of its own'.[36] Jack Brand notes that 'for many of the earliest nationalists, the Celtic culture of Scotland was what distinguished it particularly. For nationalists like Erskine of Marr, Scotland would be truly herself only when all Scotsmen used Gaelic as their everyday speech.' By contrast, 'we cannot say [. . .] that the creation or recreation of Scots constituted a language issue even on the limited scale of the situation in Wales or Ireland. There can be no question at all that, for the vast majority of Scottish nationalists, the language issue hardly existed.'[37] This was a major fault line with the cultural nationalism of the Renaissance magazines, where the 'language question' remained a central preoccupation – though not on the terms inherited from MacDiarmid and Muir's debates of the 1930s. Here it was the SNP's weak commitment to *Gaelic* which exposed its ethno-cultural vacuity. Responding to Fionn MacColla's defence of the SNP in *Scotia* 10, Seamus Mac a' Ghobhainn argued in late 1970:

> If one compares the SNP with the nationalist movements in other small nations who have managed to regain their freedom one cannot honestly even term it a nationalist party. The SNP as an organization does not seem to have any real concept as to what constitutes Scottish nationalism or Scottish nationality. [. . .] The SNP have no plans for instance to re-Celticise (which means to re-Scoticise) Scotland. They have already stated publicly that they would consider it undesirable to make Scotland's true national language A'Ghaidhlig a compulsory subject in all Scottish schools. They also have no intention of bringing into being a modern Scottish state whose life pattern would be based upon the democratic-socialist precepts which are native to all Celtic countries. A politically independent Scotland such as the contemporary SNP envisages is not worth striving for.[38]

Though consistent with an important tradition of Scottish radicalism – John Maclean's 1920 leaflet *All Hail, The Scottish Worker's Republic!* hearkened back to 'the tradition and instincts of the Celtic race' in advocating a modernised 'communism of the clans'[39] – this was an extreme view even for *Scotia*, and in a 'Supplement' issue the following month F. A. C. Boothby firmly disagreed, insisting 'the best way to kill off Gaelic is to make it compulsory in schools'.[40] Debating the ultimate ends of nationalism in the first issue of *Scotia Review*, Robert Mulholland positioned Gaelic as the *sine qua non* of the movement:

> Why does any National Independence movement exist? The 'end' surely must mirror that which is distinctively Scottish. This fundamental and enduring characteristic which gives the Scottish people any right to claim distinctiveness of nationality is centred on the Gaelic language, which was the majority language in Scotland for well over a thousand years; its reduction to the present minority has been due solely to the politics of Empires. [. . .] Any description of an independent Scotland which does not give prominence to the role of Gaelic can have little claim to being Scottish at all.[41]

Advocating 'Revolution in a Scottish-Speaking Scotland', he concluded that 'to re-Gaelicise Scotland will require a socio-political revolution as a protective counter-challenge to English imperialism and its culture; a revolution of a kind which so far only a small minority of the leading Scottish Nationalists have comprehended'.[42] This stance was strongly rejected by Tom Scott in the next issue: 'Mr Mulholland's attempt to identify the Scottish national cause with the Gaelic language [. . .] is a non-starter. That way lies only death and defeat for the cause of nationhood.'[43] In its place, Scott proposed a vision of independence where 'all languages in use in Scotland and their literatures [are] to be encouraged, each in its proper sphere: English the lingua franca for the foreseeable future, Scots for predominantly Teutonic areas and people, Gaelic for the Celtic: with the sister Eirean and Welsh given more study than at present'.[44] In this balkanised Free Scotland, tongues would be matched up with restored ethnic communities and territories.

From the standpoint of 'cultural devolution', what is missing from these ethno-symbolist pipe-dreams is more significant than their content. The class valence of vernacular Scots – with its flexible or 'nebulous' relationship vis-à-vis Standard English – would become central to the narrative of devolution as empowerment, but is overlooked almost entirely in the mid-1970s magazines. The first issue (Autumn 1977) of *Radical Scotland*'s predecessor magazine, *Crann-Tàra*, defined the national struggle as a matter of restoring identity: 'we have opted against assimilation. We are to face the crisis of identity head on. We have decided that we want an identity. [. . .] We wish to be ourselves, and not replicas of others.'[45] The magazine's Gaelic title was chosen to bolster difference from English-speaking 'others' and to evoke a context of communal hazard and self-defence, naming a 'symbol of gathering (lit. gathering stick) [. . .] to alert the people and summon them to the traditional place of assembly in time of danger'.[46] The Janus-faced qualities of this nationalism are clear – 'we join with Maclean in harking back to what he called "the communism of the clans" in order to re-establish it on a modern basis' – but the backward, romantic impulse is primary, seeking the renewal of nationhood via passionate contact with the indigenous past: 'we must return to our roots, deprived, shriveled and impoverished as they are. We must plant them once more in their native soil.'[47]

This project certainly has its Volkish resonances – its masthead reads 'liberty for the individual, independence for the nation, brotherhood for the race' – and *Crann-Tàra* is nearly as interested in questions of language and national consciousness as in foreign ownership of land. The opening salvo concludes with a 'language policy' promising Gaelic articles and translations, and insisting:

> It would be inadmissible for any new publication in this country today not to take cognizance of the language question. Every sentence published exclusively in the English language is an inadvertent blow at other languages in Scotland. The ideal of One Culture, One Language, One Nation, One State, is not one to which we subscribe.[48]

Commitment to Gaelic is positioned as resistance to the imperial dominance of 'English' language, culture and government. The editorial is followed by Lindsay Paterson's report on the second annual congress of the breakaway Scottish Labour Party (led by Jim Sillars from 1976, and a magnet to the left-nationalist intelligentsia – including Nairn – until its collapse in 1981). Writing as a member of the party's national executive committee, Paterson – himself a Highlander – claims a Scottish 'culturalist' orientation for the SLP, defining it against prevailing 'British socialist circles' (that is, the mainstream Labour movement) in which '"culture" is a dirty word', and pledging its 'commitment to official status for the gaelic [sic] language': 'This is a question of civil rights: the 90,000 folk in Scotland who speak gaelic have a democratic right to be able to use it in dealing with politicians, businesses, and bureaucrats. [. . .] As a public body seeking to represent the people of Scotland, the SLP has a duty to do so.'[49]

Here we have two rather different arguments for including and recognising Gaelic: one appealing to its ethno-symbolist function as a 'focus for kinship' like the crann-tàra itself, another centred on 'civil rights' and democratic participation.[50] One appeals to the mythscape of the ethnic past, mobilising a sense of radical (but threatened) Celtic difference in need of restoration, while the other aspires to the integration of Gaelic into modern state bureaucracies, countering the practical marginalisation of its speakers. As Duncan MacLaren put the latter case in issue three of the magazine (1978):

It is not a matter of the Government pandering to a vociferous minority but of granting people the right to speak, read and write their own language in their private and public lives to the greatest possible extent. That means: Gaelic radio and television; Government use of Gaelic in the Gaidhealtachd and occasionally outwith; giving testimony in Gaelic in courts of law; having children educated in Gaelic at all levels. This is the minimum that should be given to Gaelic speakers, not as a favour but as of right as a citizen of Scotland.[51]

The difference between these arguments – language as a 'gathering stick' to rally the race and keep the others at bay, versus language as the medium of state citizenship – traces the general pattern of *instating* Scottish civic space on the basis of a prior claim to cultural difference; but grounded in a 'different' language embodying national separateness.

Similar stirrings were manifest in the short-lived *Calgacus* magazine (1975–7), edited by Ray Burnett, and assisted by an (all-male) advisory board boasting the cream of literary nationalism including Hamish Henderson, John McGrath, Sorley Maclean and Tom Nairn. As with *Crann-Tàra*, the title evokes a militant Celtic *Volksgeist*, in the person of the hero Mons Graupius Calgacus ('they make a desolation and call it peace'): 'faced with a common enemy, the Caledonian tribes came together in a great Celtic confederation and elected as their leader a man distinguished for his valour and his military skills'.[52] Issue 2 of the magazine (Summer 1975) published a letter from Antonio Gramsci translated by Hamish Henderson, in which the imprisoned Italian radical implored his sister to let her son learn Sardinian, rather than forcing him to 'speak properly'. An editorial gloss chides 'those Marxists who would dismiss minority languages and the whole question of folk-culture as insignificant'.[53] The same issue contained a 'Tir 'is teanga' section ('Land and tongue/language') arguing that 'the "land question" is no longer the burning issue it once was in Scottish politics'; instead, 'recent stirrings in the Gaidhealtachd suggest a new found aggressiveness on the cultural and linguistic front'.[54]

Roots, nation, lingo

But the language revitalisation movement most compatible with left-nationalism was not Gaelic. By 1981, *Crann-Tàra* had abandoned its language policy, finding that its bold claim to Celtic roots infringed upon the self-determination of actual Gaels – what today would be called cultural appropriation – and also evoked the wrong sort of ethnic atavism:

> In the beginning, back in Sept. 1977, we hoped to introduce the Gaelic question to the lowland left. We wanted regular copy in Gaelic, we had a vision of a gaelic section to the

magazine. It wasn't on. We were rebuked by one notable
Gael for tokenism. It's for Gaels to create their own magazines. But we're saddled with that name: 'Crann-Tàra'. It
drives away potential readership. To potential readers we
seem like a) a Gaelic magazine (that's for teuchters, no me),
or b) an extreme pretend-gael outfit somewhere in the tri-
angle of the Scottish Republicans – the Seedsmen[55] – the
Tartan Terrorists. Needless to say our customer recoils in
horror. We're neither Gaels, nor pretending to be, and we
must find a new title to suit what we are, and not what we
once hoped to become.[56]

Neither *Crann-Tàra*'s well-meaning effort to strengthen the
Gaelic public sphere nor its ethnic flag-waving found the mark.
The quest for authentic roots ended in a queasy sense of cultural
imposter syndrome (laced with the hazard of encouraging the rac-
ist fringe), magnified by the weakness of Celticism as a mobilising
force on the urban left. It would not be Gaelic that would serve as
a 'gathering stick' to rally and unify left-nationalist cultural activism, but a Scottish linguistic tradition charged with the mass politics of class grievance, anchored in modern industrial life rather
than clannic fantasy.

In defining its profile and aims, the inaugural editorial of
Calgacus insists that

In the long run all will depend on that sole agency capable
of achieving a new social order, the Scottish working class.
[. . .] Of necessity the industrial shop-floor remains the
arena where such potential is best demonstrated, at least
for the moment. But it is not the only one. There is also
that large, amorphous area of life so vaguely referred to as
the 'cultural'. It is an area as difficult to define as are the
interconnections between politics, class and the arts. The
whole area of artistic and creative achievement sits uneasily on the mainstream of political activity yet the bonds
are there, often instinctively felt rather than formally
explained. They are perhaps most clearly seen in our vast,

rich heritage of oral tradition and popular song, an area we shall return to regularly and one at least in which socialist Scot and Scots socialist should both find common cause.[57]

The three issues of *Calgacus* went on to publish an impressive range of material answering this Gramscian interest in the national-popular: from the poetry of Sorley Maclean, Edwin Morgan and Sydney Goodsir Smith to songs of Jeannie Robertson (with music), and reviews of recorded folk ballads, Gaelic psalms and Scots poetry. The cover of issue 3 shows a famous image of Hamish Henderson recording the traveller singer Alexander Stewart of Laing, and includes reviews of Fionn MacColla, Iain Crichton Smith and Douglas Gifford on William McIlvanney's *Docherty*.

It is the territory of McIlvanney's breakthrough novel – an epic of Ayrshire class struggle, with the dialogue in dense Scots – that points up the efficacy of vernacular loyalties in neo-national mobilisation. Indeed, Gifford's review chides the novel for explaining rather too well (and too much) the cultural 'bonds' between class and nation ('often instinctively felt rather than formally explained'). In a pivotal scene with several echoes in later Scottish fiction,[58] McIlvanney has the schoolboy Conn stage a bold and instinctive claim to the validity of his natural speech, against the coercive power of his reproving schoolteacher:

'What's wrong with your face, Docherty?'
'Skint ma nose, sur.'
'How?'
'Ah fell an' bumped ma heid in the sheuch, sur.'
'I beg your pardon?'
'Ah fell an' bumped ma heid in the sheuch, sur.'
'I beg your pardon?'
In the pause Conn understands the nature of the choice, tremblingly, compulsively, makes it.
'Ah fell an' bumped ma heid in the sheuch, sur.'
The blow is instant. His ear seems to enlarge, is muffed in numbness. But it's only the dread of tears that hurts.[59]

Conn's defiance is social and national in character, and has been read as emblematic in both registers. For Cairns Craig, examining the complex role of national dialect in Scottish fiction, this scene typifies a 'descent into the gutter to discover the mouth of the nation'.[60] The violent enforcement of Standard English

> enacts the destruction of the oral culture from which Conn, like his author, derives the specificity of his identity. [. . .] In such narrative patterns and metaphoric structures, the Scottish novelist dramatizes the dilemma in which the narrative voice of the novel addresses a fundamentally English-reading (and usually English-speaking) audience across the heads of characters who are given voice only to the extent that they are encased in and, in the end, mutilated or silenced by, an alien linguistic environment.[61]

The shibboleth 'sheuch' here marks out a national boundary and claim to narrative power. Foregrounding instead the scene's class dimension, K. M. Newton finds in the same passage

> a rejection of the middle class's belief in the inferiority of the working class. Mr. Pirrie and the educational system, in refusing to accept that Ayrshire speech is proper language, implicitly devalues Conn's community, in which such language is intrinsic. The refusal of the middle class to recognize the vitality and power of working-class speech is a sign of its being trapped in a dead ideology.[62]

It was not until the 1980s, and, ironically, the reaction *against* McIlvanney's reach-me-down narrative style – poetic Standard English for the narrator, dense semi-phonetic Scots for the characters – in the work of James Kelman, that we could see clearly the bivalence of this scene. The *Docherty* set-piece asserts the legitimacy of the working-class culture embodied by Conn's speech, while associating that 'identity' with a suppressed national tradition (both celebrated and elegised by McIlvanney in the 1980s). It is in Thatcher's decade that it becomes easy to view the novel's use of dialect within a devolutionary framework that elides linguistic nationality and class oppression.

But when it first appeared in 1975, *Docherty* was something of an exception. It is striking that in the milieu of radical political debate centred on Scottish self-government and self-respect in this period, very little attention is devoted to vernacular Scots and its potential. In 1974–5 *Scottish Marxist*, the magazine of Scottish Communism, ran a three-part series on 'The Struggle for the Working-Class Novel in Scotland' by Jack Mitchell which does not dwell on 'the language question' in any sustained way, despite devoting an entire segment (part II) to Grassic Gibbon's *Scots Quair*, with its pervasive, skilful and celebrated use of dialect.[63] The author and magazine had specific priorities – working-class Scottish writers are chided for not following Gorky, for avoiding direct ideological confrontation, and so on – but the indifference towards vernacular Scots remains striking.[64] The fortunes of Scots in this period are uncertain, and clearly shift with perceptions of the political situation. In 1963, an unsigned comment in *Lines Review* – the mainstay of Renaissance poetry continuing MacDiarmid's project – was ready to grudgingly admit

> that the Lallans Movement *as such* has failed. The most plausible reason for this is surely the parallel failure of the political aspirations of Scottish nationalism. It was the dream of Albyn, directly or indirectly, that breathed life into the disparate elements of the Scottish Renaissance. For most Scottish writers today, and particularly the younger ones, that dream no longer 'lives in the mind like a vision'. What would have happened if Scotland *had* gained her independence is another question.[65]

It was political hope that kept the Lallans movement alive, and that hope was now past. In 1965 Alexander Scott struck a 'realistic' tone in surveying the condition of 'Scots in English': 'We are all Anglo-Scots nowadays. The language we use as the accepted medium of prose communication was shaped, in the main, on the tongues of Englishmen. Some of us may find that situation dreich, others may regard it as fikey, but we can scarcely ignore it. Four hundred years of history have given it undeniable authority.'[66] By 1972, the dominance of English was far from certain, and a bullish Scott now felt able to chide such defeatism (in others):

> In the middle sixties, Norman McCaig [sic] wrote of the poetical situation in Scotland that 'the language battle is over [. . .] the future will lie in the development of a poetry in English'. Since then, MacCaig has expressed his realisation that the battle is not over by any means, and the work of the new poets writing in Scots [Alastair Mackie, Donald Campbell] shows that all the victories are not being won by the big battalions who prefer the standard form to the vernacular.[67]

What changed in the interim? Not the prevailing fortunes of Scottish or English poetry, but the political context which 'breathed life' − or its opposite − into the Lallans movement.

Working-class-talking Scotland

As Scottish nationalism found a settled electoral niche in the 1970s, urban Scots acquired a new political valence and power. This was especially the case as the SNP moved toward asserting a 'coherent ideological stance', relinquishing its traditional (and electorally confusing) identity as 'a national movement rather than simply a political party (like all the others) [in which] independence took precedence over detailed policies and programmes'.[68] Peter Lynch notes that 'adopting an ideological position was attractive to centre-left Nationalists keen to take the fight to Labour in its electoral heartlands in the West of Scotland', perceived as key to electoral growth and the prospect of independence.[69] Though operating quite remotely from the SNP's growing pragmatism, the radical cultural and political reviews saw opportunities in the same terrain: leveraging the class-coded qualities of vernacular Scots both to popularise nationalism, and overcome leftist suspicion of independence. In issue three of *Calgacus* (1978), an article headed 'Get the Lingo' spoke to the need to meet traditional Labour voters half-way, ensuring that the potential upheaval of national awakening – at this point, and in these circles, many believe independence is near at hand – would be tempered by familiar accents:

> Movements can be apolitical perhaps, but parties – yes, even nationalist parties – must be founded on solid political rock. People get a queasy feeling when the sand shifts under their feet, and people in the Central belt, in the areas of old industrial prowess, get that feeling about the SNP. No escaping it – it's not as if you have to be Socialist, Labour loyalty disproves that – but you've got to seem to be working class. You've got to talk the lingo, the class lingo.[70]

A class-coded Scottish English is being positioned as a unifying electoral vehicle of the Gramscian 'national-popular'. The same article saw that 'a working-class-talking party is needed to win West Central Scotland to Nationalism, and West Central Scotland is needed to win Independence for Scotland'. These factors ensured 'class lingo' would become integral to Scottish nationality politics in the period of devolution, combining a claim to urban authenticity and political injury with a demand for unity and representation, without invoking a 'separatist' cultural tradition on the lines of Celtic revivalism.

As Benedict Anderson points out, national belonging founded 'in language, not in blood [means] one could be "invited into" the imagined community', and it was on these terms that the cultural intelligentsia helped themselves to the rhetorical value of working-class speech.[71] In the 'civic' national public sphere re-constituted by Scottish intellectuals in the 1980s, anticipated by the semi-nationalism and institutional backing of *Scottish International*, a literature of 'Scottish Speaking Scotland' would assume the mantle of class liberation under the sign of 'identity'. Once incorporated into the electoral logic of devolution, vernacular Scottishness could serve as the channel of trans-class national marginality (seeking inclusive recognition, not sovereignty) rather than a folkway to the ethnic past. Its double-coding of class and nation became indispensable to the politics of 'voice' which accompany the rhetoric of devolutionary self-representation in the 1990s: the rubric underpinning Douglas Gifford's 'paradox' of the asymmetric fortunes of literary renaissance and the SNP.

The 'new renaissance' and vernacular literary space

James Costa, Haley De Korne and Pia Lane point out that 'minoritised language standardisation efforts differ in important ways from national language standardisation projects'.[72] In Scotland the post-1979 'new renaissance' associated with James Kelman, Tom Leonard, Liz Lochhead and their followers falls somewhere between a conventional Herderian language nationalism and a phenomenon particular to what Casanova calls 'linguistically dependent regions', where 'as a result of cultural and political traditions writers have available to them only one great literary language'.[73]

> In the absence of an alternative language, writers are forced to devise a new idiom within their own language; subverting established literary usages and the rules of grammatical and literary correctness, they affirm the specificity of a popular language. [. . .] It therefore became necessary to reinstate a paradoxical sort of bilingualism by making it possible to be different, linguistically and literarily, within a given language. In this way, a new idiom was created, through the *littérarisation* of oral practices. [. . .] While remaining within the central language it becomes possible, by means of minute deviations, to break with it no less explicitly than if one had adopted another tongue.[74]

The pertinence of this model to Scottish writing of the devolutionary period is obvious. Indeed, Casanova makes a case study of the influence of James Kelman, Tom Leonard and Alasdair Gray, going so far as to compare their impact to that of Mark Twain: 'With *Huckleberry Finn* the literary world and the American public became aware of the existence of a peculiarly American oral language – and therefore a distinctive "Americanness".'[75] Kelman, she continues, 'while remaining within the English language

[. . .] managed through the illustration and defence of a popular language – affirmed as a specifically Scottish mode of expression – to create a difference that was both social and national'.[76] Here Casanova overstates the case, over-reading Kelman's 'association with the Scottish nationalist movement' and his 'radical (indeed, exclusive) use of [. . .] popular language in his novels'.[77] In fact, Kelman's fiction employs very few words or expressions you would not find in an English dictionary; the localised and class-marked qualities of his Glasgow English are achieved via subtle grammatical and discursive markers, within a narratorial language which renders a naturalistic impression of speech and thought primarily via stylised rhythmic effects.[78] In addition to the language barrier, the rising tide of vernacular nationalism itself – Casanova's study was first published in French in 1999 – may explain the over-reach of this interpretation. If so, this would prove Casanova's point at another level, reflecting the efficacy of 'the *littérarisation* of oral practices' in establishing a national frame in which to (over-) read the politics of writing identified as Scottish.[79]

Class surrogates for ethnic tradition

We can trace the social-and-national dynamic of 'linguistically dependent regions' to earlier Scottish movements with which Kelman, Leonard and Lochhead find little common ground. In his 1941 *Golden Treasury of Scottish Verse* – an effort to collect, re-conceptualise and cheaply distribute the glories of the national poetic tradition – MacDiarmid argues that 'our national spirit today sorely needs to replenish itself at its most ancient sources', Scotland being 'deep in the grip' of the 'disease' of lack of will-power, and in need of (Herderian) national awakening.[80] Notably, the 'roots' the vernacular can activate and renew are social as well as national: 'it is an important point that poetry in Scots still has access, not only to the cultured section but to the working-classes, in Scotland, that no English poetry has ever had or, to all appearances, can ever have'.[81] In a sense the Scottish working class become surrogates of *ethnic* rootedness and difference for which the Herderian model would nominate Scottish Gaeldom. While MacDiarmid's project was deeply invested in

Celtic revivalism and the Irish example, he recognised that 'a political project of re-establishing Gaelic as the vernacular of Scotland would only have been possible if the Gaels, a geographical and cultural minority, had succeeded in imposing their will on the majority'.[82] After his initial 1920s experiments with Scots – partly inspired by the poetry of Lewis Spence – MacDiarmid experienced a 'satori [. . .] an illumination, a sudden awakening': in Bob Purdie's summary, 'he now believed that a literature in Scots would lead to the kind of national revival advocated by the Gaelic revivalists, but this would be achieved by a cultural Renaissance, not state action from above'.[83] Elaborated and extended by MacDiarmid's disciples, this project constructs a modernist-primitivist paradigm in which the basis of revived peoplehood elides class experience and ethnic *geist*. Tom Scott shows the continuing influence of this stream into the early 1970s, figuring the vernacular as 'the stored memory of the experience of a people':

> it is their spiritual Records Office in which are storied not only the history of past experience but the linguistic equivalents of present and future experience, and understanding of their own natures by living and unborn members of that people. It is, in fact, a cultural heritage totally essential to organic growth, growth in the real feelings as opposed to the abstract intellect, of that people past, present and to come.[84]

But this undiluted Herderianism struggled for political traction as the decade wore on. It was the non-identity – indeed, the antipathy – between romantic-cultural and electoral nationalism in the 1970s which made their later integration in the project of devolution so politically productive. The very looseness of the ties between SNP thinking and the radical upstarts of the literary magazines was key. Indeed, one reason post-devolutionary Scotland has been open to strategically reimagining national identity and its symbols is the historic marginality of 'the cultural argument' within organised nationalism. This weak cultural basis – that is, the minimal extent to which the rationale for political independence is safeguarding and developing distinctively Scottish culture – has permitted devolved Scotland to bypass the 'traditionalist' quandary by which a narrative of cultural preservation inevitably imposes past-oriented restrictions on the nationalist imagination. Arthur Aughey observes that

> nationalist politics in Scotland, perhaps because it did not have any heavy culturist baggage, has become reasonably nimble in adapting to [post-devolutionary] self-confidence. The embrace by nationalism of an attractive popular culture rather than a single-minded attempt to make traditional culture popular may now be its strength and its appeal to youth in Scotland.[85]

Highly pertinent, here, is the appeal of an authenticated, flexible and 'unofficial' vernacular identity, eligible for all manner of re-coding and personal stylisation, and available for voluntarist display which does not imply any cast-iron ideological commitment. Not for its inheritors the quasi-ethnic loyalty tests and fear of speaking for others which marked language nationalism of the 1970s. In the 1980s, a 'working-class-talking' electoral project could dream of a 'Scottish Speaking Scotland' without needing to carefully justify the substitution of Gaelic for Scots in that formula, or in any wider vision of cultural revival and liberation.

Conclusion: devolution as vernacular statehood

Strategies of 'differentiation and dissimilation' play a strong but muted role in the production of what we may, adapting Casanova, call 'vernacular' literary space:

> Historically, the category and notion of a popular language – that is, a means of expression intrinsically linked to the nation and the people, which it defines and whose existence it justifies – emerged at the juncture of the two main conceptions of the people, as nation and as social class.[86]

We have frequently noted the elision of class and nation in arguments for devolved representation. In 1994 James Robertson noted that 'sometimes the accusation has been made that Lallans is the preserve of middle-class people who are desperate to acquire the cultural badge of Scottishness which they feel their anglicised speech patterns deprive them of, and that its literary achievements are therefore highly artificial and reflect certain individual cultural neuroses more than a genuine voice of Scotland'.[87] He goes on to cite Tom Leonard's disdain for 'the middle-class appropriation of Scots', thinking particularly of the exclusion of Glasgow urban speech from 'Scots' in dictionaries of the 1960s (see Leonard's influential poem 'Ghostie Men', and its defiant reply 'all livin language is sacred / fuck thi lohta thim').[88] As Aaron Kelly argues, the form of pluralist civic nationalism that attended Scottish devolution 'pursues the final repression of class in its discourse of cultural difference', rewriting class antagonism as 'a revalued sign of the postnation's healthy polyphony'.[89] We may regard this as a liberal, relativist, 'modernised' 1990s edition of the classic nationalist paradigm in which (as Nairn puts it) 'the middle-class intelligentsia of nationalism had to invite the masses into history; and the invitation-card had to be written in a language they understood'.[90] But there is a difference, too.

In the Herderian scheme outlined by Casanova we have a distinct nation who look to their language for inward strength and uniqueness; in devolved Scotland we find a semi-nation who look to their vernacular folk-language for proof of their subjection and marginality, and to affirm and cherish their self-difference vis-à-vis their 'other' (we might say their predominant) national tongue, namely English. It is this added dimension of viewing Scots *via* English that renders Scotland as vernacular space, a detour from the Herderian road that amounts to a reversal, forever returning 'home' to our peculiarity (whether wounded, confident or defiant) without carrying national difference into the enemy camp. This language nationalism ducks the question of separateness (from English/English Literature), to cultivate linguistic and literary difference as a flexible end in itself: institutionalising the signposts of nationality while shrugging their political warrant. Thus we find a key departure from the normative alignment between romantic linguistic nationalism and the assertion of state sovereignty. Dominique Schnapper points out that in the national state, 'language may be an ethnic marker, but it is also the essential instrument by which democratic life is instituted and maintained'.[91] Apart from a few diehards in the tradition of MacDiarmid, this is not the role envisioned for the Scottish vernacular in the period of devolution, which is not seriously nominated to serve as the supra-political language of citizenship and public administration.

A Herderian language nationalism can never launch Scotland into the space of international literary competition, because its claims to linguistic and literary autonomy are too fragile and limited. In the post-1970s period after MacDiarmid's dominant influence (and notwithstanding its extension by Tom Scott, T. S. Law and others), vernacular literary nationalism has aspired not to secure independence within world literary space – assuming the responsibilities of standardisation as the direct analogue of statehood – but has aimed to achieve a special enclave, and stylistic cachet, within the orbit of 'English'. In 1994, James Robertson figured the Scots/English predicament as 'opting for different registers [. . .] an entirely natural linguistic process in which most people engage on a daily basis', and argued that the 'very strengths' of Scots lie 'in its flexibility and its less-than-respectable status'.[92] It might be argued that this was a highly skilled writer's view of everyday bilingualism, assuming a degree of linguistic capital (and absence of linguistic insecurity) not all speakers will enjoy:

> The crux of the matter is the relationship between Scots and English. As close cousins, they already possess many similar or overlapping characteristics. This, in the late 20th century, is highly unlikely to be reversed, even in the event of a new political relationship between Scotland and England. There are, presumably, still a few pipedreamers with visions of an independent Scotland in which the citizens all speak either Gaelic or Lallans, or both. Realistically, it seems to me, the future for Scots lies in exploiting its close relationship with English, in generating positive, progressive energy from that juxtaposition and the tensions it creates.[93]

This resourceful outlook could look forward to the opportunities of devolutionary recognition and the generative frictions of difference-within-English, lightly dismissing the dream of Herderian nationhood entertained in *Crann-Tàra* and *Calgacus*. On these terms, devolved literary space constructs Scots predominantly as a marker of *subjection-as-tradition*, mobilising an ethno-national solidarity which does not seek to institute a separate cultural identity or state, or to overturn the native social hierarchy it encodes. Effectively transmuting *class into race*, this vernacular sign serves a new historical reading of national suppression within the Union: 'it is not by our colour, of course that we [Scots] have stood to be recognised as incomplete within the British context', writes Cairns Craig in 1996, 'it is by the colour of our vowels'.[94] An oppressed, quasi-racialised language is constructed to serve as the mobilising ground of demands for 'voice' which will invest the demotic with new iconic value, *irrespective* of the social power of its speakers – indeed, redoubling their dependency on the class of cultural activists and parliamentarians who conduct 'national representation' on their behalf.

Notes

1. Nairn, 'Festival of the Dead', p. 266.
2. Casanova, *The World Republic of Letters*, p. 34.
3. Fishman, *Language and Nationalism*, pp. 45, 52.
4. Nairn, *Faces of Nationalism*, p. 180.
5. Ibid. pp. 202–3.
6. Ibid. p. 206.
7. Ibid. pp. 206, 191.
8. Edwards, *A Claim of Right for Scotland*, p. 4.
9. Keitner, 'The "false promise" of civic nationalism', p. 347.
10. Nairn, *Faces of Nationalism*, p. 206.
11. Schnapper, *Community of Citizens*, p. 60.
12. Ibid. p. 61.
13. Anderson, *Imagined Communities*, pp. 145, 77.
14. Ibid. p. 90.
15. Ibid. p. 155.
16. All taxonomic debates over 'dialect v. language', Scots v. Scottish English, and continuums between Scots and English, lie beyond

my purposes (and expertise) here. These debates are of minimal relevance to the implications (for politics, for literature) of asserting and valorising Scottish *linguistic difference* within the specific context of devolution. For this reason I will not scrupulously distinguish between 'Scots', 'Ideal Scots', 'Glaswegian demotic' and 'English as spoken in Scotland', etc., except where directly relevant, comforted by Caroline Macafee's comment in 2005 that 'the view that is now predominant [. . .] embrac[es] the urban dialects as Scots' and applies 'the term "Scots" not only to the Scots pole of the continuum but to all the mixed varieties short of the English pole' (Macafee's editorial introduction to A. J. Aitken, 'The good old Scots tongue: does Scots have an identity?' [first published 1981], p. 1). The shifting 'predominance' of this inclusive view is of course not unrelated to the developments traced in this chapter.

17. Schnapper, *Community of Citizens*, p. 113.
18. 'Scotland's Census 2011'; Macafee, 'Scots in the Census', p. 36.
19. Casanova, *The World Republic of Letters*, p. xi.
20. See Orridge, 'Uneven development and nationalism'.
21. Craig, *The Wealth of the Nation*, p. 50.
22. Casanova, *The World Republic of Letters*, p. 10.
23. Ibid. p. 75.
24. Ibid. p. 76.
25. Kedourie, *Nationalism*, p. 58.
26. Casanova, *The World Republic of Letters*, pp. 105–6.
27. Ibid. p. 220.
28. Costa, 'Occasional Paper: Language, ideology and the "Scottish voice"'.
29. Aitken, 'Completing the record of Scots', p. 129.
30. MacDiarmid, *The Golden Treasury of Scottish Verse*, p. xxi.
31. McClure, 'Scots: its range of uses', p. 27.
32. Kloss, 'Interlingual communication', p. 74.
33. Aitken, 'The good old Scots tongue', p. 3. Aitken cites Stewart, 'A sociolinguistic typology for describing national multilingualism', pp. 531–45.
34. Macafee, introducing Aitken, 'The good old Scots tongue', p. 1.
35. McClure, 'Scots: its range of uses', pp. 38–9.
36. Nairn, *The Break-Up of Britain*, p. 197.
37. Brand, *The National Movement in Scotland*, p. 15.
38. Seamus Mac a' Ghobhainn, Letter, *Scotia*, 12 (December 1970), pp. 3–4.
39. Quoted in Bold, *MacDiarmid*, p. 319.

40. F. A. C. Boothby, Letter, *Scotia* Supplement, January 1971. Often described as 'enigmatic' (and frequently suspected of double-dealing with British intelligence), Major Boothby was secretary of the (SNP-banned) 1320 Club and later active in fringe nationalist groups involved in 'tartan terror'. He was jailed in 1975; see Harvie, *Scotland and Nationalism*, p. 172.

41. Robert Mulholland, 'Scotland's future – ends before means', *Scotia Review*, 1 (August 1972), pp. 16–19 (p. 17).

42. Ibid. p. 17.

43. Tom Scott, Letter, *Scotia Review*, 2 (December 1972), pp. 3–4 (p. 3).

44. Ibid. p. 4.

45. 'Editorial', *Crann-Tàra*, 1 (Autumn 1977), p. 2.

46. Ibid. p. 2.

47. Ibid. p. 2.

48. Ibid. p. 2.

49. Lindsay Paterson, 'What Kind of Scotland?', *Crann-Tàra*, 1 (Autumn 1977), p. 3.

50. 'Editorial', *Crann-Tàra*, 1 (Autumn 1977), p. 2.

51. Duncan MacLaren, 'Civil rights', *Crann-Tàra*, 3 (Summer 1978), p. 13.

52. Calgacus, 'Who was Calgacus?', *Calgacus*, 1 (Winter 1975), p. 16.

53. Neil Davidson highlights a number of contradictions and ironies in Scottish Gramscianism, in which the Italian's abiding Leninism is frequently misread or overlooked: '[Gramsci's] desire to see folk culture taught and studied, read and performed, was partly to *overcome* what he called "the separation between modern and popular culture", not to preserve the latter as a supposedly untainted expression of subaltern consciousness.' Davidson, 'Antonio Gramsci's reception in Scotland', p. 259.

54. Calgacus, 'Tir 'is teanga', *Calgacus*, 2 (Summer 1975), p. 13.

55. 'Seedsmen' refers to the racialist, self-styled 'ultranationalist' group Siol Nan Gaidheal, founded in 1978 to challenge the 'moribund devolutionism' of the SNP leadership, and proscribed from the party in 1982.

56. 'Editorial', *Crann-Tàra*, 15 (Autumn 1981), p. 3.

57. Ibid. p. 3.

58. Liz Lochhead's poem 'Kidspoem/Bairnsang' (1985) explores the same dynamic, which also features in James Kelman's *Kieron Smith, Boy* (2008).

59. McIlvanney, *Docherty*, p. 114.

60. Craig, *The Modern Scottish Novel*, p. 76.

61. Ibid. p. 77.
62. Newton, 'William McIlvanney's *Docherty*', p. 111.
63. Jack Mitchell, 'The struggle for the working-class novel in Scotland, part I', in *Scottish Marxist*, 6 (April 1974), pp. 40–52.
64. Note that the CPGB and *Scottish Marxist* were consistent supporters of Scottish devolution – more consistent than the Labour Party or SNP in this period – so we can probably discount any bias against national particularism.
65. 'Comment', *Lines Review*, 19 (Winter 1963), p. 4.
66. Alexander Scott, 'Scots in English', *Glasgow Review*, 2.1 (Spring 1965), pp. 12–15 (p. 12).
67. Alexander Scott, 'Scots in '72', *Glasgow Review*, 3.1 (Summer 1972), pp. 35–8 (p. 38).
68. Lynch, *SNP: The History of the Scottish National Party*, p. 140.
69. Ibid. p. 140.
70. 'Editorial', *Crann-Tàra*, 3 (Summer 1978), pp. 2–3 (p. 2).
71. Anderson, *Imagined Communities*, p. 145.
72. Costa, De Korne and Lane, 'Standardising minority languages', p. 11.
73. Casanova, *The World Republic of Letters*, p. 282.
74. Ibid. p. 282.
75. Ibid. p. 293.
76. Ibid. p. 294.
77. Ibid. p. 294.
78. See Müller, *A Glasgow Voice*. Müller's quantitative and qualitative analysis concludes that Kelman makes 'sparing use of identified Glasgow dialect words' and surprisingly few departures from Standard English orthography, instead utilising covert Scoticisms and non-standard grammatical features such as 'second person pronouns, and Scottish and English auxiliary verb negation' in constructing localised, working-class voices via 'high prevalence of Glasgow dialect discourse features, particularly sentence tags' (p. 328).
79. Casanova, *The World Republic of Letters*, p. 282.
80. MacDiarmid, *Golden Treasury of Scottish Verse*, pp. viii, xv.
81. Ibid. p. xxv.
82. Purdie, *Hugh MacDiarmid*, p. 64.
83. Ibid. p. 64.
84. Tom Scott, 'Characteristics of our greatest writers', *Akros*, 12 (1970), pp. 37–46 (p. 37).
85. Aughey, *Nationalism, Devolution and the Challenge to the United Kingdom State*, p. 121.

86. Casanova, *The World Republic of Letters*, p. 282.
87. Robertson, *A Tongue in Yer Heid*, p. xiii.
88. Leonard, *Intimate Voices*, p. 134.
89. Kelly, 'James Kelman and the deterritorialisation of power', p. 177.
90. Nairn, *The Break-Up of Britain*, p. 340.
91. Schnapper, *Community of Citizens*, p. 117.
92. Robertson, *A Tongue in Yer Heid*, pp. xiv, xv.
93. Ibid. p. xv.
94. Craig, *Out of History*, p. 12.

7

Devolution and the Spectacle of Voice

Irvine Welsh, A. L. Kennedy, James Kelman

The voice isn't you, and never was – or if it was *you, it was all there was of you.*

– Don Paterson[1]

In a set-piece irresistible to cultural critics, the state opening of the new Scottish Parliament found its 'truly electric moment, the moment everyone remembers' when the new intake of MSPs joined in Sheena Wellington's recital of 'A Man's a Man For a' That'.[2] 'Part of the frisson', observed Douglas Mack, 'doubtless derived from the fact that this old song gives voice to a radical egalitarianism of a kind not usually associated with royal opening ceremonies.'[3] With its noisy contempt for elite prerogative, Burns' song is difficult to square with the sanctifying presence of the Queen, the Duke of Edinburgh and Prince Charles, who 'sat in respectful silence, listening to lines about rank being merely "the guinea's stamp", about "yon birkie ca'd a lord", about the "tinsel show" of wealth and privilege'.[4] This awkwardness extends to the well-scrubbed parliamentarians, solemnly crooning vindication of their 'toils obscure' for the television cameras, ventriloquising the disdain of the powerless.

But as nobody in the chamber (or watching a recording) could mistake, in the moment of song these rhetorical glitches are as nothing – so much 'a' that' to triumphantly set aside. The contradictions of the scene are flushed away in the sensuous mutuality of collective singing. In releasing the sound and experience of latent togetherness – the force of 'unisonance' described by Benedict Anderson[5] – this song-pageant manifests a condition of national co-presence emblematised by *voice*; and on terms far exceeding those of the Scotland Act 1998.

As we have seen, 'voice' and its giving and joining have been key motifs in Scottish literary and political discourse of the past few decades. In critical thought which elides literary and democratic claims to voice during this period, Scottish vernacular writing functions both as a soulful emblem of suppressed agency, and a flexible display-identity within a spectacle of cultural difference. This concluding chapter surveys the vernacular freedoms and jointings of selected 1990s novels, and questions their affinity with the parliamentary theatre of 'representation'.

A new voice in the land

Parliamentary metaphors pervade the discourse of literary devolution, but on mutually affirmative terms. At times, Holyrood has drawn heavily on the romantic investments of voice in Scottish literary culture. The imagery of Donald Dewar's famous 1999 speech of thanks to the Queen (immediately following Wellington's recital) anchors the representative functions of the new parliament well beyond its legal remit, at the much 'deeper' and more concrete level evoked by the Burns song and by Grassic Gibbon's mystical 'Speak of the Mearns' – within shouts and cries which do not signify but embody some essential trans-historic Scottishness:

> This is about more than our politics and our laws. This is about who we are, how we carry ourselves. In the quiet moments today, we might hear some echoes from the past:
>> The shout of the welder in the din of the great Clyde shipyards;
>> The speak of the Mearns, with its soul in the land;
>> The discourse of the enlightenment, when Edinburgh and Glasgow were a light held to the intellectual life of Europe;
>> The wild cry of the Great Pipes;
>> And back to the distant cries of the battles of Bruce and Wallace.

The past is part of us. But today there is a new voice in
the land, the voice of a democratic Parliament. A voice to
shape Scotland, a voice for the future.[6]

This ritual en-soulment of Scotland's new democratic machinery, formally investing Holyrood with its deeper cultural mandate, appeals continually to 'voice' as a principle of recuperated
national substance and presence. These tropes of vocal plenitude
help to mask the constitutive separation of action from authority
in all democratic assemblies, the apparent immediacy of vernacular speech countering Holyrood's particularly complex attenu-
ation of sovereignty. In Alex Salmond's speech marking his
re-election as First Minister following the 2011 SNP landslide,
the rhetoric of voice shifts from depth to diversity. Perhaps wary
of its ethno-cultural baggage, Salmond grafts a more flexible repertoire onto the vocal imaginary constructed by Dewar:

When Donald Dewar addressed this parliament in 1999,
he evoked Scotland's diverse voices: The speak of the
Mearns. The shout of the welder above the din of the
Clyde shipyard. The battle cries of Bruce and Wallace.
Now these voices of the past are joined in this chamber
by the sound of 21st century Scotland. The lyrical Italian
of Marco Biagi. The formal Urdu of Humza Yousaf. The
sacred Arabic of Hanzala Malik. We are proud to have
those languages spoken here alongside English, Gaelic,
Scots and Doric.[7]

The effort to add a multicultural alloy to more traditionally Scottish
voice-totems goes so far as to recruit Hugh MacDiarmid as a
champion of liberal-pluralist diversity: 'Scotland's strength has
always lain in its diversity. In the poem "Scotland Small", Hugh
MacDiarmid challenged those who would diminish us with ste-
reotypes.' This laudably inclusive vocal imaginary still operates on
the logic of *displaying* pre-given 'identities', vocal icons of essentialised difference.

Salmond valorises the plurality of Scottish voices precisely to
rebut any suggestion of an exclusive or ethnic nationalism, but
it is language which is the more powerfully binding force. As

Étienne Balibar showed thirty years ago, the notion of 'language community' seems more abstract than race, 'but in reality it is the more concrete since it connects individuals up with an origin which may at any moment be actualized and which has as its content the *common act* of their own exchanges'.[8] Precisely this dynamic aspect, mediating between tradition and creation, collectivity and the individual utterance, allows nation-language 'to appear as the very element of the life of a people, the *reality* which each person may appropriate in his or her own way, without thereby destroying its identity'.[9]

This personal dimension – the anchoring and realisation of self in linguistic freedoms secured by the speech-community; in the Herderian paradigm traced by Pascale Casanova (see Chapter 6), 'national peculiarities' become 'the private property of native speakers'[10] – is crucial in grasping the rhetorical appeal of vernacular Scottishness in the period of devolution. But the primary claim of this identity is not a Herderian folkway or idiom of belonging, but a marginal, subjected condition conceived as *beyond* any re-centring or 'inclusion' within a hegemonic cultural order (such as a state, or a standardised language). It licenses a radical particularism and self-fashioning (for the individual, in the name of the group), while continuing to trade on (and exploit) the romantic 'ethnic-cultural' residues of vernacular rootedness. Thus supplying the concrete object of national attachment, the vernacular idiom of Scottishness combines an impression of *formal democracy* (a writing which textually encodes and exhibits Scottish difference), and an aura of *populist-demotic inclusiveness* (dialect as subaltern speech).[11] Its class component re-coded as ethno-national subjection, this vernacular 'arrogates the living culture of the working class and then seeks to remarket it back to them as a commodity', in the words of Aaron Kelly, effectively nationalising its symbolic capital.[12]

Representation minus society

A. L. Kennedy would later reflect that 'like being inoculated with botulism', Margaret Thatcher had done the Scots 'a lot of good'.[13] There are deep ironies in Thatcher's decisive role in the political developments which led to Scottish devolution, and in the salience of her social vision in the Scottish fiction held to embody an anti-Thatcherite national consensus. I have in mind the winnowing of 'society' to the terrain of family, work and welfarism in novels of personal crisis such as Ron Butlin's *The Sound of My Voice* (1987), Janice Galloway's *The Trick is to Keep Breathing* (1989) and Andrew O'Hagan's *Our Fathers* (1999) – though important counter-examples would include Andrew Greig's *Electric Brae* (1992), the comradely hedonism of Alan Warner's *Morvern Callar* (1995) and *The Sopranos* (1998), and the fiction of Agnes Owens. In this final chapter we consider key works by Irvine Welsh, A. L. Kennedy and James Kelman, whose connected and celebrated writing seems to illuminate the broader cultural and political developments traced in this study.

Andrew O'Hagan describes modern Scotland as 'a nation of conservatives who never vote Conservative',[14] and there is a similar disjunction in much of 1990s Scottish fiction between the presumed loyalties and social texture of the national polity. For all their influence (real *and* exaggerated) in renovating Scottish identity, there is a striking paucity of collective experience and large-scale 'we-ness' in these books. For Ian A. Bell, the unifying dynamic is not a struggle for national collectivity but for vulnerable personhood:

> Refusing to collaborate with a transcendental, totalising and finally determining sense of national identity, Scottish novelists since the 1980s have concentrated instead on individual moments of crisis, alienation and fragmentation, moments dramatising the loss and discovery of self, as they are articulated through the lives of some of those conventionally excluded from the story of Scotland.[15]

Indeed, a number of key devolutionary novels centre the Story of Scotland on 'marginal' figures of this kind, re-figured as central to a new idiom of national subalternity combining the demand for autonomy with the recognition of difference. This requires an adjustment to Benedict Anderson's familiar model of 'imagined community', whereby (in Cairns Craig's paraphrase) the archetypal hero 'becomes the bearer of a consciousness of the nation as interconnected space, which becomes in turn a sign of the interconnected consciousness of the "people" of whom he or she is now representative'.[16] With the monumental exception of Alasdair Gray's *Lanark*, the most celebrated Scottish novels of the 1980s and 1990s provide few legible co-ordinates for integrating the subjective, interpersonal and national in this way – they objectify no convincing space of the 'many' in which to locate the lyric-novelistic 'one'. Instead, much Scottish fiction of the 1980s and 1990s radically constrains our vantage point on the shareable public world, or what Anderson calls the 'socioscape', and shifts the figurative medium of national co-presence from narrative space to narrative voice.[17] Projected as a national *class speech*, vernacular writing seems to directly embody the *absent* condition of social rootedness recorded by the novels themselves. Instead of manifesting the strength of collective bonds, the vernacular functions as an index of collective disempowerment, both spurring and realising a demand for 'representative' liberation.

Cool statelessness and self-fashioning

We should attend to the wider historical context in which icons of subaltern nationality proved so attractive. Michael Keating captures the shifting complexion of 'nations without a state' in the decade prior to the establishment of Holyrood:

> The end of the Cold War weakened security concerns in Western Europe and opened new spaces for movements challenging the monopolies of the state. At the same time, the renewed emphasis on universal human rights spilled over into debates about national minorities and their collective rights to language, culture and self-government. In these circumstances, the nationalism of the stateless altered in its image. Previously labelled as backward and anti-modern, stateless nations and regions came to be identified with the modern and even post-modern.[18]

It is on these terms that vernacular prose fiction functions as a display-identity suited to Scotland's cultural and constitutional semi-detachment. As we saw in Chapter 6, markedly Scottish English is invested with special national agency and representivity, abetted by a wider (romantic) discourse which figures language as a medium of tradition and communal self-presence; but owing to the ungoverned 'flexibility' of vernacular forms, accessing this register of social groundedness does not limit or inhibit the individual's scope for self-fashioning. Indeed, the ex-centric, ungoverned valence of non-standard writing bolsters its appeal as a medium for enacting the individual as *excited particle*. Its wider appeal clearly resonates with what Graham Huggan calls *The Postcolonial Exotic*, Scottish vernacular writing satisfying 'the mainstream demand for an "authentic", readily translatable, marginal voice', feeding and re-inscribing the commodification of cultural difference.[19]

Trainspotting and spectacle

In 1956, notes Catriona M. M. Macdonald, 'Edwin Muir suggested that "the distinguishing mark of Scottish literature is conservatism". In the 1990s, few would have agreed. By tackling disturbing themes, experimenting with styles and voices and pushing back the limits of genres, writers such as Irvine Welsh, Iain Banks, Liz Lochhead and others fiercely resisted convention.'[20] Yet these very postures of defiance could become an orthodoxy with its own conservative qualities. In a prescient essay of 1992 marking the centenary of Hugh MacDiarmid, Robert Alan Jamieson noted the emergent 'brand' of Scottish urban fiction with some trepidation:

> there is a danger that the curse of success, imitation, of which there is already much evidence, may lead to an urban kailyard of inverted values, where the pub and the bookie's replace the school and the kirk, where the break-down of family and community becomes as much a cipher for the state of Scottish society in the 1990s as the fictional perpetuation of the same was a cipher for the Kailyarders a hundred or so years ago, long after the passing of the world they described into unreality.[21]

It was a frenetically hyper-realist novel from Edinburgh, published only a few months after Jamieson's essay, which cemented the pattern he feared. But *Trainspotting* contains no elegy for family and community of the kind suggested by 'urban kailyard'. This profoundly and entertainingly amoral novel ridicules every ethical narrative, including that of national liberation and renewal. The seductive power and 'attitude' of the book arises in the anarchic *self-performance* of characters whose language is at once the embodiment of their social being, and a kind of pyrotechnic special effect. This represents a mutation of the radical individualism Welsh inherits from James Kelman. Flaunting his intellectual bona fides to secure a more lenient court sentence (for stealing books), the heroin addict Mark Renton admits that Kierkegaard's

> is primarily a bourgeois, existential philosophy and would therefore seek to undermine collective societal wisdom. However, it's also a liberating philosophy, because when such societal wisdom is negated, the basis for social control over the individual becomes weakened.[22]

This ethic is directly realised in the narrative architecture of *Trainspotting*, which aggregates first-person episodes from the lives of a loose grouping of friends acquainted through the common pursuit of private (chemical) pleasures. Welsh's debut trades in heightened, lacerating details, though the novel's more banal and anecdotal dimension – banter about television, football, weekend hedonism – is arguably closer to ordinary Scottish experience than the tense and surreal meditations of Kelman or A. L. Kennedy. For Berthold Schoene, *Trainspotting*'s great achievement 'resides in its re-authentication of the Scottish tradition, paradoxically achieved by breaking with it, by asserting a local rootedness marred by deracination, and by instilling a sense of flux and mobility from claustrophobic stagnation'.[23] The novel certainly explodes fantasies of Scottishness (both tartan and Red Clydeside), but does not replace them with any reality principle available to novelistic identification, still less a toehold for resistant solidarity.[24] Here Mark Renton vividly recalls the displacements of a working-class 'schemie' traversing the postcard vistas of central Edinburgh, unable to inhabit thoroughly alienated and appropriated space:

> They say you have to live in a place to know it, but you have to come fresh tae it tae really see it. Ah remember walkin along Princes Street wi Spud, we both hate walkin along that hideous street, deadened by tourists and shoppers, the twin curses ay modern capitalism. Ah looked up at the castle and thought, it's just another building tae us. It registers in oor heids just like the British Home Stores or Virgin Records. We were heading tae these places oan a shoplifting spree.[25]

This lopsided economy of seeing and knowing, in which only the first holds any narrative interest, should alert us to the novel's complicity with the forces of consumerism it frequently castigates. Robert Morace argues that '*Trainspotting* had originally been written against the grain of the mainstream culture of spectacle which swiftly co-opted it',[26] but the novel is locked into high-street circuits of desire and display from the very start, registering in its sensibility the pre-conceived taste of the Virgin Records stores in which it would eventually appear (and frequently be stolen). In this respect *Trainspotting* is a novel of postmodern self-fashioning trading on the signs and languages of pre-modern communal rootedness, and the only mode of 'authentication' it leaves standing is that of consumption itself. 'Buying into' the various performed outbursts and identities of the novel seems the only way to engage with its savage and sexy anger.

The fourth edition of Christopher Harvie's *Scotland and Nationalism* connects the cool vacancy of 1990s Scottish identity with a sudden and dramatic loss of firm cultural anchorage: 'Scotland's renascent nationalism coincided with market and information revolutions which shattered structures and hierarchies, leaving a hyperindividuation exhausted by its technology, and overwhelmed by its data: deconstructed texts, rejected canons, literature or culture fixed in local constellations.'[27] The splintered urgency of *Trainspotting* is tied much more closely to these 'extra-Scottish' factors – including the HIV epidemic – than the gathering force of civic nationalism, and its 'hyper-individuation' makes local speech a technology of the self. If MacDiarmid's Lallans was 'a vehicle for national differentiation and political mobilisation',[28] and Ayrshire dialect signified some residual condition of solidarity in William McIlvanney's *Docherty* (1975), the restless urban argot of *Trainspotting* is exploited as a reservoir of subcultural pyrotechnics. In the ecology of Cool Britannia, Welsh's vernacular operated as a register for 'edgy', MTV Scottish difference: a pose of marginal authenticity borrowing heavily from punk and proletarian defiance. Its stylised language functioning as a quasi-ethnic badge, demanding no more than affiliation and self-assertion, the vernacular identity constituted in 1990s Scottish writing thus operates as a postmodern 'voluntarist substitute' for the nationalist object of a state, while retaining the aura – and perhaps only the aura – of class protest.[29] In this period, Christopher Whyte observed in 1998, 'the task of embodying and transmitting Scottishness is, as it were, devolved to the unemployed, the socially underprivileged, in both actual and representational contexts'.[30] In effect, the governing classes were able to quietly bank, as their own 'national' symbolic capital, the authenticating and representative value which now accrued to working-class language; a pattern culminating in the new parliamentary elite mouthing patriotic contempt for wealth and status.[31]

A more dangerous kind of class division

Though it acquired a special political valence and potential in this period, the nationalisation of class speech was of course nothing new. In a 1947 column in *Tribune* George Orwell observed that

> many Scottish people, often quite moderate in outlook, are beginning to think about autonomy and to feel that they are pushed into an inferior position. They have a good deal of reason. In some areas, at any rate, Scotland is almost an occupied country. You have an English or Anglicized upper-class, and a Scottish working-class which speaks with a markedly different accent, or even,

part of the time, in a different language. This is a more dangerous kind of class division than any now existing in England.[32]

For Orwell the linguistic identities 'Scottish' and 'working-class' are virtually coequal, but this fact does not occlude the reality (seen, not heard) of a native Anglicised elite. In the post-Thatcher period, the popular imagery of this alignment had narrowed such that 'Scottish ruling-class identity' was virtually a contradiction in terms, and could find no place in literary culture premised on a unifying 'subaltern' condition which overwrites – or, more effectively, re-codes – Scottishness in class terms. But this is not a proletarian nationhood of flat-capped commonality: on the contrary, vernacular Scottishness aligns the personal quest for liberated (aesthetic and consumer) 'choice' with the demand for national (literary and political) 'voice'. As Kirstin Innes observes, the *Trainspotting* phenomenon (including the hit film),

has become not only a cutting-edge brand signifier for a fetishised, cool version of working–class drug culture, but also the most widely globalised representation of contemporary Scottishness. As a result, the particular linguistic code developed by Welsh to articulate the experiential reality of a certain community in a certain part of Edinburgh has become standardised as *the* authentic Scottish voice, both celebrated by the media and eagerly emulated by Welsh's peers and successors.[33]

This 'liberation of voice' entails a self-exoticising performance of verbal rootedness, flirting always with a fetishism of 'identity' as essentialised difference. 'Much the most important thing about language', writes Benedict Anderson, 'is its capacity for generating imagined communities, building in effect *particular solidarities*'.[34] But when, as in *Trainspotting*, these solidarities are reduced to badges of stylistic attachment – the verbal equivalent of an Iggy Pop T-shirt – and realised in isolation from any narrative context or sharable social space in which they might be mobilised into collective action or experience, their political valence alters accordingly. The excited particles of *Trainspotting*'s swirling polyphony belong ultimately to an order of stylised self-display:

> The Bridges is hotchin wi minge. *Ooh, ooh la la, let's go dancin, ooh, ooh la la, Simon dancin* . . . There is fanny of every race, colour, creed and nationality present. Oh ya cunt, ye! It's time tae move. Two oriental types consulting a map. Simone express, that'll do nicely. Fuck Rents, he's a doss bastard, totally US.
> — Can I help you? Where are you headed? ah ask. *Good old-fashioned Scoattish hoshpitality, aye, ye cannae beat it, shays the young Sean Connery, the new Bond, cause girls, this is the new bondage* . . .
> — We're looking for the Royal Mile, a posh, English-colonial voice answers back in ma face. What a fucking wee pump-up-the-knickers n aw. *Simple Simon says, put your hands on your feet* . . . [35]

The novel's kinetic and transgressive blur of languages figure Balibar's 'common acts' in a space beyond lived action or commonality, in a totalised spectacle of difference and self-performance. We are meant to repudiate the misogynist, predatory gaze Sick Boy levels at the tourist scene, but *Trainspotting* presses the reader into a similar objectifying orientation to its own language, rendering up exotic 'voices' for touristic consumption. Surveying the ongoing boom in Scottish literary fiction in 1997, Alan Freeman observes that the hyper-realism of *Trainspotting* and its imitators produce an invigorating sense of direct contact with 'low-life reality', one curiously heightened by an equally strong sense of reading *through*, and actively experiencing, the vernacular language in which that world is realised – a sensuous encounter with 'words as objects themselves'. 'It's the relation between the street, realism; and the word, the medium of expression, which gives such energy and spectacle to contemporary fiction.'[36] The energy and excitement are 'real' – as a Canadian teenager I found these novels utterly enthralling – but we should note the continuities of this experience with the modes of touristic consumption described by David McCrone, Angela Morris and Richard Kiely in *Scotland the Brand*, serving (as they do) an appetite 'purely or largely for the signs over the content'.[37] Precisely this doubled experience of the verbal texture – both flushed with social 'presence' and materiality, and a verbal firework display only loosely tethered to the real – marks out the terrain of vernacular liberation in *Trainspotting*.

A. L. Kennedy, *Looking for the Possible Dance* (1993) and *So I Am Glad* (1995)

Writing in 1993, Gavin Wallace offers a thematic litany of 'a substantial majority of the most significant [Scottish] novels' published since the 1970s. Their 'constituent complaints' include:

> the spiritual and material deprivations of unemployment and decaying communities; failures to find – or accept – self-fulfilment in education, work, emotional relationships; inarticulacy and alienation escaped through alcoholism; destructive mental instability; the paralysing hyper-awareness of class and cultural differentiation; crippling incapacities to give love, or to receive it.[38]

With the exception of 'inarticulacy' this list could serve as a rough guide to the fiction of A. L. Kennedy, whose first novel appeared in the same year. In Kennedy's early novels, suppressed or self-conscious nationality plays a key role in the realisation of self, and the de-realisation of sociocultural 'world'. This writing tends to subordinate the codes, forms and motifs of ethno-cultural tradition to a more fundamental quest for personal agency in a society where 'community' is a scripted ritual largely divorced from lived experience. This fiction is keen to exhibit a communitarian consensus in politics, but almost devoid of ordinary sociality. In *Looking for the Possible Dance* a tormented but painfully articulate Glasgow community worker struggles in life and love under social conditions where both 'community' and 'work' seem a kind of sham. The book is structured around relations of co-dependence between

Margaret Hamilton and three outwardly respectable but quietly controlling Scottish men: her kindly father, her creepy employer, and her unreliable lover. The novel's intense introversion, observational precision and temporal misdirections would later emerge as hallmarks of Kennedy's crisp prose, recognised by the *Granta* list of Best Young British Novelists in both 1993 and 2003.

Labelling a Scottish writer British meant something slightly different the second time around, a development partly telegraphed in the dislocations of *Looking for the Possible Dance* itself. Margaret Hamilton met her (Scottish) lover, Colin, while at university in England, and their relationship is dominated by his fickle migrations between London and Glasgow. The novel's complex jigsaw of memories is framed by a southbound train journey between the same cities, during which Margaret befriends a disabled man of uncertain age who shares his name with the Scottish inventor of the steam engine. James Watt is highly dependent on others and communicates only through writing, but his wit and vitality shine through the boredom and disappointment of not directing his own life. James hates the doctors and pills, and yearns to be accepted in his difference: as 'FUC WON HUNNER PERCEN MEEEEEE'.[39] His role as the resistant passenger, probably outgrown his dependence but powerless to change it, nominates him as the iconically Scottish figure in the book, but his yearning for acceptance is quite beyond Margaret, whose selfhood seems tenuous even to herself. Some readers find the precisely rendered elusiveness of Kennedy's characters emotionally dis-involving, but Alan Freeman astutely observes that 'their vagueness is what makes her writing real'.[40]

As the novel begins, Margaret is leaving a city whose actuality is constantly in doubt. Passing through the 'curiously unconvincing' urban environment, she feels 'that she has inadvertently started to be a film', a sensation which heightens as she reaches Glasgow Central station.[41] 'The period wood-panelling and glass, ripped out several years ago, is slowly being replaced by imitation wood-panelling and glass.'[42] The novel participates in the same heritage stagecraft, repeatedly offering the reader tidily schematised recipes for Scottishness. Item two of 'THE SCOTTISH METHOD (FOR THE PERFECTION OF CHILDREN)' declares 'the history, language and culture of Scotland do not exist. If they did, they would be of no importance and might as well not.'[43] It is only at university in England that Margaret discovers her nationality (Kennedy herself studied theatre at Warwick). 'The only two Scots on an English, English literature course', Margaret and Colin had formed a 'natural pair', though their Scottishness is stagily self-conscious. 'There was a formality about them that some of their fellow students found off-putting. Even drunk or stoned, they retained a strange air of propriety.'[44] England offers a world in which Margaret's alienation can be safely anchored in her cultural difference, and projected outside her brittle inner life. One of Colin's attractions is that 'he looked far too respectable to ever be rolling a joint. A Scottish upbringing had some good points.' After berating a nocturnal horn player as a 'fucking drunken English bastard', he wonders 'do you think that's me conforming to a national stereotype?'[45]

The insistence with which the novel thematises its Scottishness, going out of its way to highlight and address conventional national signifiers, is one reason *Looking for the Possible Dance* might be read as a representative 'new renaissance' novel; another is how clearly it premises the assertion of that Scottishness on rejections of Thatcherism. The key problem in Margaret's professional life is that it is 'impossible to work with people in the community, if your boss hates people and communities are being phased out as barriers to enterprise and foreign travel'.[46] The listless drop-in centre where she spends her days is mordantly known as the 'Fun Factory'. A 'grassroots' welfarist institution networked to hundreds of others across Britain, the Community Link Centre is shown to be a largely purposeless monument to the economic inactivity whose social impact it is intended to mitigate. Institutions embodying a more generous, 'native' welfarism north of the border (schools, hospitals, community centres, the social service bureaucracy) are figured as a profound threat to the autonomy of individuals. 'These places aren't meant for people and I'm a person and I will stay that way', says Margaret's father of the hospital where he waits to die.[47]

Margaret graduates 'in the summer after Orwell's year', at the height of British class conflict when 'England seemed more and more like a foreign country, even to itself.'[48] This national estrangement is mirrored by her dislocation as a British political subject.

Disturbed to find herself 'extremely happy' at radio reports of the IRA's Brighton bombs, 'it worried her when she stood in crowds and heard herself yelling with them, "One more cut – Thatcher's throat! One more cut – Thatcher's throat!" But she yelled it.'[49] Colin and Margaret know the protest is futile; the theatrical objectification of their dissent – of standing for what they stand for – hints both at the emptiness of democratic representation and its free rejection. Their politics becomes a cunning 'dance' both ineffectual and aesthetically sovereign, with no significance beyond its own constituent actions: 'they had decided they lived in a country where pointless gestures were all they had left to make. There was almost a nobility in that.'[50]

The ennobling of 'irrelevance and defeat'[51] is a key pattern in the formation of vernacular Scottishness in the 1980–90s, where the workless urban poor and their language are iconically nationalised: as despised remainders (or even internal enemies) within the Thatcherite narrative of self-reliance and unitary Britishness, but rhetorically central to an assertion of Scottish difference, community and authenticity. A. L. Kennedy is a stylist of Standard English, and largely uninterested in dialect. Compared with Welsh or Kelman, she engages more 'traditionally' with national display-identity, while thematising the problem of Scottishness in settings of broader (British) crisis and un-belonging. In this fiction, templates of nationhood are accessed to order and stabilise the fraught selfhood of individuals. These characters face bigger problems than frustrated patriotic feeling, but the pageantry and half-belief of national belonging offers some kind of stage-direction with which to recover a speaking part.

Thus the 'possible dance' of Kennedy's title becomes the elaborated set-piece in which the values of the local working-class community – articulated via received, 'couthy' conventions of Highlandism – are shown to trump both the economic individualism of government ideology, and the life-denying strictures of Mr Lawrence, Margaret's sinister (Scottish) boss at the community centre. The novel's climax is a charity ceilidh held on his premises, but organised by an unemployed working-class intellectual, Graham, who provides a suggestive gloss on this usable (and flexible) tradition:

The purposes of the ceilidh, a uniquely unsullied flowering of Scottish culture, are many. [. . .] As the Israelites in slavery had their psalms, so we have the ceilidh. As the Africans transported to Haiti kept their voodoo, so we have the ceilidh. As every languageless, stateless, selfless nation has one last, twisted image of its worst and best, we have the ceilidh. Here we pretend we are Highland, pretend we have mysteries in our work, pretend we have work. We forget our record of atrocities wherever we have been made masters and become comfortable servants again. Our present and our past creep in to change each other and we feel angry and sad and Scottish. Perhaps we feel free.[52]

Adroitly re-casting the traditional Scottish celebration into a focus of protest, liberation and wry self-knowledge, Kennedy allows kitsch images of Scottishness to be refigured as vaguely postcolonial vehicles of resistance and self-assertion. Graham decorates the centre with tartan banners and 'a battered Saltire', but the walls are also adorned with 'new signs', handwritten quotations from 'Thoreau, Brecht, Paine, Thomas Muir, Cervantes'.[53] The usable iconography of nationality is not simply unpacked and displayed like Christmas decorations, but altered and re-versioned. This selection-box of intellectual heroes forms a new, autodidact tableau of political identification, at the centre of which is the sovereignty and self-grounding of the Western subject. Graham gestures toward one of his chosen texts:

'Look over there – René Descartes. His "Second Meditation", fucking read it. He's telling me I can be everything, the whole fucking world – telling me that I can do that. I have that inside. And I'm fed up with folk who are certain that I'm nothing but shite underfoot. Tonight, I'm backing Descartes. We all are.'[54]

Read on its own emancipatory terms, this unlikely slogan clearly exceeds the Dream narrative of democratic self-actualisation (cultural devolution), and comes closer to an anarchist or existential vision of freedom; Alan Freeman argues that Kennedy's fiction concerns nothing less than 'the struggle to construct and sustain the human subject in contemporary life'.[55] Far from the autonomy of the Cartesian subject, however, Kennedy's characters are shown to lean heavily on the props and pageants of national difference. Rather than supplying the narrative context for interconnected identity, templates of nationhood are deployed to splint and stabilise the fraught selfhood of wounded individuals. Though their injuries are ambiguously national, the advent of a Scottish Parliament seems no more likely than the ceilidh or the community centre to alleviate the 'numberless, larger failings' of a society rich in identity-rituals but seemingly devoid of ordinary *ethos*.[56]

So I Am Glad (1995)

Kennedy's next novel, *So I Am Glad*, more pointedly questions the value of cultural forms such as the *détourned* ceilidh. Rather than enacting the 'Scottish' vision of social democracy enshrined as a usable national past, a fushionless nostalgia displaces resistance:

> As far as I can understand, my entire country spent generations immersed in more and more passionate versions of its own past, balancing its preoccupations with less and less organised activity or even interest in the here and now. Far more recently the whole island of which my country forms a part was swallowed wholesale by the promise of a ravenously brilliant future.[57]

But this wistfulness is no sooner named than indulged, as the narrator measures the emptiness of that promise against a vague folk memory: 'I have the impression that forty, even thirty, years ago, people worked towards what they might all do for each other.' This is a novel protesting against the nostalgia and de-socialisation it also reflects. When we first encounter M. Jennifer Wilson, she has withdrawn from the sharable social world to 'a small, still life that fitted very snugly around nobody but me'.[58] Wary of social or sexual intimacy, but disarmingly frank in her self-narration, Kennedy's protagonist has firm control of the boundaries around and within her private world. Forced as a child to observe her parents having sex, she seeks refuge from this obscene display within the opacity of witnessing itself: 'I knew, when they looked at me, that they couldn't tell how I was inside, unless I showed them.'[59] The grown-up Jennifer gives nothing away, is self-consciously unemotional, and gradually develops 'an invincible lack of involvement' in relationships. 'Like manholes and poison bottles I was made to be self-locking and I could no longer be bothered pretending I might have a key.'[60] But Jennifer is a household name, or rather a household voice, and as David Borthwick observes the novel quickly becomes a meditation on 'the actual, hidden privacy of the public sphere'.[61]

The forced witnessing of her childhood is repeated in the novel's opening scenes, as Jennifer finds herself compelled to listen to the inexplicable story of a mysterious spectral visitor, apparently suffering from amnesia and profoundly displaced from his origins. We gradually learn that the novel is Jennifer's own retrospective account of her relationship with this man, and a loving friendship that grows alongside the stranger's recovery of 'identity' figured as historical and linguistic otherness. The man is the French author and duellist Savinien de Cyrano de Bergerac (1619–55). While critical attention to the novel has focused on the magic realist qualities of this scenario – Savinien's 'reality' is verified by other characters, and no figment of Jennifer's imagination – my interest here is how the novel grounds the problem of his reality in *vocal presence*. Savinien's physical being is unstable and bizarre, but it is his ability to converse in a strangely poetic English which fully cements his position outside the order of 'identity'. He prefers the writer/reader scenario to 'being present with these words' in face-to-face speech, but the mutuality of conversation is what anchors Savinien's existence.[62] As 'the first woman [he] hears', Jennifer is nominated both as 'mother' and an all-witnessing Berkeleyan God, guaranteeing his existence by holding the visitor constantly in her perception:

I am sure I have no natural place on this planet. In your world or mine. I feel constantly precarious and I need the weight of your attention to secure me and allow me to be justified. I cannot just be, I must do and be seen to do and be heard to do and known to do and then I can live.[63]

Perhaps because he has a great deal staked on listening, Savinien has an extravagant sense of Jennifer's power as a Glasgow radio announcer and recorder of jingles: 'Wonderful! You can speak to an entire city and the province around it immediately. No matter what you intend them to know, they will know it, hear it as if you were speaking their thoughts.'[64] Employed as a 'professional enunciator', Jennifer's speech is positioned between the psychological isolation of the 'self-locking' monad and the public world to which her voice is broadcast. Speaking the words of others to unknowable strangers, her transmitted speech embodies not her personality but her social and emotional alienation. If Savinien is 'talking his world into existence',[65] the daily litany of violence, commerce and politics Jennifer spends her days announcing as verified public reality – 'the news' – sounds arch, unlikely and without objective reference: 'every thirty minutes, I was required to tell a fat, black goosenecked microphone about traffic irregularities, mutilated children, the wreckage of peace in Europe and the weather. I felt the syllables warm and open against my teeth, I licked and pushed and breathed them, kissed them goodbye.'[66]

These syllables have sensuous mass and colour, but what they signify is absent from them, a hollowness matched by the collectivity to which 'the news' is addressed. The socio-spatial range of Jennifer's transmitted voice contains a potential for unisonance, materialising a space of simultaneous we-ness, but one that only masks the real isolation of urban life. Between announcements, Jennifer thinks

> of the night that carried my voice. Potentially I was going with it everywhere, through walls and under buildings, into all the little corners of my city and several more beyond. Very few people were actually listening of course – other back-shifty workers, the taxi-cruising, night-watching types, professional seducers and policemen, the lone insomniacs.[67]

Far from fostering imagined community, Jennifer's broadcasts and recordings re-double the imagined solitude and marginalisation of her listeners, addressing them as isolated monads beyond any true experience of co-presence. She wonders 'how many hundreds

or thousands of [her nocturnal listeners] had masturbated themselves into compromise relaxation, coincidentally listening to my
voice'; a tableaux in which the voice is *within* the listener's experience, without realising any condition of *withness*.[68] This transmitted speech reaches but does not bridge the separate lives of these
anonymous thousands, and in a voice carefully voided of Jennifer's
own personal expressivity. Announcing words scripted by others,
constituting a shared reality of non-connection and unfreedom,
this speech is without lyric action or purpose, and simultaneously
drained of all Herderian communal 'glue'.

'The voice', writes Slavoj Žižek, 'displays a spectral autonomy.
It never quite belongs to the body we see, so that even when we
see a living person talking, there is always a minimum of ventriloquism at work: it is as if the speaker's own voice hollows
him out and speaks "by itself", through him.'[69] This impression
of autonomy is heightened in a 'self-locking' subject happy to be
regarded as hollow, and to reduce voice-work to the artful realisation of prescribed effects:

> I stayed awake, thinking only of striking the ideal tone,
> of adding or losing that second or two requested and of
> the essential musicality to fake and make. My breathing
> was clear and round and utterly invisible. [. . .] I ran up
> and down the octaves like a rat in a greasy drain, I turned
> accents by minutes within the degree until they were more
> themselves than they had any right to be.[70]

Acutely conscious of her 'role as life-support system to a voice',
Jennifer is a physical conduit for words determined elsewhere, and
only registers her own subjectivity and moral stance at the level of
tone.[71] Viewed within the horizon of Scottish cultural politics, the
iconic scenes of the novel are those depicting Jennifer as an emergent political subject facing a dilemma of vocal stylisation. Toward
the end of the novel, as her growing love for Savinien gives her
a reason to care about the world she announces into shared reality, Jennifer acquires an aural attitude, a 'tone' for which she is
reproached by her superiors at the radio station.[72] Her personal
sensibility and politics begin to be realised through 'an unnecessary

colour in the voice, an air of negative comment' which reflect her accumulated outrage with government by 'born-again Nazis'.[73] But she stops short of *speaking* her mind: 'I never said a word. I only thought. My tone was the only protest I could make.'[74] Jennifer's speech embodies her (and, it would seem, Scotland's) hostility to Thacherite political values; but this meaning is carried in the gap *between* scripted words and their humanising embodiment, between 'content' and voice as the non-verbal remainder of speech. Like the sovereign gestures of the protest-dance in Kennedy's first novel, Jennifer acquires expressive agency within a media form which *empties* her voice of political subjectivity.

If Jennifer's voice-work reduces her to a dualistic 'mouth without a brain', a 'living bellows drawing and shaping air into fiction', the nature of this fiction is triple.[75] The systematic deceit of advertising and 'the news'; the unreal collectivity addressed by these broadcasts (the fiction of 'community'); and the lie of 'voicing' the words of the script, granting them a human presence in which to be vectored to the audience-market. In truth, Jennifer is better on precision than warmth. Until late in the novel, the absence from her voice of personal affect, or any trace of sociocultural specificity – the colouration of the vernacular – conveys both the hollowness of her ventriloquism and Jennifer's true inner state:

> While we recorded, each word would emerge with nothing but itself, a courageous little assembly of sibilants, fricatives, plosives – lips and teeth and tips of tongues. When I work I listen hard, inside and out, and all I could hear was loneliness, slipping and smoking under every phrase, one great lack of the noise of any other living thing. I would stare through the coloured haze of my reflection in the booth glass and feel like an astronaut peering down over the edge of for ever.[76]

This inversion of Herderian speech-community sees Jennifer imagine herself into Savinien's predicament of total displacement in space and time ('I am the loneliest man in the world'[77]), marooned in 'voice' *not* as the embodiment of self or community, but as the repertoire of techniques by which their fragile fictionality is masked.

Kelman, voice and being

Kennedy's account of her beginnings as a Scottish writer echo those of Alan Warner, Janice Galloway and many others; Alasdair Gray and *Lanark*, and then

> Gray's work led me to [the poet] Tom Leonard and James Kelman, writers who broke the most fundamental rule of my childhood – they sounded Scottish. When I was a child, if you wanted to be successful, you had to sound anglicised or English. [. . .] Leonard and Kelman produced work that celebrated their right to sound like themselves and extended that courtesy to the reader. [. . .] You can imagine the effect of feeling that if you open your mouth you will sound wrong, that you are somehow thinking wrongly in your own head. Instilling such a feeling is one of the most fundamental ways to control a population. Now imagine what happens when the feeling stops – that miracle.[78]

I conclude with the most significant and influential figure in the literary developments this book explores. In a 1995 article, Dorothy McMillan notes the authenticating appeal of demotic experience in the 'new' Scotland: 'some engagement with the folk or the people has generally been found necessary in the construction of a notion of nation and it is, of course, in the urban discourses of James Kelman and his disciples that most critics north and south of the border have found the new centre of Scottishness'.[79] Michael Gardiner's 2005 primer on *Modern Scottish Culture* installs Kelman at the heart of cultural devolution: 'dissatisfied with being politically silenced in the 1980s and 1990s, [Scots] had to find a creative solution [. . .] Kelman's rise came at a time when Scots were literally finding a political "voice" in the form of the new Parliament.'[80] But Kelman's best-known novel underscores the limits of conceiving voice as a channel for transmitting 'given' identities into pre-constituted representative space. Gardiner's reading of *How late it was, how late* as a 'direct representation of devolution' therefore strikes me as antithetical; on the contrary, Kelman's most celebrated novel is forearmed against intercessionary mechanisms of power, and pointedly refuses to conceive power *as* representation on the devolutionary model.[81] Instead *How late* constitutes voice as the medium of *being*, and pungently insists 'there's a difference between repping somebody and fucking being somebody'.[82] As in much of Kelman's fiction, the narration seems to directly embody the subjectivity and ipseity of his characters – of *The Busconductor Hines* we are told 'his language contains his brains and his brains are a singular kettle of fish'[83] – in language which is nonetheless saturated in class, place and Balibar's 'common acts' of exchange.

With extraordinary immediacy *How late* seems to enact rather than describe the drama of Sammy's inner life as he navigates the living moment, but in a relational idiom which de-centres his self-narration into a form of reportage:

> Quiet voices quiet voices, he was gony have to move man he was gony have to fucking move, now, he stepped back, pushing out the door and out onto the pavement he went left, tapping as quick as he could, keeping into the wall. He hit against somebody but battered on, just to keep going, he was fine man he was okay except this feeling like any minute the wallop from behind, the blow in the back, the quick rush of air then thud, he kept going, head down, the shoulders hunched.[84]

This hyper-naturalist effect cannot but flirt with the positivism of ethnographic writing; words that seem to 'precipitate the culture they purport to describe'.[85] Yet they also, in Kelman, enregister the particularity of the individual's lifeworld and his freedom from what ethnographic writing (and parliamentary displays of identity) would reify as 'given'.[86] Sammy is an unemployed ex-convict who wakes up on a patch of Glasgow waste ground, unaccountably assaults some undercover police officers, and is blinded soon after they take their revenge. *How late* conveys, with overpowering intensity, his efforts to navigate this predicament, one compounded by the disappearance of his girlfriend and acute police interest in friends Sammy may or may not have met during a drinking binge he cannot remember. As he navigates various circles of bureaucratic purgatory, moving from police custody to

doctors' offices to charity clinics via the state social security apparatus, Sammy encounters lawyers, fellow prisoners and his young
son. But he remains utterly alone in his struggle, and insists on a
personally authenticated confrontation with state power: 'He had
nay intention of using a rep [lawyer]. [. . .] Nay cunt was gony get
him out of trouble; nay cunt except himself.'[87]

How late it was, how late is a heroic monument to the freedom
and resilience of the individual subject – if any contemporary novelist 'backs Descartes', it is Kelman – but the fiction of psychological immersion he achieves is largely divorced from recognisable
Scottish society. Traces of contemporary Glasgow are few and
cursory, with the important exception of language: the medium
of this character's psychic being, mobilised as a literary device
which seems to embody rather than signify social rootedness. In
'obliterating' the universalist third-person narrative space from
which his characters might formerly have been 'fixed' as objects –
their lives and speech rendered as mere sociological facts by an
external, 'colonising' Standard English narrator – Kelman's narrative experiments severely attenuate the 'interconnected' spatiality
of the national imaginary. In this respect his narrative experiments
aim to realise *subjectivity* rather than nationality, and his influence
on the contemporary novel is not confined to Scotland.[88]

Unparliamentary language

In Kelman's writing, the politics of personal expression are urgently
connected to wider structures of 'representation' and governance.
In the climactic scene of his first novel *The Busconductor Hines*,
the titular hero reflects on his past experience of garage politics as
the union intervenes to prevent his sacking: 'Once upon a time
he was ejected from a Branch Meeting for applying the term
Shite to a Chairman's summing up. That kind of thing should be
beyond belief.'[89] Even after the meeting has unanimously decided
to threaten strike action over Hines' case, and his Shop Steward
has been dispatched to relay the message to management, he cannot take seriously this model of proxy action via speech: 'What is
the point. There is no point in any of it. They do not understand.
There is no point in speech. How come they speak. What do they

speak for. It is beyond belief. How come people are content to act in this manner. Are they fucking crazy.'[90]

Like Sammy's refusal to pursue a compensation claim in *How late*, Hines cannot allow himself to be drawn into a structure of representative power which would exclude both fundamental questions of justice and the personal basis of his own struggle. Both his oppression and his means of deliverance must remain within the orbit of his own self-determination, which is limited to the sphere of his own action and 'inner speech'.[91]

This stance is not compatible with the parliamentary governance of 'representative' speech. Pierre Bourdieu observes that parliament

> is a site where struggles between groups, interest groups, classes if you like, are waged according to rules of the game, meaning that all conflicts outside of these struggles have something semi-criminal about them. Marx saw this 'parliamentarization' of political life as analogous to the theatre [. . .] a kind of collective delusion that citizens allow themselves to be caught up in, a shadow-play that obscures the real struggles taking place elsewhere.[92]

In this 'site of regulated consensus, or dissension within certain limits', parliament 'may rule out both objects of dissension and perhaps above all ways of expressing dissension. People who lack the right way of expressing dissension are excluded from legitimate political life.'[93] There are clear resonances here with the controversies attending Kelman's entire critical reception, and most prominently his 'legitimation' by the 1994 Booker Prize he received for a novel (*How late*) bitterly resented by elitist commentators for its 'semi-criminal' language and social milieu.[94] It is perfectly possible to alter the parameters of inclusion, admitting new voices and expressions, without altering parliament's character as the 'juridically constituted and juridically controlled space, within which conflicts are regulated'.[95] This applies to 'new' democratic institutions quite as forcibly as to prize juries. Bourdieu emphasises that this critique of parliamentarism 'is a problem that troubled the working-class movement in the nineteenth century':

> Should we join the parliamentary game or remain outside?
> [. . .] Do we resort to strikes and demonstrations, or to the
> mediation of parliamentarians? These debates have been
> forgotten, but their outcome remains in our unconscious
> and in our institutions.[96]

This is precisely the terrain of Kelman's writing, and of his characters' inner lives.[97] As we have seen, he has no truck with a politics
of 'representation' on parliamentary terms, and the lessons of his
political activism are instructive in grasping their limits. In a 1990
essay recounting his personal experience with the Workers City
campaign group – established to contest the gentrifying re-brand
of Glasgow in the 1990 City of Culture – Kelman describes a large
group of protestors determined to confront Glasgow city council-
lors considering a proposal to privatise part of Glasgow Green.
'About 200 folk turned up. Mostly individuals unconnected to any
grouping. Very few young folk. We took it to them by entering
en masse. [. . .] we just empowered ourselves, walked through and
on up to the room in question. A good initiative this. It means we
were playing by our rules, keeping control.'[98]

On gaining entry to the council chamber ('we followed without waiting for an invitation, walking as a body'), the 'Chairman
asked for three representatives to speak on behalf of the public'.

> This was a body of people representing nobody but them-
> selves, it was not a formal grouping of any kind. That point
> was missed by every official there. They could not seem to
> comprehend the possibility of individual members of the
> public coming together to act as they were acting. The idea
> that nobody was empowered to 'represent' folk seemed
> totally alien to any of them.[99]

Here the capacity for empowered action is clearly antithetical to
'representation' on parliamentary terms (viciously satirised, in the
context of home rule politics, in his 1992 essay 'Let the Wind
Blow High Let the Wind Blow Low', discussed in Chapter 4).
This political action is 'vernacular' in the sense of retaining its
own autonomy from the protocols of the official institution, but

also crystallising its own rules and norms – of endowing its creative energies with *form*. Kelman's fiction even more clearly separates the possibility of personal agency and creativity from the
discourse of democratic stand-ins.

Inkliz spaking

A related strand of Kelman's work theatrically flouts the protocols
of verbal 'identity' for its own anarchic pleasure. Take the cartoonish blur of *déraciné* lingo in Kelman's *You Have to be Careful in
the Land of the Free*, in which a 'failed fucking immigrant' spends
a final night in the USA before flying home/hame to Glasgow.
Though the protagonist's inner speech is grounded in Glasgow,
what it says dispels any affection for homely *ethos*: 'I was an Inkliz-
spaking pink-face caucasian frae a blood-and-soil motherland heil
hitler hail mary hullo to king billy.'[100] This hyperbolic rejection of
roots is a guide to the novel's energetic de-coupling of voice and
place. The more Jerry ponders his displacement, the more playfully itinerant his language becomes:

> Nay wonder people got sick of me. Who wants to listen to
> some girning-faced furnir prick constantly moaning. Why
> dont ya fuck off hame to yer ayn country and moan. Yeh,
> precisely, le billet is booked monsieur. So gie us a smoke to
> celebrate. And a bier, où est le bier? Donde está la señorita!
> Eh hombre, gie us el brekko.[101]

This estrangement reflects not only his own personal displacement but Jerry's role as a security operative policing his fellow
'furnirs' and drifters, holders of 'Red Cards' denoting (and paradoxically securing) their status as non-citizens untrusted to settle
and naturalise: 'I am a non-integratit unassimilatit member of the
alienigenae. That to me is important.'[102] Embracing this marginal
condition and its contingency – his apparent freedom from a stable, 'given' identity authenticated by origins – a dizzying array
of territorial slangs, jargons and patois are constituted as Jerry's
pidgin of unbelonging: 'No savvy hombré, I dont fokking know,
everyting ees concealed.'[103]

When Jerry thinks of 'hame' he imagines a static, risible, tour-ist board Scotland; and since 'all that blood and soil stuff is a joke, it is a fucking joke',[104] he instead constructs himself as a 'furnir' in solidarity with the marginalised and oppressed – and perhaps parasitic upon their claims to justice and self-assertion. ('My peo-ple were slaves as well', Jerry tells his black girlfriend Yasmin, who with dry forbearance 'found that hard to believe'.[105]) With objective exclusion comes freedom from determinate 'identity', and license to roam the margins of American culture in romantic freedom. The cartoonish liberties available to those constituted outside the order of standardised language and identity blossom into Kelman's most successful exercise in surreal fancy. Here Jerry recalls some buddy movie exploits with an Iraqi friend:

> Gambling with [Haydar] I went skint umpteen times but through him I landed in some unmissable experiences, occasionally of the Keystone Cops variety.
>
> The women he favoured were no skeenee cheeks my frenn no sir these were women females with the curves and the soft places [. . .] He wasnay even handsome; a heavyset feller with a big heid and then the fucking lip growth. I thought the mountain man muslim background was all just an excuse for the moostachayo that draped its way ower his fizzog. How in tarnation he got off with women wearing one of them I dont know. He insisted on wearing it but and it was just goddam ludicrous. Like maist of us he had a tremendous regard for Pancho Villa but so what, it doesnay mean ye stop shaving.[106]

This play of language – strongly recalling the cartoon voice-work of Mel Blanc – both caters to and scrambles the appetite for col-our, otherness and idiosyncrasy which has always formed part of the appeal of vernacular writing. If this text shares in the 'kinetic' satisfactions of *Trainspotting*, it also undercuts the fetishism of roots and difference, re-materialising in its own ceaseless dodging the 'weight' and burden of *Volkssprache*, encountered not as Herderian hame territory but as a transverse space of vocal contestation and potential entrapment. The vernacular here is not simply a pliable medium with which the self-choosing subject fashions identity, but the crowded terrain *in which* political subjecthood is claimed and contested; where 'identity' is an ideological inscription with juridical repercussions. Jerry's refusal of origins, territory and everything implied by the notion of 'naturalisation' (either in language or migration) locates him, romantically, outside any fixed order. But if this leaves the character objectively paralysed in recollection, speculation and regret, his inner speech is also highly charged with vocal *actionality* – and neither discharges this freedom in 'marginal' postures of singularity, nor grounds it in pre-given 'subaltern' community. Here the vernacular subject struggles for its own protocols of belonging and unbelonging, identity and difference, through its own self-concretion as political utterance.

Inheritors

For a younger generation of novelists, the radical intensities of Welsh and Kelman *are* traditional, and viewed somewhat uncritically. Alan Bissett sees 'new Glasgow writers' such as Suhayl Saadi and Ewan Morrison as 'emulat[ing] Kelman's vernacular achievements', but in postmodern fictions 'saturated with pop culture, iPods, the internet, shopping and brand names'.[107] Recruiting the Glasgow demotic as a 'style' available to re-mixing and imaginative self-fashioning, Bissett sees this writing as 'the Scottish equivalent of hip-hop' insofar as it 'chronicles the urban experience in a politicised and vernacular mode': '"Mixing" contemporary youth culture's commodity language with a Glaswegian syntax and lexicon, they produce a new aesthetics, at once local and global, which successfully subverts late-capitalist consumerism's signifiers by appropriation and recontextualization.'[108] This strikes me as too hopeful a reading. Just as the creative 'recontextualisation' of a musical sample presupposes its prior reification – its *de*-contextualisation and reduction to an aural pose – this 'bad' aestheticisation of vernacular language, reducing it to a colourful 'idiom' available for consumption and political exploitation cannot but participate in the commodification Bissett sees this 'New Weegie' writing as counteracting. The semiotic exoticism of the vernacular, encountered in the context of international popular culture, tends to reinforce identitarian display by 'emptying' (or, to side-step tropes of romantic embodiment, *shallowing*) the ideological inscription of the vernacular sign (as subaltern speech). Far from 'eradicating political, racial and national disparities', this difference-fetishising appetite for signs, motifs and languages encrusted with historical conflict merely renders them up as exhilarating spectacle to the dislocated cosmopolitan consumer.[109]

Conclusion: solidarity's signposts

In the decade prior to legislative devolution, *authenticated marginality* became the core identity-message of a vernacular Scottishness free to refuse the hegemonic obligations of 'representation' (e.g. in the democratic order), while remaining available for display in the spectacle of 'identity'. The political limits of this paradigm will by now be clear. Scottish 'cultural demands' for national visibility and recognition were to be managed and accommodated within the existing constitutional order, inscribing 'difference' into the UK state. A neo-national Scottish literature, confidently employing language not quite Standard English and not quite 'separatist' (or Ideal) Scots, strongly resonates with the flexible management of 'national feeling' envisioned in 1970s devolutionary thinking. In effect, neo-popular vernacular writing becomes a way of disguising the limits of devolution's cultural logic, presenting a 'legitimised' medium of representation as a form of action and power in its own right. But we could equally say that vernacular writing refuses the standardising obligations of 'government' which come with settled (standard) form, preferring the provisional and un-finalised character of language developing immanently *within* culture, and eschewing any fixed civic or constitutional principle authorising – but also 'containing' – its possibilities.

Its intense particularism trumping – and co-opting – residues of demotic communion, vernacular writing exceeds the democratic claim for recognition and participation, overspilling the civic sphere and its representative forms. In Scottish writing of the devolutionary period, it seems to me, there are two main paths for this overspill: 'depth' and lyric embodiment of the romantic subject (as in Kelman's *How late it was, how late*), or the kinetic 'rush' of vocal spectacle (the exoticised lingos of Welsh's *Trains-potting*). Examining these separate flows reveals something about the limits of the democratic container itself, and the inadequacy of conflating 'voice' with second-order political cipherment (of the theatrical kinds employed in Kennedy's *Looking for the Possible Dance*). Yet shallow commodification of voice proves difficult to separate from appeals to its plenitude as an object of national attachment. The civic-democratic metonym of 'vocal' empowerment cannot reconcile or govern the vernacular's restless shuttling between romantic and postmodern registers of authenticity, its simultaneous claims to cultural rootedness and semiotic autonomy. As a vehicle separate from its expressive content, 'voice' in *So I Am Glad* mediates a fundamental projection of self onto world, without ever realising a medium of shared social being or consciousness. In this period the very condition of Scottish nationality was increasingly figured as a personal and provisional choice, and disconnected from questions of origin or ethnicity, notably in Alasdair Gray's *Why Scots Should Rule Scotland*, first published in 1992. As Linda Gunn and Alistair McCleery observed of the devolutionary ethos of *Edinburgh Review*, in 1990s writing it seems that 'a "free" Scotland would be composed of individuals',[110] on the very pattern by which communitarian 'Scottish values', effectively silenced by the voting preferences of England, were leveraged to secure institutions of distinctive government. In these circumstances the 'imaginary' qualities and carriers of national collectivity were specially freighted. Scottish vernacular writing was invested with a heightened and autonomous power: a nationalised class-speech seeming to index an imperishable communal ethos, reified as solidarity's signposts.

Writing in 2005, Carla Sassi argued that 'Scotland has gone a long way towards a full recognition of its culture, its languages and its literature', such that the defensive compulsion toward national self-definition 'belongs to an historical period that is now over'. In the more confident era of devolution, another challenge comes to the fore: 'that of checking globalization and of resisting assimilation to the falsely multicultural, "united colours" ideal promoted by glossy magazines'.[111] But these are not distinct processes or stages: the commodification of Scottish identity and 'voice', enabled by a postmodern valorisation of 'difference' and marginality, was a key means by which Scottishness was promoted and re-fashioned in the 1990s. The bazaar of shallow and stylised 'identities' Sassi evokes under the sign of globalisation – she highlights the popularity of *Braveheart* (1995) with the xenophobic Lega Nord movement in Italy – is not the 'false' after-image of some real or indigenous self-definition that came before, but the very cultural condition *in which* an image of Scottishness emerged which satisfied Huggan's 'mainstream demand for an "authentic", readily translatable, marginal voice', without breaking from the cultural logic of devolution (that is, 'full recognition' of Scottish literature and language).

As Matthew Wickman writes of the intellectual project of legitimising Scotland's distinctiveness, 'the postmodern moment in some ways comes first'.[112] Emphasis on the national sign and not its referent – or the 'dimension' and not its condition – has indeed been a major theme of the preceding history. James Mitchell notes the fetishisation of *representation* within the milieu of pro-devolution campaign groups: 'it was as if the creative energies of [the new parliament's] supporters concentrated on questions of representation. All would be well so long as the new institution embodying Scottish interests was representative.'[113] Devolved institutions, in overtly recognising (electoral) signs of national feeling, would assimilate them to the sphere of democratic spectacle. The theatre of linguistic difference in recent Scottish writing has unwittingly re-inscribed this logic, in which the very display of 'Scottish identity' is equated with neo-national liberation. Pervasive tropes of voice cement the expression of Scottishness with a demand for limited and provisional autonomy; a demand premised on romantic investments, but discharged in postmodern currency.

We should recall that parliamentary representation is founded on absence and substitution: one speaking, somewhat mysteriously, in place of many others.[114] Reified as a display-event within pre-constituted representative space, even stirring and rebellious voices saturated with 'roots', uttering the most stinging rebukes to institutional power, are incorporated within its legitimising rituals. Admitted to the regulated consensus of parliamentary theatre, the vernacular can never generate *new form* out of its own unsettled and illegible status; here 'voice' functions as a deployment of representative power, rather than *grounding* the contestation of agency, otherness and recognition.[115] Assimilated by hegemonic power as a sign of its own generous flexibility, this liberal-democratic 'voice' occludes the utopian vernacular utterance yet to come, which realises its own action and authorises its own claims to liberty and presence.

Notes

1. Paterson, *Orpheus*, p. 84.
2. Mack, 'Can the Scottish subaltern speak?', p. 148. For Wellington's performance see <https://youtu.be/5F4KdkQTKBw> (accessed 23 February 2019).
3. Mack, 'Can the Scottish subaltern speak?', p. 148.
4. McIlvanney, *Burns the Radical*, p. 1.
5. Anderson, *Imagined Communities*, p. 145.
6. Donald Dewar, 'Donald Dewar's speech at the opening of the Scottish Parliament, 1 July 1999'.
7. Alex Salmond, 'Parliament re-elects First Minister' [Alex Salmond's acceptance speech], 18 May 2011.
8. Balibar, 'The nation form: history and ideology', p. 97.
9. Ibid. p. 98.
10. Casanova, *The World Republic of Letters*, p. 106.
11. Stefanie Lehner's 'subaltern aesth*ethics*' conceives 'the aesthetic as an ongoing negative critique either side of the devolutionary event'. While the present study shares (something like) this goal, I do not here pursue Lehner's largely philosophical framing of subalternity, and have instead sought to locate its value within cultural and electoral politics. See Lehner's *Subaltern Ethics in Contemporary Scottish and Irish Literature*, p. 41.
12. Kelly, *Irvine Welsh*, p. 70. This chapter draws on Kelly's critique of devolution in 'James Kelman and the reterritorialisation of power'.
13. Quoted by Gunn and McCleery, 'Wasps in a jam jar', p. 49.
14. O'Hagan, 'Scotland's old injury', p. 24.
15. Bell, 'Imagine living there', p. 226.
16. Craig, *The Modern Scottish Novel*, p. 12.
17. Anderson, *Imagined Communities*, p. 32.
18. Keating, 'Nationalist movements in comparative perspective', pp. 206–7.

19. Huggan, *The Postcolonial Exotic*, pp. 26–7.
20. Macdonald, *Whaur Extremes Meet*, p. 297.
21. Robert Alan Jamieson, 'MacDiarmid's spirit burns on', *Chapman*, 69–70 (Autumn 1992), pp. 3–8 (p. 5).
22. Welsh, *Trainspotting*, p. 166.
23. Schoene, *The Edinburgh Companion to Irvine Welsh*, p. 1.
24. Willy Maley questions Welsh and Kelman's re-inscription of capitalist individualism in 'Denizens, citizens, tourists and others: marginality and mobility in the writings of James Kelman and Irvine Welsh'.
25. Welsh, *Trainspotting*, p. 228.
26. Morace, 'Irvine Welsh: parochialism, pornography and globalisation', p. 227.
27. Harvie, *Scotland and Nationalism*, p. 212.
28. Ibid. p. 106.
29. Ibid. p. 211.
30. Whyte, 'Masculinities in contemporary Scottish fiction', p. 275.
31. On the later evolution of 'social nationalism', see Gallagher, Scothorne and Westwell, *Roch Winds*.
32. Orwell, *Complete Works*, vol. XIX, p. 44.
33. Innes, 'Mark Renton's bairns', p. 301.
34. Anderson, *Imagined Communities*, p. 133.
35. Welsh, *Trainspotting*, pp. 28–9.
36. Alan Freeman, 'Realism fucking realism: the word on the street – Kelman, Kennedy and Welsh', *Cencrastus*, 57 (1997), pp. 6–7 (p. 6).
37. McCrone, Morris and Kiely, *Scotland the Brand*, p. 207.
38. Wallace, 'Voices in an empty house', p. 217.
39. Kennedy, *Looking for the Possible Dance*, p. 191.
40. Freeman, 'Realism fucking realism', p. 7.
41. Kennedy, *Looking for the Possible Dance*, p. 9.
42. Ibid. p. 10.
43. Ibid. p. 15.
44. Ibid. p. 38.
45. Ibid. p. 44.
46. Ibid. p. 75.
47. Ibid. p. 128.
48. Ibid. p. 38.
49. Ibid. p. 39.
50. Ibid. p. 39.
51. Ibid. p. 40.
52. Ibid. pp. 145–6.
53. Ibid. p. 172.

54. Ibid. p. 173.
55. Freeman, 'Realism fucking realism', p. 7.
56. Kennedy, *Looking for the Possible Dance*, p. 24.
57. Kennedy, *So I Am Glad*, p. 187.
58. Ibid. p. 4.
59. Ibid. p. 71.
60. Ibid. p. 4.
61. Borthwick, 'A. L. Kennedy's dysphoric fictions', p. 267.
62. Kennedy, *So I Am Glad*, p. 176.
63. Ibid. pp. 19, 44.
64. Ibid. p. 39.
65. Ibid. p. 68.
66. Ibid. p. 61.
67. Ibid. p. 61.
68. Ibid. p. 61.
69. Quoted by Dolar, *A Voice and Nothing More*, p. 70.
70. Kennedy, *So I Am Glad*, pp. 114–15.
71. Ibid. p. 132.
72. Ibid. p. 218.
73. Ibid. pp. 218, 220.
74. Ibid. p. 221.
75. Ibid. p. 217.
76. Ibid. p. 115.
77. Ibid. p. 56.
78. Kennedy, 'Scotland's cultural awakening is a terrifying prospect for politicians'.
79. McMillan, 'Constructed out of bewilderment: stories of Scotland', p. 84.
80. Gardiner, *Modern Scottish Culture*, p. 155.
81. Gardiner, 'Literature, theory, politics', p. 49.
82. Kelman, *How late it was, how late*, p. 241.
83. Kelman, *The Busconductor Hines*, p. 254.
84. Kelman, *How late*, p. 272. On the 'inner heterocentricity' of the protagonist see Craig, *The Modern Scottish Novel*, p. 102.
85. Ashcroft, *Caliban's Voice*, p. 128.
86. See Hames, 'Kelman's art speech'.
87. Kelman, *How late*, p. 245.
88. See Akbar, 'Sounds of the street'.
89. Kelman, *The Busconductor Hines*, p. 235.
90. Ibid. p. 242.
91. See Hames, 'Maybe just singing into yourself'.

92. Bourdieu, *On the State*, p. 355.
93. Ibid. pp. 355–6.
94. See McGlynn, '*How late it was, how late* and literary value'.
95. Bourdieu, *On the State*, p. 356.
96. Ibid. p. 356.
97. See Kelman's story 'Street sweeper' in *The Burn* (1991) for an example of a character's inner monologue merging with the procedural and ceremonious language of British parliamentary debate.
98. Kelman, 'Subjective account', p. 82.
99. Ibid. p. 83.
100. Kelman, *You Have to be Careful in the Land of the Free*, p. 132.
101. Ibid. p. 52.
102. Ibid. p. 151.
103. Ibid. p. 159.
104. Ibid. p. 106.
105. Ibid. p. 407.
106. Ibid. p. 64.
107. Bissett, 'The "New Weegies"', p. 63.
108. Ibid. p. 63.
109. Ibid. p. 63.
110. Gunn and McCleery, 'Wasps in a jam jar', pp. 47–8.
111. Sassi, *Why Scottish Literature Matters*, pp. 11–12.
112. Wickman, 'The emergence of Scottish Studies', p. 250.
113. Mitchell, 'Devolution without self-government', p. 30.
114. See Pitkin, *The Concept of Representation*, p. 54 and Morgan, *Inventing the People*, p. 39.
115. On 'the relationality already put in action by the simple reciprocal communication of voices', see Cavarero, *For More Than One Voice*, p. 16.

Conclusion

I began this study by highlighting Alan Warner's concern that 'the whole Scottish literature "project"' would live or die by the result of the 2014 referendum on independence. As should now be clear, this warning was less perplexing than it first appears: in 'co-constituting' a new Scotland and their hopes of cultural leadership, several generations of writers, intellectuals, journalists and politicians had established a discursive frame eliding literary and political representation. Incorporated into the ethos, theatre and self-image of devolved governance, the critical and creative endeavour called Scottish Literature was, by 2014, often difficult to separate from the political project with which it is entwined. That project is nationalist in its core logic and 'final vocabulary', but in the political circumstances of post-1960s Britain it was re-fashioned into the cause of 'identity', 'recognition' and 'distinctive government', and fulfilled these democratic aims in a condition just short of independence. From the 'cultural' point of view, the limited and expressive autonomies afforded by devolution are sufficient, and perhaps preferable to what would be entailed by a full claim to statehood and national literary space.

In this regard, it is puzzling how little interest the specific character and limits of devolution has attracted, especially viewed as a living and 'unsettled' condition (rather than a constitutional 'process' to be narrated and explained from without). If I have one simple and uncontentious conclusion to offer the reader, it is that Scottish devolution is not only a set of political structures, but a cultural condition. Indeed, the legitimacy of the political structures has been premised on the historic reality and electoral salience of cultural difference, and on these terms the 'cultural

devolution' thesis is easy to accept. But the legacy of this paradigm in forming and reproducing Scottish culture goes beyond
the history-reading public, beyond occasional confusion about
the stakes of novel-writing versus electioneering, or the broader
vagueness David McCrone highlights as a mismatch between the
influence and persuasiveness of 'cultural' explanations for socio-
political change.[1]

The rhetorical strategies by which devolved Scotland was
achieved are alive in its continuing lifeworld. Constituted as a
trans-class people-nation in the logic of 'representative' empowerment, the devolved habitus involves a specific historical formation of Scottish identity, a specific distribution of symbolic capital,
and a specific allocation of subject-positions and available 'voices'.
They are inscribed in the patterns of Scottish civic-institutional
life just as legibly as the literary quotations embedded in the walls
of the parliament. A distinctive Scottish 'identity' is the premise
of these devolved structures, but also their promised outcome,
continually fashioned and reproduced to affirm what devolution
assumes in advance. Favouring the cause of Scottish self-government (as I do) is no reason to turn away from these processes, or
to refrain from their critique.

Literary and cultural critics are well-placed to undertake this task,
and perhaps specially obligated as well. Within the shifting political
conditions surveyed in this study, and by the nature of its national(ist)
instatement, 'Scottish literary studies' tends to reproduce Scottish distinction and cultural capital on terms compatible with the
'claims of right' of the political class. It was the densely networked
and overlapping professional circles of 'Civic Scotland' who were
directly empowered by devolution, and it was via the logic of liberated 'social-and-national' identity that this governing strata secured
effective ownership of the vernacular nationhood constructed by
writers, politicians and activist-editors. Nancy Fraser reminds us that
the identity model, 'in reifying group identity [. . .] ends by obscur-
ing the politics of cultural identification, the struggles *within* the
group for the authority – and the power – to represent it'.[2] On just
these terms, the governing elite of devolved Scotland extract political 'rent' from collective symbolic capital (the half-strategic, half-
nostalgic image of national working-classness), having successfully

turned a rhetoric of mongrel resistance to non-democracy into the corporatist governing ethic of 'Team Scotland'.[3]

Viewed in this light, Warner's caution against jeopardising the 'Scottish literature "project"' evokes both the strength and ambiguity of the enterprise: the degree to which the literary intelligentsia really did play a major role in constituting the cultural warrant and political logic of Scottish devolution. In turn, the literati were able to benefit from the myths and flexibilities built into the constitutional reform in whose image they defined (and sometimes inflated) their social authority: as leaders of an audacious cultural movement which transformed the political order from 'outside' the formal system of parties and elections, creating the sociocultural conditions (of restored confidence, 'identity' and self-knowledge) which enabled Scotland to choose to democratise itself in 1999. The flexibilities were key, for devolution was nobody's dream, and such a halfway house – stalled, abandoned and jerry-rigged at several points of its construction – compels no fixed or unwavering belief. The commitment required of Civic Scotland from the late 1980s was not to full democratic empowerment but to 'representation' itself, on terms which carried few significant risks to their continuing authority (and strong prospects of its expansion). Even the stirring, categorical language of the *Claim of Right* finally shrinks from its own logic to request 'distinctive government' (expressing Scottish difference) rather than the full sovereignty of its founding premises. In this sense, its drafting author Jim Ross – a retired Whitehall official – is by some distance the most wily and consequential Scottish writer of the period. In the domain of culture, the voluntarist nature of pro-devolution consensus is matched by the object it realises – 'identity' – which is easily chosen, un-chosen or renounced as suits the occasion: a 'free-floating cultural representation', in Fraser's terms, which can be discarded like Mark Renton's Leith accent in those tricky moments where national working-classness loses its cachet.

I am conscious that this study will often seem antagonistic to the developments it examines and documents, especially in the ears of those who have devoted their own talents to a remarkably successful cultural-political project (which undoubtedly changed Scotland for the better). Adopting a critical orientation to these processes, I hope to illuminate rather than diminish them, though in ways that consciously break from the pervasive boosterism of Scottish cultural life (one of the most regrettable legacies of the nation-building process here described). This is a selective view of the writing and political movements at issue, and a study with different aims would yield a different picture of post-1979 Scottish fiction, of the periodical culture of the 1960s–80s, and of the broader civic movement for self-government. The resulting impression of the relative contribution of men and women to devolution is just as dismaying as the Canongate Wall. This is largely the consequence of my specific focus on the male-dominated print cultures and political milieus of the 1960s–80s charted in Chapters 1–4. Largely for reasons of space, I have focused on the coteries and cultural reviews of the national(ist) intelligentsia, in ways that downplay the broader coverage and discussion of home rule politics in newspapers and the popular press. If my focus on cultural nationalist commentary and activism, and the direct interface between political parties and Scottish literary culture, paints too narrow a picture of these developments – a picture that sidelines women's groups, 'new social movements', anti-nuclear and anti-racist campaigners, and which marginalises the key economic context of 'national' industrial strategy (including trade union organisation) – I trust the specific aims of my approach will be borne in mind. I look forward to more comprehensive critical studies of all these inter-related developments.

Literary Scotland and critique

The devolving motifs traced in this study have been very powerful in aligning Scottish literary studies with the optimistic energies of the new Scotland, assertively voicing and representing itself. But they have also over-determined the critical repertoire through which we view and value Scottish writing. At the level of literary history, this pattern encourages teleological readings of confidence and self-actualisation which often distort the aims and achievements of individual writers. In close analysis, these habits sponsor a dreary circular procedure in which nationhood and 'identity' are the meta-tropes of all Scottish writing, and the task is simply to find the myriad ways in which the text announces, deposits or queries its Scottishness.[4] This interpretive paradigm is a cul-de-sac for many reasons, including the tendency to inhibit critical attention to other forms and stakes of 'the political' in literature and culture.

For scholars and political operators alike, the problem is that continually affirming (thereby reproducing) the identitarian logic of devolution leaves us stranded on the surface of that cultural condition, cherishing iconic signs and displays of nationality, rather than critically examining what lies beneath. Scholars with any pretence to social engagement are obliged to glance in that direction, but it should be even more obvious that intellectuals whose role and position is (for better and worse) deeply imbricated with 'the national dimension' have special reason to contemplate the large fraction of Scottish society who have never read (or indeed heard of) the writers consecrated in the Canongate Wall. As was often remarked during the 2014 referendum campaign, if we were to conceive the writings and panel discussions of Literary Scotland as somehow representative of the public, there would have been no need to take a vote. I will conclude by re-voicing the (clearly legitimate, often noble) aims of the devolutionary intellectuals of the 1980s, on whose shoulders I have been uneasily standing: the prospects of critical renewal in Scottish literary scholarship depend – like the prospects for serious democratic change – on addressing the considerable gap between familiar display-identities and the hope of better nationhood.

Notes

1. See McCrone, 'National identity and culture in a cold climate', pp. 54–6.
2. Fraser, 'Rethinking recognition', p. 112
3. See Harvey, 'The art of rent', and Miller et al., *Tartan Pimps*.
4. See Thomson, '"You can't get there from here'; for a case study, see Hames, 'Don Paterson and poetic autonomy'.

Bibliography

NB Unsigned editorials (from periodicals) are presented at the end of this listing.

Abizadeh, Arash, 'Liberal nationalist versus postnational social integration: on the nation's ethno-cultural particularity and "concreteness"', *Nations and Nationalism*, 10.3 (2004), pp. 231–50.

Adorno, Theodor, *Minima Moralia: Reflections from Damaged Life*, trans. E. F. N. Jephcott (London: Verso, 1974).

Aitken, A. J., 'Completing the record of Scots', *Scottish Studies*, 8 (1964), pp. 129–40.

Aitken, A. J., 'The good old Scots tongue: does Scots have an identity?', in Einar Haugen, J. Derrick McClure and Derick Thomson (eds), *Minority Languages Today* (Edinburgh: Edinburgh University Press, 1981), pp. 72–90. Archived online by the Scots Language Centre, <http://media.scotslanguage.com/library/document/aitken/The_good_old_Scots_tongue.pdf> (accessed 24 February 2019).

Aitken, Keith, *The Bairns O' Adam: The Story of the STUC* (Edinburgh: Polygon, 1997).

Akbar, Arifa, 'Sounds of the street: how authors are turning to slang narratives as a more authentic mode of storytelling', *The Independent*, 4 March 2011.

Anderson, Benedict, *Imagined Communities: Reflections on the Origin and Spread of Nationalism*, revised edn (London: Verso, 1991).

Anderson, Perry, 'The antinomies of Antonio Gramsci', *New Left Review*, I/100 (November–December 1976), pp. 5–78.

Archello entry for the Scottish Parliament [architecture platform and magazine], <https://archello.com/project/scottish-parliament> (accessed 24 February 2019).

Ascherson, Neal, 'Next steps for the LCSA', 16 October [1980?]. Scottish Political Archive at the University of Stirling. SPA/GF/LCSA/2.

Ascherson, Neal, 'Seven days that exposed the black hole at the heart of Scottish politics', *Independent on Sunday*, 8 September 1996, <https://www.independent.co.uk/voices/seven-days-that-exposed-the-black-hole-at-the-heart-of-scottish-politics-1362340.html> (accessed 24 February 2019).

Ascherson, Neal, *Stone Voices: The Search for Scotland* (London: Granta, 2002).

Ashcroft, Bill, *Caliban's Voice: The Transformation of English in Post-Colonial Literatures* (London: Routledge, 2009).

Aughey, Arthur, *Nationalism, Devolution and the Challenge to the United Kingdom State* (London: Pluto Press, 2001).

Balibar, Étienne, 'The nation form: history and ideology', in Étienne Balibar and Immanuel Wallerstein, *Race, Nation Class: Ambiguous Identities*, trans. Chris Turner (London: Verso, 1991), pp. 86–106.

Bell, Eleanor, *Questioning Scotland: Literature, Nationalism, Postmodernism* (London: Palgrave Macmillan, 2004).

Bell, Ian A. 'Imagine living there: form and ideology in contemporary Scottish fiction', in Suzanne Hagemann (ed.), *Studies in Scottish Fiction: 1945 to the Present* (Frankfurt: Peter Lang, 1996), pp. 217–33.

Berridge, John and Mona Clark, 'Dundee', in John Bochel, David Denver and Allan Macartney (eds), *The Referendum Experience: Scotland 1979* (Aberdeen: Aberdeen University Press, 1981), pp. 66–77.

Billig, Michael, *Banal Nationalism* (London: Sage, 1995).

Bissett, Alan, 'The "New Weegies": the Glasgow novel in the twenty-first century', in Berthold Schoene (ed.), *The Edinburgh Companion to Contemporary Scottish Literature* (Edinburgh: Edinburgh University Press, 2007), pp. 59–67.

Bissett, Alan, 'Scotland's no vote has forced its artists to rediscover ambiguity', *The Guardian*, 15 October 2015, <http://www.theguardian.com/commentisfree/2015/oct/15/scotland-no-vote-artists> (accessed 24 February 2019).

Black, David M., Letter to Bob Tait, undated. University of Edinburgh Special Collections. Gen. 2159/3.

Black, David M., Letter to Robert Tait, 3 November 1967. University of Edinburgh Special Collections. Gen. 2159/3.

Bogdanor, Vernon, *Devolution in the United Kingdom*, revised edn (Oxford: Oxford University Press, 2001).

Bold, Alan, 'Two interviews with Alan Bold', *Scotia Review*, 4 (August 1973), pp. 39–45. Archived by David Morrison online, <http://

davidmorrisonshortstories.blogspot.com/2010/11/two-inter-views-by-alan-bold.html> (accessed 24 February 2019).

Bold, Alan, *MacDiarmid: A Critical Biography* (London: John Murray, 1988).

Boothby, F. A. C., Letter, *Scotia* Supplement, January 1971.

Borthwick, David, 'A. L. Kennedy's dysphoric fictions', in Berthold Schoene (ed.), *The Edinburgh Companion to Contemporary Scottish Literature* (Edinburgh: Edinburgh University Press, 2007), pp. 264–74.

Bourdieu, Pierre, *In Other Words: Essays Towards a Reflexive Sociology*, trans. Matthew Adamson (London: Polity, 1990).

Bourdieu, Pierre, *Language and Symbolic Power*, ed. John B. Thompson, trans. Gino Raymond and Matthew Adamson (Cambridge: Polity, 1991).

Bourdieu, Pierre 'The forms of capital', in A. H. Halsey et al. (eds), *Education: Culture, Economy, and Society* (Oxford: Oxford University Press, 1997), pp. 46–58.

Bourdieu, Pierre, *On the State: Lectures at the Collège de France, 1989–1992*, ed. Patrick Champagne et al., trans. David Fernbach (Cambridge: Polity, 2014).

Brand, Jack, *The National Movement in Scotland* (London: Routledge, 1978).

Brand, Jack, Letter to George Foulkes, 15 August 1980 ('Some considerations on strategy'). Scottish Political Archive at the University of Stirling. SPA/GF/ASSEM.

Brand, Jack, 'Defeat and renewal: the Scottish National Party in the 1980s', Autonomous University of Barcelona Working Paper 23 (1990), <https://www.icps.cat/archivos/WorkingPapers/WP_I_23.pdf> (accessed 24 February 2019).

Broom, John L., 'Candid commentary', *Scotia*, 1 (January 1970), pp. 5–6.

Broom, John L., 'Candid commentary', *Scotia*, 2 (February 1970), pp. 5–6.

Brown, Ian, '"Arts first; politics later": Scottish theatre as a recurrent crucible of cultural change', *Anglistik*, 23.2 (September 2012), pp. 95–105.

Brown, Ian, 'Processes and interactive events: theatre and Scottish devolution', in Steve Blandford (ed.), *Theatre and Performance in Small Nations* (Bristol: Intellect Press, 2013), pp. 33–49.

Brown, Wendy, *States of Injury: Power and Freedom in Late Modernity* (Princeton, NJ: Princeton University Press, 1995).

Brown, Wendy, *Politics Out of History* (Princeton, NJ: Princeton University Press, 2001).

Buchan, Tom, *Exorcism* (London: Midnight Press, 1972).

Burnett, Ray, 'Scotland and Antonio Gramsci', *Scottish International*, 5.9 (November 1972), p. 12.

Burns, Danny, *Poll Tax Rebellion* (Stirling: AK Press, 1992).

Calgacus, 'Tir 'is teanga', *Calgacus*, 2 (Summer 1975), p. 13.

Calgacus, 'Who was Calgacus?', *Calgacus*, 1 (Winter 1975), p. 16.

Cameron, Ewan A., *Impaled Upon a Thistle: Scotland Since 1880* (Edinburgh: Edinburgh University Press, 2010).

Campbell, Donald, 'A focus of discontent: Scottish literature and the Scottish Assembly', *New Edinburgh Review*, 45 (Spring 1979), pp. 3–5.

Campbell, James, 'A life in writing: James Robertson', *The Guardian*, 14 August 2010, <https://www.theguardian.com/books/2010/aug/14/james-robertson-land-still-profile> (accessed 24 February 2019).

Cartwright, T. J., *Royal Commissions and Departmental Committees in Britain* (London: Hodder and Stoughton, 1975).

Casanova, Pascale, *The World Republic of Letters*, trans. M. B. Debevoise (London: Harvard University Press, 2004).

Castle, Barbara, *The Castle Diaries 1974–76* (London: Weidenfeld and Nicolson, 1980).

Caughie, John, 'Political culture/cultural politics', *New Edinburgh Review*, 40 (Spring 1978), pp. 4–7.

Cavarero, Adriana, *For More Than One Voice: Toward a Philosophy of Vocal Expression*, trans. Paul A. Kottmann (Stanford, CA: Stanford University Press, 2005).

Costa, James, 'Occasional Paper: Language, ideology and the "Scottish voice"', *International Journal of Scottish Literature*, 7 (Autumn/Winter 2010), <http://www.ijsl.stir.ac.uk/issue7/costaOP.pdf> (accessed 28 February 2019).

Costa, James, Haley De Korne and Pia Lane, 'Standardising minority languages: reinventing peripheral languages in the 21st century', in Pia Lane, James Costa and Haley De Korne (eds), *Standardizing Minority Languages: Competing Ideologies of Authority and Authenticity in the Global Periphery* (London: Routledge, 2017), pp. 1–23.

Craig, Cairns, 'Across the divide', *Radical Scotland*, 2 (April–May 1983), pp. 24–5.

Craig, Cairns, 'Scotland 10 years on (the changes that took place while Rip Mac Winkle slept)', *Radical Scotland*, 37 (February–March 1989), pp. 8–11.

Craig, Cairns, *Out of History: Narrative Paradigms in Scottish and English Culture* (Edinburgh: Polygon, 1996).

Craig, Cairns, *The Modern Scottish Novel: Narrative and the National Imagination* (Edinburgh: Edinburgh University Press, 1999).

Craig, Cairns, 'Scotland: culture after devolution', in Edna Longley, Eamonn Hughes and Des O'Rawe (eds), *Ireland (Ulster) Scotland:*

Concepts, Contexts, Comparisons (Belfast: Cló Ollscoil na Banríona, 2003), pp. 39–49.

Craig, Cairns, *Intending Scotland: Explorations in Scottish Culture Since the Enlightenment* (Edinburgh: Edinburgh University Press, 2009).

Craig, Cairns, 'Unsettled will: cultural engagement and Scottish independence', *Observatoire de la société britannique*, 18 (2016), pp. 15–36. [My citations follow the different pagination of the file accessible online (pp. 1–16).]

Craig, Cairns, *The Wealth of the Nation: Scotland, Culture and Independence* (Edinburgh: Edinburgh University Press, 2018).

Crawford, Robert, *Devolving English Literature*, 2nd edn (Edinburgh: Edinburgh University Press, 2000).

Cross, Thom, 'Another look at the thistle (a discussion worth a dram)', *Radical Scotland*, 41 (October–November 1989), pp. 28–9.

Crossman, Richard, Letter to Harold Wilson, 25 June 1968. National Archives. CAB 164/658.

Crowther, Geoffrey (Lord), 'The Task of the Commission – Note by the Chairman', 13 May 1969. Royal Commission on the Constitution. National Archives. HO 221/335.

Cusick, James, 'How fearful Scotland stayed in its cage: Jim Sillars, the SNP's former deputy leader, believes his country "bottled it" when it rejected independence', *The Independent*, 24 August 1992, <http://www.independent.co.uk/news/uk/how-fearful-scotland-stayed-in-its-cage-jim-sillars-the-snps-former-deputy-leader-believes-his-1542310.html> (accessed 24 February 2019).

Dalyell, Tam, *Devolution: The End of Britain?* (London: Jonathan Cape, 1977).

Davidson, Neil, 'Antonio Gramsci's reception in Scotland', in *Holding Fast to an Image of the Past: Explorations in the Marxist Tradition* (London: Haymarket, 2014), pp. 253–86.

Deacon, Susan, 'Adopting conventional wisdom – Labour's response to the national question', in Alice Brown and Richard Parry (eds), *Scottish Government Yearbook 1990* (Edinburgh: Edinburgh University Press, 1990), pp. 62–75.

Derrida, Jacques, 'Declarations of independence', trans. T. Keenan and T. Pepper, *New Political Science*, 15 (Summer 1986), pp. 3–19.

Devine, T. M., *The Scottish Nation 1700–2000* (London: Penguin, 1999).

Devolution Proposals 1973–6, 'Background Paper 54' (1976) [House of Commons Library Research Division]. Scottish Political Archive at the University of Stirling. SPA/GF/ASSEM/2.

Dewar, Donald, 'Donald Dewar's speech at the opening of the Scottish Parliament, 1 July 1999', <http://www.parliament.scot/Education andCommunityPartnershipsresources/New_Parliament_Levels_ A-F.pdf> (accessed 23 February 2019).

Dixon, Keith, 'Notes from the underground: a discussion of cultural politics in contemporary Scotland', *Etudes écossaises*, 3 (1996), pp. 117–28.

Dolar, Mladen, *A Voice and Nothing More* (Cambridge, MA: MIT Press, 2006).

Dorey, Peter, *The Labour Party and Constitutional Reform: A History of Constitutional Conservatism* (Houndsmills: Palgrave, 2008).

Drucker, H. M. and N. L. Drucker (eds), *Scottish Government Yearbook 1979* (Edinburgh: Paul Harris Publishing, 1978).

Dunn, Douglas (and others), 'What it feels like to be a Scottish poet', *Aquarius*, 11 (1979), pp. 62–79.

Edwards, Owen Dudley (ed.), *A Claim of Right for Scotland* (Edinburgh: Polygon, 1989).

Elder, Murray, 'A Scottish Labour leader', in Wendy Alexander (ed.), *Donald Dewar: Scotland's First First Minister* (Edinburgh: Mainstream, 2006), pp. 84–103.

Eriksen, Helle Linné, 'Walking the tartan tightrope: the British Labour Party and the Scottish question 1974–1979', unpublished Master's thesis, University of Oslo, 2006.

Findlay, Bill, 'The voice of Scotland' [reviewing *The Proclaimers*, 'This is the Story'], *Radical Scotland*, 27 (June–July 1987), p. 33.

Finlay, Richard J., *Modern Scotland 1914–2000* (London: Profile, 2004).

Fishman, Joshua A., *Language and Nationalism* (Rowley, MA: Newbury House, 1972).

Foulkes, George, Submission to Labour Party Discussion (on Proportional Representation), 22 April 1991. Scottish Political Archive at the University of Stirling. SPA/GF/ER/5.

Fowler, Bridget, 'Pierre Bourdieu: the State, the Enlightenment and the Scottish literary field', in Lisa Adkins, Caragh Brosnan and Steven Threadgold (eds), *Bourdieusian Prospects* (London: Routledge, 2017), pp. 71–90.

Fraser, Nancy, 'From redistribution to recognition? Dilemmas of justice in a "post-socialist" age', *New Left Review*, I/212 (July–August 1995), pp. 68–93.

Fraser, Nancy, 'Rethinking recognition', *New Left Review*, 3 (May–June 2000), pp. 107–20.

Freeman, Alan, 'Realism fucking realism: the word on the street – Kelman, Kennedy and Welsh', *Cencrastus*, 57 (1997), pp. 6–7.

Fry, Michael, 'A claim of wrong', in Owen Dudley Edwards (ed.), *A Claim of Right for Scotland* (Edinburgh: Polygon, 1989), pp. 93–8.

Gallagher, Cailean, Rory Scothorne and Amy Westwell, *Roch Winds: A Treacherous Guide to the State of Scotland* (Edinburgh: Luath, 2016).

Gallagher, Tom, 'The SNP faces the 1990s', in Tom Gallagher (ed.), *Nationalism in the Nineties* (Edinburgh: Polygon, 1991), pp. 9–28.

Gardiner, Michael, *The Cultural Roots of British Devolution* (Edinburgh: Edinburgh University Press, 2004).

Gardiner, Michael, *Modern Scottish Culture* (Edinburgh: Edinburgh University Press, 2005).

Gardiner, Michael, 'Literature, theory, politics: devolution as iteration', in Berthold Schoene (ed.), *The Edinburgh Companion to Contemporary Scottish Literature* (Edinburgh: Edinburgh University Press, 2007), pp. 43–50.

Gardiner, Michael, 'Arcades – the 1980s and 1990s', in Ian Brown and Alan Riach (eds), *The Edinburgh Companion to Twentieth-Century Scottish Literature* (Edinburgh: Edinburgh University Press, 2009), pp. 181–92.

Gay, Oonagh, 'Scotland and Devolution Research Paper 97/92', House of Commons Library (29 July 1997), <https://researchbriefings. parliament.uk/ResearchBriefing/Summary/RP97-92> (accessed 24 February 2019).

Geekie, Jack and Roger Levy, 'Devolution and the tartanisation of the Labour Party', *Parliamentary Affairs*, 42.3 (1989), pp. 399–411.

Gellner, Ernest, *Nations and Nationalism* (Oxford: Blackwell, 1984).

Gifford, Douglas, 'At last – the real Scottish literary renaissance?', *Books in Scotland*, 34 (1990), pp. 1–4.

Gifford, Douglas, '"Out of the world and into Blawearie": the politics of Scottish fiction', in Edward J. Cowan and Douglas Gifford (eds), *The Polar Twins* (Edinburgh: John Donald, 1999), pp. 284–303.

Gifford, Douglas, 'Breaking boundaries: from modern to contemporary in Scottish fiction', in Ian Brown (ed.), *The Edinburgh History of Scottish Literature, Vol. III: Modern Transformations, New Identities (from 1918)* (Edinburgh: Edinburgh University Press, 2007), pp. 237–52.

Goodsir Smith, Sydney, 'Millennial Ode to Hugh MacDiarmid on yet another Birthday Occasion', *Lines Review*, 25 (Winter 1967–8), pp. 20–5.

Gow, David, 'Devolution and democracy', in Gordon Brown (ed.), *The Red Paper on Scotland* (Edinburgh: EUSPB, 1975), pp. 56–68.

Gray, Alasdair, 'A modest proposal for by-passing a predicament', *Chapman*, 35–6 (1983), pp. 7–9.

Gray, Alasdair, *1982 Janine* (London: Penguin, 1984).

Gray, Alasdair, *Why Scots Should Rule Scotland* (Edinburgh: Canongate, 1992).

Gunn, Linda and Alistair McCleery, 'Wasps in a jam jar: Scottish literary magazines and political culture 1979–1999', in Aimee McNair and Jacqueline Ryder (eds), *Further From The Frontiers: Cross-currents in Irish and Scottish Studies* (Aberdeen: AHRC Centre for Irish and Scottish Studies, 2009), pp. 41–52.

Haider, Asad, *Mistaken Identity: Race and Class in the Age of Trump* (London: Verso, 2018).

Hames, Scott, 'On vernacular Scottishness and its limits: devolution and the spectacle of "voice"', *Studies in Scottish Literature*, 39.1 (2003), pp. 201–22.

Hames, Scott, 'Don Paterson and poetic autonomy', in Berthold Schoene (ed.), *The Edinburgh Companion to Contemporary Scottish Literature* (Edinburgh: Edinburgh University Press, 2007), pp. 245–54.

Hames, Scott, 'Kelman's art speech', in Scott Hames (ed.), *The Edinburgh Companion to James Kelman* (Edinburgh: Edinburgh University Press, 2010), pp. 86–98.

Hames, Scott (ed.), *Unstated: Writers on Scottish Independence* (Edinburgh: Word Power, 2012).

Hames, Scott, 'Maybe just singing into yourself: James Kelman and vocal communion', in Scott Lyall (ed.), *Community in Modern Scottish Literature* (New York: Brill/Rodopi, 2016), pp. 196–213.

Hames, Scott 'The new Scottish renaissance?', in Peter Boxall and Bryan Cheyette (eds), *The Oxford History of the Novel in English, Volume Seven: British and Irish Fiction Since 1940* (Oxford: Oxford University Press, 2016), pp. 494–511.

Hanham, H. J., *Scottish Nationalism* (London: Faber, 1969).

Hart, Matthew, *Nations of Nothing But Poetry: Modernism, Transationalism, and Synthetic Vernacular Writing* (London: Oxford University Press, 2010).

Harvey, David, 'The art of rent: globalisation, monopoly and the commodification of culture', *Socialist Register*, 38 (2002), pp. 93–110.

Harvie, Christopher, 'Beyond bairns' play: a new agenda for Scottish politics', *Cencrastus*, 10 (Autumn 1982), pp. 11–14.

Harvie, Christopher, 'Tasks for self-governing socialists', *Radical Scotland*, 2 (April–May 1983), p. 16.

Harvie, Christopher, 'Nationalism, journalism and cultural politics', in Tom Gallagher (ed.), *Nationalism in the Nineties* (Edinburgh: Polygon, 1991), pp. 29–45.

Harvie, Christopher, 'The devolution of the intellectuals', in Lindsay Paterson (ed.), *A Diverse Assembly: The Debate on a Scottish Parliament* (Edinburgh: Edinburgh University Press, 1998), pp. 88–91 [reprinting Harvie in the *New Statesman*, 28 November 1975].

Harvie, Christopher, *Scotland and Nationalism: Scottish Society and Politics from 1707 to the Present*, 4th edn. (London: Routledge, 2004).

Hassan, Gerry and Peter Lynch, *The Almanac of Scottish Politics* (London: Politico's, 2001).

Hassan, Gerry and Eric Shaw, *The Strange Death of Labour Scotland* (Edinburgh: Edinburgh University Press, 2012).

Hearn, Jonathan, *Claiming Scotland: National Identity and Liberal Culture* (Edinburgh: Edinburgh University Press, 2000).

Heath, Edward, 'The Declaration of Perth', in Lindsay Paterson (ed.), *A Diverse Assembly: The Debate on a Scottish Parliament* (Edinburgh: Edinburgh University Press, 1998), pp. 26–30.

Hendry, Joy, 'Editorial', *Chapman*, 35–6 (1983), p. 1.

Hepburn, Ian, 'The Foulkes Memorandum', *Radical Scotland*, 4 (August–September 1983), p. 16.

Herdman, John, 'Politics III', in Duncan Glen (ed.), *Whither Scotland?* (London: Gollancz, 1971), pp. 103–11.

Herdman, John, 'What Kind of Scotland? A view of the conference', *Scottish International*, 6.5 (May–June–July 1973), pp. 10–15.

Herdman, John, *Another Country: An Era in Scottish Politics and Letters* (Edinburgh: Thirsty, 2013).

Hologa, Marie, *Scotland the Brave? Deconstructing Nationalism in Contemporary Scottish Novels* (Trier: WVT, 2016).

Huggan, Graham, *The Postcolonial Exotic: Marketing the Margins* (London: Routledge, 2001).

Ichijo, Atsuko, 'Entrenchment of unionist nationalism: devolution and the discourse of national identity in Scotland', *National Identities*, 14.1 (March 2012), pp. 23–37.

Innes, Kirstin, 'Mark Renton's bairns: identity and language in the post-*Trainspotting* novel', in Berthold Schoene (ed.), *The Edinburgh Companion to Contemporary Scottish Literature* (Edinburgh: Edinburgh University Press, 2007), pp. 301–9.

Introna, Arianna, 'Reveries of a progressive past: the missing Scotland as indyref heritage', *Journal of Scottish Thought*, 8 (2016), pp. 117–29.

Introna, Arianna, 'Avoiding disability in Scottish literary studies? Scottish studies, ablenationalism, and beyond', in David Bolt and Claire Penketh (eds), *Disability, Avoidance and the Academy: Challenging Resistance* (London: Routledge, 2017), pp. 153–63.

Jackson, Alan, 'The knitted claymore', *Lines Review*, 37 (1971), pp. 2–38.

Jackson, Ben, 'The political thought of Scottish nationalism', *Political Quarterly*, 85.1 (January–March 2014), pp. 50–6.

Jameson, Fredric, *The Antinomies of Realism* (London: Verso, 2013).

Jamieson, Robert Alan, 'MacDiarmid's spirit burns on', *Chapman*, 69–70 (Autumn 1992), pp. 3–8.

Jamieson, Robert Alan, 'Review: *And the Land Lay Still*', *The Bottle Imp*, 8 (2010), <https://www.research.ed.ac.uk/portal/en/publications/review-of-and-the-land-lay-still-by-james-robertson(b7d87e34-b7dc-4d48-b9a4-b6bd4d728701).html> (accessed 24 February 2019).

Kane, Pat, 'A Day for Scotland', *Radical Scotland*, 46 (August–September 1990), p. 15.

Kane, Pat, 'Banality, solidarity, spectacle' in *Tinsel Show: Pop, Politics, Scotland* (Edinburgh: Polygon, 1992), pp. 117–31.

Kay, Billy, 'Interview with Billy Kay', *Radical Scotland*, 25 (February–March 1987), pp. 33–5.

Keating, Michael, Letter to George Foulkes MP, dated 30 June 1981. Scottish Political Archive at the University of Stirling. SPA/GF/ASSEM/5.

Keating, Michael, *Nations Against the State: The New Politics of Nationalism in Quebec, Catalonia and Scotland* (London: Macmillan, 1996).

Keating, Michael, 'Nationalist movements in comparative perspective', in Gerry Hassan (ed.), *The Modern SNP: From Protest to Power* (Edinburgh: Edinburgh University Press, 2009), pp. 204–18.

Keating, Michael and David Bleiman, *Labour and Scottish Nationalism* (London: Macmillan, 1978).

Kedourie, Elie, *Nationalism*, 4th edn (Oxford: Blackwell, 1993).

Keitner, Chimène I., 'The "false promise" of civic nationalism', *Millennium: Journal of International Studies*, 28.2. (1999), pp. 341–51.

Kellas, James G., 'On to an assembly?', in John Bochel, David Denver and Alan Macartney (eds), *The Referendum Experience: Scotland 1979* (Aberdeen: Aberdeen University Press, 1981), pp. 147–52.

Kellas, James G., 'Restless natives' [reviewing *A Claim of Right for Scotland*], *Radical Scotland*, 39 (June–July 1989), p. 37.

Kellas, James G., *The Scottish Political System*, 4th edn (Cambridge: Cambridge University Press, 1989).

Kelly, Aaron, *Irvine Welsh* (Manchester: Manchester University Press, 2005).

Kelly, Aaron, 'James Kelman and the deterritorialisation of power', in Berthold Schoene (ed.), *The Edinburgh Companion to Contemporary*

Scottish Literature (Edinburgh: Edinburgh University Press, 2007), pp. 175–83.

Kelman, James, 'Subjective account', in Farquhar McLay (ed.), *The Reckoning: Beyond the Culture City Rip Off* (Glasgow: Clydeside Press, 1990), pp. 82–6.

Kelman, James, 'Let the wind blow high let the wind blow low', in *Some Recent Attacks: Essays Cultural and Political* (Stirling: AK Press, 1992), pp. 85–91.

Kelman, James, *How late it was, how late* (London: Secker and Warburg, 1994).

Kelman, James, *You Have to be Careful in the Land of the Free* (London: Penguin, 2004).

Kelman, James, *The Busconductor Hines* ([1984] Edinburgh: Polygon/Birlinn, 2007).

Kemp, Arnold, *The Hollow Drum: Scotland Since the War* (Edinburgh: Mainstream, 1993).

Kennedy, A. L., *So I Am Glad* ([1995] London: Vintage, 1996).

Kennedy, A. L., *Looking for the Possible Dance* ([1993] London: Vintage, 2005).

Kennedy, A. L., 'Scotland's cultural awakening is a terrifying prospect for politicians', *The Guardian*, 9 October 2011, <https://www.theguardian.com/politics/2011/oct/09/scotland-cultural-awakening-terrifies-politicians> (accessed 23 February 2019).

Kennedy, Michael D. and Ronald Grigor Suny (eds), *Intellectuals and the Articulation of the Nation* (Ann Arbor, MI: University of Michigan Press, 2001).

Kerevan, George, 'Labourism revisited', *Chapman*, 35–6 (1983), pp. 25–31.

Kerevan, George, 'The cultural consequences of Mr Keynes', *Radical Scotland*, 4 (August–September 1983), pp. 23–6.

Kerr, John, 'Bomb attack during Tattoo', *The Guardian*, 30 August 1971.

Kidd, Colin, *Union and Unionisms: Political Thought in Scotland 1500–2000* (Cambridge: Cambridge University Press, 2008).

Kidd, Colin, 'The end of Labour?', *London Review of Books*, 34.5 (2012), pp. 3–5.

Kidd, Colin, 'Scottish independence: literature and nationalism', *The Guardian*, 19 July 2014, <http://www.theguardian.com/books/2014/jul/19/scottish-independence-literature-nationalism> (accessed 24 February 2019).

Kloss, Heinz, 'Interlingual communication: danger and chance for the smaller tongues', *Scottish Studies*, 4 (1984), pp. 73–7.

Kravitz, Peter, 'It began slowly, with a distinct interval between each blow . . . or, Towards a parallel culture', *Edinburgh Review*, 80–1 (1988), pp. 3–8.

Kravitz, Peter, 'Nations can't be beautiful, only people can', *Edinburgh Review*, 82 (Winter 1989), pp. 5–8.

Kymlicka, Will, *Politics in the Vernacular: Nationalism, Multiculturalism and Citizenship* (Oxford: Oxford University Press, 2001).

'Labour campaign for a Scottish Assembly – a Scottish Socialist initiative', no date [1980?]. Scottish Political Archive at the University of Stirling. SPA/GF/LCSA/4.

Labour Party in Scotland, *Why Devolution* [pamphlet] (Glasgow: Labour Party in Scotland, 1976).

Labour, Co-Op, STUC, 'Speaker's Notes', Labour Movement Yes Campaign [Labour, Co-Op, STUC], 1979. Scottish Political Archive at the University of Stirling. SPA/GF/REF79/1.

Law, Alex and Gerry Mooney, 'Devolution in a "stateless nation": nation-building and social policy in Scotland', *Social Policy & Administration*, 46.2 (April 2012), pp. 161–77.

Lawson, Alan, 'Has anybody been taking notes?', *Radical Scotland*, 46 (August–September 1990), pp. 24–5.

Lehner, Stefanie, *Subaltern Ethics in Contemporary Scottish and Irish Literature: Tracing Counter-Histories* (London: Palgrave Macmillan, 2011).

Leishman, David, 'A parliament of novels: the politics of Scottish fiction 1979–1999', *Revue Française de Civilisation Britannique*, 14.1 (Autumn 2006), pp. 123–36.

Leonard, Tom, Letter to 'John', 12 June 1989, archived on Leonard's website, <http://www.tomleonard.co.uk/selected-letters/selected-letters-1988-1989.html> (accessed 24 February 2019).

Leonard, Tom, *Intimate Voices: Selected Work 1965–83* (Hastings: Etruscan, 2003).

Lindsay, Isobel, 'Nationalism, community and democracy', in Gavin Kennedy (ed.), *The Radical Approach: Papers on an Independent Scotland* (Edinburgh: Palingenesis Press, 1976), pp. 21–6.

Lindsay, Isobel, 'Divergent trends', *Radical Scotland*, 29 (October–November 1987), pp. 14–15.

Lukács, Georg, *The Historical Novel*, trans. Hannah and Stanley Mitchell (London: Merlin, 1962).

Lukács, Georg, *Theory of the Novel*, trans. Anna Bostock (London: Merlin, 1971).

Lyall, Scott, '"The man is a menace": MacDiarmid and military intelligence', *Scottish Studies Review*, 8.1 (Spring 2007), pp. 37–52.

Lynch, Michael, *Scotland: A New History* (London: Pimlico, 1992).

Lynch, Peter, 'The Scottish National Party: the long road from marginality to blackmail and coalition potential', in Lieven De Winter et al. (eds), *Autonomist Parties in Europe: Identity Politics and the Revival of the Territorial Cleavage*, vol. I (Barcelona: Institut de Ciències Polítiques i Socials, 2006), pp. 227–51.

Lynch, Peter, *SNP: The History of the Scottish National Party*, 2nd edn (Cardiff: Welsh Academic Press, 2013).

McAdam, David, 'Canongate Wall' [pamphlet for Lothian and Borders GeoConservation] (Edinburgh: Edinburgh Geological Society, 2011), <https://edinburghgeolsoc.org/downloads/lbgcleaflet_canongate-walla4.pdf> (accessed 24 February 2019).

Mac a' Ghobhainn, Seamus, Letter, *Scotia*, 12 (December 1970), pp. 3–4.

Macafee, Caroline, 'Scots in the Census: validity and reliability', in Janet Cruickshank and Robert McColl Millar (eds), *Before the Storm: Papers from the Forum for Research on the Languages of Scotland and Ulster Triennial Meeting, Ayr 2015* (Aberdeen: FRLSU, 2017), pp. 33–67, <https://www.abdn.ac.uk/pfrlsu/documents/Macafee_Scots_in_the_Census.pdf> (accessed 27 February 2019).

McClure, J. Derrick, 'Scots: its range of uses', in A. J. Aitken and Tom McArthur (eds), *Languages of Scotland* (Edinburgh: Chambers, 1979), pp. 26–48.

McCrone, David, *Understanding Scotland: The Sociology of a Stateless Nation* (London: Routledge, 1992).

McCrone, David, 'Cultural capital in an understated nation: the case of Scotland', *British Journal of Sociology*, 56.1 (2005), pp. 65–82.

McCrone, David, 'National identity and culture in a cold climate: the case of Scotland', *Journal of Irish and Scottish Studies*, 2.2 (2009), pp. 53–65.

McCrone, David, Angela Morris and Richard Kiely, *Scotland the Brand: The Making of Scottish Heritage* (Edinburgh: Polygon, 1995).

MacDiarmid, Hugh, *The Golden Treasury of Scottish Verse* (London: Macmillan, 1941).

MacDiarmid, Hugh [C. M. Grieve], Letter to *Scottish International*, 9 October 1967. University of Edinburgh Special Collections. Gen. 2159/2.

MacDiarmid, Hugh, 'Programme for a Scottish Fascism' [1923], in *Selected Prose*, ed. Alan Riach (Edinburgh: Carcanet, 1992), pp. 34–8.

MacDiarmid, Hugh, *Selected Poetry*, ed. Alan Riach and Michael Grieve (Manchester: Carcanet, 1992).

MacDiarmid, Hugh, *Contemporary Scottish Studies*, ed. Alan Riach (Manchester: Carcanet, 1995).

Macdonald, Catriona M. M., *Whaur Extremes Meet: Scotland's Twentieth Century* (Edinburgh: Birlinn, 2009).

McGlynn, Mary, 'How late it was, how late and literary value', in Scott Hames (ed.), *The Edinburgh Companion to James Kelman* (Edinburgh: Edinburgh University Press, 2010), pp. 20–30.

McIlvanney, Liam, *Burns the Radical: Poetry and Politics in Late Eighteenth-Century Scotland* (East Linton: Tuckwell, 2002).

McIlvanney, Liam, 'The politics of narrative in the post-war Scottish novel', in Zachary Leader (ed.), *On Modern British Fiction* (Oxford: Oxford University Press, 2002), pp. 181–208.

McIlvanney, William, *Surviving the Shipwreck* (Edinburgh: Mainstream, 1991).

McIlvanney, William, *Docherty* ([1975] Edinburgh: Canongate, 2014).

Mack, Douglas, 'Can the Scottish subaltern speak? Nonelite Scotland and the Scottish Parliament', in Caroline McCracken-Flesher (ed.), *Culture, Nation, and the New Scottish Parliament* (Lewisburg, PA: Bucknell University Press, 2007), pp. 141–57.

MacLaren, Duncan, 'Civil rights', *Crann-Tàra*, 3 (Summer 1978), p. 13.

McLean, Bob, *Getting it Together: The History of the Campaign for a Scottish Assembly/Parliament 1980–1999* (Edinburgh: Luath, 2005).

McMillan, Dorothy, 'Constructed out of bewilderment: stories of Scotland', in Ian A. Bell (ed.) *Peripheral Visions: Images of Nationhood in Contemporary British Fiction* (Cardiff: University of Wales Press, 1995), pp. 80–99.

McMillan, Joyce, 'The predicament of the Scottish writer', *Chapman*, 35–6 (1983), pp. 68–71.

Macwhirter, Iain, 'After Doomsday . . . The Convention and Scotland's constitutional crisis', in Alice Brown and Richard Parry (eds), *Scottish Government Yearbook 1990* (Edinburgh: Edinburgh University Press, 1990), pp. 21–34.

Maley, Willy, 'Denizens, citizens, tourists and others: marginality and mobility in the writings of James Kelman and Irvine Welsh', in David Bell and Azzedine Haddour (eds), *City Visions* (Harlow: Longman, 2000), pp. 60–72.

Marks, Peter, *Literature of the 1990s: Endings and Beginnings* (Edinburgh: Edinburgh University Press, 2018).

Marr, Andrew, *The Battle for Scotland* ([1992] London: Penguin 2013).

Maxwell, Stephen, Letter, *Scottish International*, 6.5 (May–June–July 1973), p. 9.

Maxwell, Stephen, 'The trouble with John P. Mackintosh', in Henry Drucker (ed.), *John P. Mackintosh on Scotland* (New York: Longman, 1982), pp. 142–7. [Reprinted from *Question*, 18 March 1977.]

Maxwell, Stephen, 'Scotland's Claim of Right', in Owen Dudley Edwards (ed.), *A Claim of Right for Scotland* (Edinburgh: Polygon, 1989), pp. 119–25.

Maxwell, Stephen, *Arguing for Independence: Evidence, Risk and the Wicked Issues* (Edinburgh: Luath, 2012).

Menges, Karl, 'Particular universals: Herder on national literature, popular literature, and world literature', in Hans Adler and Wulf Köpke (eds), *A Companion to the Works of Johann Gottfried Herder* (Rochester, NY: Camden House, 2009), pp. 189–214.

Michaels, Walter Benn, *The Trouble with Diversity: How we Learned to Love Identity and Ignore Inequality* (New York: Henry Holt, 2006).

Miller, Mitch and Johnny Rodger, *The Red Cockatoo: James Kelman and the Art of Commitment* (Dingwall: Sandstone Press, 2011).

Miller, Mitch, Johanny Rodger and Owen Dudley Edwards, *Tartan Pimps: Gordon Brown, Margaret Thatcher and the New Scotland* (Glendaruel: Argyll, 2010).

Miller, William L., *The End of British Politics? Scots and English Political Behaviour in the Seventies* (Oxford: Clarendon, 1981).

Mitchell, Jack, 'The struggle for the working-class novel in Scotland, part I', *Scottish Marxist*, 6 (April 1974), pp. 40–52.

Mitchell, James, 'Factions, tendencies and consensus in the SNP in the 1980s', in Alice Brown and Richard Parry (eds), *Scottish Government Yearbook 1990* (Edinburgh: Edinburgh University Press, 1990), pp. 49–61.

Mitchell, James, *Strategies for Self-Government: The Campaigns for a Scottish Parliament* (Edinburgh: Polygon, 1996).

Mitchell, James, 'The evolution of devolution: Labour's home rule strategy in opposition', *Government and Opposition*, 33.4 (October 1998), pp. 479–96.

Mitchell, James, 'Devolution without self-government', in Gerry Hassan and Rosie Ilett (eds), *Radical Scotland: Arguments for Self-Determination* (Edinburgh: Luath, 2011), pp. 29–39.

Mitchell, James, *The Scottish Question* (Oxford: Oxford University Press, 2014).

Mitchell, James, *Hamilton 1967* (Edinburgh: Luath, 2017).

Mitchell, James, 'Devolution', in David Brown, Robert Crowcroft and Gordon Pentland (eds), *The Oxford Handbook of Modern British Political History, 1800–2000* (Oxford: Oxford University Press, 2018), pp. 173–88.

Morace, Robert, 'Irvine Welsh: parochialism, pornography and globalisation', in Berthold Schoene (ed.), *The Edinburgh Companion to*

Contemporary Scottish Literature (Edinburgh: Edinburgh University Press, 2007), pp. 227–35.

Morgan, Edmund S., *Inventing the People: The Rise of Popular Sovereignty in England and America* (New York: Norton, 1988).

Morgan, Edwin, 'The future of the antisyzygy', *Bulletin of Scottish Politics*, 1.1 (1980), pp. 7–29.

Morgan, Edwin, *The Midnight Letterbox: Selected Correspondence 1950–2010*, ed. James McGonigal and John Coyle (Manchester: Carcanet, 2015).

Mulholland, Robert, 'Scotland's future – ends before means', *Scotia Review*, 1 (August 1972), pp. 16–19.

Müller, Christine Amanda, *A Glasgow Voice: James Kelman's Literary Language* (Newcastle upon Tyne: Cambridge Scholars Press, 2011).

Murray, Alex, 'Whither Kilbrandon?', *Scottish Marxist*, 6 (April 1974), pp. 56–68.

Nairn, Tom, 'Festival of the Dead', *New Statesman*, 1 September 1967, pp. 265–6.

Nairn, Tom, 'The three dreams of Scottish nationalism' [1968], *New Left Review* (May–June 1968), pp. 3–18.

Nairn, Tom, 'The three dreams of Scottish nationalism' [1970], in Karl Miller (ed.) *Memoirs of a Modern Scotland* (London: Faber and Faber, 1970), pp. 34–54.

Nairn, Tom, 'Culture and nationalism: an open letter', *Scottish International*, 6.4 (April 1973), pp. 7–9.

Nairn, Tom, 'The modern Janus', *New Left Review*, I/94 (November–December 1975), pp. 3–29.

Nairn, Tom, 'After the referendum', *New Edinburgh Review*, 46 (Summer 1979), pp. 3–10.

Nairn, Tom, *The Break-Up of Britain* (London: Verso, 1981).

Nairn, Tom, 'The timeless girn', in Owen Dudley Edwards (ed.), *A Claim of Right for Scotland* (Edinburgh: Polygon, 1989), pp. 163–78.

Nairn, Tom, *Faces of Nationalism: Janus Revisited* (London: Verso, 1997).

Nairn, Tom, *After Britain: New Labour and the Return of Scotland* (London: Granta, 2000).

Nairn, Tom, 'The radical approach' [*Question Magazine*, July 1976], in Jamie Maxwell and Pete Ramand (eds), *Old Nations, Auld Enemies, New Times: Selected Essays* (Edinburgh: Luath, 2014), pp. 162–8.

Newton, K. M., 'William McIlvanney's *Docherty*: last of the old or precursor of the new?', *Studies in Scottish Literature*, 32.1 (2001), pp. 101–16.

O'Hagan, Andrew, 'Homing: the anti-kailyard aesthetic of Bill Douglas', *Edinburgh Review*, 89 (Spring 1993), pp. 75–85.

O'Hagan, Andrew, 'Scotland's old injury', in *The Atlantic Ocean: Essays on Britain and America* (London: Faber, 2008), pp. 19–30.

O'Hagan, Andrew, 'Scotland your Scotland' (speech at the Edinburgh International Book Festival, 16 June 2017), <https://www.edbookfest.co.uk/news/scotland-your-scotland-andrew-o-hagan-delivers-keynote-lecture-at-book-festival> (accessed 20 February 2019).

O'Rourke, Donny (ed.), *Dream State: The New Scottish Poets*, 2nd edn (Edinburgh: Polygon, 2002).

Orridge, A. W., 'Uneven development and nationalism: I', *Political Studies*, 29.1 (March 1981), pp. 1–15.

Orwell, George, *The Complete Works of George Orwell, Vol. XIX*, ed. Peter Davison (London: Secker and Warburg, 1998).

Paterson, Don, *Orpheus: A Version of Rilke* (London: Faber, 2006).

Paterson, Lindsay, 'What Kind of Scotland?', *Crann-Tàra*, 1 (Autumn 1977), p. 3.

Paterson, Lindsay, 'Are the Scottish middle classes going native?', *Radical Scotland*, 45 (June–July 1990), pp. 10–11.

Paterson, Lindsay, *The Autonomy of Modern Scotland* (Edinburgh: Edinburgh University Press, 1994).

Paterson, Lindsay (ed.), *A Diverse Assembly: The Debate on a Scottish Parliament* (Edinburgh: Edinburgh University Press, 1998).

Paterson, Stuart A., 'Naw', *The Poets' Republic*, 1 (May 2015), <https://poetsrepublic.org/back-pages-poems/> (accessed 20 February 2019).

Phillips, Jim, *The Industrial Politics of Devolution: Scotland in the 1960s and 1970s* (Manchester: Manchester University Press, 2008).

Pitkin, Hannah F., *The Concept of Representation* (Berkeley, CA: University of California Press, 1972).

Pittin-Hedon, Marie-Odile, *The Space of Fiction: Voices from Scotland in a Post-Devolution Age* (Glasgow: Scottish Literature International, 2015).

Pollock, David, '*And the Land Lay Still* [Review]', *The List*, 23 July 2010, <https://www.list.co.uk/article/27344-and-the-land-lay-still-james-robertson/> (accessed 25 February 2019).

Possum, 'Who will kill the Commission?', *Scottish International*, 6.4 (April 1973), pp. 3–4.

Purdie, Bob, *Hugh MacDiarmid: Black, Green, Red and Tartan* (Cardiff: Welsh Academic Press, 2012).

'Queen's Speech – Debate on the Address', 30 October 1968. National Archives. CAB 221/335.

Rancière, Danielle and Jacques Rancière, 'The philosopher's tale' [1978], in *The Intellectual and His People*, trans. David Fernbach (London: Verso, 2012), pp. 75–124.

Report of the Royal Commission on the Constitution 1969–1973 [Kilbrandon Report], 2 vols (London: HM Stationery Office, 1973).

Robb, David, *Auld Campaigner: A Life of Alexander Scott* (Edinburgh: Dunedin Academic Press, 2007).

Robertson, Douglas and James Smyth, '*Radical Scotland*: articulating, arguing, pursuing and presenting the case for Scottish self-government in Thatcher's Britain', unpublished essay, 2009.

Robertson, James, 'A culture of diversity' [reviewing Cairns Craig (ed.), *The History of Scottish Literature*, vol. 4], *Radical Scotland*, 31 (February– March 1988), p. 32.

Robertson, James, 'The construction and expression of Scottish patriotism in the Works of Walter Scott', unpublished doctoral dissertation, University of Edinburgh, 1988. University of Edinburgh Archives.

Robertson, James (ed.), *A Tongue in Yer Heid: A Selection of the Best Contemporary Short Stories in Scots* (Edinburgh: Black and White, 1994).

Robertson, James, *Voyage of Intent: Sonnets and Essays from the Scottish Parliament* (Edinburgh: Scottish Book Trust/Luath, 2005).

Robertson, James, *And the Land Lay Still* (London: Hamish Hamilton, 2010).

Robertson, James, 'The republic of the mind' [1993], in *Republics of the Mind: New and Selected Stories* (Edinburgh: Black and White, 2012), pp. 131–51.

Rokkan, Stein and Derek W. Urwin, *Economy, Territory, Identity* (London: Sage, 1983).

Ross, Jim, 'Grasping the Doomsday nettle – methodically', *Radical Scotland*, 30 (December 1987–January 1988), pp. 6–9.

Royal Commission on the Constitution – Papers. Minutes of 9 December 1971 meeting. National Archives. HO 221/361.

Royal Commission on the Constitution – Papers. Minutes of 16 November 1972 meeting. National Archives. HO 221/360.

Ryan, Ray, *Ireland and Scotland: Literature and Culture, State and Nation, 1966–2000* (Oxford: Oxford University Press, 2002).

Salmond, Alex, 'Parliament re-elects First Minister' [Alex Salmond's acceptance speech], 18 May 2011, <https://www2.gov.scot/News/ Releases/2011/05/18104940> (accessed 23 February 2019).

Salmond, Alex, MSP, Official Report (Scottish Parliament), 21 March 2013, <http://www.parliament.scot/parliamentarybusiness/report. aspx?r=8383#ScotParlOR> (accessed 24 February 2019).

Sandbrook, Dominic, *Seasons in the Sun: The Battle for Britain, 1974–1979* (London: Penguin, 2012).

Sassi, Carla, *Why Scottish Literature Matters* (Edinburgh: Saltire Society, 2005).

Schnapper, Dominique, *Community of Citizens: On the Modern Idea of Nationality*, trans. Séverine Rosée (London: Transaction, 1998).

Schoene, Berthold, *The Edinburgh Companion to Irvine Welsh* (Edinburgh: Edinburgh University Press, 2010).

Scothorne, Rory, unpublished doctoral research, University of Edinburgh, 2016–19. Used with permission.

Scotland on Sunday, 'Books of 2010: Authors, actors, politicians, sports stars and more reveal their top reads of the year', 12 December 2010.

'Scotland's Census 2011' (National Records of Scotland) [Table QS212SC – Scots language skills], <https://www.scotlandscensus.gov.uk> (accessed 27 February 2019).

Scott, Alexander, 'Scots in English', *Glasgow Review*, 2.1 (Spring 1965), pp. 12–15.

Scott, Alexander, Letter to *Scottish International*, 8 October 1967. University of Edinburgh Special Collections. Gen. 2159/2.

Scott, Alexander, 'Scots in '72', *Glasgow Review*, 3.1 (Summer 1972), pp. 35–8.

Scott, Tom, 'Observations on Scottish Studies', *Studies in Scottish Literature*, 1.1 (1963), pp. 5–13.

Scott, Tom, Letter to *Scottish International*, dated 11 October 1967. University of Edinburgh Special Collections. Gen. 2159/2.

Scott, Tom, 'Characteristics of our greatest writers', *Akros*, 12 (1970), pp. 37–46.

Scott, Tom, Letter to David Morrison, 18 August 1971, archived online by David Morrison, <http://davidmorrisonshortstories. blogspot.com/2010/11/3-duddingston-park-send-me-your. html> (accessed 24 February 2019).

Scott, Tom, 'Epistle to David Morrison', *Scotia Review*, 1 (August 1972), pp. 3–9.

Scott, Tom, Letter, *Scotia Review*, 2 (December 1972), pp. 3–4.

Scott, Tom, 'Supplement to No. 4', *Scotia Review*, 4 (August 1973).

Scottish International, 'Commentary: Scottish writing and the individual writer', *Scottish International*, 9 (February 1970), pp. 18–27.

Scottish International, Draft advertisements for *Scottish International*. University of Edinburgh Special Collections. Gen. 2159/1.

Scottish Labour, 'Devolution is dead: the constitutional status of the Assembly' [Scottish Labour Action report], undated, but shortly after the formation of the Scottish Constitutional Convention in Spring 1989. Scottish Political Archive at the University of Stirling. SPA/ JMC/SN/SLA/10.

Scottish Labour, 'Labour and a Constitutional Convention' [Scottish Labour Action report], undated, but probably July 1989. Scottish

Political Archive at the University of Stirling. SPA/JMC/SN/ SLA/10.

Scottish Parliament, 'Canongate Wall', <http://www.parliament.scot/ visitandlearn/21012.aspx> (accessed 24 February 2019).

Smith, Alexander, *Devolution and the Scottish Conservatives: Banal Activism, Electioneering and the Politics of Irrelevance* (Manchester: Manchester University Press, 2011).

Smith, Anthony D., *National Identity* (London: Penguin, 1991).

Smith, Elaine C., 'A Day for Scotland', *Radical Scotland*, 46 (August– September 1990), pp. 14–15.

Smith, Sarah, ITN News broadcast, 29 April 1999, <https://www. gettyimages.co.uk/detail/video/scottish-assembly-election-campaign-scotland-edinburgh-news-footage/803580108> (accessed 24 February 2019).

Stewart, David, *The Path to Devolution and Change: A Political History of Scotland Under Margaret Thatcher* (London: Tauris, 2009).

Stewart, William A., 'A sociolinguistic typology for describing national multilingualism', in Joshua A. Fishman (ed.), *Readings in the Sociology of Language* (New York: Mouton, 1968), pp. 531–45.

Tait, Bob, 'Facts sacred, comment free, and art for everybody's sake', *Scottish International*, 6.5 (May–June–July 1973), p. 33.

Thomson, Alex, '"You can't get there from here": devolution and Scottish literary history', *International Journal of Scottish Litera-ture*, 3 (2007), <http://www.ijsl.stir.ac.uk/issue3/thomson.htm> (accessed 24 February 2019).

Tierney, Stephen, 'Giving with one hand: Scottish devolution within a unitary state', *International Journal of Constitutional Law*, 5 (2007), pp. 730–53.

Torrance, David, *'We in Scotland': Thatcherism in a Cold Climate* (Edinburgh: Birlinn, 2009).

Various [Janice Galloway, Duncan McLean, Alan Warner et al.], 'Poet's Parliament', *Edinburgh Review*, 100 (1999), pp. 71–7.

Waite, Lorna, 'Self-determination and power event', *Radical Scotland*, 44 (April–May 1990), pp. 26-7.

Wallace, Gavin, 'Voices in an empty house: the novel of damaged identity', in Gavin Wallace and Randall Stevenson (eds), *The Scot-tish Novel Since the Seventies: New Visions, Old Dreams* (Edinburgh: Edinburgh University Press, 1993), pp. 217–31.

Wallace, Gavin and Randall Stevenson (eds), *The Scottish Novel Since the Seventies: New Visions, Old Dreams* (Edinburgh: Edinburgh University Press, 1993).

Warner, Alan, 'Scottish writers on the referendum – independence day?', *The Guardian*, 19 July 2014, <http://www.theguardian.com/books/2014/jul/19/scottish-referendum-independence-uk-how-writers-vote> (accessed 24 February 2019).

Webb, Keith, *The Growth of Nationalism in Scotland* (London: Pelican, 1978).

Welsh, Irvine, *Trainspotting* ([1993] London: Minerva, 1994).

White, Benjamin Thomas, 'Landscape for a decent bloke [review of *And the Land Lay Still*]' (2015). Personal blog, <https://singularthings.wordpress.com/2015/08/30/landscape-for-a-decent-bloke/> (accessed 24 February 2019).

Whyte, Christopher, 'Out of a predicament', *Radical Scotland*, 5 (October–November 1983), pp. 20–1.

Whyte, Christopher, 'Masculinities in contemporary Scottish fiction', *Forum for Modern Language Studies*, 34.2 (1998), pp. 274–85.

Whyte, Christopher, 'Nationalism and its discontents: critiquing Scottish criticism', in J. Derrick McClure, Karoline Szatek and Rosa E. Penna (eds), *"What Countrey's This? And Whither Are We Gone?"* (Newcastle upon Tyne: Cambridge Scholars Press, 2010), pp. 23–39.

Wickman, Matthew, 'The emergence of Scottish Studies', in Gerry Carruthers and Liam McIlvanney (eds), *The Cambridge Companion to Scottish Literature* (Cambridge: Cambridge University Press, 2012), pp. 248–60.

Williamson, Kevin, 'Language and culture in a rediscovered Scotland', in Mark Perryman (ed.), *Breaking Up Britain: Four Nations After a Union* (London: Lawrence and Wishart, 2009), pp. 53–67.

Wolfe, William, 'SNP and the Arts', *Scottish International*, 2 (April 1968), pp. 5–6.

Unsigned editorials (grouped by publication)

'Editorial: Presenting the *Bulletin*', *Bulletin of Scottish Politics*, 1.1 (Autumn 1980), pp. i–iv.

'Editorial', *Calgacus*, 1 (February 1975), p. 1.

'Editorial', *Crann-Tàra*, 1 (Autumn 1977), p. 2.

'Editorial', *Crann-Tàra*, 3 (Summer 1978), pp. 2–3.

'After the 79' [Editorial], *Crann-Tàra*, 8 (Autumn 1979), p. 2.

'Editorial', *Crann-Tàra*, 15 (Autumn 1981), p. 3.

'Editorial', *Edinburgh Review*, 68–9 (1984), p. 3.

'Editorial', *Edinburgh Review*, 75 (November 1986), pp. 3–5.

'Editorial', *Edinburgh Review*, 76 (February 1987), pp. 3–4.

'Comment', *Lines Review*, 19 (Winter 1963), p. 4.

'Editorial: A hope and a prayer', *Radical Scotland*, 1 (February–March 1983), p. 3.

'In the red corner' [Editorial], *Radical Scotland*, 4 (August–September 1983), pp. 7–8.

'Hoping for the best ... preparing for the worst' [Editorial], *Radical Scotland*, 25 (February–March 1987), pp. 9–11.

'Responding to Doomsday' [Editorial], *Radical Scotland*, 28 (August–September 1987), p. 3.

'Why this is the last issue' [Editorial], *Radical Scotland*, 51 (June–July 1991), p. 3.

'Editorial', *Scotia Review*, 1 (August 1972), p. 1.

'Editorial', *Scottish International*, 1 (January 1968), cover to p. 3.

Index